Presented to Purchase College
by
Gary Waller, PhD Cambridge

State University of New York
Distinguished Professor

Professor
of Literature & Cultural
Studies, and Theatre &
Performance, 1995-2019
Provost 1995-2004

Philip Stubbes,

The Anatomie of Abuses

Medieval and Renaissance Texts and Studies

Volume 2 4 5

Renaissance English Text Society

Seventh Series
Volume XXVII (for 2002)

Philip Stubbes,

The Anatomie of Abuses

edited by

MARGARET JANE KIDNIE

Arizona Center for Medieval and Renaissance Studies
in conjunction with
Renaissance English Text Society
Tempe, Arizona
2002

Library of Congress Cataloging-in-Publication Data

Stubbes, Phillip.
 [Anatomie of abuses]
 Philip Stubbes, The anatomie of abuses / edited by Margaret Jane Kidnie.
        p. cm. — (Medieval & Renaissance texts & studies ; v. 245) (Renaissance
    English Text Society ; v. 27)
    Includes bibliographical references and index.
    ISBN 0-86698-287-6 (hardcover : alk. paper)
    1. England — Social life and customs — 16th century. 2. Theater — Moral
and ethical aspects — Early works to 1800. 3. Theater — England — Early
works to 1800. I. Kidnie, Margaret Jane. II. Title. III. Medieval & Renaissance
Texts & Studies (Series) ; v. 245. IV. Renaissance English Text Society (Series);
vol. 27.
DA320.S876 2002
942.05—dc21   2002074614

∞

This book is made to last.
It is set in Caslon,
smythe-sewn and printed on acid-free paper
to library specifications.

Printed in the United States of America

This book is dedicated to my parents,

Marjory and Hugh Kidnie.

Table of Contents

List of Illustrations

All illustrations immediately follow page 27.

Preface

Philip Stubbes is not a writer given to subtlety of expression. In his *Anatomie of Abuses* he exposes to view and, he hopes, correction, the supposed vices of Elizabethan society. Very little escapes his gaze. Popular entertainments and traditional rural festivals are subject to the same scrutiny as gluttony and promiscuity, all such activities standing condemned as behavior unbefitting a true Christian. It is precisely the scope of this critique which has ensured the book's enduring interest: scholars researching nearly any custom or practice of Elizabethan England will at some point find themselves turning to *The Anatomie of Abuses*.

But Stubbes is no dispassionate chronicler, and his account is something more — or, depending on one's perspective, something less — than an eye-witness record. Not only is it an example of early modern polemic, but also of popular literature, filled with gossip and tales of encounters with the devil. The *Abuses* captured its readers' imaginations, going through four editions and two issues between 1583 and 1595. However, despite its complexity and importance, scholars without access to the original printed editions have previously had to depend on facsimiles and microfilms, or on inadequate and scarce nineteenth-century editions. This edition, aimed at a broad audience with widely diverse needs, will make *The Anatomie of Abuses* accessible to a modern readership.

The earliest version of this edition was submitted in 1996 as a doctoral thesis at the University of Birmingham, England. This work would not have been possible without the financial support provided prior to that date by the University of Birmingham, the Committee of Vice-Chancellors and Principals of the Universities of the United Kingdom, the Canadian Women's Club, and the Social Sciences and Humanities Research Council of Canada. I am further indebted to a number of scholars and friends who have in different ways aided my research. John Jowett read and offered comments on the introduction and was always willing to explore ideas about editorial theory, pointing me in important new directions at various key stages. Susan Brock, the former Head Librarian at the Shakespeare Institute, expertly supervised my editing of Stubbes's Latin and the use of Latin quotations in the commentary. I would also like gratefully to acknowledge assistance offered by the late Janet Arnold, who provided prompt insight into my questions about sixteenth-century costume construction, and to thank J. W. Binns, Desmond Costa, Leslie S. B. MacCoull, and Sergio Mazza-relli for helping me to sort out obscure or garbled Greek and Latin passages.

Lisa Jardine was an exemplary external examiner, making clear and helpful suggestions about revisions that might be made to the thesis for future publi-cation. Tom Berger was likewise of huge assistance in this process of revision; it was a pleasure and a privilege to work with him so closely on this project. I am further indebted to other Renaissance English Text Society Council Members — Arthur F. Kinney, Suzanne Gossett, and David Kastan, in particular — for their feedback and assistance. James Purkis at different stages of the edition's prepara-tion for publication read and offered invaluable comments on the introduction and commentary. Karen Lemiski, Production Manager for Medieval and Renais-sance Texts and Studies, provided reliable and capable support as the edition went into print. I was also blessed with the choice of copy-editor made by MRTS: Leslie S. B. MacCoull checked the typescript with care and diligence, sharing with me in many instances her own outstanding scholarship. Stephen Baker, Caroline Cakebread, and Kristin Lukas helped keep it all in perspective. My parents, Marjory and Hugh Kidnie, offered a seemingly endless supply of good advice and moral support from beginning to end.

My "but for whom" thanks, however, are extended to my doctorate supervi-sor, Stanley Wells. Stanley's quiet humor, encouragement, and sound scholarly advice sustained me through years of research at the Shakespeare Institute, and made the preparation of this edition an enjoyable and rewarding pursuit.

M.J.K.

Abbreviations

Biblical quotations, unless indicated otherwise, are taken from the Geneva Bible
(*The Geneva Bible: A Facsimile of the 1560 Edition*. With an introduction by
Lloyd E. Berry. Madison: University of Wisconsin Press, 1969).

Arber,   Edward Arber, ed. *A Transcript of the Registers of the Company*
Company of *of Stationers of London; 1554–1640 A.D.* 5 vols. London and
Stationers   Birmingham: Privately Printed, 1875–1894.

Dent,   R. W. Dent, *Proverbial Language in English Drama Exclusive*
Proverbial   *of Shakespeare, 1495–1616: An Index.* Berkeley: University of
Language   California Press, 1984.

Erasmus,   Desiderius Erasmus, *Adages*, trans. Margaret Mann Phillips and
Adagia   R. A. B. Mynors. In *Collected Works of Erasmus*, vols. 31–34.
Toronto: University of Toronto Press, 1982–1992.

OED   *The Compact Oxford English Dictionary.* 2nd ed. Oxford: Clarendon Press, 1991.

PG   *Patrologiae cursus completus*, gen. ed. J. P. Migne. Series Greca.
Paris, 1857–1866.

PL   *Patrologiae cursus completus*, gen. ed. J. P. Migne. Series Latina.
Paris, 1844–1862.

Sermons   *Certain Sermons or Homilies Appointed to be Read in Churches in*
the Time of Queen Elizabeth of Famous Memory. London: Society
for Promoting Christian Knowledge, 1851.

Statutes   John Cay, ed. *The Statutes at Large, from Magna Charta, To the*
Thirtieth Year of King GEORGE the Second, inclusive. 6 vols.
London: Thomas Baskett and Henry Lintot, 1758.

STC   Pollard, A. W., and G. R. Redgrave, *A Short-Title Catalogue of Books Printed in England, Scotland and Ireland and of English Books Printed Abroad, 1475–1640*. 2nd ed. Revised W. A. Jackson, F. S. Ferguson, and Katharine F. Pantzer. 3 vols. London: The Bibliographical Society, 1976–1991.

Tilley,   Morris Palmer Tilley, *A Dictionary of the Proverbs in England in*
Proverbs   *the Sixteenth and Seventeenth Centuries*. Ann Arbor: University of Michigan Press, 1950.

TRP   Paul L. Hughes and James F. Larkin. *Tudor Royal Proclamations*. 3 vols. New Haven: Yale University Press, 1964–1969.

Walther,   Hans Walther, *Proverbia Sententiaeque Latinitatis Medii Aevi.*
Proverbia Carmina Medii Aevi Posterioris Latina. 5 vols. Göttingen: Vandenhoeck & Ruprecht, 1963–1967.

Walther,   Hans Walther, *Proverbia Sententiaeque Latinitatis Medii ac Re-*
Proverbia, n.s. *centioris Aevi.* Carmina Medii Aevi Posterioris Latina. Nova series. 3 vols. Göttingen: Vandenhoeck & Ruprecht, 1982–1986.

Introduction

BIOGRAPHY AND CANON

What little we know about the life of Philip Stubbes — and it is very little indeed — has mostly been surmised from the author's published works. At the beginning of *The Anatomie of Abuses* the character Philoponus mentions that he has led "the life of a poore Traueller, in a certaine famous Iland ... called **Anglia**, wherein I haue liued these seuen winters and more, trauelling from place to place, euen all the land ouer indifferently" (211–16).[1] Reading this information as autobiographical rather than as the literary device it probably is, and, further, assuming that Stubbes began this journey around England upon reaching his majority at the age of twenty-one, F. J. Furnivall works back from the date of the first publication of the *Abuses* in 1583 to suggest that Stubbes was born in the year 1555 (*Abuses*, ed. Furnivall [London, 1879], 2:50, n. 2). Equally speculative reasoning lies behind the author's supposed date of death. Believing that Stubbes wrote nothing more after *A Motiue to Good Workes* in 1593, J. P. Collier concludes in the introduction to his edition of the *Abuses* that "we may presume, from various circumstances, that he was carried off by the plague, which raged in 1592" (*Abuses*, ed. Collier [London, 1870], ii). But if we assume that the revised version of *A perfect Pathway to Felicitie* was enlarged by Stubbes just prior to its publication in 1610, and that it is not a reprint of an earlier, now lost, edition, then it seems likely that Stubbes lived well into the seventeenth century.

Attempts to identify Stubbes's parents and place of birth have met with even less success. Stubbes appears in the second edition of Anthony à Wood's *Athenae Oxonienses* (ed. and revised Bliss, 1813–1820). Here the claim is made that John Stubbes, the Protestant Englishman whose right hand was chopped off in punishment for writing *The discouerie of a gaping gulf* (1579) in opposition to the projected marriage between Queen Elizabeth I and the Duke of Anjou, was

---

[1] Unless indicated otherwise, all references to the *Abuses* have been keyed to this edition.

"[n]ear of kin, if not brother, or father to this Philip" (1:646). Philip, however, is not mentioned in the wills of either John Stubbes or his father (*Abuses*, ed. Furnivall, 2:53–55), and à Wood's speculation seems prompted by nothing more concrete than a shared surname. Terry Pearson confirms that there is likewise no evidence in the university records to support à Wood's claim that Stubbes "was mostly educated in Cambridge, but having a restless and hot head, left that university, rambled thro' several parts of the nation, and setled for a time in Oxon, particularly, as I conceive, in Glocester-hall" (*Athenae Oxonienses*, 1:645, cf. Pearson, "The Life and Works," 28–29). Described by both à Wood and Furnivall as a gentleman and titled as such in a number of his works from 1584, Stubbes was mocked by Thomas Nashe in the anti-Martinist pamphlet *An Almond for a Parrat* for having only pretensions to gentility.[2] If Nashe's purpose in mentioning Stubbes had not been to deride him as a zealous hypocrite, one might be tempted to credit his claim that "his mastershippe in his minority plaide the Reader in Chesshire for fiue marke a yeare and a canuas dublet" (*Works*, ed. McKerrow, 3:357).[3] This detail provokes some scepticism, however, printed alongside less plausible reports of Stubbes gambling on the Sabbath and attempting — unsuccessfully — to persuade a widow to have sex with him in return for a Geneva Bible.

But while the biographical information is sketchy, evidence of Stubbes's literary output is ample. His earliest known publication is a ballad dated 1581 entitled "A fearefull and terrible Example of Gods iuste iudgement executed vpon a lewde Fellow, who vsually accustomed to sweare by Gods Blood." This ballad is no longer extant. J. P. Collier claimed to own a copy of it, and included it in his 1868 collection of *Broadside Black-letter Ballads* (42–47). Although Collier's history of forgery raises suspicions about the authenticity of this work, corroboration of its previous existence is provided by W. Carew Hazlitt. Hazlitt describes the ballad in *Collections and Notes 1867–1876* (1:410), claiming in his Preface to

---

[2] "Learning is a iewel, my maisters, make much of it, and *Phil. Stu.* a Gentleman euery haire of his head, whom although you doe not regard according as he deserues, yet, I warrant you, *Martin* makes more account of him then so, who hath substituted him long since (if the truth were well boulted out) amongst the number of those priuy *Martinists*, which he threatens to place in euery parish" (Nashe, *Works*, ed. McKerrow, 3:358).

[3] Pearson argues from internal evidence that Stubbes may have been born in the Cheshire area. In addition to this passage from *An Almond for a Parrat*, Stubbes details in the *Abuses* the untimely end of a swearer whom he knew "a dozen or sixteen yeares togither" in the town of Congleton in Cheshire (5136–46). Pearson was unable, however, to find any record of the birth of a Philip Stubbes in the parish records ("The Life and Works," 24–26).

have personally seen every work included in the compilation (6–7). The story also features as part of a longer pamphlet by Stubbes probably printed later in 1581 entitled *Two wunderfull and rare Examples* (*STC* 23399.7).[4] Moralized as true examples of God's just punishment of sinners, these sensationalist accounts of the gruesome death of a swearer and the assault made by the devil on a covetous woman were undoubtedly written as much to capitalize on the public's horrified fascination with the grotesque as to provide readers with suitably edifying literature. A third pamphlet entitled *A View of Vanitie*, entered in the Stationers' Register on 9 October 1582 (Arber, *Company of Stationers*, 2:415) and printed in octavo by T. Purfoot the same year, is described by W. Carew Hazlitt in his 1867 *Hand-Book to the Popular, Poetical and Dramatic Literature of Great Britain* (581), but no copy of it survives today.

Stubbes's next publication, *The Anatomie of Abuses* (*STC* 23376), is a wide-ranging social critique presented in the form of a dialogue between Philoponus, the educated, worldly-wise traveler, and Spudeus, the country yokel, who chat as they walk along about the manners of the people who live in the foreign land of England. Licensed to Richard Jones on 1 March 1583, *The Abuses* was in print by May, and its immediate success prompted Stubbes to revise and expand the book for a second edition in August.[5] He then wrote a sequel to it which was registered to William Wright on 7 November (Arber, *Company of Stationers*, 2:428), and entitled *The Second part of the Anatomie of Abuses, conteining The display of Corruptions* (*STC* 23380). The date printed in the collophon to this edition is 1583. The *Second part* continues the castigation of Elizabethan vice seemingly exhausted in the previous work, focusing in particular in the last half of the book on "The Corruptions and Abuses of the Spiritualitie." This chapter is especially valuable for the light it sheds on the author's attitudes towards the English Protestant Church. Before writing the sequel to the *Abuses*, Stubbes compiled *The Rosarie of Christian Praiers and Meditations* which was entered in the Stationers' Register on 3 August 1583 (Arber, *Company of Stationers*, 2:426). Seen by Hazlitt and recorded in his *Hand-Book* as printed by John Charlewood in octodecimo (582), the work is no longer extant. *The Anatomie of Abuses* was thoroughly revised twice more for publication, once in October, 1584, and again in 1595.

---

[4] The story of the blasphemer was recycled yet again in 1583, the author incorporating it into a chapter on swearing found in all of the revised editions of *The Anatomie of Abuses* (5102–35).

[5] The title pages of the first and second editions are dated "1.Maij.1583" and "16 August.1583" respectively.

After contributing in 1583 a Latin poem to the introductory material of the fourth edition of John Foxe's *Actes and Monuments* (*STC* 11225) with the title "In sanguisugas Papistas" ("The Papist Bloodsuckers") and a preface to *A Godlie and fruitfull Treatise of Faith and workes* by "H. D." (*STC* 6168), Stubbes wrote two pamphlets rabidly anti-Catholic in content. The first, printed in 1584, vilifies all things Catholic under the title *The Theater of the Popes Monarchie* (*STC* 23399.2). Maligning the Pope as "that great Antichrist ... whom the Lorde shall destroy with the glory of his comming" (sig. C7v), Stubbes caricatures the ceremonies, vestments, and institutions of the Catholic Church as "a Satyricall stage playe of fooles consecrated to the Diuel" (sig. E1). The second pamphlet, *The Intended Treason, of Doctor Parrie: and his Complices, Against the Queenes moste Excellent Maiestie* (*STC* 23396), probably published in 1585, describes the manner in which William Parry was suborned by the Pope to assassinate the Queen. After printing in full a letter to Parry written by the Cardinal of Como dated 30 January 1584, Stubbes draws the categorical conclusion that "all papists are traitors in their harts, how soeuer otherwise they beare the world in hand" (sigs. A3v–A4).

No record of any publication survives from 1586 to 1590, the period corresponding to Stubbes's marriage to the fifteen-year-old Katherine Emmes. Their marriage licence, dated 6 September 1586, reads "Philip Stubbes, Gent., of S[t] Mary at Hill, London, & Katherine Emmes, Spinster, of same, dau. of William Emmes, late of S[t] Dunstan in the West, Cordwaynor, dec[d]; Gen. Lic." (*Harleian Society Publications*, 25:153).[6] Katherine died of a fever four and a half years later, six weeks after bearing their first child, John. The parish registers of Burton-upon-Trent record his baptism: "John Stubs filius Philippi baptized the 17th November 1590" (*Abuses*, ed. Furnivall, 2:51). These registers also record that Katherine was buried on 14 December 1590, apparently the same day she died.[7] As Furnivall comments, it would be unusual for a body to be interred on the day of death, and Pearson clarifies that the entry is "in a different hand and ink to the rest of the register, and is inserted between the lines" ("The Life and Works," 53). It seems likely that this entry was added to the parish register at a later date, perhaps by a reader of Stubbes's pamphlet, and that no independent record of Katherine's burial survives. Thus the only non-literary documentary

---

[6] Katherine's father died in 1583, and his widow, also named Katherine, received a licence to marry Richard Tompkyns on 18 January 1584 (*Harleian Society Publications*, 25:127); Katherine Emmes, senior, died a widow in 1591 (*Abuses*, ed. Furnivall, 2:52–53).

[7] Her date of death is printed on the title page of the earliest editions of *A Christal Glasse for Christian Women*.

evidence we have of the life of Philip Stubbes is a marriage licence, and an entry in the parish registers of Burton-upon-Trent, Staffordshire, recording the baptism of his son.

Within six months of his wife's death Stubbes had written a biography entitled *A Christal Glasse for Christian Women Containing, A most excellent Discourse, of the godly life and Christian death of Mistresse Katherine Stubs* (1591, *STC* 23381).[8] This pamphlet was revised for a second edition which was published the following year (*STC* 23382). *A Christal Glasse* was even more successful than the *Abuses*, achieving at least twenty-four editions by 1637.[9] Stubbes also compiled a collection of prayers under the title *A perfect Pathway to Felicitie, Containing godly Meditations, and praiers, fit for all times* (*STC* 23398) which was licensed to Humfrey Lownes on 22 March 1592 (Arber, *Company of Stationers*, 2: 606).[10] In this small book are printed prayers befitting all conceivable circumstances: there are prayers against idleness and covetousness, prayers for pregnant women, travelers, and servants, and prayers to be said while washing one's hands and face. Another edition of this work, enlarged by fifteen prayers, was printed in 1610.

Stubbes's final pamphlet, *A Motiue to Good Workes* (*STC* 23397), revisits many of the same issues found in the *Abuses*. Entered in the Stationers' Register on 14 October 1593 (Arber, *Company of Stationers*, 2:638), the text has a dedication in which the author explains that after travelling around England for three months and finding many things badly out of order, he was moved to "stirre vp the mindes of men ... if not to doe goodworkes themselues, yet to maynteyne those which our predecessors haue left behinde them" (sig. A4v). His ensuing complaints about such faults as neglected churches and corrupt lawyers are familiar to the reader from his attack on English society published ten years earlier. Ironically, in light of the scorn heaped on him by Thomas Nashe in *The*

---

[8] The pamphlet was entered in the Stationers' Register on 15 June 1591 (Arber, *Company of Stationers*, 2:585).

[9] In *Cheap Print and Popular Piety* (Cambridge: Cambridge University Press, 1991), Tessa Watt suggests that the pamphlet may have been designed to replace the lives of saints: "If Protestant women in labor could no longer appeal to Saint Margaret or the virgin Mary in childbirth, they had the companionship and inspiration of Katherine Stubbes" (284).

[10] Hazlitt suggests that this is perhaps just a different name for *The Rosary of Prayers*, printed in 1583 (*Second Series*, 586), but this seems unlikely, despite the apparent congruence of subject-matter, since in his dedicatory letter to Katherine Milward dated 10 April 1592, Stubbes mentions that he has only now agreed to publish *A perfect Pathway to Felicitie* on the insistence of a friend who paid for its printing (sigs. ¶3v–¶4).

Anatomie of Absurditie and *An Almond for a Parrat*, Stubbes also finds space to criticize those "scummes of the worlde" who slander other authors in "railing pamphlets, and paltrie libels" (sigs. N2v–N3). At the time of writing this pamphlet Stubbes was resident in London, his dedicatory letter dated "From my lodging by Cheapeside this 8. of Nouember. 1593" (sig. A6).[11]

With the success of the *Abuses* in the early 1580s and *A Christal Glasse for Christian Women* in the early 1590s, Philip Stubbes emerges as a populist writer of some repute. This is not to say that everyone who bought a copy of Stubbes's work agreed with his opinions, but simply that he achieved a certain notoriety, as suggested by Nashe's justification in 1592 of the format of *Pierce Penilesse his Supplication to the Divell* with the tongue-in-cheek explanation that "I bring *Pierce Penilesse* to question with the diuel, as a yoong nouice would talke with a great trauailer; who, carrieng an Englishmans appetite to enquire of news, will be sure to make what vse of him he maie, and not leaue anie thing vnaskt, that he can resolue him of. If then the diuell be tedious in discoursing, impute it to *Pierce Penilesse* that was importunate in demanding" (*Works*, ed. McKerrow, 1: 240). Other writers show evidence of Stubbes's influence by drawing extensively on his published work. The *Abuses* is quoted in both William Prynne's expansive *Histriomastix* (1633) and I. G.'s *A Refutation of the Apology for Actors* (1615), Prynne referring throughout his tome to "*Mr. Philip Stubs*, his Anatomy of Abuses", and "I. G." (John Greene) quoting at length from Stubbes's account of the London theaters shaken by an earthquake in 1580 (sigs. F3–F3v).[12] *The Second part of the Anatomie of Abuses* was an important source for both the anonymous *Defence of Conny-Catching* (1592) and for Robert Greene's *A Quip for an Upstart Courtier* (1592).[13] And *A Christal Glasse for Christian Women* was well-known enough to be alluded to on stage by Richard Brome and William Cartwright sixty years after its first publication.[14] Stubbes, albeit a relatively minor Elizabethan literary figure, clearly had a not inconsiderable impact on the work of subsequent writers.

---

[11] Anthony à Wood also attributes to Stubbes a tract entitled "Praise and Commendation of Women", noting that he has not yet seen it (*Athenae Oxonienses*, 1:646); as no other record of the work exists, it has not been included here as part of the canon.

[12] Elsewhere in his pamphlet Greene pays Stubbes the backhanded compliment of silently reprinting much of his chapter on stage-plays (sigs. G3–I2v).

[13] Parallels among these three texts are traced by Brian Parker in his edition of *A Quip for an Upstart Courtier* (Ph.D. Diss., University of Birmingham, 1958, ccii–ccvii).

[14] *The Court Beggar* (1653), III.i; *The Ordinary* (1651), III.v.

STUBBES'S REPUTATION AS A PURITAN

Despite our limited knowledge of his life, Stubbes is popularly known today as a sixteenth-century Puritan. François Laroque, in his study of Elizabethan festivity, introduces Stubbes's views on the lords of misrule as those of a "Puritan pamphleteer" (*Shakespeare's Festive World*, 95), while Joan Larsen Klein in her preface to excerpts from *A Christal Glasse for Christian Women* printed in *Daughters, Wives and Widows* suggests that Stubbes "was a Puritan, but perhaps not an extreme one" (139). Jonas Barish, commenting on such writers as Stubbes, John Northbrooke, and Stephen Gosson as "English Puritans of the sixteenth century", acknowledges in a footnote that the classification is ambiguous, and in the case of Gosson, inaccurate, but he opts to use the word anyway as a "convenient shorthand term ... [standing] for a complex of attitudes best represented by those strictly designated as Puritans" (*Antitheatrical Prejudice*, 82, n. 5). These three scholars have been singled out not because their assumption that Stubbes was a Puritan is in any way unusual, but rather because they indicate the extent to which this belief has become widely accepted.

But the label is hardly accurate. The only really undisputed application of the term "Puritan" is in the context of those who continued to push for further reform of the English church after the Elizabethan religious settlement of 1559: these critics of the Establishment were dissatisfied by the extent to which vestiges of Catholic doctrine perceived to be inconsistent with Protestantism had been carried over and incorporated into the reformed church (Collinson, "William Shakespeare's Religious Inheritance," 238). However, when Stubbes comes to address this controversy in *The Second part of the Anatomie of Abuses* it becomes clear that his own theological opinions are entirely orthodox. Far from calling for the abolition of the episcopacy, Stubbes, citing the example of Christ's apostles, baldly states that "[t]o doubt whether there ought to be bishops in the churches of christians, is to doubt of the truth it selfe" (sig. O1). Moreover, while maintaining that bishops are not superior in calling, function, or office to less exalted ministers, Stubbes confidently argues that it is fitting for them to assume a greater majesty and pomp as a necessary means to reinforce their honor and authority (sig. O2v). With regard to the controversy surrounding ecclesiastical vestments, Stubbes's view is that they are a cause of offence only when particular holiness is attached to them; when commanded to be worn by a Christian prince, they should be tolerated by ministers (sig. P2v).

As Alexandra Walsham likewise argues in "'A Glose of Godlines': Philip Stubbes, Elizabethan Grub Street and the Invention of Puritanism," Stubbes was no presbyterian (198).[15] The term "Puritan", however, as used in Elizabethan England was not restricted to careful or objective assessments of doctrinal views: "the evidence of reported speech at a more popular level suggests that from at least the 1570s, and certainly toward 1580, 'Puritan' was a gibe hurled, as it were, in the vernacular at all too evidently religious persons, Protestants, by their less obviously religious or crypto-Catholic neighbors" (Collinson, *Puritan Character*, 20). Stubbes, it seems certain, would not have applied the label to himself. Intended, and taken, as an insult, the word was a polemical ruse by which Elizabethans of a less godly bent tried to undermine moral opposition to such popular activities as dancing, theatrical performances, and seasonal festivals. The author of *The Anatomie of Abuses* was exactly the sort of busy, interfering killjoy, set apart from the rest of the community by extreme moral fervor and godly zeal, who was liable to be branded a Puritan.

So describing Stubbes as a Puritan perhaps tells us little more than that he was identified as such by his enemies. And yet to imply that he simply fell victim to bad press is perhaps to beg the question. Pamphlets such as *The Anatomie of Abuses*, *A Christal Glasse for Christian Women*, and *A Motiue to Good Workes* give the strong sense that this author held a perspective on Elizabethan life which was in some manner distinct from that of his neighbors; even if we choose to avoid labelling him a Puritan, a satisfactory account of the ideology informing the work of Stubbes must address the fact that the word seemed — and still seems — to fit.

Peter Lake argues that "both puritans and their contemporaries could recognize a member of the godly when they saw one", and that their identifying characteristic was "the seriousness with which they took entirely orthodox doctrines of election and reprobation and applied them to their own lives and experience" ("Puritan Identities," 116). According to this construction, Puritans are exceptionally keen Protestants who are known by the extent of their religious fervor — what Stubbes in his dedicatory letter to the *Abuses* describes as "the zeale of my God." What distinguishes a writer such as Stubbes from other Elizabethans is the intensity with which he expresses conventional Protestant standards of morality and behavior.[16] And certainly, the impassioned commitment

---

[15] *Belief and Practice in Reformation England: A Tribute to Patrick Collinson*, ed. Susan Wabuda and Caroline Litzenberger (Aldershot: Ashgate, 1998), 177–206, esp. 198.

[16] In his review of *Society and Religion in Elizabethan England* by Richard L. Greaves, Lake reflects on the extent to which Puritan attitudes towards morality and behavior were consistent with those held by committed Protestants: "Broadly, they were all opposed to sin and shared many common definitions of what, in fact, constituted sin ... Dr

with which he embarks on a relentless denunciation of sin is remarkable to a reader of the *Abuses* today. The severity with which he wishes to see sin punished further testifies to the militancy of his attitudes. Railing against the current tendency to "rappe out othes at euery worde" (4995), Stubbes argues that this vogue would quickly pass if swearers were stoned to death as commanded in the Bible or had their tongues cut out (5074–91). While the potential for an increased burden on poor rates implicit in the birth of children to unwed mothers caused parish authorities to adopt a particularly intolerant view of extra-marital sex between men and women, the punishment exacted by the ecclesiastical courts in the period suggests that few would agree with Stubbes that offenders should either be put to death or seared with a hot iron, "to the ende that the Adulterous children of Sathan, might be discerned from the honest and chast Christians" (3582–84).[17] Stubbes's enduring reputation as a Puritan, therefore, seems to result from the vehemency and didacticism with which he expresses an uncompromising agenda of social and moral reform.

Lake's interpretation of puritanism is appealing since it allows for the existence in sixteenth-century England of a broad group of people who may not have been presbyterian or separatist but who were nonetheless regarded as hotter sorts of Protestants. As early as 1941, however, William Ringler pointed out the drawbacks of identifying strict morality as the distinguishing mark of Puritanism: "We already have a word, asceticism, which refers to this attitude; to restrict or equate Puritanism to it would be a careless and uneconomical use of language" ("The First Phase," 418). Moreover, readers of the *Abuses* need to keep in mind the derogatory overtones of the term. As Collinson puts it, "a certain nastiness was inherent in the idea of puritanism, since the word was a broad and sticky brush with which to tar those who usually denied that they were puritans and insisted that they were nothing but orthodox and loyal protestant Christians, which they believed was more than could be said of those who defamed them as puritans" ("Ecclesiastical Vitriol," 155). Stubbes's status as a Puritan may well have resulted from his forcefulness of opinion on a wide variety of social and moral issues, but such a label nonetheless presupposes conflict and tension.

Greaves's book represents a massively documented disproof of the notion that under Elizabeth either puritans or Anglicans had anything like a distinctive social theory" ("Puritan Identities," 115).

[17] The punishments set in place by the Elizabethan "bawdy courts" to deter adultery and pre-marital sex included fines and public penance in the church or marketplace (Laslett, *World We Have Lost Further Explored*, 156).

Even now "a certain nastiness" adheres to the word Puritan: used deliberately in the sixteenth and early seventeenth centuries to stigmatize and engender ridicule, its modern application to a writer such as Stubbes reflects the extent to which we find ourselves in agreement with his opponents. *The Anatomie of Abuses* is perhaps best remembered today for the stand it takes against the theaters. In a short chapter consisting of just over five quarto pages, the author cites Scriptural and classical authority to prove the wickedness of theaters and players; raging against licentious audiences and pranked-up actors, Stubbes aggressively calls for immediate action. Returning to the larger issue of neglect of the Sabbath, the author moves from a discussion of the theaters to a similar condemnation of lewd dancing, idolatrous May games, and murderous football play. These so-called abuses, however, may not appear from a modern perspective as quite so heinous as Stubbes suggests. Four hundred years on, the sight of morris dancers at a local village fête is more likely to provoke antiquarian interest in Old World traditions than outraged mutterings against the dance of the devil. The sense that Stubbes expends a great deal of energy attacking what are now regarded as essentially harmless pastimes inclines a reader of the *Abuses* to accept the view of Stubbes as a sometimes amusing, but nonetheless narrow, Puritan.

If, however, the consensus of opinion fell on Stubbes's side, or rather, if he were best known not for his desire to close the theaters but for some other of his proposed social reforms, then one might see this popular estimation of him begin to break down. Condemning, for example, the bewildering variety and costly sumptuousness of clothing owned by a few individuals, Stubbes draws a clear correlation between such luxury and unrelieved poverty in the streets of London, bluntly asking his readers how they can justify having "millions of sutes of apparell lying rotting by them, when as the poore members of Iesus Christ dye at their doores for want of cloathing" (1802–5). In a later chapter Stubbes interrupts a discussion of usury to advocate reform of the penal system, arguing that there is no mercy in imprisoning men and women for debt without any hope of recovery (4742–66). Although the zeal with which Stubbes documents vice encourages a perception of him as a sixteenth-century Puritan, it is the readiness of his audience either to affirm or to resist his attitudes which is also at issue.

The problems with continuing to refer to this author as Puritan are threefold. First, the imprecision with which the term is applied means that one might wrongly assume that Stubbes was in some way opposed to the Establishment when in fact his church politics were strongly conformist. In this case, the usage would not only be ambiguous but misleading. Secondly, describing Stubbes as a Puritan in even a carefully qualified sense risks perpetuating the rhetorical tactic by which his views were undercut by contemporary opponents. Used as a term of abuse in his own lifetime, the word remains polemically loaded. Finally, such terminology flattens out the complexity of the dynamics surrounding issues of religion in late sixteenth-century England. Exploring, in particular, the interconnections between the commercial book trade and what she describes as "fervent" Protestantism, Alexandra Walsham argues that Stubbes emerges as a "shadowy" character, a semi-professional author of popular literature whose literary persona was at least partly shaped in response to the demands of a well-defined reading public ("Invention of Puritanism," 177–206). This edition avoids narrow categorization in order to allow readers the opportunity to assess for themselves the complex and often controversial attitudes towards Elizabethan England held by this extraordinary writer.

THE MULTIPLE TEXTS OF
THE ANATOMIE OF ABUSES

Readers of the present edition should take careful note that its text is that of the fourth edition of *The Anatomie of Abuses*. The *Abuses* was entered in the Stationers' Register on 1 March 1583, and the title page of the first octavo reads "1. Maij.1583.". A variant issue appeared soon after, its title page dated 29 May. This first edition rapidly led to the publication of a second dated 16 August, and a third in the following year dated 12 October, both printed in octavo. A variant issue of this third edition appeared in 1585. The fourth and final edition of the *Abuses* appeared in quarto ten years later in 1595. According to their imprints and colophons, all four editions were printed in London by Richard Jones, but J. A. Lavin has demonstrated by means of the ornament on sig. B1 and the ornamental letter "R" on sig. A2 that the 1595 quarto edition of the *Abuses* was "printed in whole or in part" by John Danter for Jones ("John Danter's Ornament Stocks," 39–40). *The Short-Title Catalogue* further suggests, without citing any supporting evidence, that the first and second editions were printed by John Kingston for Jones (*STC*, 2:370).

The Entry in the Stationers' Register
   The Anatomie of Abuses was entered in the Stationers' Register as licensed to Richard Jones on 1 March 1583:

Anno Domini 1582 [1583]. Annoque R. Rne. Eliz. xxv^{to}
primo die Martij

Rich. Jones   Licenced vnto him vnder thandes of the Bishop

of london and both the wardens. *The Anatomye*
of abuses. by Phillipe stubbes.   vj^d

[Liber B, 194; Arber, *Company of Stationers*, 2:421]

The First Edition (O1)
Collation: 8°: ¶^{8}, A^2, B–P^8 (missing P8), Q^4, R^2 = 127 leaves unnumbered
Type-faces: predominantly black letter with some Roman for proper names,
     Latin, proverbs, etc.

There are eight known copies of the first edition (*STC* 23376; cf. figure 1).
Four of these are held at the Bodleian, while the National Library of Wales, the
Folger Shakespeare Library, the Huntington Library, and the Rosenbach Foundation in Philadelphia each owns one copy. I have examined all of the Bodleian
copies and the Huntington copy. Of these five copies two are imperfect. Both
damaged copies are at the Bodleian, S.269 Art missing signature P6, and Douce
S655 missing signatures ¶1–¶4^v and O3–R2^v. Although I was unable to detect
a watermark on any leaf, the direction of the chain-lines in gatherings A, Q, and
R supports the suggestion that the last two leaves of the preliminaries (A) were
printed on the same sheet as the last two gatherings of the book.

The variant issue of this edition (*STC* 23376.5; cf. figure 2), the only copy
of which is owned by Peterborough Cathedral and is on long-term deposit at
University Library, Cambridge, is nearly identical to the first edition. Besides the
change of date on the title page to "29.Maij.1583" (the colophon is invariant),
the only difference between this issue and O1 is that the page heading and running-title to sig. H7^v read "**Knowen whores keept openly. The Anat.**" instead of
"**Impunitie for whordome. The Anatomie**".

A point of further bibliographical interest in the first edition is that the final leaf of gathering P, missing in other copies, was accidentally bound in one of
the Bodleian copies (Crynes 833). The recto of the leaf is blank, but on the
verso is printed a full page of text complete with running-title, page heading,
and catchword (cf. figure 3, and Appendix I, Passage F). While the style, vocabulary, and subject-matter of the text printed on sig. P8v are typical of the *Abuses*,
these lines are not found in any of the four early editions of the book, nor indeed, in any other of Stubbes's extant works. What seems most probable is that
this material represents a false start that was marked for deletion by Stubbes
himself. The compositors, overlooking indications for deletion in the manuscript,
realized their mistake only after setting P8v. Instead of resetting the page, they
left the recto blank and marked the leaf for omission. This page of cancelled text

is important because it offers us evidence of an Elizabethan author at work. Not only can Stubbes's revising hand be traced between the four editions of the *Abuses*, but the process of revision is apparent within the first edition itself.[18]

The Second Edition (O2)

Collation: 8°: ¶⁴, B–R⁸, [8 leaves unnumbered] fols. 1–125 [124] (= 132 leaves)
Type-faces: predominantly black letter with some Roman and italic for proper names, Latin, proverbs, etc.

The second edition (*STC* 23377; cf. figure 4) is extant in eight copies. I have examined the two copies at the British Library and the two copies at the Bodleian. The Bodleian copies are damaged, but while one — Mal. 526 — is complete, Mal. 528 is missing gathering A and signatures R7–R8ᵛ. Three other copies are in the United States at the Folger Shakespeare Library, the Huntington Library, and the Newberry Library. The *Short-Title Catalogue* suggests that of the American copies, only the Folger is imperfect. The *STC* also records another British copy in the John R. Hetherington Collection, Birmingham; this collection having been partly dispersed, however, the location of the copy is unknown.

O2 is significantly different from the first edition. Most notably, it is much longer. Stubbes's decision to enlarge the text for the second printing and thereafter to publish even more material in *The Second part of the Anatomie of Abuses* (1583) was presumably prompted by an enthusiastic reception of O1. Key passages added to O2 include the commendatory poem by "C.B.", two anecdotes about drunkards who were punished by God, an anecdote about a woman whose ruff was set by the devil, and the chapters on gardens, swearing, and the daily exercises of women in England. This revised edition, however, lacks the "Preface to the Reader". In O1, this preface had afforded Stubbes the opportunity to explain that he is not opposed to dancing, gaming, the theaters, and sumptuary excesses as such, but merely to their abuse. Furnivall argues that the preface was omitted after the first edition as inconsistent with the rest of the book (*Abuses*,

---

[18] I have published a fuller discussion of this anomaly in Margaret Jane Kidnie, "Evidence of Authorial Revision in the Earliest Edition of *The Anatomie of Abuses*," *Papers of the Bibliographical Society of America* 92 (1998): 75–80. See also Terry P. Pearson, "The Composition and Development of Phillip Stubbes's 'Anatomie of Abuses,'" *Modern Language Review* 55 (1961): 321–32, 326. Pearson further argues for the late addition to the original manuscript of some of Stubbes's more topical reports by comparing the May publication date of the *Abuses* to the dates of those events which can be verified through external sources, and speculating about the time it would take to write a book of this length (323–26).

ed. Furnivall, 1:62). Terry Pearson instead suggests that a passage in the newly
written chapter on gardens sufficiently clarified Stubbes's moderate position,
making the preface redundant ("Composition and Development," 322, cf. 3098–
202). The motivation behind the omission of the preface cannot finally be
known. All additions and omissions introduced to the second edition were carried over with further revisions into the last two editions.

The Third Edition (O3)
Collation: 8°: A⁴, B–Q⁸, R⁴, [8 leaves unnumbered] fols. 1–124 [120] (= 128
   leaves)
Type-faces: predominantly black letter with some Roman and italic for proper
   names, Latin, proverbs, etc.

There are only two extant copies of the third edition (*STC* 23377.5; cf.
figure 5), at Harvard University and the University of Illinois. I have examined
the Harvard copy on microfilm. Beyond the partial or complete revision of individual words, sentences, and paragraphs typical of all of the revised editions, the
third edition supplements much of the new material found in O2 with sidenotes
and page headings. A variant issue of this edition was subsequently published
which, beyond altering the date of publication both on the title page and in the
colophon to "1585", is identical to O3 (*STC* 23378; cf. figure 6). There are five
copies of this variant issue. Two are in the United States, at the Folger Shakespeare Library and at Yale University. The other three copies, all of which I have
examined, are at the British Library, The Shakespeare Centre, Stratford-upon-
Avon, and University Library, Cambridge. The BL copy lacks sig. Q6, and the
Cambridge copy has been badly damaged, missing sigs. E6, F6, F8, and P4–R4.

The Fourth Edition (Q1)
Collation: 4°: A–T⁴ [8 pages unnumbered] pp. 1–144 (= 152 pages)
Type-faces: predominantly black letter with some Roman and italic for proper
   names, Latin, proverbs, etc.

The fourth edition (*STC* 23379; cf. figure 7) is the only one printed in
quarto. All twelve extant copies of Q1 were examined and collated in the course
of preparing this modern edition. Four of the copies are in the United States at
the Folger Shakespeare Library, the Huntington Library, Harvard University,
and the University of Wisconsin Library. Four more are spread among the British Library, St. John's College, Oxford, Emmanuel College, Cambridge, and the
Birmingham Reference Library, while the last four are lodged in the Bodleian.

Examination of each of these copies shows that five are imperfect: Douce S221 at the Bodleian replaces gathering O with handwritten pages, while Mal. 707, also at the Bodleian, lacks the top corners of sigs. K1–K2 with the subsequent loss of the first two sidenotes printed on sig. K1. Wood 653, a third copy held at the Bodleian, is slightly mutilated at sig. O3, while the bottom of the pages of the copy held at St. John's College, Oxford, have been badly cropped and the final line of text on some pages is missing. The Folger copy appears on microfilm to be cropped where the signatures should appear on sigs. L2–M3.

The printing of this edition was of a usual standard for the period — there are a number of obvious misprints (i.e., "exaseperate" for "exasperate" at line 2992, and "lhing" for "thing" at line 1431) as well as readings that appear to be compositor's errors (i.e., "faire" for "fairer" at 937.5 and "Numer. 24" for "Numer. 25" at 3374.1). In three places the type has shifted, in one instance as the result of a pulled letter, and these variant readings are recorded below after the press-corrections. Collation of all of the copies of Q1 resulted in the discovery of a handful of press-variants. Only eleven formes show evidence of press-correction: the outer formes of gatherings A, B, F, and M, the inner forme of gathering E, and the inner and outer formes of gatherings K, L, and Q. All of the variants are grouped below by forme:

Sig.	Line Number[19]	Corrected Reading	Uncorrected Reading
A3	93	holdeth	holdeıh
B3	running title	Abuses	Absues
	page heading	charitie	charitei
	407	Philo.	Philip.
E2	1540	speech prefix before and on same line as chapter title	chapter title on line above speech prefix
E3ᵛ	1665.2–3 SN	diuers & sundrie	di- and sundrie

---

[19] The line numbers cited here are those of this edition. Where a line is either not included or is unnumbered in this edition, the location of the press-correction has been described (i.e., running title, page heading, page number, signature).

F1	1821	There is a certaine	Ther is a ceitaine
	1835–36	Hell, and sealed an Obligation	hell, and sealed an an obligation
F2^v	1962	Womens	Womans
	1977	I be vnable	I be be vnable
F3	2004.2	faces	fnces
	2017–18	& a Cobbler should presume	and a Cobler should presum
F4^v	2161	& cunningly	and cunning-
	2179	faces	faaces
	2200	owne natural Haire:	owne owne natural haire:
	2200–1	and vppon . . . Haire	and vpon . . . haire
K1^v	3501	feare it	feare it it
K3	page heading	delicate	delicaɟē
K4^v	3838.3	those	••those[20]
L2	page number	75	74
L4^v	page number	80	88
M1	4259	M1	omitted
Q3	page heading	followed	followəd
Q4	6233	thinke	tinke
Q4	6234	dances	daunces

The following differences between the extant copies of the quarto are examples of drifting and/or pulled type. These variant readings have been silently emended:

Sig.	*Line Number*	*Variant Readings*
A2^v	47	wh•ether, whether

---

[20] A bullet signifies a gap in the text approximately equal to one em.

| D3 | 1205 | speciall, •peciall, pe•ciall |
| N2ᵛ | 4844 | dish•onoured, d•ishonoured, d•ish•onoured |

As in the second and third editions, the fourth edition has been thoroughly revised. Fewer page headings are needed as a result of the larger quarto format, but this change is compensated for by the incorporation of more chapter breaks within the main body of the text. Some further additional passages have been included in the chapters on men's fashion, but otherwise the book shows signs of streamlining. The previously extensive prefatory material is reduced to include only the dedicatory epistle and a short commendatory poem by "I. F.", while the example of two adulterers burned in London along with a brief digression on the consequences of a luxurious diet are omitted. Proper names are no longer spelled backwards and in Latin as they were for the most part in the earlier editions, and the text, previously dedicated to Philip Howard, Earl of Arundel, is rededicated to the Magistrates of England. This particular revision was presumably prompted by the Earl's secret conversion to Roman Catholicism in 1584 and aborted flight to the Continent in 1585 which led to a sentence of life imprisonment (Granville, *Life of Saint Philip Howard*, 12, 24–25); it is unknown whether Q1 was published before the Earl's death in the Tower on 19 October 1595 (cf. 20–21n.). In light of the consistent nature of the changes made to each edition after the first and the fact that the third and fourth editions explicitly state on their title pages that these extensive revisions are authorial, there seems little reason to doubt that all four versions were written and revised by Stubbes.

Modern Editions

This is the first critical edition of *The Anatomie of Abuses* undertaken since the nineteenth century. The earliest modern edition of the *Abuses* is a reprint of the text of O3 produced in 1836 under the superintendence of W. B. D. D. Turnbull in a limited issue of one hundred copies. A reprint of O1 was published in 1870 with an introduction by J. P. C[ollier] as part of *Miscellaneous Tracts Temp. Eliz. & Jac. 1*. F. J. Furnivall's quirky edition for The New Shakspere Society, a text which is based on O1 but includes some of the variants from the three later editions either within the main text or footnoted at the bottom of the page, followed in 1877–1879 and was reprinted in 1965 by Kraus Reprint Ltd. Two facsimile reprints of O1 were published in 1972. The first, a reproduction of Crynes 833 held at the Bodleian Library, was published by the Johnson Reprint Corporation with an introductory note by Peter Davison, and the second, a reproduction compiled from all four copies of O1 held at the Bodleian Library, was published as part of the English Experience Series (no. 489). Another facsimile of O1, prepared from the Huntington copy, was published for the Garland Press in 1973 with a preface by Arthur Freeman.

STUBBES AS STYLIST

Stubbes's strength as a polemicist lies in his ability to engage the reader's interest in his subject, and he excels at enlivening his description of Elizabethan England with verbal pictures which vividly capture an instance of the particular abuse under examination. Thus, for example, he not only criticizes current trends in men's footwear by outlining the extravagant choice of colors, materials, and styles of trimming currently available to consumers, but also illustrates his argument with an image of the smartly dressed man forced to hobble down city streets in elevated slippers which "goe flip flap vp and downe in the dirt" (1762–72). This rhetorical technique can backfire, of course, as the author's lively accounts at times have the unintended effect of attracting readers to, rather than repelling them from, the focus of attack. His vignette of a minister's sermon abruptly interrupted when the church congregation jump up on their pews to stare at the sudden entrance of the Lord of Misrule's unruly entourage is perhaps the best example of this (5639–79). The more powerfully Stubbes portrays the excitement of such events, the more difficult it is to turn one's back on them.

The vitality and urgency of his prose style is reinforced through the strong visual impact of the words on the page. Foreign words and phrases with their translations, many neologisms and quotations, and expressions on which he has decided to place added rhetorical emphasis are set apart from the rest of the text in each of the four versions through the use of contrasting type.[21] This interrupts the smooth flow of words past the reader's eye, imposing on the work heavy verbal inflections which influence one's reception of the views being expressed. Stubbes, that is, not only controls the words that constitute his book, but also attempts to control the manner in which they are read. The number of passages highlighted in this manner steadily increased throughout the process of revision, particularly between the second and third editions.

The accessibility of Stubbes's prose to a modern readership might potentially encourage the sense that the *Abuses* offers an unmediated window onto late Elizabethan culture. The book is in fact a carefully contrived piece which blends

---

[21] Shifts in typeface have in all cases been reproduced in the present edition.

a variety of literary traditions. Stubbes calls it an "anatomy", a genre of writing which was popular in the sixteenth century as a means by which writers strove, in Devon Hodges' words, "to strip away false appearances and expose the truth" (*Renaissance Fictions of Anatomy*, 1–2). Certainly, an almost scientific urge to catalogue and dissect abuses provides a strong organizing influence. "You haue borne me in hande of many and grieuous abuses, raigning in **England**", Spudeus comments after listening to Philoponus's disquisition on pride, "but ... I pray you describe vnto me more particularly, the sundrie abuses of apparell there vsed, running ouer by degrees, the whole state thereof, that I may see, as it were, the perfect anatomie of that Nation in apparell" (1389–96). The dialogue to this point is little more than an extended introduction; only with Spudeus's demand for exhaustive detail, for a "perfect anatomie", does Stubbes's critique begin in earnest.

This self-proclaimed anatomy shades in a number of places into a style which approaches modern tabloid journalism. The period from 1580 to 1640 witnessed the emergence of the news pamphlet, a form of popular writing which, while ostensibly leading its readers away from sin, in fact provided writers with the opportunity to relate unusual happenings in sensationalist and graphic detail.[22] As Stubbes published such topical pamphlets throughout his career, it is not surprising to find him incorporating this type of attention-grabbing material into a longer work. Reports of events such as the collapse of Paris garden, the supposedly true account of drunkards who were served alcohol by the devil, and startling natural phenomena ranging from blazing stars to monstrous births to wheat falling from the sky are scattered throughout the *Abuses* as evidence of God's wrath towards those who flout his power. Expected, presumably, to draw customers and boost sales, these news stories were advertised on the title page of each of the editions, every edition printing a variation of the promise made in O1 that the book includes "**most fearefull Examples of Gods Iudgementes, executed vpon the wicked for the same, aswell in AILGNA of late, as in other places, elsewhere**" (cf. figures 1–7).

Other features of the book such as the chance encounter between the world traveler and a local inhabitant, the dialogue format, the discussion of the peculiar manners of a remote land, and (at least in the first three editions) the spelling of proper names such as "London" and "Congleton" in reverse and often in Latin

---

[22] Sandra Clark offers a comprehensive discussion of the pamphlet genre in *The Elizabethan Pamphleteers: Popular Moralistic Pamphlets 1580–1640* (London: The Athlone Press, 1983).

(i.e., "Munidnol" and "Notelgnoc") are strongly reminiscent of the conventions of Utopian literature.[23] The *Abuses*, however, differs significantly from more typical examples of Utopian writing in that instead of recounting a visit to an idealized and imaginary land where the traveler is shown around by a local guide, Philoponus, the author's mouthpiece, assumes the powerful roles of both traveler and guide, introducing his fellow countryman to the corrupt and immoral customs practiced in the far-away country of England (known as "Ailgna" prior to the fourth edition). Instead of positing the merits of what might be, Stubbes berates the wickedness of what is.[24]

The *Abuses* thus partakes of literary genres as diverse as anatomies, Utopian writing, and news pamphlets; but one of the most illuminating generic influences is the tradition of Complaint. English Complaint literature, unlike formal Satire which took as its model classical Latin exempla, was a homegrown genre. John Peter identifies four recurrent moral themes in Complaint: attacks on professions, attacks on groups of people associated by a particular abuse, attacks on abuses, and discussion of the general principles on which the whole attitude of Complaint is founded, a category which might include, for example, human mortality and sinfulness. In addition to this, Complaint writers place before one's imagination a vivid awareness of Death and Judgment Day, pointing ahead to the inevitable retribution which will result to those who fail to heed their warnings (Peter, *Complaint and Satire*, 60–80). Bewailing present wickedness and driven by an earnest desire to incite the reader to amendment of life, the complainant rehearses a set of standard *topoi* while nostalgically looking back to better days. This was the standard format of Complaint as it was perpetuated for over three hundred years, and significantly, the genre altered very little over that period of time.

The boundaries among Complaint, Satire, and anatomy are notoriously fluid, and it would be misleading to present generic distinctions between them as clear-cut. Northrop Frye, for example, introduces the term "Menippean Satire" in his *Anatomy of Criticism* to describe a form of writing with apparently a

---

[23] The characteristic features of Utopian literature are analysed by Northrop Frye in "Varieties of Literary Utopias," in *Utopias and Utopian Thought*, ed. Frank E. Manuel (Boston: Beacon Press, 1965), 25–49.

[24] In her survey of sixteenth-century Utopian literature, Helen C. White tracks a shift from the sort of creative and imaginative speculation found in More's *Utopia* to a dissatisfied acceptance of the current social order typical of a writer such as Stubbes (*Social Criticism in Popular Religious Literature of the Sixteenth Century* [New York: Macmillan, 1944, repr. New York: Octagon Books, 1965], 81).

number of the same characteristics as Complaint, only to substitute for it the less unwieldy label "anatomy", choices which make clear the overlap among the three genres (310–11). But without making these various related categories either unnecessarily or arbitrarily fixed, it is possible to highlight certain key conventions within which Stubbes is working. The constancy of tone and subject-matter to which Peter refers in his discussion of Complaint, for example, is particularly relevant when one comes to evaluate the extent to which Stubbes can be read as a witness to the practices and attitudes of late sixteenth-century England. Far from engaging with the particulars of his society in an original or unique manner, Stubbes reworks a familiar and age-old literary tradition. Although he introduces specific details about Elizabethan life ranging from clothing trends to rent-racking, the *Abuses* lacks the sharp focus or cutting edge usually associated with Satire, and the commentary repeatedly slips from precisely observed details to sweeping complaints about a universal moral deterioration. The book's position within a tradition of Complaint, moreover, explains how Stubbes could publish the fourth edition of the *Abuses* in 1595 — eleven years after the previous edition, twelve years after the first edition — without significantly updating it to account for the intervening decade: the priority of Complaint is not to present accurate social observation, but to condemn more generally a perceived downward slide in social morals.

The genre of the anatomy perhaps had the greatest impact on the manner in which Stubbes writes Complaint. Literary anatomies, as suggested previously, are premised on careful and detailed examination of the subject under study: abundance and amplification are inherent in the form. But it is this very excess which undermines the effectiveness of the *Abuses* as Complaint. Attempting to control social excess, Stubbes is himself swept away by an excessive prose style, caught up in the very debasement he is struggling to contain.[25] This is the greatest irony of Stubbes's work: passionately committed to stamping out the abuses of Elizabethan England, Stubbes is remembered for having preserved in print the very practices he so strongly opposed, and his usefulness as a witness to a style of life now lost to modern scholars results from a near obsessive concern for description and detail. Indeed, the most remarkable feature of the language

---

[25] Writing of anatomies more generally, Devon Hodges comments that it is not unusual to find the literary form subverting the moral purpose in this manner: ". . . the cure had all the symptoms of the disease it was to heal . . . In the process of stripping away excess, the anatomist creates it. In the end, an anatomy makes the physical dominant over the abstract, the parts more important than any abstract unity" (*Renaissance Fictions of Anatomy* [Amherst, MA: University of Massachusetts Press, 1985], 39–40).

of the *Abuses* is its proliferation of words, paralleling the book's proliferation of abuses. The extent to which he savors, even revels in, his writing is obvious. Stubbes is a severe critic of disorder, whose unchecked verbal profusion reveals him to be himself tainted by the very abuse against which he writes. The immense energy of his prose style derives from the tension which exists between his imaginative identification with, yet intellectual rejection of, excess.

It is by means of this insistent verbal excess, however, that the *Abuses* is as forward-looking as it is nostalgic. The sixteenth century was a period of extreme social, economic, and religious change in England; seemingly everything was in flux, and a writer such as Stubbes provides striking evidence of the personal and social anxieties such a period of transition could occasion. But the *Abuses* also, paradoxically, provides the language through which change can be conceptualized. Not simply reflecting disorder, Stubbes contributes to the process by which that disorder is resolved over time.[26] The importance of the *Abuses* thus rests partly in the role Stubbes played at a historic moment in the construction of an intellectual framework through which Elizabethan society could make sense of itself.

About the time of the publication of the fourth edition of the *Abuses* in 1595, this sort of social debate moved into the realm of the formal Satire, and from there, onto the stage in city comedy. Complaint disappeared, or rather, mutated into something different, as the traditional literary form became increasingly regarded, in Peter's words, as passé (*Complaint and Satire*, 111). Stubbes's novelty as a writer therefore derives neither from the particulars of his account of Elizabethan vice, nor from his tone of moral criticism, both of which were well-known, and well-practiced, generic conventions in the Complaint tradition. If Stubbes stands out from other writers of his time, this is probably because his scrutiny of the age is by far the most idiosyncratic.

More ambitious claims to originality one might wish to advance for the *Abuses* are further challenged by the relation of the book to its source-texts. In his dedicatory letter to the fourth edition, Stubbes writes that he "collected" his book "with paines & good will ... for the benefit of [his] cuntry, the pleasure of the godly, and amendment of the wicked" (113–15). His choice of verb is apt:

---

[26] Lawrence Manley makes a similar point with reference to the manner in which the genre of Complaint gave shape to the growing political dominance of urban life. Manley argues that it "invent[ed] a vocabulary that 'naturalized' or normalized the urbanizing process as a result of attacking, from a traditional, non-urban point of view, the maldistributions resulting from the urban concentration of wealth and power" (*Literature and Culture in Early Modern London* [Cambridge: Cambridge University Press, 1995], 76).

Stubbes not infrequently incorporates into his own work lengthy passages from other writers' published material. It is well known that the antitheatricalists lifted blocks of text from each other as a matter of course, but Stubbes freely appropriated material on any aspect of English society in which he was interested. It would be misleading, however, to refer to this activity as plagiarism. Sandra Clark comments that ". . . the Elizabethans, and the pamphleteers in particular, had a conception of literary borrowing that is not necessarily to be identified with stealing . . . They had not yet developed the sense of exclusive rights that belongs to the professional attitude, and they seemed also to feel that using someone else's material, especially if it was older, would lend their own work an extra authority" (*Elizabethan Pamphleteers*, 33). It seems to have been this desire for "extra authority" which led Stubbes to dip into relevant secondary material to copy down those excerpts which reinforced his views on Elizabethan life. The precise extent of his dependence on such texts is worth closer discussion for the light it sheds on his manner of composition.

Stubbes scatters *sententiae*, either in Latin and English or only in English, throughout the *Abuses*. Often these sayings derive from the classics, patristic authors, and the writings of contemporary church leaders, and where possible, I have identified sources for them in the commentary. However, original sources for what is in effect commonplace material are not always available. In these instances, I have instead made an effort to demonstrate the proverbial status of the saying through reference to scholarly collections of proverbs.[27] Lengthier references, on the other hand, to named authorities such as the church father John Chrysostom (c. 347–407), the Roman emperor Alexander Severus (222–235), and the Greek rhetorician and philosopher Maximus Tyrius (second century C.E.), cited explicitly as corroboration for Stubbes's own views, were for the most part lifted from intermediary texts.[28] Consequently, although such prompting is not always necessary, interest expressed by Spudeus in the judgements of

---

[27] In English these include M. P. Tilley, *A Dictionary of the Proverbs in England in the Sixteenth and Seventeenth Centuries* (Ann Arbor: University of Michigan Press, 1950), and R. W. Dent, *Proverbial Language in English Drama Exclusive of Shakespeare, 1495–1616: An Index* (Berkeley: University of California Press, 1984). For the purposes of tracing proverbs in Latin I have mainly relied on A. Otto, *Die Sprichwörter und sprichwörtlichen Redensarten der Römer* (Leipzig: Teubner, 1890), and Hans Walther, *Proverbia Sententiaeque Latinitatis Medii Aevi* (Göttingen: Vandenhoeck and Ruprecht, 1963–1967) and its *Nova series* (Göttingen: Vandenhoeck and Ruprecht, 1982–1986).

[28] The only such authorities cited in the *Abuses* which I have not been able to trace to immediately contemporary secondary sources are the words of St. Cyprian and St. Ambrose on face-painting (cf. 2016–211, and notes).

"Fathers and Councelles" (6514–15) or in the opinions of "good men from the beginning" (5418) invariably signals a transition from original to borrowed material. The text to which Stubbes turned most frequently for such erudition is Northbrooke's *Treatise wherein Dicing, Dauncing, Vaine playes or Enterluds with other idle pastimes &c . . . are reproued* (c. 1577).

The *Treatise*, like the *Abuses*, is written "dialogue-wise" between two characters who happen to meet in the road. There is a strong possibility that Stubbes's choice of format was influenced by Northbrooke, but as the dialogue tradition was by this time well-established, the resemblance may be only coincidental.[29] Whereas Northbrooke's speakers are called "Age" and "Youth", Stubbes gives his characters names which translate from the Greek into English as "hard worker" (Philoponus) and "earnest student" (Spudeus). These particular names would have had scholastic resonances for many of Stubbes's readers. The former alludes to John Philoponus, the sixth-century Alexandrian philosopher who confuted scholarly commentaries on Plato and Aristotle that were inconsistent with the tenets of Christian belief (Schmitt et al., 786). His writings were becoming available in Latin from about 1535 and were influential on the thought of, for example, Benedetti and Galileo.[30] Spudeus (Greek *Spoudaios*), by contrast, was a name familiar from Aristotle's *Nicomachean Ethics* (3.4, 1113a). Originally a word to describe "the zealous good man", it eventually came to mean "scholar".

As the title of the *Treatise* suggests, Stubbes and Northbrooke address a number of the same issues, and it is in those chapters that the parallels between the two books are most obvious. Stubbes's method, for example, of refuting Scriptural support for dancing by having the evidence voiced by Spudeus and examined and subsequently discredited by the more knowledgeable Philoponus is a technique picked up from Northbrooke. Likewise, the laws cited against gaming at 6928–87 and the holy and secular decrees against dancing at 6523–96 were all first printed in the *Treatise*. The arguments presented in opposition to the theaters at lines 5394–490, on the other hand, were cobbled together from

---

[29] Virginia Cox analyzes Latin dialogues with particular reference to the development of the genre in Italy in *The Renaissance Dialogue: Literary Dialogue in Its Social and Political Contexts, Castiglione to Galileo* (Cambridge: Cambridge University Press, 1992). Other English social commentaries that make use of the form in the vernacular are Thomas Lupton's *Siquila. Too good, to be true* (1580) and Christopher Fetherston's *A Dialogue agaynst light, lewde, and lasciuious dauncing* (1582).

[30] Philoponus as a character name also appears in Juan Luis Vives's *Dialogues* (1539), and in the drama *Hecastus* (1539) by the Dutch humanist Georg Macropedius.

extracts copied out of both the *Treatise* and Gosson's *Playes Confuted in Fiue Actions* (c. 1582).[31]

The extent of Stubbes's borrowing from *Playes Confuted* is almost entirely limited to this single chapter on stage-plays and interludes. The one exception to this is a sentence inserted in the chapter on women's apparel entitled "Doublets for Women in England", where Stubbes modifies Gosson's attack on the transvestite boy actor to apply it to the cross-dressed woman in the streets of London (cf. 2424–28n.). Oddly enough, although Stubbes inveighs at length against the theaters much later in the book, he fails to return to the issue of cross-dressing, making no mention of the boy actors. This omission is surprising in itself, but especially so given that he found Gosson's views on the subject memorable enough to adapt them to the issue of women in men's clothing.

The influence of another work by each of these same two authors can also be traced. Gosson's first antitheatrical pamphlet, *The Schoole of Abuse* (1579), provided a few examples from the classics against music at 6673–87, while testimonies against usury printed in Northbrooke's *The poore mans garden* (1571) were fitted into Stubbes's discussion of the same topic at 4795–809. Northbrooke's text further suggested the series of comparative statements which begins, "An Vsurer is worse then a Theefe" (4767–94). The citation of the words of St. Ambrose at 4795–96 demonstrates that Stubbes must have been working from one of the later editions of *The poore mans garden*, as this quotation was not included prior to the third edition of about 1575.

The classical authorities cited in the opening chapter on pride (1219–50) were taken from the *Homily against Excess of Apparel*. Stubbes adapted his source only slightly by making some of the examples, which in the sermon are specific to women, pertain to both sexes. Other less lengthy echoes of this homily have been noted in the commentary (cf. esp. 1184–91 and 1367–83). While passages from other Church homilies and the *Book of Common Prayer* were not worked into the *Abuses* to quite the same extent, their influence is discernible. The explanation of animals' disobedience to humans at 7159–75, for example, can be traced to a sentence printed at the beginning of the *Homily against Disobedience and wilful Rebellion*, and the purposes of matrimony which are set out at 3201–10 form part of the traditional wedding ceremony.

The influence of the Bible on the language and imagery of the *Abuses* is pervasive, but, as in the passages which draw on Northbrooke's and Gosson's

---

[31] Precise verbal similarities between the *Abuses* and its source-texts are explored at length in the commentary and will not for the most part be repeated here.

treatises, Stubbes's use of biblical authority tends to follow a certain recognizable pattern. The chapters on whoredom, drunkenness, and covetousness begin with a debate as to whether these features of English society should be considered an abuse. In each instance Spudeus half-heartedly attempts a brief defense before being swayed to Philoponus's reasoning. Then he requests his traveling companion to show him "out of the word of God, wher this so detestable a vice is reprooued" (4417–19; see also 3918–22 and 3271–74). This evidence is followed by examples from the Bible of people who were punished for such faults. Sometimes one or the other half of this basic formula will be left out: in the chapters on pride and gluttony, for example, only lists of punishments are rehearsed, whereas in the material on usury, the reader is provided with only the words of God against the practice.[32] Stubbes collects material out of the Bible in the same manner as he borrows material from contemporary writers; the effect is to overwhelm the reader with classical, patristic, and biblical testimony.

Although Stubbes does not commonly misquote the Bible out of ignorance, he does at times stretch his interpretation of a passage in order to make it better suit his argument. In his discussion of punishments of whoredom, for example, Philoponus states that Judah "vnderstanding that his daughter in Lawe was **impregnate**, and great with childe, and not knowing by whome, commaunded that she should be burned, without any further delay" (3347–50). What Stubbes neglects to mention is that Tamar, Judah's daughter-in-law, was in fact pregnant with Judah's child. Far from being burned, Tamar is in the end justified, Judah acknowledging that she "is more righteous then I: for *she hath done it* because I gaue her not to Shelah my sonne" (Gen. 38:26). Similarly, in the chapter on gluttony, Philoponus implies that Belshazzar's kingdom was taken from him solely as a result of his sumptuous banqueting when in fact the Lord was angered by the king's idolatry and pride in eating and drinking from the temple vessels (cf. 3733–39 and Dan. 5:22–23).

Biblical and classical authority in the *Abuses* is set alongside news events which demonstrate the judgement of the Lord on unrepentant sinners. Most of these tales either cannot be traced at all, Stubbes's immediate sources for them having long since disappeared, or else they surface in so many extant pamphlets and chronicle histories that it is impossible to identify which — if any — the author read. It seems likely that in many instances these reports circulated

---

[32] The one major exception to this pattern is found in the chapter on dancing where Philoponus refutes biblical evidence cited by Spudeus in support of the activity; as already discussed, the particular format of this chapter was probably suggested to Stubbes by Northbrooke's *Treatise*.

throughout London and even the country through ballads and word of mouth.[33] Stubbes also borrowed material from his own work, the description of the death of the man who swore by God's blood having been published separately, as Stubbes points out, "about two yeares agoe in verse" (5108).[34]

Finally, we might be led to think that there may have existed a book by Iacobus Stuperius entitled "lib. de diuersis nostrae aetatis habitibus" ("the book about the different apparel of our age") on which Stubbes drew heavily in the chapters on pride of apparel. This is the second of only two source-texts which the author acknowledges (the other being his own ballad), and he refers to it repeatedly to demonstrate the contrast between the simple attire worn by foreigners and the gorgeous clothing worn by the English (592–609, 2777–828). I have not been able to identify this book. It seems likely that it is a deliberate fiction, Stubbes coining the name Stuperius from the Latin verb "stupere", meaning "to be astonished" or "to be stupefied". Tellingly, Stuperius surfaces again in one of Stubbes's later dialogues, *The Theater of the Popes Monarchie*, as a character name.

Stubbes's habit of incorporating into his own work passages from other tracts, sometimes verbatim, was not exceptional. Northbrooke's *Treatise*, a text which proved so useful to Stubbes, itself prints material which can be traced to Sir Thomas Elyot's *The Boke Named the Gouernour* and Rychard Hyrde's translation of Lodovicus (Juan Luis) Vives's *The Instruction of a christen woman* (cf. 6928–48n. and 6545–63n.).[35] Passages of borrowed authority in the *Abuses* represent what seems to have been considered legitimate engagement with current moral and political debates. Instead of being dismissed out of hand as derivative and even unethical, they are perhaps more appropriately viewed in terms of the author's attempt to gain credibility for his attack on sixteenth-century English society. Stubbes's stand on certain key issues and some of the preoccupations which can be seen to underlie his polemic form the subject of the next section.

---

[33] Possible sources for some of them are suggested in the commentary. Verbal parallels, for example, between the account of the collapse of Paris Garden found in the *Abuses* and *A godly exhortation* by John Field (January 1583) strongly suggest that Stubbes based his report on Field's pamphlet (cf. 7053–55n.).

[34] The ballad to which Stubbes refers, "A fearefull and terrible example of Gods iuste iudgement", is no longer extant, but what we know of it is discussed at pp. 2–3.

[35] William Ringler, who describes Northbrooke as "a quotation-monger of some industry", cites further sources for the *Treatise* in his biographical and critical study of Stephen Gosson (*Stephen Gosson* [Princeton: Princeton University Press, 1942], 59).

The Anatomie
of Abuſes:

Contayning
A DISCOVERIE, OR BRIEFE
Summarie of ſuch Notable Vices and Im-
perfe&tions, as now raigne in many Chriſtian Countreyes of the VVorlde : but (eſ-
peciallie) in a verie famous ILANDE
called AILGNA : Together, with
moſt fearefull Examples of Gods Iudgementes, executed vpon the wicked for the
ſame, aſwell in AILGNA of late, as in
other places, elſewhere.

Verie Godly, to be read of all true Chꝛiſtians,
euerie where : but moſt needefull, to
be regarded in ENGLANDE.

Made dialogue-wiſe, by Phillip Stubbes.

Seene and allowed, according to order.

MATH. 3. ver. 2. Repent, for the kingdome of God
is at hande.
Lve. 13. ver. 5. I ſay vnto you (ſaith Chriſt) except
you repent, you ſhall all periſh .

¶ Pꝛinted at London , by Richard
Iones. 1. Maij, 1583.

Figure 1.
Title page from *The Anatomie of Abuses* by Philip Stubbes,
May 1, 1583. Reference (shelfmark): 8° S.269 Art. Actual size.
By permission of the Bodleian Library, University of Oxford.

The Anatomie
_hɸ:_ of Abuſes: _Kennet_

Contayning

A DISCOVERIE, OR BRIEFE
Summarie of ſuch Notable Vices and Im-
perfeċtions, as now raigne in many Chriſtian Countreyes of the Worlde : but (eſ-
peciallie) in a verie famous ILANDE
called AILGNA : Together, with
moſt fearefull Examples of Gods Iudgementes, executed vpon the wicked for the
ſame, afwell in AILGNA of late, as in
other places, elſewhere.

Uerie Godly, to be read of all true Chʒiſtians,
euerie where : but moſt needefull, to
be regarded in ENGLANDE.

Made dialogue-wiſe, by Phillip Stubbes.

Seene and allowed, according to order.

MATH. 3. ver. 2. Repent, for the kingdome of God
is at hande.
LVC. 13. ver. 5. I ſay vnto you (ſaith Chriſt) except
you repent, you ſhall all periſh .

¶ **Pʒinted** at London , **by** Richard
Jones. 29. Maij. 1 5 8 3. _17_

And which is moꝛe, I pꝛay God there be not
ſome vile Atheiſts,ꝗ Nullifidians amõgſt thē,
who iñ their harts ſay non eſt Deus, there is
no God at all , and with the filthie ſwiniſhe
Epicures cry out.Emoi theos tou parou theou
to mallon. that is: giue me ỹ fruition of theſe
tempoꝛall ioyes pꝛeſent,ꝗ foꝛ the reſt that are
ſo come, let God alone: as though indǽd,they
belǽued there were none ſuch. And ỹ there
be ſome ſuch,their liues ſhowe plaine: foꝛ be-
ſides all theſe (with infinit the like Abuſes.)
what colde ȝeale, what ſmall deuotion , and
what froȝen affection is their now a dayes to
the woꝛd of God?

In time of palpable ignoꝛance , I mean. in
time of papiſtrie, when their Temples were
ſtuffed with Idolatrie,ſuperſticion,Imagery
and ſuch like:when God was diſhonoꝛed euerie way, his ſacraments pꝛoſtituted,his bleſſed woꝛd conculcate, andtroden vnder fǒt ,
and when they them ſelues vnderſtǒde nothing that they heard: then I ſay, euen then,
was there moꝛe ȝeale,feruencie and deuotion
to the ſame,moꝛe then Mahometicall heathē-
rie ꝗ hethnicall diuitrie , then is now to the
bleſſed woꝛd of God,the fǒd of our ſaluation.

So that it falleth out vith them, as it dǒth
with a man that hauingſoꝛe eyes , is not a-
ble to abide the bꝛight ſeames of the Sun.

Foꝛ their liues being wicked,and deteſtable,
they

Figure 3.
Signature P8v (cancelled page) from *The Anatomie of Abuses* by Philip Stubbes,
May 1, 1583. Reference (shelfmark): 8º Crynes 833. Actual size.
By permission of the Bodleian Library, University of Oxford.

The Anatomie
of Abuses:

Containing,
A DISCOVERIE, OR BRIEFE
Summarie of such Notable Vices and Imperfections, as now raigne in many Countreyes of the World: but (especiallye) in a
famous ILANDE called AILGNA:
Together, with most fearefull Examples
of Gods Iudgements, executed vppon the
wicked for the same, afwel in AILGNA
of late, as in other places, elsewhere.

Uery Godly, to be reade of all true Christians;
but most nædefull to be regarded
in ENGLANDE.

¶ Made Dialogue-wise by Phillip Stubbes.

Scene and allowed, according to order.

Math. 3. Verf. 2.
Repent, for the Kingdome of God is at hande.

Lvc. 13. Verf. 5.
I say vnto you (saith Christ) except you
repent, you shall all perish.

¶ Printed at London, by Richard
Iones, 16. August, 1583.

Figure 4.
Title page from *The Anatomie of Abuses* by Philip Stubbes,
August 16, 1583. Reference (shelfmark): G.10369. Actual size.
By permission of the British Library.

The Anatomie

of Abuſes:

Containing

A Diſcouerie, or briefe Sum-
marie of ſuch Notable Vices and Corruptions, as nowe raigne in many Chriſtian Countreyes of the Worlde : but(eſpecially)in the
Countrey of A I L G N A: Together,with moſt
fearefull Examples of Gods Iudgementes, executed vpon the wicked for the ſame,aſ-
well in A I L G N A of late, as in
other places,elſe-
where.

Uery godly,to be read of all true Chri-
*ſtians,euery where: but moſt chiefly,to be
regarded in England.*

Made Dialogue-wiſe by P H I L L I P   S T V B S.

**And now newly reuiſed recognized, and aug-
mented the third time by the ſame Author.**

MATH.3.Ver.2.
Repent, for the kingdome of God is at hande.
LVKE 13.Ver.5.
I ſay vnto you,except you repent you ſhall all periſh.

Printed at *London,* **by** *Richard*
Iones 12. October. 1 5 8 4.

Figure 5.
Title page from *The Anatomie of Abuses* by Philip Stubbes,
October 12, 1584. Reference: *STC* 23377.5. Actual size.
By permission of the Houghton Library, Harvard University.

The Anatomie

of Abuſes:

Containing

A Diſcouerie, or briefe Sum-

marie of ſuch Notable Vices and Corruptions, as nowe raigne in many Chriſtian Countreyes of the Worlde : but(eſpecially)in the
Countrey of A I L G N A: Together,with moſt
fearefull Examples of Gods Iudgementes, executed vpon the wicked for the ſame, aſwell in A I L G N A of late, as in
other places, elſe-
where.

Uery godly, to be read of all true Chri=
ſtians, euery where: but moſt chiefly, to be
regarded in England.

Made Dialogue-wiſe by P H I L L I P S T V B S.

And now newly reuiſed recognized, and augmented the third time by the ſame Author.

MATH.3.ver.2.
Repent, for the kingdome of God is at hande.

LVKE.13.ver.5.
I ſay vnto you, except you repent you ſhall all periſh.

¶Printed at London, by Richard
Iones 1 5 8 5.

The Anatomie

of Abuses.

Containing

A Description of such nota-

ble Vices and enormities, as raigne in many Countries of
the world, but especiallie in this Realme of England: Together
with most fearefull examples of Gods heauie Iudgements inflicted vpon the wicked for the same
as well in *England* of late, as in other
places else where.

Uerie godly to be read of all true Christians
euery where, but most chiefly, to bee
regarded in England.

Made dialogue-wise by Philip Stubs, *Gent.*

Now, the fourth time, newly corrected and
inlarged by the same Author.

Imprinted at London by Richard Iohnes, at the sign of the
Rose and Crowne next aboue S. *Andrewes* Church
in Holborne. 1595.

Figure 7.
Title page from *The Anatomie of Abuses* by Philip Stubbes,
1595. Reference (shelfmark): C.25.c.12. Actual size.
By permission of the British Library.

THE *ANATOMIE* OF *ABUSES* AND
ELIZABETHAN SOCIETY

The *Abuses* opens with a lengthy and astoundingly detailed scrutiny of sixteenth-century fashion. Itemizing first men's and then women's clothing and working systematically from their embroidered taffeta hats down to their pinked velvet pantofles, Stubbes denounces the rich apparel of those who do not belong to the nobility, gentry, or magistracy as wicked extravagance which will in the end lead to dearth and financial ruin throughout England. The sin out of which this excess has grown is pride, specifically pride of apparel, which is demonstrated by the wearing of clothing "more gorgeous, sumptuous, and precious then our state, calling, or condition of life requireth, whereby we are puffed vp into Pride, and induced to think of our selues, more then we ought, being but vile earth and miserable sinners" (536–41). As such statements make clear, it is not sumptuous clothing in itself to which Stubbes is opposed, but rather its indiscriminate use by low-ranking members of society. Pride of apparel is a far more dangerous fault than either mental or verbal glorification of one's condition since it remains written on the body for all to see (541–54). This visual transgression, as Marjorie Garber observes, was especially disturbing in a culture in which ideally, "a person's social station, social role, gender and other indicators of identity in the world could be *read*, without ambiguity or uncertainty" (*Vested Interests*, 26). Adorned in their finery, social upstarts — or "dunghill gentlemen" as Stubbes calls them — not only tempt others to similar excess, but, more frighteningly, are impossible to situate within the social hierarchy: "there is such a confuse mingle mangle of apparell in **England**, and such horrible excesse thereof, as euery one is permitted to flaunt it out, in what apparell he listeth himselfe, or can get by any meanes. So that it is very hard to knowe, who is noble, who is worshipfull, who is a Gentleman, who is not . . . And this I accompt a great confusion, and a generall disorder in a Christian common wealth" (711–26).

The hierarchy of degree, which assigned to each person a social ranking which was construed as an essential and immutable aspect of identity, provided Elizabethans with a comprehensive and popular model of a stable, well-ordered society.[36] The supposedly rigid boundaries of rank separating the "better" from

---

[36] The transition made in England in the sixteenth and early seventeenth centuries from the language of a society of estates to the hierarchy of degree and the more informal notion of "sorts" of people is traced by Keith Wrightson in "Estates, Degrees, and Sorts: Changing Perceptions of Society in Tudor and Stuart England," in *Language, History and Class*, ed. Penelope J. Corfield (Oxford: Basil Blackwell, 1991), 30–52.

the "meaner" sort of person were blurred, however, when commoners dressed themselves in the silks and velvets appertaining to the upper orders; exceeding the prescribed limits, these social aspirants seemed in danger of erasing the boundaries altogether. Struggling against the chaos threatened by such cross-dressing, Stubbes attempts to impose order by insisting that apparel is abused when it no longer stands as the true outward manifestation of social position. In this, his thinking was consistent with that of the state authorities. Sumptuary proclamations issued throughout the Tudor reign carefully limited the use in clothing of certain fabrics and forms of trimming on the basis of wealth and status, while the *Homily against Excess of Apparel* read out in churches around the country during the reign of Elizabeth I drove home to its listeners the precept that "all may not look to wear like apparel, but every one, according to his degree, as God hath placed him" (*Sermons*, 326–27).[37]

The end of the sixteenth century, however, was marked by widespread movement both up and down the social scale.[38] As luxury consumer goods became increasingly affordable to many outside of the nobility and gentry, the premise that everyone's position in society was fixed and God-given began to appear less self-evident. On the contrary, wealthy commoners dressed in the clothes assigned to the gentry were regularly demonstrating that admission to the élite depended on little more than having the resources to perform the role with conviction.[39] Stubbes's single-minded determination to preserve the function of clothing as a clear marker of social rank thus serves to put off the more deeply disturbing possibility that degree may not in fact be fixed at all — that individuals could shape or even transform their status simply by changing their clothes. The irony of this tactic, as Jean Howard points out, is that an insistence on costume as an accurate visual projection of one's essential identity highlights further the performative dimension of social station (*Stage and Social Struggle*, 33).[40]

---

[37] The attempts to restrict legally the use of luxury consumer goods were intended not only to preserve distinctions between social ranks but also to alleviate the detrimental economic consequences of buying products manufactured for the most part abroad (Elizabeth Baldwin, *Sumptuary Legislation and Personal Regulation in England* [Baltimore: Johns Hopkins University Press, 1926], 212, 224); Stubbes's advocacy at 649–66 of domestic wools and kerseys over foreign silks and velvets reflects this concern to "buy British".

[38] Increased social mobility in the period is discussed by Laslett, *World We Have Lost Further Explored*, chaps. 2, 10; Lawrence Stone, *Crisis of the Aristocracy 1558–1641* (Oxford: Clarendon Press, 1965), chap. 2; and Keith Wrightson, *English Society 1580–1680* (London: Routledge, 1993), chap. 1.

[39] Wrightson, "Estates, Degrees, and Sorts," 39–40.

[40] Ann Rosalind Jones and Peter Stallybrass likewise draw attention to the precarious

Committed to policing transgressions of dress, Stubbes begins his campaign by stigmatizing excessively rich clothing as an unnatural perversion: "doe not the most of our **fond Inuentions**, and **newfangled fashions** rather deforme, then adorne vs: disguise [i.e., disfigure] vs, then become vs: making vs rather to resemble sauage beastes, and bruitish monsters, then continent, sober and chast Christians?" (563–68). What represents lawful display of birth and authority in the nobility, gentry, and magistracy becomes shameful deformity in anyone else, a cloak contrived to conceal one's true social identity which only succeeds in making the offender monstrous. The language of disfigurement and deception runs throughout the chapters on apparel. However, as the author embarks on his inventory of Elizabethan costume, concerns about the blurring of distinctions of rank become overlaid with equally pressing anxieties about the blurring of gender differences. Pampered in luxurious and richly ornamented clothing, men, Stubbes claims, are becoming effeminate and weak. Thus, after describing the gorgeously embroidered shirts made out of cambric, holland, or lawn supposedly worn by nearly all men in England, Philoponus comments that such indulgence "transnatureth" them, making them "weaker, tenderer, and nesher [more delicate], then otherwise they would be if they were vsed to hardnesse" (1577–603). The sight of men dressed, albeit not in woman's apparel, but nonetheless in beautiful and delicate and therefore *womanish* apparel, provokes the fear that men are adopting not only the clothing but also the manners and characteristics of the opposite sex.

The sense in which Stubbes uses the term "effeminate" to disparage male dandies needs careful qualification. While the adjective could at times imply that men who dress and behave in a luxurious fashion are attracted to other men, it could also suggest the exact opposite, that such men are overly inclined to women (*OED*, adj. 3). The context in which it appears in a later chapter confirms that Stubbes was familiar with this alternative sense. Stubbes criticizes music — using terminology similar to that with which he describes the effect of costly linen shirts on men — as "alluring the hearers to a certaine kind of **effeminacie**, & **pusillanimitie**" (6659–60). When used to facilitate "filthy dauncing" between men and women, music literally maddens a man: losing all control over his mind and heart, a man who dances to music with a woman becomes both effeminate and lecherous, and is driven to satisfy his furious lust through sexual inter-

---

relation between costume and identity: "Stubbes wants clothes to place subjects recognizably, to materialize identities for onlooker and wearer alike. But he is forced to recognize what he deplores: that clothes are detachable, that they can move from body to body" (*Renaissance Clothing and the Materials of Memory* [Cambridge: Cambridge University Press, 2000], 5).

course.[41] Stubbes's recommendation that this spark of lust should be contained through men dancing by themselves and women dancing by themselves (6485–505) suggests that in his view, "womanish" men are not so much in danger of engaging in sexual relations with other men as of becoming inordinately given to sexual pleasure with women. The effeminate man is thus defined in the *Abuses* not by homosexual desire but by a more general proclivity to material and sexual indulgence; virility, in contrast, resides in a stoic renunciation of luxury, beauty, and passion.[42] According to Stubbes, a slavish adherence to fashion makes men victim to an enervating voluptuousness. The loss of authority and status which ensues is figured in the powerful metaphorical image of men degenerating into women.

By contrast, lavishly dressed women are read not as men, but whores. Berating parents' misguided indulgence of their daughters' desire for luxurious apparel, Stubbes fumes that this "ouer great lenity . . . may rather be counted an extreame cruelty, then a fatherly loue or pittie of them towards their children: For what maketh them so soone Whoores, Strumpets, Harlots and Baudes, as that cockering of them doeth?" (2526–33). Stubbes adds two new concluding chapters to the material on costume in the second edition of the *Abuses* printed in August 1583: "**The dayly exercises of the Women of England**" and "**Gardens in Englande**".[43] Although introduced in the context of Elizabethan fashion excesses, these revisions in fact constitute an attack on fashionably dressed women who wilfully assert their independence from male control. Forever arguing with their family and neighbors, sitting in their doorways to see and be seen, going out in public to participate in illicit, extra-marital trysts, these assertive, self-possessed women appropriate to themselves the power perceived to have been lost by their male counterparts. Stubbes's additional material reveals more explicitly what in the first edition is only glanced at with the abusive epithet "whore": the immense

---

[41] Ian Frederick Moulton argues that a perception of eroticism, with its attendant disorders, underlies Stubbes's sense of the corrupting influence not just of music in the form of ballads but of "wicked bookes" more generally (7301 ff). He explains that "the rhetoric of effeminacy addressed itself to all poetic forms, from street verse and ballads to vernacular translations of classical texts and aristocratic coterie verse" (*Before Pornography: Erotic Writing in Early Modern England* [Oxford: Oxford University Press, 2000], 85).

[42] This point is supported by Gary Spear's analysis of the manifold connotations and implications of the idea of effeminacy in the early modern period in "Shakespeare's 'Manly' Parts: Masculinity and Effeminacy in *Troilus and Cressida*," *Shakespeare Quarterly* 44 (1993): 409–22, esp. 416–18.

[43] Included in the last three versions of the book, these additions were only separated with chapter headings from the rest of the text in the fourth edition.

anger directed towards women who are perceived as a challenge to patriarchal authority.

The threat of woman's usurpation of male power is imagined most vividly in a chapter entitled "Doublets for Women in England". Apoplectic at the sight of women dressed in masculine apparel, Stubbes storms that "if they could as wel change their sexe, and put on the kind [sex] of man, as they can weare apparell assigned only to man, I thinke they would as verily become men indeed, as now they degenerate from godly sober women" (2413–17). The violence of Stubbes's reaction is explained by Lisa Jardine: "It was not that the doublet was indecent — it was actually more decorous than a 'feminine' low-cut gown. But it was morally indecent because it announced absence of difference between the sexes in a language only too readily understood by a contemporary" (*Still Harping on Daughters*, 155). Not content merely to dress beyond their degree, which would be bad enough, these women desire to "verily become men indeed". Thinking herself the equal of man, woman inscribes on her body through costume the sin of overweening pride. But female-to-male cross-dressers, according to Stubbes, are neither men nor women, nor even — despite his accusations of lewd and dissolute behavior — whores, but monsters. Paraphrasing a line from Stephen Gosson's discussion of the transvestite boy actor in *Playes Confuted in Fiue Actions*, Stubbes asserts that "Our apparell was giuen as a signe distinctiue, to discerne betwixt sexe and sexe, and therfore one to weare the apparell of another sexe, is to participate with the same, and to adulterate the veritie of his owne kinde. Wherefore these women may not improperly bee called **Hermaphroditi**, that is Monsters of both kindes, halfe women, half men" (2424–31).

Laura Levine argues that writers against the stage perceived the self as fundamentally unstable, "inherently monstrous and inherently nothing at all" (*Men in Women's Clothing*, 12). The lack of any sense of a fixed identity coincided with a belief in magic to generate the notion that "doing" what another person does inevitably leads to "being" that person; specifically, that doing what a woman does — dressing in woman's clothes or becoming sexually aroused watching an all-male theatrical performance — transforms a man into a woman. Positing that it is specifically the masculine identity which is presented in these pamphlets as under threat of dissolution (8), Levine takes the position that writers such as Stubbes dealt with their fears about the self by fixating on the issue of effeminacy (24).

This thesis, while thought-provoking, is limited by the fact that the crucial passage Levine repeatedly quotes from Stubbes's work is the one quoted above from the chapter on doublets for women — a chapter which attacks female, not male, cross-dressers. Although his claim that costume has the power to alter gender is undoubtedly relevant to the controversy surrounding the boy actor, Stubbes notably makes no mention at any point in the *Abuses* of the male actor dressed in woman's clothes, a silence which sometimes seems overlooked or ignored in studies of Renaissance antitheatricality. Stubbes's chapters on womanish shirts for men and masculine doublets for women clearly express the anxiety that both male *and* female gender could be perverted through clothing: where men risk degenerating into women (the inferior sex), women risk degenerating into hermaphrodites (the monstrous sex). This view of gender as radically unstable is related to anxieties about social position: in both instances, a fearful concern that the self is infinitely malleable and therefore susceptible to transformation through apparel underlies an obstinate demand that costume must be the true and clear expression of personal identity.

Violations of the hierarchies of degree and gender open the floodgates to further social abuses, the common feature of which is excess. The English are groping after too much money, too much food and drink; they swear incessantly about the slightest trifling matters; they flock to bear-baitings, dancing schools, and theatrical performances night and day, day in and day out. Pursuing sensual gratification and material indulgence, the English neglect the more sober pleasures on which their spiritual well-being depends. Not surprisingly, many forms of popular recreation fail to meet Stubbes's austere standards, but he is particularly apprehensive about activities which entail casual and unsupervised interaction between the sexes. His concern in this regard is especially noticeable in the chapters grouped together as abuses of the Sabbath.

May games, for example, provide an unaccustomed opportunity for sexual licence as they involve men and women of all ages departing overnight into the hills and groves (5722–66). Similarly, the author's primary criticism of modern forms of dancing is that the practice of pairing men and women together in large assemblies of people provokes lechery and lustful love: "For what clipping, what culling, what kissing and bussing, what smouching & slabbering one of another? what filthy groping & vnclean handling is not practised euery where in these dauncings?" (6015–19). Asserting that he is not opposed to dancing altogether, Stubbes maintains that the activity would be "more tollerable" if it were practiced not every day but occasionally, in praise of God's mercies rather than for our own wanton enjoyment, each person either alone or in groups consisting of men by themselves or women by themselves (6460–97).

The spectre of uncontrolled and uncontrollable sexual appetite is perhaps summoned with most force in the author's comments on the theaters. Stubbes's complaints against both plays and players are numerous: religious plays abuse the word of the Lord (5351–405), secular plays tend to idolatry and sin (5405–16),

all plays draw crowds away from sermons and offer a bad example to life (5515–
29, 5548–74), and actors, no better than beggars, dress sumptuously in apparel
above their rank (5601–3). Stubbes further insists that the theaters give rise to
lewd activity in the audience itself. A long passage describing the improprieties
of spectator behavior concludes: "Then these goodly **Pageants** being ended, euery
mate sortes to his mate, euery one brings another homeward of their way very
friendly, and in their secret conclaues (couertly) they play the **Sodomits**, or
worse" (5542–47). Stubbes's evocative charge of sodomy has been interpreted by
some critics as alluding specifically to sexual intercourse between men.[44]

As in the chapters on May games and dancing, however, this description
of post-performance behavior is focused primarily on interaction between members of the opposite sex. I am anticipated in this point by Jonathan Goldberg
who likewise takes issue with readings of this passage as referring to sex between
men, arguing that the very idea of same-sex intercourse is beyond Stubbes
(*Sodometries*, 120–21). This perhaps overstates the case, as Stubbes would have
almost certainly known of such relations from the Bible, where it is made explicit that this is the sin which epitomized the disorder in human relations in
Sodom and Gomorrha (Rom. 1:27). But it does seem significant that he chooses
nowhere else in the *Abuses* to address this as an issue, even when citing passages
from the Old Testament in which this is of primary concern. In the chapter on
whoredom, most strikingly, the crime committed at Judg. 19:22–28 is glossed as
"the Adultery done with one **Leuits** wife" (3359–60), Stubbes remaining silent
about the fact that the men of Gibeah originally intended to gang-rape the Levite himself. This selective use of biblical authority is indicative, not of any lack
of awareness, but rather of a preoccupation with supposed abominations committed between men and women.

Returning then to the chapter on stage-plays, to "play the sodomites" is
probably no different than to "play the filthy persons", an activity Stubbes ac-
cuses women of indulging in with their lovers in banqueting houses in the liberties of the city (3075–76). This also explains Stubbes's use of almost exactly the

---

[44] See, for example, Alan Bray, *Homosexuality in Renaissance England* (London: Gay
Men's Press, 1982), 54; Levine, *Men in Women's Clothing*, 22; and Stephen Orgel, "Nobody's Perfect," *South Atlantic Quarterly* 88 (1989): 7–29, here 16–17: Orgel subsequently
revised his interpretation of this passage in *Impersonations* (Cambridge: Cambridge University Press, 1996), 29. Claiming that the passage in question immediately follows
Stubbes's description of transvestites as hermaphroditic monsters, Levine silently elides
more than fifty quarto pages of text, implying that the concept of sodomy in the *Abuses*
is presented by the author himself as intimately tied up with fears of gender instability.

same phrase when recounting the supposedly true story of William Bruster and Mary Breame, who were struck dead by the Lord in an instant as they were "playing the filthie **Sodomites** together" (App.1–E, 27–28). Included in the version of the chapter on whoredom printed in the first three editions, this anecdote has as its overt purpose to warn the reader away from adulterous affairs. For Stubbes, extra-marital sexual intercourse between men and women clearly constitutes a form of sodomy.

Stubbes's vision, then, is of spectators enflamed with sexual desire who leave a play to engage in not necessarily homoerotic, but sodomitical, activity; that is, they have sex for fun with someone to whom they are not married. The likelihood is that sexual attraction between men was a feature of the public theaters, and it seems unnecessary to rule out entirely the possibility that Stubbes at least nods towards same-sex relations in his use of the term "Sodomits". But the heavy and exclusive emphasis placed on transgressive sexual interaction between men and women elsewhere in the book strongly suggests that in this chapter on stage-plays the possibility of lewd behavior between men is not the author's primary concern. Stubbes's obsessive determination to control lust between the sexes — whether it erupts in the woods in May, while dancing the cinque-pace, or while attending a theatrical performance — stems from a conviction that such intimate association has the same deleterious effect as dressing in luxurious, fashionable clothing. The disorder and confusion to society threatened by gorgeously dressed men and women who are victim to their own ungoverned sexual desire is figured in the *Abuses* in the vision of the effeminate man and whorish woman "playing the sodomites" together.

Editorial Procedures

THE PROCESS OF REVISION

Even a superficial perusal of the four versions of *The Anatomie of Abuses* makes it clear that each successive edition is heavily dependent on previous versions. Stubbes added, cut, and rephrased, but his revisions always grew out of existing work. Although one can therefore conclude that the first edition must have been printed from either an authorial or scribal manuscript, and the second edition from a revised manuscript or printed copy of the first edition, the copy underlying the revised third and fourth editions is less immediately apparent. As the provenance of the versions influences editorial decisions about copy-text and emendation, this section tracks the development of the book from its first publication in 1583 to its last in 1595 and from this evidence establishes the nature of the copy used in the printing-house for each of the revised editions.[45]

When preparing the *Abuses* for press the third time, Stubbes had two printed versions of the book on which he could base his revisions. What quickly emerges through comparison of the first three editions is that most of the revisions made in the second edition also appear in the third.[46] Most importantly, O3 follows O2 in omitting the preface and in including a number of large blocks of text that did not appear in the *Abuses* until publication of the second edition.[47] This fact in itself proves that O3 could not have been based on the first edition without at least recourse to O2, or the copy from which O2 was printed,

---

[45] A fuller version of this section, "Printer's Copy Underlying the Four Editions of Philip Stubbes's *Anatomie of Abuses*," has been published separately in *Analytical and Enumerative Bibliography* n.s. 8 (1994): 159–75.

[46] Spelling and punctuation vary greatly from one edition to the next, and a systematic study of these features does not produce an immediately meaningful pattern, alterations apparently being introduced to maintain line justification or resulting from compositorial whim. Consequently, I will focus on substantive changes made to the text, and when citing examples from each edition, spelling and punctuation will be treated as significant only if they affect meaning.

[47] The longest of these added passages are noted in the description of O2 (pp. 13–14).

to retrieve the passages not available in O1. The third edition also reproduces many small additions, substitutions, and deletions found in the second edition but not in the first. For example, Spudeus's second speech on the first page of the first edition reads: "I am glad to see you in good health, for it was bruted abroad euery where in our countrey (by reason of your discontinuance, I thinke) that you were dead, long agoe" (sig. B1). In the second edition, the words "euery where" have been omitted and the words "from thence" added after "discontinuance" (sig. B3^v). The third edition (sig. B3^v) accepts these revisions and adds one of its own. There are also instances where sentences have been completely reworked for the second edition, and it is significant that it is always the revised reading that is reproduced in some form in O3. An example of this occurs in the chapter on May games, where Philoponus says in the first edition that "Against **May, Whitsonday** or other time, all the yung men and maides, olde men and wiues run gadding ouer night to the woods, groues, hils & mountains" (sig. M3^v). In O2, this passage is revised and expanded to read: "Against Maie, Whitsondaie, or some other tyme of the yeare, euery Parishe, Towne, and Village, assemble themselues together, bothe men, women, and children, olde and yong, euen all indifferently: and either goyng all together, or deuidyng themselues into companies, they goe some to the Woodes and Groues, some to the Hilles and Mountaines, some to one place, some to an other" (sig. N8). The third edition repeats the version of the sentence found in O2.

Stubbes was in a similar position when he came to revise the *Abuses* for the final edition of 1595; presumably, he could have prepared any one of his three previous editions for publication of the fourth. However, Q1 not only includes the blocks of text first printed in O2 (thus, as in the third edition, making it impossible for O1 to have been the sole text underlying Q1), but also reproduces or further revises the revisions that had been newly printed in the third edition. Similarly, words and phrases found in O1 and O2, but taken out of O3, very rarely reappear in Q1.

Close examination of the four versions of *The Anatomie of Abuses* indicates that, with one exception discussed below, O3 and Q1 consistently reproduce the revisions made in the version of the book that had been last printed (O2 in the case of O3 and O3 in the case of Q1). If one hypothesizes that the new revisions printed in O3 and Q1 were appended to any editions other than O2 and O3, respectively, then it becomes difficult to explain how the revisions that had been newly printed in O2 and O3 find their way into O3 and Q1 respectively. The scale on which the text was revised for each edition precludes the possibility that Stubbes happened to make all of the same changes more than once. The least complicated and most likely explanation for this pattern of revision is that the third edition of the *Abuses* was largely based on a marked-up copy of O2, while the fourth edition was entirely based on a marked-up copy of O3.

Only once did Stubbes not base his revisions on the text that immediately preceded the edition he was preparing. Both the second and third editions print revised versions of the title page and "Epistle Dedicatorie". However, unlike the pattern that is found in the rest of the book, where a revision made in O2 is picked up and built on in O3, the third edition in these two sections ignores most of the changes made in O2 and reverts to the readings found in O1, while making a number of completely different revisions of its own. The second edition makes twenty-eight revisions to O1 and the third edition makes fifty-six: only three of these revisions are common to O2 and O3, and each of these could have been made in O3 without reference to O2.[48] Clearly, the title page and "Epistle Dedicatorie" of O3 have been printed from a revised copy of O1, rather than from a revised copy of O2. Whatever Stubbes's motivation was for basing the title page and "Epistle Dedicatorie" of O3 on the versions found in O1, it did not affect his treatment either of the rest of the third edition, which was based on O2, or his treatment of Q1, which was based on O3.[49]

Working with the conclusion that each successive edition of *The Anatomie of Abuses* was printed from a marked-up copy of the edition immediately preceding it (the title page and "Epistle Dedicatorie" of O3 set aside), it emerges that the development of the *Abuses* from the first to the last edition was a process of cumulative change, each revised edition building on revisions that had been made previously. However, it is possible — if unlikely — that instead of sending a printed copy of the book containing manuscript revisions to the printing house, he copied out a manuscript version of the whole book, complete with revisions, from which the new edition was to be printed. Furthermore, in the case of the second edition, Stubbes might have appended his revisions to the original manuscript, rather than to a printed copy of the first edition.[50] Both of these possi-

---

[48] The three revisions to O1 common to both O2 and O3 are the substitution of "consulting with himself" for "aduysing himselfe" (O3, sig. A2), the printing of the word "MICROCOSMOS" in Greek characters (O3, sig. A2), and the addition of the word "this" in the phrase "accept of this my poore contribution" (O3, sig. A2^v).

[49] The Latin poem, "Candido Lectori", remained unchanged in the first three editions, and it is therefore impossible to determine whether it was a copy of O1 or O2 that was used in the setting of O3. The rest of the prefatory material in O3 preserves revisions made in O2.

[50] Given the extent to which the *Abuses* was reworked for each new edition, it is unrealistic even to speculate that the original MS could have been revised a second or third time and used in the printing-house after the publication of O2. Such a document would be illegible.

bilities are ruled out, however, by the reappearance of printing errors in subsequent editions, textual traces which prompt the conclusion that O2, O3, and Q1 were set from marked-up printed copies of O1, O2, and O3 respectively. This finding is consistent with what we know of contemporary printing-house practices.[51]

One might also consider that during the process of revision Stubbes occasionally, or even consistently, consulted either his manuscript or editions other than the one most recently printed. If this were the case, then O1 readings not found in O2 could sometimes appear in O3, and similarly, O1 and O2 readings not found in O3 could sometimes be found in Q1. There are sixteen O1 readings which reappear in O3 after having been dropped in O2. Although this figure may initially appear significant, it represents a tiny proportion of the total revisions made to O3, and moreover, all of the sixteen revisions could have been made in O3 without reference to O1 or the manuscript, especially since the corrector/author presumably had a disposition to his own original readings. What often happened is that O2 made a poor substitution for a word in O1, which is simply replaced in O3 with a better reading that happens to be the reading given in the first edition. For example, in the chapter on pride in the first edition, Philoponus compares pride of heart to "the polluted cloth of a menstruous woman" (sig. B6^v). In O2, this reading is changed to "a polluted clothe, of a menstruous woman" (sig. B8^v), but is changed back in O3 (sig. B8). The O1 and O3 reading is less generalized than the one given in O2 and therefore is arguably the more powerful image.

Sometimes Stubbes makes an indifferent revision in O2 that is reversed in O3. For example, in the chapter on church-ales, Spudeus asks in O1 and O3 if it were not better that "euery one contributed somewhat according to his abilitie" (sigs. M5^v, N7). In O2, however, "contribute" is substituted for "contributed" (sig. O2^v). The verb form has little substantive impact on the meaning of the sentence, yet it was changed twice. This example, however, does not necessarily imply that Stubbes was aware when he was revising O2 for O3 that he was

---

[51] J. K. Moore discusses the use of printed editions as printer's copy, saying that "Authors of the sixteenth and seventeenth centuries would annotate a printed copy of their work to serve as printer's copy for the next corrected edition ... [This was] felt to be preferable to rewriting the work and incorporating the changes. Despite the cramped pages that resulted, the printer may have asked for the annotated copy because the ease of working from type would have compensated for slowness in setting manuscript additions and because a corrected copy also eliminated decisions about design": *Primary Materials Relating to Copy and Print in English Books of the Sixteenth and Seventeenth Centuries* (Oxford: Oxford Bibliographical Society, 1992), 31.

returning to the original reading of O1: hundreds of revisions were made every time a new edition came out after O1, and it is reasonable to expect that in a few instances an earlier indifferent revision would be reversed.

Similar cases can be found in the printed text of Q1, where readings found in O1 and O2, but not in O3, turn up in the last edition. None of these reinstated readings provides convincing evidence that Stubbes revised O3 for the printing of Q1 with one eye on the first edition, second edition, or manuscript. The only instance that might seem to need discussion involves a phrase revised out of O1 which reappears in Q1. At the very beginning of the book in its first edition, Spudeus tells Philoponus not to worry about the men in England "for they are such, as the Lord hath cast of into a reprobat sence, & preiudicat opinion, & preordinat to destruction" (sigs. B3^v–B4). In the second edition, the words "reprobat sence, &" are dropped (sig. B6). This is also the version picked up by O3 (sigs. B5^v–B6). In the fourth edition, however, "reprobate sence" is substituted in place of "preiudicat opinion" (sig. B2^v, 348–49). It at first seems unlikely that Stubbes could have happened to have made this substitution without reference to the first edition or manuscript since "reprobate sence" is not a necessary or obvious synonym for "preiudicat opinion". However, these two expressions in the context of the idea of the Lord "casting off" sinners seem to have been coupled in Stubbes's mind since he repeats the phrase "the Lord hath cast off into a reprobate sence" a few pages later in the same chapter, a phrase which is found in the last three editions (sigs. C8^v, C8, C4^v). Moreover, in the fourth edition, at this later point in the text, Stubbes adds the words "and preiudicate opinion" (975–76). The repeated use of these same expressions in a similar context indicates that they formed part of the author's usual vocabulary and were interchangeable.

What emerges from detailed study of the four versions of the text is that O2, most of O3, and Q1 were printed from marked-up printed copies of the previous edition. That each of the revised editions was set from a printed text explains how printing errors introduced in one version could be carried over into later versions; Stubbes simply failed to catch these mistakes while he was revising the copy. Inferring that Stubbes chose not to consult his manuscript or versions of the text printed before the one he was currently revising explains why there are so few instances where one finds previously-abandoned readings in a later edition and why the author was sometimes unable to correct compositorial errors (cf. 2246–47n., 6335–38n.). Barring the anomalous use of the first edition's title page and "Epistle Dedicatorie" as copy for the revised third edition, Stubbes's working attitude towards his text was that a new, revised edition made obsolete any version that preceded it.

COPY-TEXT

The majority of Stubbes's revisions are relatively minor, mostly involving the rephrasing of sentences and substitution of one synonym for another. Although one does not often get the sense that these changes reflect a revised viewpoint, Stubbes's endless tinkering nonetheless has an impact on one's reception of the book. The third and fourth editions, for example, print increasingly more words and phrases in contrasting Roman type rather than in the standard black letter type, causing the reader to attribute particular importance to words that may have been skimmed over lightly in the previous editions. Similarly, while few readers of the first three editions would be unaware that "Ailgna" is really "England" in Latin (Anglia) spelled backwards, the discarding of this device in the quarto edition creates the effect of a more direct commentary on contemporary life in England. Further, the direction taken during the process of revision was towards the use of an increasingly colloquial vocabulary, as unusual, bookish terms were replaced with more familiar synonyms. As F. J. Furnivall notices in the introduction to his edition of 1877–1879, "inkhorn terms" such as "acuate" and "introite" were consistently replaced in later editions with words such as "whette" and "entrance" (*Abuses*, ed. Furnivall, 2:62–63). The cumulative impact of Stubbes's revisions in each successive edition of the *Abuses* after the first has impressed on me the need to present this work not as a single text but as a series of four related, but distinct, versions. Rejecting, therefore, the idea of a conflated edition, yet concerned to present an easily readable text, I chose to edit only one of the versions. The extent and nature of the changes, characterized by an incremental process of sentence and paragraph revision and not just straightforward substitutions of individual words, make a comprehensive tabular listing of authorial alterations nearly impossible. However, the book's unstable textual character is highlighted and discussed in some of its details in the introduction, commentary, and appendices.[52]

---

[52] I considered a parallel-text edition or the development of a system of markers which would allow the simultaneous display of variant readings of all four versions in the main body of the edition, but both of these alternatives seemed cumbersome and alienating to the reader interested not so much in the textual status of the book as in its content. Although not ideally suited to my purposes, immensely useful and important editions of other writers' work have been constructed on these models. See, for example, Michael Warren, *The Complete "King Lear" 1608–1623* (Berkeley: University of California Press, 1989); Paul Bertram and Bernice W. Kliman, *The Three-Text Hamlet* (New York: AMS Press, 1991); and H. W. Gabler, ed. with Wolfhard Steppe and Claus Melchior, *James Joyce, Ulysses: A Critical and Synoptic Edition* (New York: Garland, 1984).

Arguments can be presented in favor of editing any one of the four versions of the *Abuses*. The first edition has the merit of most closely embodying the text as originally written by Stubbes, but it does not include many passages found in the three later versions, and facsimiles and reprints of it are already available. The second edition, as noted elsewhere, marks a major departure from the original version, with large passages of text newly incorporated into the book and inconsistencies ironed out. Printed just months after the first edition, O2 has much to recommend it; indeed, F. J. Furnivall worked the major additions found in the second edition of the *Abuses* into his text of O1 in square brackets, thus creating an edition of O1 that in fact looks much like O2. The third edition is interesting given its placement in the sequence and original date of publication: it was the last edition published in rapid succession between 1583 and 1584. While it incorporates many of Stubbes's revisions, it can still be seen as engaging and participating in the events and issues of the early years of that decade. The fourth edition, finally, is interesting both by merit of the book's reappearance in a new format with revised preliminaries a decade after its third publication and because Q1 is the version which incorporates the author's final revisions. Any of these versions would provide a suitable copy-text for a modern critical edition; the priority when putting together a single-version edition is to keep that version distinct from the others. In the end, I chose to edit the quarto text of 1595.[53] The original spelling and punctuation of the copy-text have been reproduced with printing errors emended and noted in the collation.

EMENDATION

A consequence of Stubbes's practice of correcting and revising the version that had been most recently printed without consulting either his original manuscript or the printer's copy is that non-authorial readings passed unnoticed into the next printed edition. The 1595 text of the *Abuses* is a palimpsest of at least four different compositorial habits of spelling and punctuation and includes a number of other potentially non-authorial alterations such as the transposition of words and word substitution. Since the hand of the finicky author is often indistin-

---

[53] The extent to which a variety of influences can be brought to bear on choice of copy-text is discussed by Hans Zeller: "From a historical point of view the different versions are in theory of equal value ... [F]or the historian, for the editor, the alterations mean an adaptation of the work to suit the altered circumstances, ideas and purposes of the author. For the editor there is no 'best version'": "A New Approach to the Critical Constitution of Literary Texts," *Studies in Bibliography* 28 (1975): 231–64, here 245.

guishable from that of the careless compositor, it is difficult to determine with certainty the provenance of every new reading and impossible to quantify with precision the extent of the compositors' impact on the text.[54] But by consistently choosing to send to the printing-house for publication a marked-up printed copy of the most recent version of his book, the author tacitly, if not explicitly, accepted the readings introduced during the previous printing. The fact that Stubbes chose to correct only those changes that appear manifestly wrong in the context of the particular version currently under revision suggests that he did not consider it necessary to weed out every instance of non-authorial alteration. Consequently, the revised versions cannot be regarded as becoming progressively more corrupt simply because of the probability of compounded compositorial input.

And yet, while the author tolerated printing-house input — and for all we know, even actively collaborated with the printing-house — neither the author nor the printers deliberately perpetuated manifest error. Their concern to remove faults from the printed text is amply demonstrated by the errata sheet appended to the first edition, the series of press-corrections made to the fourth edition, and the ongoing efforts to catch printing mistakes made in one version before publication of the next. The problem for the editor is to develop a consistent definition of error that balances a desire for textual accuracy with an awareness of the important and pervasive role of the printing-house in the production of the work. Correcting only those mistakes that could be discerned without reference to a previous edition would necessarily lead to the loss of a number of passages almost certainly omitted through eye-skip.[55] Determined to maintain to a large extent the highly socialized character of the quarto edition, I nonetheless felt that these unintended changes were a form of corruption that should not be carried over into a modern edition.

I thus define error as changes to the text that either obscure or impoverish meaning. This subjective definition isolates four separate categories of error: straightforward misprints such as turned or wrongly placed letters or misassigned speech prefixes; mistakes in punctuation such as misplaced brackets and turned question marks; omissions from the text which apparently result from eye-skip

---

[54] The possibility that even minor changes may represent deliberate revision is supported by E. A. J. Honigmann's work on authorial revision in *The Stability of Shakespeare's Text* (London: Edward Arnold, 1965): "quite often trivial substitutions outnumber those with any real significance; less apparent, because my extracts are short, is the fact that one substitution often leads to another" (63).

[55] Compare, for example, the passages at 1151–64, 2223–27, and 7273–80 with the accompanying commentary.

or faulty memory on the part of the compositor(s) and which damage the sense
of the passage; and errors introduced by the author himself during the process of
revision. Overlooked mistakes perpetuated in subsequent authorized editions
have been emended in the same manner as those errors introduced for the first
time in the fourth edition. Potential examples of compositorial misreadings and
eye-skip which do not impair meaning — the substitution of "wel fitting" for
"wel sittyng" at 7046, or "plague" for "torture" at 2883, for example — have on
the whole been left as printed in the quarto since the new readings may equally
represent authorial revision. Such substitutions are noted and discussed in the
commentary.

Instances of apparently corrupt spelling have been determined through reference to similar usages elsewhere in Stubbes's canon, and through recourse to
the second edition of the *Oxford English Dictionary* (1989; compact edition,
1991). No similarly comprehensive resource exists to which one can appeal in instances of punctuation. The text of the *Abuses* as printed in the quarto edition is
for the most part meaningfully pointed with commas, colons, full-stops, question
marks, and parentheses, but the non-standardized use of these symbols can appear strange and even whimsical to a modern reader. Aware that the particular
complexion of the quarto punctuation is a composite of usages introduced by the
Q1 compositor(s) and inherited from earlier versions, I have emended the punctuation with due regard to the evolving usages of the time and to the manner in
which these symbols are generally applied throughout the book.[56]

Although there is no reason to assume that mistakes in the quarto would
necessarily have been replaced with the originally intended reading since subsequent versions of the *Abuses* were corrected without benefit of the printer's copy,
for lack of a better alternative most errors in Q1 have been emended on the
authority of one or more of the previous editions on the grounds that these corrected readings are known to have formed constituent parts of the author's vocabulary and manner of usage. This policy has been of particular use in resolving
those instances where an emended reading is not immediately apparent from
context. In the chapter on usury, for example, Philoponus complains that the
scrivener "hath a great more Vsurie to himselse [sic], of him who borroweth the

---

[56] My editorial practice in this regard is particularly indebted to the discussions of the
use and development of punctuation in the Elizabethan period found in Anthony
Graham-White, *Punctuation and Its Dramatic Value in Shakespearean Drama* (Newark,
DE: University of Delaware Press, 1995); M. B. Parkes, *Pause and Effect: An Introduction
to the History of Punctuation in the West* (Aldershot: Scolar Press, 1992); Anthony G.
Petti, *English Literary Hands from Chaucer to Dryden* (London: Edward Arnold, 1977);
and Percy Simpson, *Shakespearian Punctuation* (Oxford: Clarendon Press, 1911).

money" (sig. N2ᵛ). The word that "great" is supposed to qualify is missing. I restore the reading found in O3, the edition which provided the printer's copy for the quarto. The emended passage thus reads, "hath a great deale more Vsurie to himselfe, of him who borroweth the money" (4834–36).

I have not returned to a previous reading, however, when it can be argued that corruption has been introduced as a direct consequence of authorial revision. In these cases, I have instead tried to make sense of the process of revision init- iated by the author. An example of this occurs in the section on apparel, where Philoponus says, "the **Egyptians** are said neuer to chaunge their fashion, or al- tered the form or fashion of their attire" (Q1, sig. C1). This same line in the third edition reads, "the **Egyptians** are saied, neuer to haue changed their fas- hion, or altred the forme of their first Attire" (sig. C2). It seems that Stubbes decided to put this sentence in the present rather than in the past tense, but only incompletely executed the revision. Rather than reinstate the O3 reading, the text has been corrected through the substitution of the verb "alter" for the past participle "altered".

While prepared to correct manifest printing errors and concerned to emend passages showing evidence of incomplete authorial revision in keeping with the author's inferred intentions, I have been careful not to correct errors that result from Stubbes's ignorance of his material. As previously discussed, passages of varying length in the *Abuses* can be traced to the printed works of authors such as John Northbrooke and Stephen Gosson, and it is not unusual to find Stubbes either misquoting his sources or unquestioningly reproducing their errors. At lines 4802–5, for example, Philoponus alludes to the "sharpe lawes against Vsu- rie" passed by **"Claudius Vespatianus"** and **"Alexander Seuerus"**, apparently una- ware that Claudius and Vespasian were in fact two different Roman emperors. This is a careless corruption of *The poore mans garden* which reads, **"Claudius,** and after him **Vespasian,** and after him **Alexāder Seuerus,** made sharpe lawes against vsurers, which were put in execution with all diligence, and seuerytie" (sig. LL6). Since this mistake almost certainly results from an authorial mis- representation, I have noted it in the commentary and left the text uncorrected. Errors such as these have been preserved as integral features of the text, being characteristic of the author's scholarship and manner of composition.

LAYOUT

The layout of the quarto has not been exactly reproduced in this edition. Side- notes, page and chapter headings, and the use of multiple type-faces and type- sizes have been preserved, albeit in a slightly different form than in the quarto.

Sidenotes have been positioned, as in the quarto, in the outer margins of the page, and their placement relative to the text corresponds as closely as possible with the quarto printing. Each sidenote is numbered from line one, and keyed to the line of text in the main body of the book at which the sidenote begins. So, a six-line sidenote which starts opposite line 2718 will be numbered 2718.1–2718.6. Page headings, conversely, are printed at the foot of the page in order to avoid interrupting the flow of the text in its modern format.

The variety of type-faces found in the quarto is reflected through a parallel use of modern fonts. The edited text has been printed in Caslon: black letter in regular Caslon, italic in italic Caslon, and roman in bold Caslon. Ten point has been chosen to stand for the pica type-size used in the main body of the text, with semibold eight point representing the long primer found in the sidenotes, and twelve point representing the English type-size used in the prefatory material and most chapter and page headings. The size of type found in speech prefixes has been standardized since smaller type was only occasionally used as a space-saving measure; otherwise, all shifts in type-face and type-size printed in the quarto have been reproduced, with instances of apparently unintentional shifts emended and noted in the collation.

Other features, such as running-titles, page numbers, catchwords, and original line breaks, have not been indicated, and conventional capital letters have been substituted for ornamental letters.[57] Variant catchwords are listed at the end of Appendix II. Although the Latin ligatures "œ" and "æ" have been preserved, all other ligatures in Latin and English have been separated, and the long "s" has been adapted to its modern equivalent. Page breaks are indicated with a double slash, and page signatures are printed in the margin. Where the page break occurs in the middle of a word, I have positioned the slashes at the end of the word; this change is not recorded in the collation line.

End-stop punctuation of page and chapter headings, and sidenotes has been left as found in the quarto or emended and noted in the collation. Spaces between words, and between words and punctuation, have been standardized, and unambiguous examples of two words being run together ("&creation", "clogged-with") have been silently emended. The gap between a chapter title and the text above it has also been standardized since the tendency of the compositor(s) was to place a variant number of empty lines between the two to create the effect of a double space; instances in the quarto where no gap is left between the two

---

[57] Press-corrected running titles and page numbers are noted along with other quarto press corrections at pp. 15–16.

apparently result from the need to conserve space on a cramped page. Appendix III contains a list of words split over a line break in Q1 without hyphenation, and indicates which ones have been elided in this edition. A separate list notes which words hyphenated over a line break in the modern edition are hyphenated in Q1 and should be quoted with the hyphen.

All facsimile reproductions of pages from the sixteenth-century editions are actual size.

COLLATION NOTE

Minor correction of compositorial error such as the replacement of missing letters as well as more substantive editorial changes such as the substitution of "Bastardes" for "Bastardes a peece" at line 3428 have been noted in the collation, located in Appendix II. The corrected reading printed in the edited text is placed after the number of the line on which it appears within a closing square bracket, followed by the authority for the emendation, a semi-colon, and the uncorrected Q1 reading. Emendations have been based primarily on the readings found in O3, the text that provided the printer's copy for Q1, but if O3 is also incorrect, I have defaulted to the O2 reading and in turn to the O1 reading. If editions previous to the one on which the emendation is based print the same correct reading, they are also cited. When none of the previous editions can provide the grounds for emendation either because all are incorrect or the passage in question incorporates authorial revision between O3 and Q1, then, unless the corrected quarto reading has already been provided in the footnotes to Furnivall's text of O1, the emendation is marked in the collation with the abbreviation "*This ed.*" ("this edition").

Readings in the fourth edition have been emended as far as possible without disturbing the spelling, punctuation, capitalization, or font type of that edition, and therefore, where the emended reading has been based on, but is not identical to, the evidence found in one or more of the earlier editions, the abbreviation "*subst*" ("substantively") is included in the collation. For example, in "2602. Perfumes] O1–O3 *subst*; Persumes" the word "Perfumes" at line 2602 originally read "Persumes" in Q1 and has been corrected on the evidence provided in all of the previous editions, one or more of which printed the word in a slightly variant manner, perhaps using a different type face or spelling, or without the upper case letter. If a reading was corrected at press, then the corrected state is placed within the closing square bracket followed by the abbreviation "*cor*" ("corrected"), and the uncorrected state is placed after the semi-colon followed by the abbreviation "*uncor*" ("uncorrected"), as in the following: "1821. There is a certaine] *cor*; Ther is a ceitaine *uncor*". Where a long "s" appears to have been printed in place of an "f", the reader is warned in square brackets after the emended reading of the possibility of broken type. Shifts in type face and font size found in the text are not reproduced in the collation.

The Anatomie
of Abuses.

Containing

A Description of such nota-

ble Vices and enormities, as raigne in many Countries of
the world, but especiallie in this Realme of England: T*ogether*
with most fearefull examples of Gods heauie Iudgements inflicted vpon the wicked for the same
as well in E*ngland* of late, as in other
places else where.

Verie godly to be read of all true Christians
euery where, but most chiefly, to bee
regarded in England.

Made dialogue-wise by **Philip Stubs,** *Gent.*

Now, the fourth time, newly corrected and
inlarged by the same A*uthor.*

[PUBLISHER'S DEVICE]

Imprinted at London by Richard Iohnes, at the sign of the
Rose and Crowne next aboue S. *Andrewes* Church
in Holborne.   1595. //

To the Christian Magistrates

and godly Gouernors of England, whose authority & offi-

ces are to reforme vice and maintain vertue, **P.S.** *wisheth*

the fauour of God, increase of godly honour,

reward of laudable vertue, and eternal

felicity through Iesus

Christ.

Right Honourable, worshipfull and welbeloued, the Lord our
God hauing by the power of his worde, created heauen and
earth with all other thinges, for the benefit, comfort and vse of
man: the last of all other (euen the sixt day) he made man after
his owne similitude and likenesse, to this end, that in him he
might be glorified aboue all other creatures. And therefore,
whereas in making of other things, he vsed onely this word
Fiant, bee they made, or let them be made: when he came to
make man, consulting with himselfe, and as it were, asking
counsell at his wisedome, he said, *Faciamus hominem*, let vs
make man, that is, a woonderfull creature, and therefore is
called in Greeke *Microcosmos*, a little world in himselfe. And
truly he is no lesse, whether we consider his spirituall soule, or
his humaine body. For what Creature is there vpon the face of
the earth comparable to man, either in body or soule? For what
creature hath an immortall soule but only man? what Creature
can foresee things to come, remember thinges past, or iudge of
thinges present, but only man? what creature beareth the Image
of God but man? what creature is made so erect to behold the
heauens as man? what creature may bee likened to // man,

whether we respect the lineaments, the demensions, and proportion of the body, or the giftes and graces of the mind. And
finally, what creature hath the promise of the resurrection and
glorification of their bodies, and of eternall life, but only man.   50
Then seeing the Lord hath made man thus glorious, & pre-
ferred him by many degrees, aboue all other creatures (the Angelicall creatures set apart,) it is manifest he hath done it to
some end and purpose, namely, that he might be glorified in
him, & by him aboue all other his works, according to the mea-   55
sure of his integrity, excellency and perfection. And hereby we
may learne that it is the wil of God, that we should bend al our
force to the aduancing of his glory, the edification of his people,
and the building vp of his Church, which he hath redeemed
with the blood of his deare sonne.   60

Which thing (me thinke) is notably figured foorth vnto vs
in the 25. of *Exodus*, where the Lord commanded M*oises* to
build him a Tabernacle, or house of prayer, to this ende & purpose (doubtlesse) that therein his Law might be read and
preached, his ceremonies duly practized, his Sacrifices and of-   65
ferings faithfully performed, and his glorious name called vpon
& obeyed. To the erection wherof, euery one conferred somwhat, some brought gold, some siluer, & som brasse, lead &
tin: other brought silk, purple, skarlet, and other ornaments,
and the meanest brought somewhat, namely skins, haire, sand,   70
lime, morter, wood, stone, and such like. Euen so wold the lord
haue euery one to confer somwhat, euẽ such as he hath, to the
building vp of his spiritual house the Church purchased with
the bloud of Christ. Wherfore seeing it is so, that euery one is
to further this spirituall building to his possible power: I haue   75
rather chosen with the simplest & meanest sort to bring,
though but haire, sand, skinnes, lime, morter, wood and stones,
then altogether to sit idle and contribute nothing. //   A3

Not doubting, but that the chiefe Maister and builder of
this house, Christ Iesus will not dislike, but rather accept of   80
this my poore contribution, no lesse thẽ he did of the poore

widowes Mite, to whome it was imputed that she had cast more
into the treasury of the Temple, then all the rest: for what she
wanted in effect, that she supplied in affect. And for that also
85   the Lord our God committing his talents to euery one, whether
more or lesse, not onely requireth of vs the same againe simply,
but also, as a straite computist, demaundeth interest and gaine
of euery one of vs: and for that not onely, he is a murtherer and
a Homicide before God, who slayeth or killeth a man with ma-
90   teriall sworde, but hee also, who may preuent the same murther, and will not. And for that not only, he is guilty of hainous
transgression that committeth any euill actually, but also he
who consenteth to it, as he doth, who holdeth his peace, or he
who by any means might auoid it, & either through negligence
95   will not, or for feare of the world dare not. Therefore, albeit,
that I haue receiued, but one poor talent, or rather but the
shadow of one yet least I might be reprooued (with that vnprofitable seruaunt) for hiding my small talent in the earth, not
profiting therewith at all, either my self or others, I haue ad-
100   uentured the contriuing of this litle treatise, intituled, *The
Anatomie of Abuses*, hoping that the same (by diuine assistance)
shall somwhat conduce to the building vp, and erection of this
spirituall house of the Lord.

And although I be one, that can doe least in this godlie
105   course of life, palpable barbarisme forbidding me so much as
once to enter into wisedomes schoole, yet for that some wil not,
for feare of loosing worldly promotion (though in the meane
time they loose the kingdome of heauen) other some dare not
for displeasing the worlde: I say, for these and semblable causes
110   together, with the zeale and goodwill I beare vnto my countrie,
A3ᵛ   & feruent desire of their conuersiō // and amendement, I haue
taken vpon me the publishing of this booke. Which God grant
may be with like plausible alacrity receiued, as with paines &
good will, I haue collected it, for the benefit of my cuntry, the
115   pleasure of the godly, and amendment of the wicked. And I
doubt not, that as none, but the wicked and peruerse, whose

gawld backs are tutched, will repine against me, so the Godlie
and vertuous, will accept of this my labour, and trauell herein
sustained, whose gentle fauour and goodwil, shall counterpoize
the maligne stomackes and austere countenances of the other.   120

After that I had fullie perfected this book, I was minded
notwithstanding, both in regard of the strangenesse of the matter it intreateth of, and also in respect of the rudenesse of my
pen, to haue suppressed it for euer, for diuerse and sundry
causes, and neuer to haue offered it to the viewe of the world.   125
But notwithstanding, being ouercome by the importunate
request, and infatigable desire of my friends, I graunted to
publish the same, as now you see it extant.

And because this my booke is subiect to as many re-
proches, taunts, and reproofes, as euer was any little book   130
subiect vnto (for that few can abide to heare their faults discouered) I thought it most meetest to be dedicated to all good
Magistrates and men in authoritie, to reforme vice, & maintaine vertue: Vnto whom, in al humble dutie I doe willinglie
present the same. And therefore, as the Lorde God in mercy   135
hath giuen you his power & authority to reforme vices and
abuses, so I beseech him to giue euery one of you a hungry desire to accomplish the same: for as you know, reformation of
manners and amendement of life, was neuer more needfull. For,
was pride (the chiefest argument of this booke) euer so ripe?   140
Doe not both men and women (for the most part) euerie one in
generall goe attired in Silkes, Velvets Damasks, Sattens, and
what not els? which are attire only for the Nobility and Gentrie,
and not for the other at any // hand. Are not vnlawfull games,   A4
playes, Enterludes, and the like euery where frequented? Is not   145
whoredome, couetousnesse, vsurie and the like dayly practized
without all punishment of lawe? Was there euer seene lesse
obedience in Youth of all sortes, both men-kinde and women-
kind towardes their superiours, Parents, Masters and gouernors?

But hereof I need to say no more, referring the good   150
consideration as well of these as of the rest, to your Godlie

Wisedomes, beseeching you to pardon my presumption in
speaking thus much, for, *Zelus Domini huc adegit me*, the zeale
of my God hath driuen me hither.

155   Thus I cease to mollest your eares any further with my rude
speaches, most humbly beseeching you, not onely to admit this
my booke into your protection, but also to persist, the iust defenders thereof, against the swinish crue of railing and slaun-
derous tongues, so shall I acknowledge my selfe most bounden
160   to pray vnto god for the prosperous & good estates of you all,
whom I beseech for Christ his sonnes sake, to blesse and prosper you in all your godly procedings now and for euer.

Your Honours and Wisdomes
most bounden,

165   P. S. //

I.F. In commendation of the Authour and his Book.   A4ᵛ

Shall men prophane, who toyes haue writ
    and wanton Pamphlets store:
Which onely tend to nourish vice,
    and wickednes the more: 170
Deserue their praise, and for the same,
    accepted be of all:
And shall not this our Authour then,
    receiue the Laurell palle?
Who for good will in sacred breast,   175
    he beares to natiue soile,
Hath published this godlie booke,
    with mickle paine and toile?
Wherein, as in a mirrour pure,
    thou maist beholde and see   180
The vices of the world displaid,
    apparent to the eie.
He flattereth none, as most men doe,
    in hope to get a price:
But shewes to all their wickednesse,   185
    and Gods diuine Iustice.
A Godlier booke hath not beene made,
    nor meeter for these dayes:
Oh reade it then, thanke God for it,
    let th'Authour haue his praise. //   190

The Anatomie of A-
buses in England.

The Interlocutors, or Speakers:

SPVDEVS.   PHILOPONVS.

195 God giue you good Morrow, Maister **Philoponus.**

Philo. And you also good Brother **Spudeus.**

Spud. I am glad to see you in good health, for
it was reported in our country (by reason of your
200 discontinuance from thence I thinke) that you
were dead, long agone.

*Flying fame
oftentimes a
lyer.*

Philo. Indeed, I haue spent some time abroad
els where, than in my natiue countrey (I must
needs confesse) but, how false that report is (by
205 whomsoeuer it was first broched, or how farre so
euer it be dispersed) your present eies can witnesse.

Spud. I pray you what course of life haue you
led in this your long absence, foorth of your
210 owne countrey?

Philo. Trulie (brother) I haue led the life of a
poore Traueller, in a certaine famous Iland, once
named **Albania**, after **Britania**, but nowe present-
lie called **Anglia**, wherein I haue liued these seu-
215 en winters and more, trauelling from place to
place, euen all the land ouer indifferently.

*The place
where the
Author hath
trauelled.*

Spud. That was to your charges I am sure, was
it not I pray you?

Phi. It was so: but what then? I thank God, I

haue atchiued it, and by his diuine assistance   220
prosperously accomplished it, his glorious name,
(worthy of all magnificence) bee eternally praised
therefore.

Trauelling
chargeable.

Spud. To what end, did you take in hand this
great trauell, if I may be so bold as to aske   225
you? //

Phil. Trulie to see fashions, to acquaint my   B1ᵛ
self with the natures, qualities, properties and
conditions of all men, to break my selfe to the
world, to learne nurture, good demeanour, and   230
ciuill behauiour: to see the goodly scituation of
Cities, Townes, & countries, with their pros-
pectes, and commodities: and finallie, to learne
the state of all things in generall: all which, I
coulde neuer haue learned in my owne countrey   235
at home. For (in my poore iudgment) hee that
sitteth at home, euer abiding in one place, knoweth nothing, in respect of him, that trauelleth
abroad: and he that knoweth nothing, is a bruit
beast. But he that knoweth all things (which   240
thing none doth but God alone) he is (as it were)
a God amongst men. And seeing there is a perfection in knowledge, as in euery thing els, euery
man ought to desire that perfection aboue al
other things: for in my iudgment, there is as   245
much difference betwixt a man that hath trauelled much, and him that hath dwelt euer in one
place (in respect of knowledge, and science of
things) as is betweene a man liuing, and one
dead in graue. And therfore I haue had a great   250
felicitie in trauelling abroad all my life long.

The causes
that mooued
the Author to
take this
trauel
in hand.

The differēce
betwixt a mā
that hath
trauelled, and
a man that
hath not.

Spud. Seing that by diuine prouidence, we are
met togither, let vs (vntill we come to the end of
our iourney) vse some conference of the state of
the world now at this day, as wel to recreate our   255

B1ᵛ. PH: *The Author, a* Traueller.

mindes, as to cut off the tediousnesse of our
iourney.

    Phil. I am very wel content so to do, reioyc-
ing not a little of your good company: For
260 **Comes facundus in via, pro vehiculo est.** A good
companion to trauell withall, is in steed of a
wagon or Chariot. For as the one doeth ease the
painfulnesse of the way, so doeth the other al-
leuiate the yrkesomnesse of the Iourney intended.

265   **Spud.** But before I enter into dispute with
you, (because I am a Countrey man, rude and
vnlearned: and you a **Ciuilian**, indued with great
wisdome, knowledge, and experience) I most
humblie beseech you, that you will not bee of-
270 fended with me, though I talke with you somewhat rudelie, without either pollished wordes, or
filed speeches, which your wisedome peraduenture doth require, and my insufficiencie and inability being such, is not able for to yeelde.

275   **Philo.** Your speeches (I put you out of doubt)
B2 shall not bee // offensiue to me, if they be not
offensiue to God first.

    Spud. I pray you then, what manner of
Countrey is **England**, where you say you haue
280 trauelled so much?

    Phil. A pleasant and famous Ilande, immured
about with the sea, as it were with a wall, wherein the aire is temperate, the ground fertile, the
earth abounding with all things, either needfull
285 for man, or necessarie for beast.

    Spud. What kinde of people are they that in-
habite that Countrey?

    Philo. A strong kind of people, most audaci-
ous, bolde, puissant, and heroicall, and of great
290 magnanimitie, valiancie, and prowes, of an in-
comparable feature of body, of an excellent com-

The benefite of a good Companion to trauel withall.

A request to auoid scandal or offence.

England a goodlie Countrie.

The people of England.

B2. PH: *England described,*

plexion, and in all humanitie, inferiour to none
vnder the Sunne.

Spud. This people whome God hath thus
blessed, must needs be a very godly people, either   295
els they be meerlie vngratefull to God, the authour of all grace, and of these their blessinges
especially?

Philo. It grieueth me to remember their liues,
The liues of
the people of
England.
or to make mention of their workes: for notwith-   300
standing that the Lorde hath blessed them, with
the knowledge of his truth aboue all other Lands
in the worlde, yet is there not a people more corrupt, wicked, or peruerse, liuing vpon the face of
the earth.   305

Spud. From whence spring all these euils in
man? for wee see euerie one is inclined to sinne
naturallie, and there is no flesh which liueth, and
sinneth not.

Phil. All wickednesse, mischiefe, and sinne   310
From whence
all euilles
spring in
mã.
(doubt you not brother **Spud.**) springeth from
our auncient enemie the deuill, the inueterate
corruption of our nature: and the intestine malice
of our owne hearts, as from the efficient causes,
and stinking puddles of all vncleannes and filthi-   315
nesse whatsoeuer. But wee are now new crea-
tures, and the adopted children of God created in
Christ Iesus to good workes, which God hath
prepared for vs to walke in, and therefore we
ought to haue no fellowship with the workes of   320
We ought
to haue no
dealing with
the works of
the flesh.
darknesse, but to put on the armour of light, to
walk in newnes of life, *and to work our saluation
with fear and trembling*, as the Apostle speaketh.
And our sauior Christ biddeth vs, *so to work as
our works may glorify our heauenly father*. But the   325
contrary is most true, // for there is no sin, which   B2ᵛ
was euer broached in any age, that flourisheth not

now. And therefore the fearefull day of the Lord
cannot be farre off: at which day, all the world
330   shall stand in flashing fire, and then shall Christ
our Sauiour come martching in the cloudes of
heauen, with this dreadfull **Tara tantara** sound-   The daie of
ing in each mans eare: A*rise you dead, and come to*   Dome not
iudgment, and then shal the Lord reward euerie   regarded.
335   man according to his workes. But how little this
day is feared, and how slenderlie regarded in
England, it would grieue any Christian hart to
consider.

    Spud. It is but a follie to grieue for them,
340   who sorrow not for themselues. Let them sinke
in their owne sinne: liue wel your self and you
shall not answer for them, nor they for you. Is it
not written? **Vnusquisque portabit onus suum.**   Euerie man
Euerie one shall beare his owne burthen. **Anima**   must answer
345   **quæ peccauerit, ipsa morietur.** The soule that   for himselfe.
sinneth shall die? Wherefore cease to sorrow or
grieue any more for them: for by all likelihood
they are such, as the Lord hath cast into a reprobate sence, and destinate to destruction, that his
350   power, his glorie, and his iustice, may appear to
al the world.

    Phil. Oh brother, there is not any Christian
man, in whose heart shineth **scintillula vlla pieta-
tis**, any spark of Gods grace, but will grieue, see-
355   ing his brethren and sisters in the Lord, members
of the same bodie, coheires of the same kingdome, and purchased with one and the same inestimable price of Christ his blood, to run desperately headlong into the gulfe of destruction
360   and perdition both of body and soule for euer. If
the least or meanest member of thy whole body
be hurt, wounded, cicatrized, or bruised, doth   The mutuall
not the heart, and euery member of the bodie   harmonie of
feele the anguish and paine of the grieued part,   one member
365   seeking and endeuouring by all means possible   with another
(euery one in his office & nature) to repaire the

same, & neuer ioying, vntil it be restored again
to his former integritie & perfection? Which
thing in the ballance of Christian charitie considerately weighed, moueth me, and ought to   370
mooue any good Christian man to mourne for
their defection, assaying by all means possible to
reclaime them, and to bring them home againe,
that their soules may be saued in the day of the
Lord. And the Apostle commaundeth vs, to the   375
vttermost of our power, **vt simus alteri emolu-**
mento. That we should be an aid and help one
to another. And that we do good to all men,
dum tempus habemus, // whilest we haue time.   B3
To weep with them that weepe, to mourne with   380
them that mourne, and to be of like affection
one towards another. And common reason
teacheth vs, that we are not borne for our selues

No man
borne for
himselfe.

onelie: for **Ortus nostri partem patria, partem**
amici, partem Parentes vendicant. Our countrey   385
challengeth a part of our birth, and brethren and
friends require another part, and our parents (and
that **optimo iure**) do vendicate a third part.
Wherefore I will assay to doo them good (if I
can) by discouering their abuses, & laying open   390
their enormities, that they seeing the grieuousnes
of their maladies, & daunger of their diseases,
may in time seek the true physition of their
souls, Christ Iesus, of whome onelie commeth all
health and grace, and so eternally be saued.   395

Spud. Seeing that so many and so hainous
inormities doe raigne and rage in **England**, as
your words do import, & which mooue you to
such intestine sorrow and griefe of minde: I pray
you describe vnto me more particularly some of   400
those capitall abuses, and horrible vices which are

B3. PH: *Of Christian charitie.*

there frequented, and which displease the Maiesty of God most in your iudgment?

A particular discription of
405   ## Pride, the principall
abuse in **England,** *and how manifold it is.*
Philo.

You do wel to request me to describe vnto you
some of those great abuses, and Cardinall vices
410   which are vsed in **England,** for no man (in any
competent volume) is able to comprehend the
sum of all the abuses there practised. And where-   The number
as you would haue me to speake of those capitall   of abuses in
and chiefe abuses, which both are deadly in their   England
infinite.
415   own nature, and which offend the Maiesty of
God most: Me think you herein shake hands,
with the sworne enemies of God the Papists,
who say, there are two kinds of sins, the one **Ve-**
nial, the other **lethal** or deadly. But you must vn-   Al sinne in it
420   derstand, that there is not the least sinne that is   owne nature
committed, either in thought, word or deed (yea,   is mortal.
Væ vniuersæ iustitiæ nostræ si remota miseri-
cordia iudicetur. Wo be to al our righteousnes, if
mercie put away, it shuld be iudged) but it is
425   damnable, **Dempta misericordia Dei,** if the mercie of God be taken away. And againe, there is
no sinne so **lethall** or deadly, nor yet any offence
B3ᵛ   so // grieuous, but the grace and mercie of God
is able to pardon and remit, if it be his good
430   pleasure so to do. So that you see nowe, there is
no sinne so **Veniall,** but if the mercie of God bee
not extended, it is damnable: nor yet any sinne so
mortall, which by the grace and mercie of God,
may not be done away. And therefore, as we are
435   not to presume of the one, so are wee not to
dispaire of the other. But to returne again to the

B3ᵛ. PH: *Pride the roote of all vices.*

The greatest
abuse which
offēdeth
God most,
is pride

satisfying of your request. The greatest abuse,
which in my iudgement both offendeth God
most, and is there not a little aduanced, is, the
execrable sinne of **Pride**, and excesse in **Apparell**,   440
which is there so rotten ripe, as the filthy dregges
thereof, haue long since presented themselues,
before the throne of the Maiestie of God, calling
and crying for vengeance day and night inces-
santlie.   445

    Spu. Wherfore haue you intended to speak of
Pride the first of all, giuing it the first place in
your discourse? because it is euil in it self & the
efficient cause of euill, or for some other purpose?

Pride the
beginning
of all euils.

    Philo. For no other cause, but for that I   450
thinke it, not onely euill and damnable in it
owne **Nature**, but also the very efficient cause of
all euils, and therefore the wise man was bolde to
call it, **Initium omnium malorum**. The begin-

Eccle.10.

ning and welspring of all euilles. For, as from the   455
roote all naturall things doe grow, and take their
beginning: so from the cursed roote of pestifer-
ous **Pride**, do all other euils sproute, and thereof
are ingenerate. Therefore, may **Pride** be called
not improperly, **Matercula & origo omnium vi-**   460

What is it but
Pride dares
attempt it.

tiorum, The Mother and nurse of all mischief.
For, what fact so haynous, what crime so flagicious, what deede so perillous, what attempt so
venterous, what enterprize so pernicious, or what
thing so offensiue to God, or hurtfull to man is   465
there in all the worlde, which man will not willinglie commit, to maintaine his pride withall?
Hereof euery dayes successe ministreth proofe
sufficient.

Pride is three
fold, pride of
the heart,
pride of the
mouth, and
pride of
apparell.

    Spud. How manifold is this sinne of Pride,   470
whereby the glorie of God is defaced, & his
Maiestie so grieuously offended?

    Phil. Pride is threefold: namely, the pride of
the hearte, the pride of the mouth, and the pride
of apparell, the last whereof (vnlesse I be deceiued)   475

offendeth God more then the other two. For as
the pride of the hearte, and of the mouth, are
not opposite to the eye, nor visible to the sight,
B4   and therefore cannot intice others // to vanitie &
480   sin (notwithstãding they be grieuous sins in the
sight of God) so the pride of apparell which is
obiect to the sight, as an *exemplary* of euill induceth the whole man to wickednes & sinne.

    Spud. How is the pride of the heart com-
485   mitted?

    Philo. Pride of the heart is committed, when
as a man lifting himselfe on high, thinketh of
himselfe, aboue that which he is: dreaming of a
perfection in himselfe, when there is nothing
490   lesse: and in respect of himself contemneth and
despiseth al others thinking none comparable to
himselfe, whose righteousnesse, notwithstanding,
is like to the polluted cloth of a menstruous
woman. Therefore the pride of the heart, may be   Isaias 50.
495   saide to be a rebellious elation, or lifting vp of
the mind, against the Lawe of God, attributing   What pride of
and ascribing that vnto himselfe, which is proper   the heart is
to God onelie. And although it be the Lord, **Qui**
operatur in nobis & velle & posse, Who work-
500   eth in vs both the will and power to doe good.
Ne gloriaretur omnis Caro, least any flesh
should boast of his owne power and strength: Yet
Pride with his Cosin germain *Philautia*, which is
Self-loue, perswadeth him, that he hath need of
505   no mans help but his owne: that hee standeth by
his owne proper strength and power, and by no
mans els, and that he is all in all, yea, so perfect
and good as no more can be required of him in
this life.

510   **Spud.** How is the pride of wordes, or the
pride of the mouth committed?

B4. PH: *Three sorts of* Pride.

How pride of
words, or of
the mouth is
committed.

Philo. Pride of the mouth, or wordes, is,
when we boast, bragge, or glorie, either of our
selues, our kindred, affinitie, consanguinitie,
birth, parentage, and such like: or when we extol   515
our selues in respect of some vertue, sanctimony,
synceritie, integrity or perfection, which either is
in vs, or which we pretend to be in vs. In this
kind of Pride (as in the other) almost euery one
offendeth: For shall you not haue all (in a maner)   520
boast and bragge of their auncestors and progenitors? Saying and crying **aperto ore**, With open
mouth: I am a Gentleman, I am worshipful, I am
Honourable, I am Noble, & I cannot tel what:
My father was this, my father was that: I am   525
come of this house, and I am come of that: I was
born of this race, & I was borne of that, I am
descended of this stocke, and I of that: Whereas
Dame **Nature** bringeth vs all into the world after
one sort, & receiueth // al againe, into the womb   B4ᵛ
of our mother (the bowels of the earth) all in one
and the same order and maner, without any difference or diuersitie at all, whereof more hereafter shal be spoken.

vainglorious
ostentation
of births,
and parentage,
&c

Spud. How is pride of Apparell commited?   535

Phi. By wearing of Apparell more gorgeous,
sumptuous, and precious then our state, calling,
or condition of life requireth, whereby we are
puffed vp into Pride, and induced to think of our
selues, more then we ought, being but vile earth   540
and miserable sinners. And this sin of Apparell
(as I haue saide before) hurteth more then the
other two, for the sin of the heart hurteth none
but the **Authour** in whom it breedeth, so long as
it bursteth not forth into outward shew and ap-   545
pearance. And the pride of the mouth, though it
be meere vngodly in it own nature, yet is it not

How pride of
apparel is
perpetrate &
committed,

B4ᵛ. PH: *Pride vainglorious.*

550

so permanent (for **Verba citò auolant, & euane-
scunt in aerem**, words soone fly away, and vanish
in the aire, not leauing any **print or Character**
behind them to offend the eies withal.) But this
sinne of the excesse of Apparel, remaineth as an
example of euill before our eyes, & is a **prouocation** to sin, as experience dayly prooueth.

555

Spud. Would you not haue men to obserue a
decency, a comlines, and a **decorum** in their Attire? Doth not the word of God commaund all
things to be done **decenter, & secundum ordi-
nem ciuilem**: decently and after a ciuill order.

*A Decorum to
be obserued.*

560

Phi. Yea trulie. I would wish, that a decency,
a comely order, and as you say, a **decorum** were
obserued, as well in attire, as in all thinges els:
But wold God the contrare were not true: For
doe not the most of our **fond Inuentions**, and

565

newfangled fashions rather deforme, then adorne
vs: disguise vs, then become vs: making vs rather
to resemble sauage beastes, and bruitish monsters, then continent, sober and chast Christians?

*Our apparel
rather
deformeth then
adorneth vs.*

Spu. Hath this contagious infection of Pride

570

of Apparel, infected & poysoned any other countries besides **Englãd** suppose you?

Phil. No doubt, but this poyson of Pride hath
shed foorth his influence, and poured forth his
stinking dregs ouer all the face of the earth, but

575

yet I am sure, there is not any people vnder the
face of heauen, how sauage or brutish soeuer, so
poysoned with this **Arsnecke** of Pride, or that
hath drunke so deep of this impotionate cup, as
England hath, with griefe of conscience I speak

*Circes cups and
Medeas pottes
haue made
England
drunkẽ with
pride.
No country
so drunken
with pride as
England.*

580

it, with sorrow I see it, and with teares I lament
it. //

C1

Spud. But I haue heard them say, that other
nations passe them for exquisite finenesse and

C1. PH: *Newfanglenesse in England.*

brauery in apparell: as the **Italians**, the **Athen-**
ians, the **Spaniards**, the **Chaldeans, Heluetians,**   585
Zuitzers, Venetians, Muscouians, and such like:
Nowe whether this be true or not, I greatly desire to know.

 Philo. This is but a visour or cloak, to couer
their own shame withall: onely spoken, not   590
prooued: forged in the deceiptfull mint of their
own lying braines: for (if credit may bee giuen to
auncient writers) the **Egyptians** are said neuer to
chaunge their fashion, or alter the form or fashion of their attire, frõ the beginning of the world   595

Stuperius.

to this day: as **Iacobus Stuperius, lib.de diuersis**
nostræ ætatis habitibus.pag.16. affirmeth. The
Grecians are saide to vse but one kind of apparel
without any change: that is to wit, a long gown,
reaching down to the ground. The **Germaines**,   600
are thought to be so precise, in obseruing one
vniform fashion of apparel, as they haue neuer
receeded from their first originall: as the said
Stuperius saith in these wordes: **Non enim**
mores leuiter mutare vetustos, Germanus vn-   605
quam consueuit incola: which in English verse is
thus much in effect,

  The Germaine people neuer vse at all to
   chop and chaunge,
  Their customes old, or els attire, wherein
   abroade they raunge.

 The **Muscouians, Athenians, Italians, Brasil-**   610
ians, Affricanes, Asians, Cantabrians, Hungar-

Al Nations
inferiour to
England for
pride of
apparell.

ians, Ethiopians, Dutch, French, or els what
nations soeuer vnder the Sunne, are so farre behinde the people of **England** in exquisitnesse of
apparell, as in effect, they esteeme it little or   615
nothing at all, so it repell the colde, and couer
their shame: yea, some of them are so smally ad-
dicted thereto, that setting apart all honestie and
shame, they go cleane naked. Other some meanly
apparelled, some in beasts skinnes, some in haire,   620

and what euer they can, some in one thing, some
in another, nothing regarding either hosen,
shooes, bandes, ruffes, shirts, or any thing els.
And the ciuilest nations that are, be so farre es-
625 traunged from the pride of apparell, that they esteeme him as brauely attired, that is cloathed in
our Carzies, Frizes, Rugges, and other kindes of
cloath, as we do him that is clad all ouer in
silkes, Veluets, Satens, Damaskes, Grograins,
630 Taffaties, and such like. So that hereby you see,
that they speake vntruly that say, that other Nations exceed them in brauery of apparell. For it is
C1ᵛ manifest that all // other nations vnder the
Sunne, how strange, how new, how fine, or how
635 comely soeuer they thinke their fashions to be,
when they bee compared with the diuers fashions, and sundry formes of apparel in **England**,
are most vnhandsome, brutish and monstrous.
And hereby it appeareth, that no people in the
640 worlde are so curious in newfangles, as they of
England be. But graunt it were so, and admit
that others excelled them (which is false) shall
wee doe euill, because they do so? Shall their
wickednesse excuse vs of sinne, if we commit the
645 like & worse? shal not the soule that sinneth dy?
Wherfore let vs not sinne of presumption with
the multitude, because they doe so, least we be
plagued with them, because we doe the like.
Moreouer, those countries are rich and wealthy
650 of themselues, abounding with all kind of precious ornaments, and rich attire, as Silkes, Veluets, Satens, Damaskes, Sarcenet, Taffeta,
Chamlet, and the like (for all these are made in
those forren countreyes) and therefore if they
655 weare them, they are not to be blamed, as not
hauing any other kinde of clothing to couer
themselues withall. So if we would content our

No people so
curious in
newfangles
as they of
England.

Other countries
not to be
blamed,
though they
go in Silkes,
Veluets, and
why.

C1ᵛ. PH: *Brutish fashions in England.*

Other
Countries
esteeme not
so much
of Silkes,
veluets, as
we do

selues with such kinde of attire as our owne
countrie doeth yeeld vs, it were somewhat tol-
lerable. But we are so captiuate in Pride, that if it   660
come not from beyond the seas, it is not woorth
a strawe. And thus we impouerish our selues in
buying their trifling Merchandizes, more pleasant
than necessary, and inritch them, who laugh at vs
in their sleeues, to see our great folly in affecting   665
of trifles, and parting with good wares for them.
And how little they esteeme of Silkes, Veluets,
Satens, Damaskes Taffetaes, and such, we may
easily see, in that they sell them to vs for our
Woolles, Frizes, Rugges, Carzies, and the like,   670
which they would neuer, if they esteemed of
them as we doe. So that you see they are forced
of necessitie, to weare such rich attire, wanting
other thinges (whereof wee haue store) to inuest
themselues withall. But who seeth not (except   675
wilfullie blinde) that no necessitie compelleth vs
to weare them, hauing aboundance of other
thinges to attire our selues with all both hand-
somner, warmer and comelier then they in euery
respect? but farre fetched and deare bought, is   680
good for Ladies, they say.

    Spu. Doe you thinke it not permitted to any,
hauing store of other necessarie cloathing, to
weare Silkes, Veluettes, Taffaties, // and other   C2
such rich attire, of what calling soeuer they be.   685

Euerie man
may weare
apparel
according to
his calling.

    Philo. I doubt not, but it is lawfull for the
nobilitie the gentry and the **Magistery**, to weare
rich attire, euery one in their calling. The Nobilitie and Gentrie to inoble, garnish, and set foorth
their birthes, dignities and estates. The **Magiste-**   690
rie to dignifie their callinges, and to demonstrate
and shew foorth the excellencie, the Maiestie and
worthynesse of their offices and functions, there-

C2. PH: *Sumptuous Attire.*

695

700

705

710

715

720

725

730

by to strike a terrour and feare into the hearts of
the people, to offend against their office and authority: but yet wold I wish, that what so is superfluous or ouermuch, either in the one, or in
the other, shuld be distributed and erogate, to
the help and subuention of the poore members of
the body of Christ Iesus, of whom an infinite
number dayly perish, through want of necessary
refection, & due sustentation to their bodies.
And as for priuate subiectes, it is not at any hand
lawfull that they should weare silkes, Veluets,
Satens, Damaskes, golde, siluer, and what they
list (though they be neuer so able to maintaine
it) except they being in some kind of office in
the common wealth, doe vse it for the dignifying
and innobling of the same: Or at the commandement of the chiefe Magistrate for some speciall
consideration, or purpose. But now there is such
a confuse mingle mangle of apparell in **England**,
and such horrible excesse thereof, as euery one is
permitted to flaunt it out, in what apparell he
listeth himselfe, or can get by any meanes. So
that it is very hard to knowe, who is noble, who
is worshipfull, who is a Gentleman, who is not:
for you shall haue those, which are neither of the
Nobilitie, Gentilitie, nor Yeomanrie, no, nor yet
any Magistrate or officer in the common wealth,
goe daylie in silkes, Veluettes, Satens, Damaskes,
Taffaties, and such like: notwithstanding, that
they be both base by birth, meane by estate, and
seruile by calling. And this I accompt a great
confusion, and a generall disorder in a Christian
common wealth.

   Spud. If it be not lawfull for euery one to
weare silks, veluets, Satens, Damasks, Taffaties,
gold, siluer, precious stones, & what not, wherfore did the Lord make and ordaine them?

   Phil. I deny not, but they may be worne of
them, who want other things to cloath themselues

The nobilitie
may weare
gorgious attire,
and why

Magistrates
may weare
sumptuous
atire,
& why.

Not lawfull
for priuate
subiectes
to weare
sumptuous
attire.

hard to know
a gentleman
from another
by apparell.

withal, or of the Nobility, Gentry, or magistery,
for the causes aboue said, but not of euery proud
Thraso indifferẽtly, that hath store of other attire   735

**Wherfore
the Lord
made rich
ornaments.**

ynough: & yet did // not the Lord ordaine these
rich ornaments, & glorious vestiments, to be
worne of all men, or of any, so much as to splendish, beautifie, and set foorth **the maiestie and
glorie** of this his earthly kingdom: for, as cloath   740
of **gold, Arase, Tapestrie,** and such other rich
ornaments, pendices, and hangings in a house of
estate, serue not onely to manuall vses and seruile
occupations, but also to decore, to beautifie, and
adorne the house, and to shew the rich estate   745

**Whereto rich
ornaments
do serue.**

and glorie of the owner: so these rich ornaments,
& sumptuous vestments of the earthly **territorie**
of this world, do not only serue to be worn of
them, to whome it doth appertaine (as before)
but also to shewe foorth the power, wealth,   750
dignitie, riches, and glorie of the Lorde, the
author of all things. And herein the Prouidence
and mercie of God appeareth most plainlie, for
where there is store of other clothing, there hath
he giuen lesse store of silks, Veluets, Satens   755
Damaskes, and such like: and where there is
plenty of them, there is no clothing els almost,
and thus the Lord hath dealt, for that euery
country should be content with their owne kind
of attire: except necessity inforce the contrary, for   760
then wee are to vse our libertie in the feare of
God.

    Spud. I pray you let me intreat you, to shewe
me wherefore our apparel was giuen vs, and by
whom?   765

    Philo. Your request is both diffuse and intri-
cat, and more then my weake and infirme knowl-

---

edge is able to performe: yet least I might be ad-
iudged vnwilling to doe good, I will assay to doe
770 the best that I can.

When, where
and for what
cause our
apparell was
geuen vs.

When the Lord our God, **a spirituall, intellectible vnderstanding substance, incomprehen-
sible, immensurable, and inaccessible,** had by his
word and heauenly wisdome Christ Iesus, created
775 and made the world, and all things therein contained, the sixt day he created man, after his
owne similitude and likenesse, in innocencie,
holinesse righteousnesse, and all kind of perfection: And placing him in Paradice terrestriall,
780 commanded him to till and manure the same.
Then the deuill, an old maligner of mankind,
who before was an Angell in heauen, and
through the sinne of Pride, in arrogating to himselfe the seate and throne of Gods Maiesty, cast
785 downe into the lake of Hell, enuying mans glorious estate, which he then had lost, came vnto
man in Paradise, and inticed him (like a torteous
Serpent) to eat of the forbidden fruit, whereof
C3 the Lord // God had forbidden him to taste, on
790 paine of his life: notwithstanding **Adam** condescending to the perswations of his wife, or rather
of the serpent in his wife, hauing buzzed his
venemous suggestions into her eares, tooke of the
Apple, and did eat, contrary to the expresse com-
795 mandement of his God. This done, their eies
were opened, they saw their nakednesse, and
were not a little ashamed (and yet before sinne
was committed, they being both naked, were not
ashamed, but sinne once contracted, they became
800 vncleane, filthy, lothsome, and deformed) and
sewed them garments of **Figge leaues** together,
to couer their shame withall. Then the Lord pit-

The fal of
man by the
malice of
the deuill.

C3. PH: T*he fall of Adam*

tying their miserie, and loathing their deformitie,
gaue them beasts felles and skinnes to make
Impudent
beastes that
them garmentes withall, to the ende that their   805
shew their
shamefull parts might lesse appeare: Yet some are
priuities,
so brazen faced, and so impudent, that to make
the deuill and his members sport, will not sticke
to make open shew of those parts, which God
commandeth to be couered, Nature willeth to be   810
hid, and honestie is ashamed once to behold or
looke vpon.

Spud. I gather by your words three speciall
points. First, that sinne was the cause why our
apparel was giuen vs. Secondly, that God is the   815
author, and giuer therof. Thirdly, that it was
giuen vs to couer our shame withall, and not to
feed the insatiable desires of mens wanton and
luxurious eyes?

Wherefore   **Phil.** Your collection is very true. Then see-   820
our apparel   ing that our apparell was giuen vs of God to
was giuen vs,   couer our shame, to keepe our bodies from cold,
and to be as prickes in our eyes, to put vs in
minde of our miseries, frailties imperfections and
sinne, of our backsliding from the commande-   825
ments of God, and obedience of the highest, &
to exercise vs the rather to **contrition**, and **com-**
punction of spirite, to bewaile our misery, and to
craue mercie at the mercifull handes of God, let
vs be thankfull to God for them, be sory for our   830
sinnes (which were the causes thereof) and vse
them to the glorie of our God, and the benefit of
our bodies and soules at the last. But (alas) these
good creatures, which the Lord our God gaue vs
for the respectes before rehearsed, we haue so   835
peruerted, as nowe they serue in steed of the
Mens bodies   deuils nets, to intangle poore soules in: For euery
liuing   one now adayes (almost) decke and paint their
sepulchres.   sepulchres (their bodies I meane) with all kinde
of brauerie, whatsoeuer can be deuised, to delight   840
the eyes of the vnchaste beholders, whereby

C3ᵛ   // God is dishonored, offence ministred, and much sin dayly committed, as in further discourse shall plainly appeare.

845   **Spud.** Did the Lord cloath our first Parents in leather, as not hauing any thing more pretious to attire them withall, or for that it might be a perpetual rule or patterne vnto vs (his posterity) for euer whereafter we are of force to make all
850   our garmentes, so as it is not nowe lawfull for vs to goe in rich attire, without offending his Maiestie?

        Phil. Although the Lord did not cloath them so meanly, for that he had nothing els, more pre-
855   cious to attire them withall (for **Domini est terra & plenitudo eius,** The earth is the Lordes, and the fulnesse thereof, saith the Lord by his **Psalmist,** and by his **Prophete, Gold is mine, siluer is mine, and all the riches of the world is mine**
860   **owne**) yet no doubt, but he woulde that this their meane and base attire should be as a rule or **pedagogie** vnto vs, to teach vs that we ought rather to walke meanly and simply, then gorgeously or pompouslie: rather seruing present ne-
865   cessity, thẽ regarding the wanton appetites of our lasciuious mindes: notwithstanding, I suppose not, that his heauenly maiesty woulde, that those garments of leather, should stand as a rule or pattern of necessity vnto vs, whereafter we should
870   be bound to shape all our apparell for euer, or els grieuously to offend: but yet by this we may see his blessed wil was then, & is now, that we shuld rather go an ace beneath our degree then a iote aboue. And that any simple couering pleaseth the
875   Godly, so that it repell the colde, and couer the shame, it is more then manifest, as well by the legendes of prophane Historiographers, Chron-

In our apparel we ought rather to obey necessity, thẽ to feed vanitie,

ologers, and other Writers, as also by the censures, examples & liues of all Godly since the be-

Adam his
mean kind of
attire was
a signe of
mediocrity
vnto vs in
our apparell.

ginning of the worlde: and if the Lord would not   880
that the attire of **Adam** should haue bene a signe
or patterne of mediocritie vnto vs, hee both in
mercy would, and in his mighty power could
haue inuested them in silks, Veluets, satens, gro-
gaines, gold, siluer, and what not els? But the   885
Lord our God foresaw, that if he had clothed
man in rich and gorgious attire: (such is our proanesse to sinne) he would haue bene proud
thereof, and so purchase to himselfe, his bodie
and soule eternal damnation.   890

Spud. Then it seemeth a thing material, and
of great moment that we resemble our first Parentes in austerity of apparell and // simplicity of   C4
attire, so much as may be possible, doth it not?

No religion
reposed in
apparel.

Phil. I put no religion in going, or not going   895
in the like simple attire of our parents **Adam** and
Eua (as the Sorbonicall Papists doe, placing all
their religion in heathen garmentes and **Romish**
ragges) so that we obserue a meane, and exceed
not in pride. But notwithstanding, if we ap-   900
proched a little nearer them, in godlie simplicity
and Christian sobriety, both of apparell and
maner of liuing, we should not only please God
a great deale the more, and enrich our countrey,
but also auoyd many scandalles and offences,   905
which growe dayly by our excessiue riote, and

The fruit of
pride.

riotous excesse in apparel. For doth not the apparel stir vp the heart to pride? doth it not intice
others to sinne? and doeth not sinne purchase
hell the guerdon of pride.   910

Spud. But they say they please God, rather
then offend him in wearing this gorgious attire,

C4. PH: *Hell the reward of Pride.*

915

920

925

930

935

940

C4ᵛ

for thereby the glory of his workemanship in
them doth more brauely appeare. Besides that, it
maketh a man to be accepted, and esteemed of in
euery place: whereas otherwise, they should be
nothing lesse.

    Philo. To thinke that the Lorde our God is
delighted in the splendent shew of outward apparell, or that it setteth foorth the glory of his
creatures, and the maiesty of his kingdome, I
suppose there is no man (at least no perfect
Christian man) so bewitched or assotted. For
that were as much, as to say, that stinking pride,
and filthy sinne, tended to the glory of God, so
that the more we sinne, the more we increase his
praise and glorie. But the Lord our God is so
farre from delighting in sinne, that he adiudgeth
them to eternall death and damnation, that commit the same. Then who is hee that will take
pleasure in vaine apparell, which if it be worne
but a while will fall to ragges, and if it bee not
worne, will soone rot, or els bee eaten with
Mothes. **His wayes are not our waies, his Iudge-**
mentes are not our Iudgementes, as hee sayeth
by his Prophete: And whereas they holde, that
apparell setteth foorth the glory of his Maiestie
in his creatures, making them to appeare fairer,
then otherwise they woulde of themselues, it is
blasphemouslie spoken, and much derogateth,
from the excellencie and glory of his name. For
saith not God by his Prophete **Moises,** that after
he had made all creatures, hee behelde them all,
and beholde, they were (and especiallie man the
excellentest // of all other his creatures, whom he
made after his own similitude and likenesse) exceeding good. And were all creatures good and
perfect, and onely man not perfect nor faire

The Lord
accepteth no
man after his
apparell.

No attire can
make the
creature of
God seeme
fairer.

C4ᵛ. PH: *Man comelie of himselfe.*

ynough? If these their speeches were true (which
in fulnesse of their **blasphemy** they shame not to   950
speake) then might we easily conuince the **Lord**
of vntruth, who in his sacred word teacheth vs,
that man is the perfectest creature, and the fayrest of all others that euer he made (excepting the
heauenlie Spirites, and **Angelicall creatures**) as   955
before. **But O man, who art thou that reasonest**

with thy creator? Shall the clay say vnto the
Potter, why hast thou made me thus? Or can
the clay make himselfe better fauoured then the
Potter, who gaue him his first stampe and pro-   960
portion? Shall wee thinke that stinking Pride can
make the workmanship of the Lord seem fayrer?
Then why did not the Lord cloath vs so at the
first? or at least, why gaue he not commandement in his will and testament, which he sealed   965
with the blood of his Sonne, to cloth our selues
in rich and gorgeous apparel, to set foorth this
glory the more? But away with these sauage
dogges and hellish hagges, who are of this mind,
that cursed pride glorifieth God, and setteth   970
forth or beautifieth his workmanship in his creatures. In vaine is it, for me to **expostulate** with
them, for doubtlesse none holde this, but such
miscreants (or deuils incarnate) as the Lord hath
cast off into a reprobate sence, and preiudicate   975
opinion, whom I beseech the Lorde in the bowels of his mercy, eyther speedily to conuert that
they perish not, or els confound, that they hurt
not, that peace may be vnto Israell. Thus hauing
sufficiently, I trust refelled their false supposi-   980
tions, I leaue them to the Lord, beseeching them,
as they tender their owne saluation, **Linguas**
compescere digitis, to stoppe their sacrilegious
mouthes with their fingers, & not to spit against

heauen, or kicke against the pricke, as they doe,   985
any longer. For the Lord our God is a consuming fire, and vpon obstinate sinners shall raine

downe fire and brimstone, and consume them in
his wrath. This is their portion acquired by sinne.

990   **Spud.** But what say you to the other branch
of their conclusion namely, that apparel maketh
them to be accepted, and weltaken in euery
place?

Philo. Amongst the wicked, & ignorant **pez-**
995   **ants**, I must needes confesse, they are the more
D1   esteemed, in respect of their apparel, but // nothing at al the more, but rather the lesse amongst
the godly wise. So farre off wil all wise men be,
from accepting of any for his gay apparell onely,
1000   that (be he neuer so gallantly painted, or curiously plumed in the deceiptfull feathers of Pride)
they will rather contemne him a great deale the
more, taking him to be a man, puffed vp with
pride and vaineglorie, a thing both odious before
1005   men, and detestable before God. And seeing it
can not stand with the rule of God his iustice, to
accept or not to accept of any man after his apparell, or any other externe shew of deceiptfull
vanity, it is manifest, that man doing the con-
1010   trary, is a **Iudas** to the trueth, a **traitor** to **Iustice**,
and an enemie to the **Lord**: wherefore far be that
from all good Christians. And if those that goe
richly clothed shuld be estemed the rather for
their rich apparel, then **à contrario** must those
1015   that goe in meane and base attire bee the more
contemned and despised for their pouerty. And
then should Christ Iesus our great **Ambassadour**
from the King of heauen, bee contemned: for he
came in poore and meane aray: but Christ Iesus
1020   is blessed in his poore ragges, and all others are
contemned in their rich and precious attire.
Vnder a simple coate many times lieth hid great
wisdome and knowledge: and contrarily, vnder

Marginal notes:

fire, to
destroy all
impenitent
sinners.

The wise wil
not accept of
anie, after
apparell.

Wisdom not
tied to
exterior
pompe
of apparell.

D1. PH: N*o estimation due to apparell.*

braue attire sometime is couered great idiocie and
folly.   1025

Spud. Wherefore would you haue men accepted, if not for apparell?

Phil. If any be so foolish to imagine, that he
shal be worshipped, reuerenced, or accepted the
rather for his apparel, he is not so wise as I pray   1030
God make me. For surely, for my part, I will
rather worship and accept of a poore man in his
ragged cloutes, hauing the gifts and ornaments of
the mind, then I will doe him that roisteth and
flaunteth it out dayly and hourely, in his Silks,   1035
Veluets, Satens, Damasks, Gold or siluer whatso-
euer, without the induments of Vertue, whereto
only all reuerence is due. And therfore as any
man is indued, or not indued with Vertue, and

All reuerence
due to vertue
and not to
rich attire.

true Godlinesse, so will I reuerence or not reuer-   1040
ence, accept or not accept of him: Wherfore, if
any gape after reuerence, worship, or acceptation
let him thirst after vertue, as namely, **feare of**
God, zeale to religion, wisedome, knowledge,
discretion, modestie, sobrietie, affabilitie, gentle-   1045
nesse, & such like, then can they be without reuerence & acceptation, no more then the sun can
be without light, the Fire // without the heat, or   D1ᵛ
the water without his naturall moisture.

Spud. Then I gather you would haue men ac-   1050
cepted for vertue and true godlinesse onely,
would you not?

Philo. I would not only haue men to be accepted and reuerenced for their vertue (though
the cheifest reuerence is only to be attributed to   1055
him, whose sacred breast is so fraught with ver-

Wherefore
man is to bee

tue, as it may well be called the **promptuary** or
storehouse of true wisedome and godlinesse)

but also in part, for their birthes sake, parentage
1060 and discent, and not onely for that, but also, in
respect of their callings, offices and functions,
whether it be in the temporall **Magisterie**, or **Ecclesiasticall presbyterie** (so long as they gouerne
godly and well:) For the Apostle saith, that **those**
1065 **Elders that gouerne well amongst vs, are woor-
thie of double honour:** But yet the man whome
God hath blessed with vertue and true godlinesse, though hee bee neither of great birth nor
calling, nor yet any Magistrate whatsoeuer, is
1070 woorthy of more reuerence and estimation then
any of the other, without the ornamentes of the
minde, and giftes of vertue aboue sayd. For what
preuayleth it to be borne of Worshipfull progenie, and to be destitute of al vertue, which mak-
1075 eth true Worship? What is it els then to carie a
**golden Sworde in a Leaden Scabberd? Is it anie
thing els than a golden Coffin, or painted Sep-
ulchre**, making a faire shewe outwardly, but in-
wardly is full of all stinch and lothsomnesse? I
1080 remember once I read a certaine story of one, a
Gentleman by birth and Parentage, who greatlie
reproached, and withall disdained another, for
that he was come to great authority onely by vertue, being but a poore mans childe by byrth:
1085 What? quoth the Gentleman, art thou so lustie?
Thou art but a Coblers sonne, and wilt thou
compare with me, being a Gentleman both by
birth and calling? To whome the other replying,
said: Thou art no Gentleman, for thy Gentility
1090 endeth in thee, and I am a Gentleman, in that
my Gentility beginneth in mee. Meaning (vnlesse
I bee deceiued) that the want of vertue in him
was the decay of his Gentility, and his vertue was
the beginning of true Gentility in himselfe: for
1095 vertue therefore, not for apparell, is euerie one to
be accepted. For if we should accept of men after
apparell onely respecting nothing els, then should

Side notes:

worshipped
and had in
reuerence.

Gentilitie
without
vertue is no
Gentilitie,

An excellent
Apothegme.

The exordiũ
of vertue, is
the exordiũ
of Gentilitie
and worship,
and want of
the one, is
the decay of
the other.

it come to passe, that wee might accept of one,
both meane by byrth, base in vertue, seruile by //
calling, and poore in estate, more then of some,   D2
by birth noble, by vertue honourable, and by calling venerable. And the reason is, because euery
one, tagge and rag, go brauer, or at least, as
braue as those that be both noble, honorable and
Worshipfull.   1105

Spud. But I haue heard say, there is more
holinesse in some kind of apparell, then in other
some, which makes them so much to affect variety of fashions, I thinke.

Phil. Indeed I suppose that the summe and   1110
substance of their religion, doth consist in apparell. And to speake my conscience, I thinke there
is more or as much holinesse in the apparell, as
in them, that is iust none at all. But admit that
there be holinesse in apparell (as who is so in-   1115
fatuate to beleeue it) then it followeth that the
holinesse pretended is not in them, and so bee
they plaine Hypocrites, to make shewe of that
which they haue not. And if the holinesse by
their attire presaged be in themselues, then is it   1120
not in the garmentes: and why doe they then attribute that to the garmentes, which is neither
adherent to the one, nor yet inherent in the
other? Or if it were so, why doe they glorie of it
to the world but I leaue them to their folly, hast-   1125
ing to other matters more profitable to speak of.

Spud. But I haue heard them reason thus.
That which is good in it owne nature, cannot
hurte: Apparell is good and the good creature of
God, **ergo** no kind of apparel can hurt. And if   1130
there be any abuse in it, the apparel knoweth it

No holinesse
in apparell.

An argumēt
trimly
continued.

---

not. Therefore take away the abuse, and let the
apparell remaine still, for so it may (say they)
without any hurt at all.

1135   **Philo.** These be well seasoned reasons, and
substantial asseuerations indeed, but if they haue
no better arguments to leane vnto then these,
their kingdome of Pride will shortly fall, without
all hope of recouerie againe. The apparell in it

1140 owne nature is good and the good creature of
God (I will not denie) and cannot hurt except it
be through our owne wickednesse abused. And
therefore, woe be them that make the good
Creatures of God instrumentes of damnation to

1145 themselues, by not vsing them but abusing them.
And yet notwithstanding, it may be said to hurt,
or not to hurt, as it is abused or not abused. And
whereas they would haue the abuse of apparell (if
any be) taken away, and the apparal to remain

1150 stil, it is impossible to supplant the one, without
D2ᵛ   the extirpation of // the other also. For it is truly
sayd, **Sublata causa, tollitur effectus.** But not,
Sublato effectu, tollitur causa. *Take away the*   Vnpossible
cause and the effect fayleth, but not contrarily, *take*   to take away

1155 *away the effect, and the cause fayleth.* The externe   pride, except
efficient cause of pride, is gorgeous attire, the   sumptuous
effect is Pride it selfe, ingenerate by attyre: but to   apparell be
begin to plucke away the effect, to wit, Pride,   taken away
and not to take away the cause first, namely   also.

1160 sumptuous attire, is as if a man intending to supplant a tree by the rootes, should begin to pull
the fruit and branches onely, or to pull downe
heauen, should dig in the earth working altogether preposterously, indirectly, and contrarily.

1165   And the reason is, for that these two collat-

D2ᵛ. PH: *Apparel the mother of pride.*

Apparell
and pride
combined
together as
mother &
daughter.

Vnpossible
not to be
proud of
rich attire.

erall cosins **Apparell** and **Pride** (the mother and
daughter of mischiefe) are so combinate togither,
and incorporate the one in the other, as the one
can hardly be plucked from the other, without
the destruction of them both. For the accomp-   1170
lishment wherof, God grant that those wholsome
lawes, sanctions, and statutes, which by our most
gracious and serene Princesse (whom Iesus preserue for euer) and her noble and renowmed progenitors, haue bene promulgate and enacted   1175
heretofore, may be put in execution. For in my
opinion, it is as impossible for a man to weare
precious apparell and gorgious attire, and not to
be proud thereof (for if he be not proud therof,
why doth he weare such rich attire, whereas   1180
meaner is both better cheape, easier to be had, as
warme to the body, and as decent and comely to
any chast Christians eie?) as it is for a man to
cary fire in his bosome, and not to burne. Therfore, would God euerieman might be compelled   1185
to wear apparell according to his degree, estate
and condition of life: which if it were brought to
passe, I feare least some, who ruffle now in
silkes, Veluets, Satens, Damasks, Gold, siluer and
what not els, should be glad to weare Frize   1190
coates, and glad if they might get them too.

    Spud. What is your opinion? Did the people
of the former world so much esteeme of apparell,
as we doe at this present day, without respect
had either to sex, kind, order, degre, estate or   1195
calling?

    Philo. No doubt but in all ages they had their
imperfections, blemishes and faults, for **Hominis
est errare, labi, & decipi,** *It is incident to man, to
erre, to fall, and to be deceiued.* But notwithstand-   1200
ing as the wicked haue alwaies affected, not onely
pride in apparell, but also all other vices whatsoeuer, so the chaste, godly and sober Christians,
haue euer eschewed this excesse of apparell,

D3   hauing a // speciall regard to weare such attire, as   The godly
haue euer
detested pride
of apparell.
        might neither offende the Maiestie of God, pro-
        uoke themselues to pride, nor yet offend their
        godly brethren in any respect. But (as I haue
        saide) not onlie the Godly haue detested and
1210   hated this vaine superfluity of apparell, in all
        times since the beginning of the worlde, but also
        the very **Painyms**, the Heathen **Philosophers**,   The very
heathen haue
contemned
sumptuous
apparell.
        who knewe not God, (though otherwise, wise
        Sages and great Clearkes) haue contemned it, as
1215   a pestifferous euill: insomuch as they haue writ
        almost whole volumes against the same, as is to
        bee seene in most of their bookes yet extant.
            Spud. Are you able to prooue that?
            Philo. That I am, very easily: but of an infin-
1220   ite number, take a taste of these fewe, **Democra-**   Testimonies
of heathen
people who
derided rich
attire.
        tes being demaunded, wherein the beautie and
        comely feature of man or woman consisted? an-
        swered, **In fewnesse of speeches well tempered**
        together, in vertue, in integritie of life, and such
1225   **like.** **Sophocles** seeing one weare gorgious appar-
        ell, sayd to him, **Thou foole, thy apparell is no**
        ornament to thee, but a manifest shew of thy
        follie. **Socrates** beeing asked what was the great-
        est ornamẽt in a woman? answered, **That which**
1230   **most sheweth her chastitie, and good demean-**
        our of bodie and mind, and not sumptuous at-
        tire, which rather sheweth her adulterate life.
        Aristotle is so strict in this point, that he woulde
        haue men to vse meaner apparell then are per-
1235   mitted them by the law. The wife of **Philo** the   Vertue is the
comliest
ornament
of al.
        philosopher, being vppon a time demaunded,
        why she ware not golde, siluer, and precious gar-
        ments? sayd: **She thought the vertues of her**
        husband sufficient ornamẽts for her. **Dionisius**
1240   the King sent the richest garments in all his

D3. PH: *The godlie abhorre Pride.*

Wardrobes, to the noble women of the **Lacede-**
monians, who returned them from whence they
came, saying, **They would bee a greater shame**
to them then honour. King **Pirrhus** sent rich
attire to the Matrones of **Rome,** who abhorred   1245
them, as menstruous cloutes. The conceiued opinion amongst **the Grecians** to this day is, that it
is neither gold nor gorgious attire that adorneth
either man or woman, but vertuous conditions,

Diogenes his
austeritie.

and such like. **Diogenes** so much contemned   1250
sumptuous apparell, that he chose rather to dwell
in wildernesse amongst bruite beastes, all his life
long, then in the pompous Courtes of mighty
Kinges one day to be resiant. For he thought if
he had the ornaments of the minde, that he was   1255
// then faire ynough, and fine ynough also, not   D3ᵛ

The example
of a
Philosopher
deriding
pride,

needing any more. A certaine other **Philosopher,**
adressed himself towardes a Kinges Court in his
Philosophers attire, that is in meane, base, and
poore aray: But so soon as the Officers espied   1260
him, they cried away with that rogue, what doth
he so nie the kinges Maiesties Court. The poore
philosopher seeing it lighten so fast, retired
backe, for feare of their thunderboltes, and repairing home, apparelled himselfe in rich attire,   1265
came againe martching towards the Court, he
was no sooner in sight but euery one receiued
him plausiblie, & with great submission and reuerence. When he came in presence of the King,
and other mighty Potentates, he kneeling down,   1270
ceased not to kisse his garments. The King &
Nobles maruelling not a little thereat, asked him
wherefore he did so. Who answered, O noble
King, it is no maruell, for that which my vertue
and knowledge coulde not do, my apparell hath   1275
brought to passe. For I comming to thy gates in

my Philosophers weed, was repelled, but hauing
put vpon me this rich attire, I was brought to thy
presence with as greate veneration and worship as
1280   could be. Whereby it is to be seene in what de-
testatiō he had the stinking pride of apparel, taking this occasion to giue the King to vnderstand
the inormous abuse therof and so to remooue the
same as a pestilent euill out of his whole domin-
1285   ion and kingdome. I read of a certaine other **philosopher** that came before a King, who at the
same time had inuited his Nobles to a feast or
banquet, the Philosopher comming in, and seeing
no place to spit in (for euery place was hanged
1290   with cloth of gold, cloth of siluer, Tinsell, Aras,
Tapestry, and the like) came to the King and
spat in his face, saying, it is meet, O King, that
I spit in the foulest place. This good **philosopher**
(as we may gather) went about to withdraw the
1295   King from taking pleasure or delight in the vaine
glistering shew either of apparell, or of any thing
els, but rather to haue cōsideration of his own
filthines, misery & sin, not rising vp into pride,
& spitting against heauen, as he did, by delight-
1300   ing in proud attire & gorgious ornamentes. Thus
wee see the very Painims, and heathen people,
haue from the beginning despised this excesse of
apparell, both in themselues and in others, whose
examples herein God graunt wee may follow.
1305   **Spud.** But you are not able to prooue that
any good Christians, euer set lightlie by precious
D4   attire, but alwayes esteemed // it as a speciall ornament to the whole man. As for these Heathen,
they were fooles, neither is it materiall what they
1310   vsed or vsed not?

The example
of a
philosopher,
deriding
the pompe
of the world.

The example
of a
philosopher,
who spat
in the
Kings face.

D4. PH: *The base attire of the former age.*

Phil. I am able to prooue, that euen from the
beginning of the world, the chosen and peculiar
people of God haue contemned gorgious apparell, as thinges (not onely) not necessary, but also
as verie euilles themselues, and haue gone both   1315
meanly and poorly in their vsuall attire? What
say you to our Grandfather **Adam** and **Eua** our
mother? Were they not clothed in Peltes and
skinnes of beastes? Was not this a meane kinde
of apparell thinke you? Was it not straunge to   1320
see a woman couered all ouer in Leather? But yet
the Lorde thought it precious, and seemelie
ynough for them. What say you to the noble
Prophete of the world **Elias**, did he not wallke in
the solitude or wildernesse of this world in a   1325
simple plaine mantell or gowne, girded to him
with a girdle of Leather? **Elizeus** the Prophete,
did not he in a maner the verie same? And what
say you to **Samuell** the golden mouthed Prophet,
not withstanding that hee was an Archprophete,   1330
and a chiefe Seer of that time, did he not walk
so meanly, as **Saule** seeking his fathers Asses,
could not knowe him from the rest, but asked
him, where was the seers house? This must needs
argue that he went not richer then the common   1335
sort of people in his time. The children of **Israell**
being the chosen people of God, did they not
weare their fathers attire fourtie yeares together
in the Wildernesse? Was not **Iohn** the **Baptist**
cloathed with a garment of Camels haire, girded   1340
with a thong of the skinne of the same, in steede
of a girdle or succinctorie about his loynes? **Peter**
the deare Apostle of our Sauiour, was not des-
tinct from the rest of his fellow Apostles by any
kind of rich apparell, for then the maid would   1345
not haue said **I know thee by thy tongue**, but
rather by thy apparell. The Apostle **Paule** writing
to the **Hebrewes** saith, that the persecuted Church
both in his time, and before his dayes were

Marginalia:

Probation,
that the
former
world hath
contemned
pompous
attire.

Elias.

Elizeus.

Samuell

The children
of Israll.

Iohn Baptist.

Peter.

1350   cloathed, some in Sheepes skinnes, and some in
        Goates skinnes, some in Camelles haire, some in
        this, and some in that, and some in whatsoeuer
        they could get, for if it would hide their shameful
        parts, and keepe them from the colde, they
1355   thought it sufficient, they required no more: but
        to speake in one word for all: did not our Saui-
        our Iesus Christ weare the very same fashion of
D4ᵛ   apparell, that his // Country men vsed, that is, a   The humility
        coate without a seame either knit or wouen?   and pouertie
1360   which fashions the **Palestinians** vse there yet to   of Christ
        this day, without any alteration or change, as it is   vpon earth.
        thought. This his attire was not very handsome
        (one would thinke) at least it was not curious, or
        newe fangled as ours is: For of vs that **poeticall**
1365   **Apothegme** may very well be verefied, **Nitimur**
        in vetitum semper cupimusque negata: *We desire*
        things forbid, and couet things denied vs. We lothe
        this simplicity of Christ, and abhorring the
        Christian pouertie and godly mediocrity of our
1370   forefathers in apparell, wee are neuer content ex-
        cept we haue sundrie suits of apparell, one diuers
        from another, so as our presses cracke withall,
        our coffers burst, and our backes sweat with the
        cariage thereof: we must haue one suite for the
1375   forenoone, another for the afternoone, one for   Superfluitie
        the day, another for the night, one for the   of apparell
        workeday, another for the holiday, one for Sum-   with diuersity
        mer, another for winter, one of the new fashion,   of fashions.
        another of the old, one of this collour, another of
1380   that, one cut, another whole, one laced, another
        without, one of golde, another of siluer, one of
        Silkes and Veluets, another of cloath, with more
        difference and variety then I can expresse: God
        be mercifull vnto vs, and hasten his kingdome for
1385   his Elects sake.

D4ᵛ. PH: *Christ his example for apparell.*

A particular Description of Apparell in
England by degrees.

Spud.
You haue borne me in hande of many and grie-
uous abuses, raigning in **England**, but nowe set-   1390
ting apart these impertinent and superfluous
vagaries, I pray you describe vnto me more particularly, the sundrie abuses of apparell there
vsed, running ouer by degrees, the whole state
thereof, that I may see, as it were, the perfect   1395
anatomie of that Nation in apparell, which thing
I greatly desire to know.

    Philo. Your request seemeth both hard and
intricate, considering the innumerable **Meryades**
of sundry fashions dayly inuented amongst them.   1400
But yet, least I might be iudged vnwilling, to
shew you what pleasure I can, I will assaie, **pro
virili mea**, with all the might and force I can, to
satisfie your desire. Wherefore to begin first with
their Hattes. //   1405

A Description of the Hattes   E1
of England.

Sometimes they vse them sharpe on the crowne,

The diuersitie   pearking vp like the speare or shaft of a steeple,
of hats in   standing a quarter of a yard aboue the crowne of   1410
England.   their heades, some more, some lesse, as please
the fantasies of their wauering mindes. Other
some be flat and broad on the crowne, like the
battlement of a house. Another sort haue round
crownes, sometimes with one kind of bande,   1415
sometimes with another, now blacke, now white,
now russet, now red, now greene, now yellowe:
now this, nowe that, neuer content with one collour or fashion, two moneths to an end. And
thus in vanity they spend the lord his treasure,   1420

E1. PH: V*arietie of hattes.*

consuming their golden yeers, and siluer dayes in
wickednesse and sinne. And as the fashions be
rare and strange, so is the stuffe whereof their
hattes be made diuers also: for some are of silke,
1425   some of Veluet, some of Taffeta, some of Sarcenet, some of Woolle, and which is more curious,
some of a certaine kind of fine haire: These they   The sundrie
call Beuer hattes of xx. xxx. or xl. shillings a   things
peece, fetched from beyond the seas, from   where of hats
1430   whence a great sort of other vanities do come be-   be made.
sides. And so common a thing it is, that euery
seruing man, countreyman, and other, euen all
indifferently doe weare of these hattes. For he is
of no accompt or estimation amongst them, if he
1435   haue not a Veluet or Taffeta Hat, and that must
be pinked, and cunningly carued of the best fashion. And good profitable Hattes bee these, for
the longer you weare them, the fewer holes they
haue. They haue also Taffeta hattes of all col-
1440   lours quilted, and imbroydered with golde, siluer,
and silke of sundrie sortes, with monsters, antiques, beastes, foules, and all maner of pictures
and images vpon them, woonderfull to behold.
Besides this, of late there is a new fashion of
1445   wearing their hattes sprung vp amongst them,
which they father vpon the **French men**, namely,
to weare them without bands, but how vnseemly   Wearing of
(I will not say how Assie) a fashion that is, let   hats without
the wise iudge: Notwithstanding how euer it be,   bandes.
1450   if it please them, it shall not displease me. And
another sort (as fantasticall as the rest) are
content with no kind of Hatte, without a great
plume of feathers of diuers and sundrie collours,   Wearing of
peaking on top of their heads, not vnlike (I dare   Feathers in
1455   not say) Cockscombs, but fooles bables if you   hattes.
E1ᵛ   list: And yet notwithstanding // these fluttering

E1ᵛ. PH: *Great ruffes and supportasses.*

sailes, and fethered flagges of defiance to vertue
(for so they be) are so aduanced in **England**, that
euery child hath them in his hat or cap: many
get good liuing by dying and selling of them, and   1460
not a few prooue themselues more then Asses in
wearing of them.

    Spud. These Feathers argue the lightnes of
their fond imaginations, & plainly conuince them
of instabilitie and follie, for sure I am, hansome   1465
they cannot be, therefore **Ensignes** of **Pride** they
must needes be, which I thinke none will weare,
but such as bee like themselues. But to your intended discourse.

Of great Ruffes in England.   1470
Philo.

Great ruffes
deformed &
ill fauoured.
They haue great and monstrous Ruffes, made
either of Cambricke, Holland, Lawn, or els of
some other the finest cloth that can be got for
money, wherof some be a quarter of a yard deep,   1475
yea some more, very few lesse: so that they stand
a full quarter of a yard & more from their necks,
hanging ouer their shoulder points, in steed of a
Pentise. But if it happen that a shoure of raine
catch them before they can get harbour, then   1480
their great ruffes strike sayle, and downe they fall
as dishcloutes fluttering in the winde, like Windmill sayles. But wot you what? The deuill, as he
in the fulnesse of his malice, first inuented these
great Ruffes, so hath he now found out also two   1485

Two arches
or pillers to
vnderprop
the kingdom
of great rufs
withall,
videlicet
Supportasses
and Startch.
great pillers to beare vp and vphold this his kingdome of **Pride** withall (for the Deuill is King and
Prince ouer all the children of **Pride**.) The one
arch or piller wherewith his kingdome of great
Ruffes is vnderpropped, is a certaine kind of liq-   1490
uid matter, which they call Startch, wherin the
Deuil hath learned them to wash and diue their
Ruffes, which being drie, wil then stand stiffe
and inflexible about their neckes. And this startch

1495   they make of diuers substances, sometimes of
Wheate flower, of branne, and other graines:
sometimes of rootes, and somtimes of other
thinges: of all collours and hewes, as White,
Redde, Blewe, Purple, and the like.

1500   The other piller is a certaine deuise made of
Wiers, crested for the purpose, whipped ouer
eyther with Golde, Thred, Siluer or Silke, and
this hee calleth a Supportasse or Vnderpropper:
This is to be applyed rounde about their neckes

E2   vnder // the Ruffe vpon the outside of the
Bande, to beare vp the whole frame and bodie of
the Ruffe from falling and hanging downe.

        Spud. This is a deuise passing all the deuises
that euer I sawe or hearde of. Then I perceiue

1510   the Deuill not onely inuenteth mischiefe, but also
ordayneth instrumentes and meanes to continue
the same. These Bandes are so chargeable, that
(as I suppose) but fewe haue of them, such as are
of the richer sort?

1515   **Philo.** So few haue of them, as almost none
is without them, for euerie one, howe meane or
simple soeuer they bee otherwise, will haue of
them three or foure a peece for fayling. And as
though **Cambricke, Hollande, Lawne,** and the

1520   finest cloath that may be gotte any where for
money, were not good ynough, they haue them
wrought all ouer with silke woorke, and peraduenture laced with Golde and siluer, or other
costly Lace of no small price: And whether they

1525   haue **Vnde** to maintaine this geare withall or not,
it is not greatly materiall, for they will haue it by
one meane or other, or els they will sell or at the
least morgage their lands, on **Suters hill, Stangate hole,** and **Salisburie plaine,** with losse of

1530   their liues at **Tyborn** in a rope: & in sure token

Euerie pesant
hath his
statelie
Bandes, &
monstrous
ruffes, how
costly soeuer
they be.

New kind of
Ruffes, called

E2. PH: *Costly shirts & bands in England.*

Three stepps
and a halfe to
the Gallowes

therof, they haue now newly found out a more
monstrous kind of ruffe of .xii. yea, xvi. lengthes
a peece, set 3 or 4 times double, & is of some,
fitlie called: **Three steppes and a halfe to the
Gallowes.**   1535

Spud. The state and condition of that Lande
must needes be miserable, and in time growe to
great scarcity and dearth where such prodigality
and vaine excesse of thinges is vsed.

Philo.   Of costly Shirtes in England.   1540

The shirts
vsed in
Englād

Their Shirtes, which all in a manner doe weare
(for if the Nobilitie or Gentrie onely did weare
them, it were more tollerable) are eyther of **Camericke, Hollande, Lawne,** or els of the finest
cloth that may be got. And of these kinds of   1545
Shirts euery one now doth weare alike: so as it
may be thought our forefathers haue made their
Bandes and Ruffes, (if they had any at all) of
grosser cloath and baser stuffe then the worste of
our Shirtes are made of now a dayes. And these   1550
Shirtes (sometimes it happeneth) are wrought
throughout with Needle woorke of Silke, and
such like, and curiously stitched with open
seame, and many other knackes besides, more
then I can recount: Insomuch // as I haue heard   E2ᵛ
of shirtes that haue cost, some ten shillings, some
twentie, some fourty, some fiue pound, some
twenty Nobles & (which is horrible to heare)
some ten pound a peece, yea, the meanest shirt
that commonly is worne of anie, doth cost a   1560
crowne, or a noble at the least: and yet this is
scarsly thought fine ynough for the simplest person that is.

Spud. These be goodly Shirtes indeed, and
such I trust, as will neither chafe their tender   1565

E2ᵛ. PH: N*ice apparel make tender bodies.*

skinnes, nor yet fret their delicate bodies, or if it
doe, it will not be much to their grieuances I
dare be bound. Is it any maruel, **Si Cristas
erigant & cornua attollant,** *if they stand vpon*
1570 *their Pantoffles, and hoise vp their sailes on high,*
hauing these diamond Shirtes on their backes?
but howsoeuer it is, I gather by your words, that
this must needes be a nice, and womannish kind
of people, who thus pamper their bodies in such
1575 daintie attire.

    Philo. It is very true, for this their curiositie,
and nicenesse in apparell (as it were) **transnatur-**
eth them, and maketh them weak, tender and infirme, not able to abide such blustering stormes
1580 and sharpe showers, as many other people, both
abroad far from them, and in their **confines** nie
to them, do dayly beare and sustaine. I haue
heard my father and other wise Sages affirme,
that in his time within the compasse of foure or
1585 fiue score yeares, when men went cloathed in
blacke or white Frize coates, in hosen of huswiues Carzie of the same collour that the sheepe
bare them (the want of making and wearing of
which cloth, together with the excessiue wearing
1590 of silkes, Veluets, Satens, Damaskes, Taffetaes,
and such like, hath and doth make many a thousand in **England,** to beg their bread) whereof
some were streight to the thigh, other some little
bigger: and when they ware shirtes of hempe or
1595 flaxe (but now these are too grosse, our tender
stomackes cannot easily disgest such rough and
hard meates) men were stronger, healthfuller,
fairer complectioned, longer liued, and finally,
ten times harder then we be now, and abler to
1600 endure any sorrow, or paines whatsoeuer. For be
sure, this pampering of their bodies makes them
weaker, tenderer, and nesher, then otherwise they
would be if they were vsed to hardnesse, and
more subiect to receiue any kind of infection or

Nicenesse of
Apparel
maketh the
bodie tender.

Our
predecessors
wearing
meaner
apparell
were
stronger
then we.

malady, & doth rather shorten our dayes by   1605
many years, then extenuate our liues one minut
of an hower. //

　　Spud. I thinke no lesse: for how strong men   E3
were in times past, how long they liued, and how
healthfull they were, before such nicenesse and   1610
vaine pampering curiosity was inuented, wee may
read, and many that liue at this day can testifie.
But now through our fond toyes and nice inuentions, wee haue brought our selues into such a
pusillanimity and effeminat condition, as we may   1615
rather seeme nice dames, and wayrish girles then
puissant, valorous and hardy men, as our forefathers haue bene.

English Doublets.

Philo.   1620

The
monsterous
dublets
in England.

Their Doublets are no lesse monstrous then the
rest: for now the fashion is, to haue thẽ hang
down to the midle of their thighes, or at least to
their priuie members, being so hard quilted,
stuffed, bombasted and sewed, as they can neith-   1625
er worke, nor yet well play in them, through the
excessiue heat and stifnesse thereof: and therefore
are forced to weare them loose about them for
the most parte, otherwise they could very hardly
either stoupe or bowe themselues to the ground,   1630
so stiffe and sturdy they stand about thẽ. Now
what handsomnesse can be in these **Doublets**,
which stand on their bellies as big or much bigger then a mans codpeece, (so that their bellies
are thicker then all their bodies beside) let wise   1635
men iudge. For my part, handsomnesse in them,
I see none, and much lesse profit. And besides
that, I see no good end whereto they serue, ex-

Great bellied

cept it bee to shew the disposition of the wearer,

E3. PH: *Monstrous doublets in England.*

1640 how he is inclined, as namely, to gluttony, gourmandice, riote, drunkennesse, and excesse: For
what may these great bellies signifie els, then that
eyther they are such, or els would be thought to
be such. This is the truest signification, that I
1645 could euer gather of them. And this may euery
one iudge of them that seeth them: For certain I
am there was neuer any kind of apparell euer inuented, that could more disproportion the bodie
of man, then these **Doublettes** with great bellies
1650 do, hanging down beneath their **Pudenda**, (as I
haue said) and stuffed with foure, fiue or sixe
pound of Bombast at the least: I say nothing of
what their **Doublets** be made, some of Saten,
Taffeta, Silke, Grograine Chamlet, gold, siluer,
1655 & what not? slashed, iagged, cut, carued, pinked,
and laced with all kind of costly lace of diuers
and sundry collours, of all which if I could stand
E3ᵛ vpon particularlie, rather time // then matter
would be wanting.
1660 **Spud.** These be the strangest Doublets that
euer I heard of, and the furthest from handsomnesse in euery respect, vnlesse I be deceiued.

Costly Hosen in Englande.
Philo.
1665 Then haue they Hosen, which as they bee of diuers fashions, so are they of sundry names. Some
be called French hose, some Gallie hosen, and
some Venetians. The French hose are of two diuers makings, for the common French hose (as
1670 they liste to call them) containeth length,
breadth, and sidenesse sufficient, and is made
very round. The other contayneth neither length,
breadth, nor sidenesse (being not past a quarter
of a yard side) whereof, some be paned, cut and

dublets
betoken
gourmãdice
gluttony
& such like.

Dublets
of diuers
fashiõs

Hosen of
diuers &
sundrie
fashions.

French hosen
of two sorts.

drawn out with costly ornaments, with Canions   1675
adioyned, reaching downe beneath their knees.

Gally hosen   The Gallie hosen are made very large and wide,
reaching downe to their knees onely, with three
or foure gardes apeece laide downe along either
hose. And the Venetian hosen, they reach be-   1680
neath the knee to the gartering place of the
legge, where they are tyed finely with silke
poyntes, or some such like, and layd on also with
rowes or guardes, as the other before. And yet
notwithstanding all this is not sufficient, except   1685
they be made of Silke, Veluet, Saten, Damaske,
and other like precious stuffe beside: yea euery
one, Seruingman, and other inferiour to them in

The great   euery condition, will not stick to flaunt it out in
excesse vsed   these kinde of Hosen with all other their apparell   1690
in hosen.   sutable thereunto. In times paste, Kinges (as olde
Historiographers in their Bookes yet extant doe
record) would not disdaine to weare a paire of
Hosen of a Noble, ten shillinges, or a Marke
price, with all the rest of their apparell after the   1695
same rate: but now it is a small matter to bestowe twentie Nobles, ten pounde, twentie
pound, fourty pounde, yea a hundred pound of
one paire of Breeches: (**God be mercifull vnto
vs**) and yet is this thought no abuse neither.   1700

Spud. This is a woonderfull excesse as euer I
heard of, woorthy with the Rodde of Iustice
rather too bee punished, then with paper and pen
to be confuted. //

Costly Nether Stockins in England.   E4
Philo.

Then haue they Neyther-stockes to these gay ho-
The   sen, not of cloth (though neuer so fine) for that
diuersity of   is thought too base, but of **Iarnsey, Worsted,**

1710 **Crewell, Silke, Thred**, and such like, or els at the   netherstockes
least of the finest **Yarne** that can be got, and so   worn in
curiously knit with open seame downe the legge,   England
with quirkes and clockes about the Anckles and
sometime (haplie) interlaced with golde or siluer
1715 threds, as is woonderfull to beholde. And to such
impudent insolency, and shamefull outrage it is
now growne, that euery one almost, though otherwise verie poore, hauing scarce fourtie shillings
of wages by the yeare, will not sticke to haue two
1720 or three paire of these silke netherstockes, or els
of the finest Yarne that may be got, though the
price of them be a royal or twenty shillings or
more, as commonly it is, for how can they be
lesse? when as the very knitting of them is worth
1725 a noble or a royall, and some much more. The
time hath bene, when one might haue clothed all
his body wel from top to toe for lesse then a
paire of these netherstocks will cost.

Spud. I haue seldome heard the like, I thinke   The miserie
1730 verily that **Sathan**, Prince of Darknesse and fath-   of these
er of Pride, is let loose in that land, els it could   daies
neuer so far exceed as it doth, for the like pride
(I am fully perswaded) is not vsed vnder the
Sunne of any Nation or people how barbarous
1735 soeuer: wherefore woe bee to this age and thrise
accursed be these dayes, which bringeth foorth
such vnsauorie fruits, and vnhappy are that people, whome Sathan hath so bewitched and captiuate in Pride.

1740   **Corked shooes in England.**
Philo. To these their Netherstockes they haue   Corked shoes
Corked shoes Pinsnets, and fine **Pantoffles**,   pantoffles, &
which beare them vp two inches or more from   Pinsnets
the ground, wherof some be of white leather,
1745 some of blacke, and some of red: some of blacke
Veluet, some of white, some of red, some of
greene, razed, carued, cut, and stitched all ouer

with silk, and laid on with gold, siluer, and such
like: yet notwithstanding I see not to what good
vses these Pantoffles doe serue, excepte it bee to   1750
weare in a priuate house, or in a mans Chamber,
// to keep him warm? (for this is the only vse   E4ᵛ
wherto they best serue in my iudgement) but to
goe abroad in them as they are now vsed alto-

Pantoffles, &
slippers are a
let to those
that go abrod
in them

gether, is rather a let or hinderance to a man   1755
then otherwise: for shall he not be faine to
knocke and spurne at euerie wall, stone, or poste
to keepe them on his feet? And therefore to tell
you what I iudge of them, I think they be rather
worne abroad for nicenesse, then eyther for any   1760
ease which they bring (for the contrarie is most
true) or any handsomnesse which is in them. For
how should they be easie, when a man cannot

Pantoffles
vneasie to
go in

goe stedfastlie in them without slipping & sliding
at euerie pace ready to fall downe. Againe, how   1765
should they be easie whereas the heele hangeth
an inch or two ouer the slipper from the ground?
Insomuch, as I haue knowne diuers mens legs
swell with the same. And handsome how should
they be, when they goe flip flap vp and downe in   1770
the dirt, casting vp mire to the knees of the
wearer.

    Spud. Those kind of **Pantoffles**, can neither
be so handsome, nor yet so warme as other common shooes be, I thinke. Therefore the wearing   1775
of them abroad rather importeth a nicenesse (as
you say) in them that weare them, then bringeth
any other commoditie els, vnlesse I be deceiued?

Coates and Ierkins in England.
Philo.   1780
Their **Coates** and **Ierkins**, as they be diuers in
collours, so be they diuers in fashions, for some

E4ᵛ. PH: *Coates and Ierkins.*

be made with collours, some without, some close
to the bodie, some loose, which they call **Man-**
1785   **dilians**, couering the whole body down to the
thigh, like bags or sackes that were drawne ouer
them, hiding the dimensions and lineaments of
the body: some are buttened downe the breast,
some vnder the arme, and some down the backe,
1790   some with flaps ouer the breast, some without,
some with great sleeues, some with smal, and
some with none at all, some pleated and creasted
behind, and curiously gathered, some not, and
how many dayes in the yeare, so many sortes of
1795   apparell some one man will haue, and thinketh it
good prouision in fair weather, to lay vp against
foule. But if they would consider that their
cloathes (except those that they weare vpon their
backs) be none of theirs, but the poores, they
1800   would not heape vp their Presses and **Wardrobes**
as they doe. Doe they thinke that it is lawfull for
F1   thẽ // to haue millions of sutes of apparell lying
rotting by them, when as the poore members of
Iesus Christ dye at their doores for want of
1805   cloathing? God commaundeth in his law, that
there bee no miserable poore man nor begger
amongst vs, but that euery one bee prouided for,
and maintained of that store which God hath
blessed vs withall: But wee thinke it a great mat-
1810   ter if wee giue them an olde ragged Coate, Dou-
blette, or a paire of hosen, or els a pennie or two,
whereas notwithstanding we flow in aboundance
of all things: Then we thinke we are halfe way to
heauen, and we need to doe no more. If wee giue
1815   them a peece of browne bread, a messe of pottage (nay the stocks and prison, with whipping
cheare now and then, is the best portion of almes
which many Gentlemen giue) at our dores, it is

The varietie
of Coates &
Ierkins,

The poore
ought to be
prouided for.

Our smal
regard to
the poore.

F1. PH: *Cold charitie in* England.

counted meritorious, and a work of supereroga-
tion, when we fare full delicately our selues, feed-   1820
ing on many a daintie dish. There is a certaine
Citie in **England**, called **London**, whereas the
poore lie in streetes, vppon pallets of strawe, and
well if they may haue that too, or els in the mire

Cold charitie
to the poore.

and dirt, as commonly it is seene, hauing neither   1825
house to put in their heads, couering to keepe
them from the cold, nor yet to hide their shame
withall, penny to buy them sustenance, nor any
thing els, but are suffered to die in the streets
like dogges or beasts, without any mercy or com-   1830
passion shewed to them at all. And if any be
sicke of the plague (as they call it,) or any other
mortall disease, their maisters and Mistresses are
so impudent (hauing made as it shuld seem a
league with Sathan, a couenant with Hell, and   1835
sealed an Obligation with the Deuill, neuer to
haue to do with the works of mercie) as straight
way, they throw them out of their doores: and so
being caried foorth either in cartes, or otherwise,
are layd down eyther in the streets, or els con-   1840
uayd to some old house in the fields or gardens,
where for want of due sustentation and good

The Turkish
impietie of
some toward
the poore
diseased.

tending they end their liues most miserablie.
Truly brother if I had not seene it, I would scarsly haue thought that the like Turkish cruelty had   1845
bene vsed in any place of the world. But they
say, **Vnus testis occulatus plus valet quam mille
auriti. One eye witnesse is better to be beleeued
then a thousand eare witnesses besides.** But to
leaue these excursions, and to returne from   1850
whence I haue digressed, I thinke it best: for I
am perswaded they will regard as much my
wordes (or amend their maners) as the former
world did the preaching // of **Noah**, or the latter   F1ᵛ

F1ᵛ. PH: *Costly Cloakes in England.*

1855 world the preaching of our Sauiour Christ Iesus,
that is iust nothing at all.

  Spud. Wel then, seeing they are such a stiff-
necked people, leaue them to the Lord, and proceed to your former discourse.

Cloakes in Englande.

1860

Philo.

They haue Clokes there also in nothing different
from the rest, of diuers and sundry collours,   The sundrie
white, red tawny, black, greene, yellow, russet,   fashions of
1865 purple, violet, and infinite other collours: some of   Cloakes.
cloath, silke, Veluet, Taffeta, and such like,
whereof some be of the Spanish, French and
Dutch fashions: some short, scarsly reaching to
the girdlestead or waste, some to the knee, and
1870 other some trailing vppon the grounde almost,
liker gownes then Cloakes: Then are they garded
with Veluet gards, or els laced with costly Lace,
either of golde, siluer, or at the least of silke,
three or foure fingers broade, downe the backe,
1875 about the skirtes, and euery where els. And now
of late they vse to gard their Cloakes round
about the skirtes with **Bables**, I shoulde say **Bu-**   Bugled
gles, and other kind of glasse, & al to shine to   clokes.
the eie. Besides al this they are so faced, and
1880 withall so lined, as the inner side standeth almost
in as much as the outside: some haue sleeues,
other some haue none, some haue hoodes to pull
ouer the head, some haue none: some are hanged
with points and tassels of golde, siluer, or silk,
1885 some with out al this. But how euer it be, the
day hath bene, when one might haue bought him
two clokes for lesse, then now he can haue one
of these cloakes made, they haue such store of
workmanship bestowed vpon them.

1890 **Spud.** I am sure they neuer learned this of
our sauiour Christ Iesus, nor of any other that   The coũting
euer liued godly in the lord: but rather out of the   house of all

euill, is mans
braine.

deceiptfull forge of their owne braines haue they
sucked this filthy poyson to their owne confusion
in the end, except they repent.   1895

Boothose in England.

Philo. They haue also Boothose, which are to
be woondred at, for they be of the finest cloath
that may be got, yea fine ynough to make any
bande, ruffe or shirt of, needful to be worne: yet   1900
this is bad ynough to weare next their greasie
bootes. And would to God // this were all too: F2
But (fie for shame) they must be wrought all
ouer, from the gartering place vpward, with
needle worke, clogged with Silke of all collours,   1905
with birdes, Foules, beasts, and Antiques purtrayed all ouer in sumptuous sorte, yea and of
late, imbroydered with Golde and Siluer very
costly. So that I haue known the very needle
work of some one paire of these Boothoose to   1910
stand some in foure pound, sixe pound, and some
in ten pounde a peece. Besides this, they are
made so wide to drawe ouer all, and so long to
reach vp to the waste, that as little or lesse cloath
woulde make one a reasonable large shirte. But   1915
tushe, this is nothing in comparison of the rest.

The variety
of fashions
conuince vs
of folly.

Spud. I would thinke that Boothosen of
grosser Linnen, or els woollen cloth, were both
warmer to ride in, as comely as the other though
not so fine, and a great deal more durable. And   1920
as for those gewgawes wherewith you say they
bee blaunched and trimmed, they serue to no
ende, but to feede the wanton eies of gazing
fooles, and plainely argue the vertiginy, and instabilitie of their more then phantasticall braines.   1925

F2. PH: *Great excesse in Bootehose.*

Rapiers, Daggers, Swords, gilte in Englande.

Philo.

To these haue they their Rapiers, Swordes and
1930   Daggers gilte, twise or thrise ouer the hiltes with
good Angell golde, or els argented ouer with siluer both within and without: and if it be true, as
I heare say it is, there be some hilts made all of
pure siluer it selfe, and couered with gold. Oth-
1935   ersome at the least are Damasked, Vernished,
and ingrauen meruellous goodly: and least any
thing should be wanting to set foorth their prid,
their scaberds and sheathes are of Veluet, or the
like: for leather though it be more profitable and
1940   as seemly, yet wil it not cary such a Maiesty or
glorious shewe as the other. And will not these
golden Swordes and Daggers almost appale a
man thinke you (though otherwise neuer so stout
a **Martialist**) to haue any dealing with them? for
1945   either to that end they be worne, or els other
swordes, Daggers and Rapiers of bare Iron and
steele were as handsome as they, and much more
auaileable to that ende, whereto Swordes and
Rapiers shoulde serue, that is, for a mans lawfull
1950   and godlie defence, against his aduersarie in time
F2ᵛ   of necessitie. // But wherefore they be so clogged
with golde and siluer I knowe not, nor yet wherto this excesse serueth I see not, but certaine I
am, a great shew of pride it is, an infallible token
1955   of vaine glorie, and a grieuous offence to God, so
prodigally and wastfully to lauish foorth his
treasure, for which we must render accompts at
the day of iudgement, when it shall be sayd to
euery one, **Redde rationem Villicationis tuæ,**
1960   *Come giue accomptes of thy stewardship.*

Swords and
Daggers gilt,
& damasked.

Why gilt
swords and
Daggers be
worne.

Luke 16

F2ᵛ. PH: *Abuse of the female sexe.*

A particular Description of the Abuses
of Womens apparell in England.

Philo.

Thus hauing giuen thee a taste or view (but not
discouered the hundreth part) of the guises of   1965
England in mens apparell onlie, and of the
abuses contained in the same, now will I with ex-
pedition impart vnto thee, the guise and seuerall
abuses of the apparell of women there vsed also:
wherfore giue attentiue eare.   1970

    Spud. My eares be prest to heare, begin when
you will & truly herein you shall pleasure me
much, for I haue greatly desired to know thorowly the state of that lande, euen à **crepundiis**
(as they say) from my tender yeares, for the great   1975
praise I haue heard therof. Wherefore I pray you
to proceed to the same, and though I be vnable
with any benefite to counteruaile your great curtesie, yet the Lord I doubt not, wil supply my
want.   1980

    Philo. The Lord our God is a mercifull God,
and a bountiful rewarder of euery one that trust-
eth in him, but yet (such is the munificencie &
liberalitie of that gentle sex) that I trust I shal
not be vnrewarded at their hands, if at the least   1985
to be called **a thousand knaues**, be a sufficient
guerdon for my paines. But though it may be
perhaps a **corrasiue** to their tender stomackes,
and a **nippitatum** to their haughty minds, to
heare their dirty dregs ript vp and cast into their   1990
diamond faces, yet hoping that they, seeing the
horrour of their impieties, and tragicall abuses,
layd open to the world for now they sleep in the
dust of silence and graue of obliuion, will at the
last, like good **Conuertes**, become the faithfull   1995
Penitentiaries of Christ Iesus, leaue off their
wickednesse, call for mercie at the handes of
God, repent and amende, I will proceed to my
intended purpose. //

The rewarde
of the female
sexe.

Collouring of womens faces
             ## in England.

The Women of **England**, many of them, vse to
collour their faces with certaine **Oyles, Liquors,**
Vnguents, & waters made to that end, whereby   *Colloring of*
2005 they thinke their beautie is greatlie decored: but   *faces with*
who seeth not that their soules are thereby de-   *ointments*
formed, and they brought deeper into the dis-   *and waters,*
pleasure and indignation of the Almightie, at
whose voice the earth doth tremble, and at whose
2010 presence the heauens shall liquifie and melt
away? Doe they thinke thus to adulterate the
Lord his workmanship, and to be without blame?
Doe they not know that he is **Zelotipus Deus**, *a*   *Adulteration*
iealous God, and cannot abide any alteration of   *of the*
2015 his workes, otherwise then he hath made them?   *Lord his*
If an artificer or Craftesman should make any   *workmanship*
thing belonging to his arte or science, & a Cob-   *in his*
bler should presume to correct the same: would   *creatures.*
not the other think himself abused, and iudge
2020 the reproouer worthy of reprehension? And doe
these women think to escape the iudgment of
God, who hath fashioned them to his glorie,
whẽ their great and more then presumptuous au-
dacity dareth to alter and change his workman-
2025 ship in them? Doe they suppose that they can
make themselues fairer, then God that made vs
all? These must needs be their suppositions, or
els they wold neuer go about to collour their
faces with such slibbersauces. And these being
2030 their intentions, what can derogate more from
the Maiestie of God in his creation? For in this
doing, they plainely conuince the Lorde of **vn-**
trueth in his worde, who sayth, hee made man
glorious, **after his owne likenesse**, and the fayrest   *They that*
2035 of all other terrestriall creatures. If he be thus faire, *colour their*

F3. PH: *Collouring of faces in England.*

faces deny the
lord of glory
to be true
God and so
no God at al.

then what neede they to make them fayrer?
Therefore this their collouring of their faces importeth (as by probable cōiecture may be presup-
posed) that they thinke themselues not faire
ynough, els why doe they goe about to make   2040
themselues fairer? And then must God needes be
vntrue in his word.

And also they denie the Lord to be either
mercifull, or almightie, or both, & so consequently no God at all: for if he could not haue   2045
made them faire, then is he not almightie, and if
he could & would not, then is he not a mercifull
God, and so euery way they stumble at the stone
of offence, which one day will crush them all to
peeces, // except they repent. And as they be   F3ᵛ
ashamed of the good creation of the Lord in
them, so it is to be feared, least at the day of
Iudgment the Lord will be ashamed of them, and
in his wrath denounce this heauy and ineuitable

Sentence
condemnatory
against those
that collour
their faces

sentence condemnatory against them: **Depart**   2055
from me you cursed into euerlasting fire, pre-
pared for the Deuill, and his Angels. I know
you not: I say, depart, for you were ashamed of
me, and of my creation.

Spud. Wherof do they make these waters and   2060
vnctions, wherwith they besmeare their faces, can
you tell?

Phil. Truly I am not so skilful in their dealings. But I hold this for a **maxime**, that they are
made of many mixtures, & sundry simples, both   2065
farre fetched and deare bought, cunningly mingled together, and artificially tempered with many
goodly condiments and holsome confections, I
warrant you, els you may be sure they would not
applie them to their amiable faces, for feare of   2070
harming or blemishing the same.

F3ᵛ. PH: *Coloured faces abhord of God.*

Spud. I pray you shewe the iudgementes, and opinions of the Fathers, concerning these col-lourings of faces with ointmentes and waters,
2075 that I may the better know, what to iudge of them my selfe.

Philo. S. Cyprian amongst the rest saith, a woman through painting and dying of her face, sheweth her selfe to bee more then whorish. For
2080 (saith he) she hath corrupted, and defaced (like a filthy strumpet or brothell) the workemanship of God in her, what is this els, but to turne trueth into falshood, with painting and slibbersauces, wheras the Lord saith, **Thou canst not make one**
2085 **haire white or blacke.** In another place he saith, **Qui se pingunt in hoc seculo, aliter quàm crea-uit Deus, metuant ne cum dies resurrectionis venerit, artifex creaturam suam, non recogno-scat.** Those that paint or collour themselues in
2090 this worlde, otherwise then God hath made them, let them feare least when the day of iudg-ment commeth, the Lord will not knowe them for his creatures. Againe, **Fœminæ crines suos inficiunt malo præsagio, capillos enim sibi flam-**
2095 **meos auspicare non metuunt.** Whosoeuer doe collour their faces or their haire with any vnnat-ural collour, they begin to prognosticate of what collour they shall be in hell. Saint **Ambrose** saith, that from the colloring of faces spring in-
2100 ticements to vices, and that they which collour
F4 their faces, doe purchase to // themselues the blot and staine of chastity. For what a dotage is it (saith he) to change thy naturall face which God hath made thee, for a painted face which
2105 thou hast made thy selfe? If thou beest faire, why paintest thou thy selfe to seeme fairer? and if thou bee not faire, why doest thou hypocritically

Inuectiues of the fathers against painting and collouring of faces.

No painting

F4. PH: *Collouring of faces detestable.*

can make any
to seem fairer
but fouler.

desire to seeme faire, and art nothing lesse? Can
those thinges which (besides that they be filthie,
doe cary the brande of God his curse vppon their   2110
backes for euer) make thee to seeme fayrer? I
could shewe you the sharpe inuections and
grounded reasons of manie moe, as of **Augustine,
Hierome, Chrysostom, Gregorie, Caluin, Peter
Martir, Gualter,** and of an infinite number moe: 2115
yea, of all generally since the beginning of the
world, against those whorish and brothellous
painting and collouring of faces, but to auoide
prolixitie, I will omit them, deferring them to
further opportunitie, for **Pauca sapienti, To a**   2120
wise man few words are sufficient.

Spud. It must needs be granted, that the
dying and collouring of faces, with artificiall collours, and vnnaturall oyntmentes, is most offensiue to God, and derogatorie to his Maiesty. And   2125
when they haue done all that they can, and the
cunningest Artist that euer liued besides, yet shal
they neuer be able to make so splendent, so orient, and so naturall a collour, as **Dame Nature**
hath giuen to the hearbes of the fielde. Then if   2130
God hath imprinted such an excellent collour in
the grasse of the fielde, which to day standeth,
and to morrowe is cut downe: howe much more
hath he ingrauen a beautifull collour in man, the
excellentest creature of all other? Therefore ought   2135
euery one to content himselfe with that shape
that God hath giuen him, without seeking for alteration or chaunge. For, doe they thinke, that
the God of all glory, and who only decketh and
adorneth the Sunne, the Moone, the starres and   2140
all the hoste of heauen with vnspeakeable glorie
and incomperable beauty, cannot make them

Collouring
of faces the
deuils nets.

beautifull and faire ynough (if it please him,)
without their slibbersauces? And what are they
els but the deuils inuentions, to intangle poore   2145
soules in the nets of perdition.

Attiring of womens heades in England.

Philo. Then followeth the trimming and
tricking of their heades, in laying out their hair

2150 to the shew, which of force must be curled, frizled and crisped, laide out, (a worlde to see) on

F4ᵛ wreathes // and borders, from one eare to another. And least it should fall down it is vnderpropped with forks, wiers, and I cannot tell what,

2155 like grim and sterne Monsters, rather than chaste
Christian matrones. Then on the edges of their
bolstered haire (for it standeth crested round
about their frontiers and hanging ouer their faces
like **pendices** or vailes, with glasse windowes on

2160 euery side) there is laide great wreathes of gold
and siluer curiously wrought, & cunningly applyed to the temples of their heads. And for feare
of lacking any thing to set foorth their pride
withall, at their haire thus wreathed and crested,

2165 are hanged **Bugles**, (I dare not say **Bables**)
Ouches, Ringes, Gold, siluer, glasses, and such
other childish gewgawes, and foolish trinkets besides, which for that they be innumerable, and I
vnskilfull in womens tearmes, I cannot easily re-

2170 compt. But God giue them grace, to giue ouer
these vanites, & study to adorne their heades
with the incorruptible ornaments of vertue and
true godlinesse.

Spud. The Apostle **Paule**, as I remember

2175 commandeth women to cherish their haire, saying that it is an ornament to them, and therefore
me thinke, this abuse of curling and laying it
forth, (if either were lawfull) is much more tollerable, then dying their faces.

2180 **Philo.** If curling, and laying out their owne
naturall haire were all (which is impious, and at
no hand lawfull, being as it is an Ensigne of

*Trimming of
their heads.*

*Simia erit
simia etiamsi
aurea gestat
insignia.*

*Laying out of
their haire*

*Gold wreaths
circumgiring
the tēples of
their heads.*

*Gewgawes
hāged about
their frōtiers.*

*Curling,
crisping, &*

F4ᵛ. PH: *Laying out of colloured haire.*

laying out
of haire.

Pride, and the standerd of wantonnesse, to all
that behold it) it were the lesse matter, but they
are not simplie content with their own haire, but   2185
buy other haire, either of Horses, mares, or any
other strange beasts, dying it of what collour they
list themselues. And if there be any poore woman (as nowe and then, we see God doeth blesse

Bought haire
& colloured
vsed to be
worne.

them with beautie as well as the rich) that hath   2190
faire haire, these nice Dames will not rest, till
they haue bought it. Or if any children haue faire
haire, they wil intice them into a secrete place,
and for a pennie or two they wil cut off their
haire: as I heard that one did in the city of Lon-   2195
don of late, who meeting a little childe with verie
faire haire, inueighled her into a house, promised
her a pennie, and so cut off her haire. And this
they weare in the same order as you haue heard,
as though it were their owne natural Haire: and   2200
vppon the other side, if any haue Haire of her
owne naturall growing, which is not faire
ynough, then will they // die it in diuers collours,   G1
almost chaunging the substance into accidents by
their deuillish, and more then thrise cursed de-   2205
uises. So whereas their haire was giuen them as a
signe of subiection, and therefore they were commanded to cherish the same, now haue they
made it an ornament of pride, and destruction to
themselues, except they repent.   2210

Spud. This is a stiffenecked people, and a rebellious, I see wel that thus dareth in euery respect, to peruert the straite waies of the Lord,
digging vp to themselues **Cisternes** of iniquitie,
which in the end without the great mercie of   2215
God will be their vtter confusion.

G1. PH: *Capital ornaments for heads.*

French Hoodes in England.

Phil.

Then on toppes of these stately turrets (I meane
2220   their goodly heades, wherein is more vanity, then
true Philosophy nowe and then) stand their other
capitall ornamentes, as French-hood, Hatte,
Cappe, Kercher, and such like, whereof some bee
of Veluet, some of Taffatie, some (but few) of
2225   Wooll, some of this fashion, some of that, and
some of this colour, some of that, according to
the variable fantasies of their serpentine mindes.
And to such excesse it is grown that euery Artificers wife, almost, will not sticke to goe in her hat
2230   of Veluet euery day, euery Marchants wife, and
meane Gentlewomen, in her french-hood, and
euery poore Cottagers daughter in her Taffeta
hat, or els of Wooll at least, well lined with Silk,
Veluet, or Taffeta. But how they come by this
2235   (so they haue it) they care not, who paieth for it
they regard not, nor yet what hurt both to themselues, and others it bringeth they feare not: but
run dayly **a malo, ad peius**, (as they say) **from
one mischief to another**, vntill they haue filled
2240   vp the measure of their iniquity, to their own
confusion at the last.

    They haue also other ornaments besides these
to furnish foorth their ingenious heades, which
they call (as I remember) **Cawles**, made Netwise
2245   to the end, as I think, that the cloth of golde,
cloth of Siluer, or els Tinsel (for that is the
worst) wherwith their heads are couered and attired vnder their Cawles, may the better appeare,
and shew it selfe in the brauest maner. So that a
2250   man that seeth them (their heads glister and
shine in such sort) he would think them to haue
golden heads. And some weare Lattice cappes
with three hornes, three corners I should say, like

Marginal notes:

Capitall
ornaments
for the head.

Hats of
Veluet,
Taffeta,
worne in
common.

*Trahit sua
quenque
voluptas.*

Cawles made
netwise.

Goldē heades
fraught with
leaden wit.

the forked cappes of // Popish Priestes, with   G1ᵛ
their perriwinckles, Chitterlings, and the like Ap-   2255
ish toyes of infinit variety. Thus lauish they forth
the goods of the lord, which are none of their
owne (but lent them for a time) vpon Pride and
naughtinesse, delighting (as it seemeth) in nothing so much, as in the stinking puddle of vanitie   2260
and sinne, which wil be their owne decay in the
end. Another sort of dissolute **Minions**, and
wanton **Sempronians** (for I can terme them no
Making of   better) are so farre bewitched, as they are not
holes in their   ashamed to make holes in their eares, whereat   2265
eares, to hang   they hang ringes, and other Iewels of Golde and
rings, &   precious stones. But what this signifieth in them,
iewels by.   I will holde my peace, for the thing it selfe
speaketh sufficiently. There is a certaine kinde of
people in the **Orient** (as writers affirme) that are   2270
such *Philautoi*, **louers of themselues**, and so
proude withall, that hauing plentie of precious
stones, and **Margarites** amongst them: they cut
A people   & lance their skins and flesh, setting therin these
who cut their   precious stones to the end they may glister &   2275
skin to   shine to the eie: so, except these womẽ were
set precious   minded to tread their paths, and to follow their
stones in   direful waies in this cursed kind of pride, I won-
themselues.   der what they meane. But because this is not so
much frequented amongst women as men, I will   2280
say no more thereof, vntil further occasion be
offered.

    Spud. Except it were a people wedded to
Pride (for I thinke **Humility** amongst them may
dwell a Virgin, for any that wil marie her) and   2285
giuen ouer of God, I neuer heard the like. I am
perswaded that neither the **Libertines, the Epi-**
cures, nor yet the vilest **Atheists** that euer liued,

G1ᵛ. PH: *Golden heads with leaden wits.*

exceeded this people in pride. **God be merciful**

2290 **vnto them.**

Great Ruffes
Neckerchers
and Partlets
vsed of
women.

    Philo. You heare not the tenth part, for no
pen is able so well to describe it, as the eye is to
discerne it. The women there vse great ruffes,
and Neckerchers of **Hollande, Lawne, Cammer-**

2295 **icke,** and such cloath, as the greatest thread shall
not bee so big, as the least haire that is: And
least they should fall downe, they are smeared
and starched in the Deuils liquor, I meane

startch: after that dried with greate diligence,

Startch the
Deuils liquor

2300 streaked, patted, and rubbed very nicely, and so
applyed to their goodly neckes, and withall vnderpropped with **Supportasses** (as I tolde you before) the stately **Arches** of Pride: beyond all this,

Supportasses
the pillers of
Pride.

they haue a further fetch, nothing inferiour to

2305 the rest, as namely three or foure orders or degrees of **minor** Ruffes, placed **gradatim,** one be-

Minor ruffes.

G2 neath another, and al vnder // the maister Deu-
ill-ruffe, the skirtes then of these great ruffes are
long and side euery way pleated, and crested ful

2310 curiously, God wot. Then last of all, they are
eyther clogged with golde, siluer, or silke lace of
stately price, wrought all ouer with needle worke,
speckled and sparkled here and there with the
Sunne, the Moon, the starres and many other

2315 Antiques strange to beholde. Some are wrought
with open worke, downe to the midst of the
ruffe and further, some with close worke, some
with purled lace so cloyed, and other gewgawes

The great
curiositie in
Ruffes and
Neckerchers.

so pestered, as the Ruffe is the least part of it

2320 selfe. Sometimes, they are pinned vp to their
eares, sometimes they are suffered to hang ouer
their shoulders, like flagges or Windmill sayles
fluttering in the wind, and thus euery one pleaseth her selfe in her foolish deuises, for **Suus**

G2. PH: *Great ruffes and minor ruffes.*

cuiusque crepitus sibi bene olet, as the Prouerbe   2325
sayth, **Euery one thinketh his owne foist the
sweetest.** But amongst many other fearful examples of Gods wrath against Pride, I would wish
them to set before their eies the fearful iudgment
of God, shewed vpon a Gentlewoman of **Ant-**   2330
werpe of late, euen the **27.** of Maie. **1582.** the
fearefull sound whereof is blowne through all the
world, & is yet fresh in euery mans memory.
This Gentlewoman being a very rich Marchant-
mans daughter, vpon a time was inuited to a bri-   2335
dal or wedding, which was solemnized in that
towne, against which day she made great preparation for the pluming of her selfe in gorgious
aray: that as her body was most beautiful, faire,
and proper, so her attire in euery respect might   2340
be answerable to the same. For the accomplish-
ment whereof she curled her haire, she died her
lockes, and laid them out after the best maner:
she colloured her face with waters and Oint-
ments, but in no case could she get any (so curi-   2345
ous and dainty she was) that could startch and
set her Ruffes and Neckerchers to her minde:
wherfore she sent for a couple of Laundresses,
who did the best they could to please her hu-
mors, but in any wise they could not: Then fell   2350
she to sweare, and teare, to curse and ban, casting the ruffes vnder feete, and wishing that the
Deuill might take her, when shee did weare any
of those Neckerchers againe. In the meane time
(through the sufferance of God) the Deuill trans-   2355
forming himselfe, into the shape of a yong man,
as braue, & proper as she in euery point in outward appearance, came in, faining himself to be
a woer or suter vnto her: and seeing her thus
agonized, & in such a pelting // chafe, he de-   G2ᵛ

A fearful
example
against
pride, shewed
vpon a
Gentlewoman
in Antwerpe.

Womens
lubricious
minds neuer
content with
any thing
when it
is wel

G2ᵛ. PH: *The deuill found setting of ruffes.*

maunded of her the cause thereof, who straight-
way told him (as women can conceal nothing
that lieth vpon their stomacks) how she was
abused in the setting of her ruffes, which thing
2365   being heard of him, he promised to please her
mind, and so tooke in hande the setting of her
Ruffes, which he performed to her great contentation and liking, in so much, as she looking her
selfe in a glasse (as the Deuill bad her) became
2370   greatly inamoured with him. This done, the
yoong man kissed her, in the doing whereof, hee
writhed her neck in sunder, so she dyed misera-
bly, her body being straight waies changed into
blew and black collours, most vgglesome to be-
2375   holde, and her face (which before was so amorous) became most deformed, and fearfull to looke
vpon. This being knowne in the cittie, great
preparation was made for her buriall, a rich Coffin was prouided, and her fearfull body was laid
2380   therein, & couered very sumptuously. Foure men
immediately assayed to lift vp the corpes, but
could not mooue it, then sixe attempted the like,
but could not once stirre it from the place where
it stood. Whereat the standers by maruelling,
2385   caused the coffin to be opened, to see the cause
thereof. Where they found the body to be taken
away, and a blacke Catte very leane & deformed
sitting in the Coffin, setting of great ruffes, and
frizling of haire, to the great feare and woonder
2390   of all the beholders. This wofull spectacle haue I
offered to their view, that by looking into it in
stead of their other looking glasses, they might
see their own filthinesse, and auoid the like offence, for feare of the same or worser iudgment:
2395   which God graunt they may doe.

    Spud. As in a **Camilion** are said to be al col-
lours saue white, so I thinke, in these people are
all thinges saue vertue and Christian sobrietie.
Proteus that monster, could neuer change him-

*The deuil
pleaseth
women better
then any
body els.*

*The deuill
found setting
of great
ruffes.*

Proteus.	self into so many forms & shapes, as these 2400 women do, belike they haue made an obligation with hell, and are at a league with the deuill, els they would neuer outrage thus, without either feare of God, or respect to their weake brethren, whome herein they offend. 2405

Doublets for Women in England.

Women
wearing
Dublets
and Ierkins.

Philo. The women also there haue Doublets and Ierkins, as men haue here, buttoned vp the breast, and made with wings, weltes and pinions on the shoulder pointes, as mans apparel is in all 2410 respectes, and although this be a kind of attire, proper onely to man, yet they blush not to wear it: and if they could as wel change // their sexe, G3 and put on the kind of man, as they can weare apparell assigned only to man, I thinke they 2415 would as verily become men indeed, as now they degenerate from godly sober women, in wearing this wãton leud kind of attire, proper only to

A curse to
them that
wear contrary
apparel to
their sexe.

man. It is written in the **22.** of **Deuteronomy,** that **what man so euer weareth womans apparell** 2420 **is accursed, and what woman weareth mans apparell, is accursed also.** Now whether they be within the compasse of that curse, let they themselues iudge. Our apparell was giuen as a signe distinctiue, to discerne betwixt sexe and 2425 sexe, and therfore one to weare the apparell of another sexe, is to participate with the same, and to adulterate the veritie of his owne kinde. Wherefore these women may not improperly bee

Herma-
phroditi.

called **Hermaphroditi,** that is Monsters of both 2430 kindes, halfe women, half men. Who if they were naturall women, and honest Matrones, woulde blush to go in such wanton & leud attire, as is incident only to man.

G3. PH: *A cursse for apparell.*

2435   **Spud.** I neuer read nor hard of any people,
except drunken with **Circes** cups, or poysoned
with the **Exorcismes** of **Medea** that famous and
renowmed Sorceresse, that euer would wear such
kind of attire, as is not onely stinking before the
2440   face of God, and offensiue to man, but also such
as painteth out to the whole world the dissolutenesse of their corrupt conuersation.

Womens Gownes in England.

    Philo. Their Gownes be no lesse famous then
2445   the rest, for some are of silke, some of Veluet,
some of Grograine, some of Taffatie, some of
Scarlet, and some of fine cloath, of x. xx. or xl.
shillinges a yard. But if the whole gowne be not
Silke or Veluet, then the same must be layd with
2450   lace, two or three fingers broad all ouer the
gowne, or els the most part. Or if not so (as lace
is not fine ynough now and then) then it must be
garded with great gardes of Veluet euery garde
foure or sixe fingers broad at the least, and edged
2455   with costly lace, and as these gownes be of diuers
and sundry collours, so are they of diuers fashions, chaunging with the **Moone:** for some be of
the new fashion, some of the olde, some of this
fashion, some of that, some with sleeues hanging
2460   downe to their skirtes trayling on the ground,
and cast ouer their shoulders like Cow tailes.
Some haue sleeues much shorter, cut vp the
arme, drawne out with diuers and sundry collours, and poynted with silke Ribbons verye //
G3ᵛ   gallantly, tyed with true Loues knottes (for so
they call them.) Some haue Capes reaching
downe to the midst of their backes, faced with
Veluet, or els with some fine wrought Taffeta, at
the least, and fringed about very brauely: and (to

The diuersity of gownes.

Simiæ in purpuris.

Costly Gownes.

Diuers fashions of gowns

G3ᵛ. PH: *The impudencie of Harlots.*

shut vp all in a word) some are pleated and   2470
creasted downe the backe woonderfully, with
more knackes then I can expresse. Then haue
they **Peticoates** of the best cloath that can be

Peticotes.   bought, and of the fayrest die that can be made.
And sometimes they are not of cloath neyther,   2475
for that is thought too base, but of Scarlet, Grograine, Taffeta, Silke, and such like, fringed
about the skirtes with Silke Fringe of chaungea-
ble collour. But which is more vaine, of whatso-
euer their **Peticoates** be, yet must they haue **Kir-**   2480

Kirtles.   **tles** (for so they call them) eyther of Silke, Veluet, Grograine, Taffeta, Satten, or Scarlet, bor-
dered with gardes, Lace, Fringe, and I cannot tel
what besides. So that when they haue all these
goodlie robes vpon them, women seem to be the   2485
smallest part of themselues, not naturall women,

Women the   but artificiall women, not women of flesh and
least part of   bloud, but rather **Puppits** or **Mawmettes** consist-
themselues.   ing of ragges and clowtes compact togither. Yea,
so farre hath this Canker of Pride eaten into the   2490
body of the Common wealth, that euery poore
Yeoman his daughter, euery Husbandman his
daughter, and euery Cottager his daughter, will

Poore mens   not sticke to flaunt it out, in such **Gownes, Peti-**
daughters   **coates,** and **Kirtles** as these. And notwithstand-   2495
excesse.   ing that their Parentes owe a brace of hundred
pounds more then they are worth, yet will they
haue it, **quo iure quaue iniuria,** *either by hook or*
by crook, by right or wrong as they say, wherby it
commeth to passe, that one can scarsly know,   2500
who is a Noble woman, who is an honourable, or
worshipfull woman, from them of the meaner
sorte.

Parents to   **Spud.** Their parentes and friendes are much
blame   to be blamed, for suffering them to go in such   2505
wanton attire. They should not allow them such
large pittance, nor suffer them to measure their
apparell after their owne licencious yardes of

2510 selfe-wil and wicked desires: then could they not
so far exceede as they doe.

Phil. Then shal theyr Parents be sure neuer
to haue good day with them. For they are so impudent, that all be it, their poore parentes haue
but one cow, horse or sheepe, they will neuer let
2515 them rest til they be sold, to maintaine them in
G4 their braueries beyonde // all measure. And to
say the truth, some Parents (worthy to be inaugured for fooles with the Laurell crowne of tripple
folly) are so buxome to their shamlesse desires
2520 and so **exorable** to their **prostitute** requests, that
they grant to their too too nice daughters more
than they doe desire themselues, taking a singular
felicity and far surmounting pleasure in seeing
them decked and plumed in the **Feathers** of de-
2525 ceitful vanity.

Spud. This ouer great lenity, and remisse liberty of theirs in the education of youth, in respect of the euent, and successe that it bringeth
in the end, may rather be counted an extreame
2530 cruelty, then a fatherly loue or pittie of them towards their children: For what maketh them so
soone Whoores, Strumpets, Harlots and Baudes,
as that cockering of them doeth? What maketh
them apt and prone to all kind of naughtines,
2535 but this? Nothing in the world so much. For
giue a wild horse the liberty of the head neuer so
litle and he will run headlong to thine and his
own destruction also. So long as a sprig, a twist
or a branch is young, it is flexible and bowable
2540 which way a man can desire, but if we tary till it
be a great tree, it is inflexible and vnbowable: If
Waxe be taken whilest it is hot, any **Character**
may be easily imprinted in it, but tarying till it be
hard, it receiueth no print at all. So correct chil-

The
impudēcie
of proud
Harlots.

Ouer remisse
lenity of
Parents
to their
children.

G4. PH: *What makes youth wicked.*

dren in their tender yeares, and you may bow   2545
them to what good lore you will yourself, but
tary till they be old, then it is to late, as
experience teacheth dayly.

Netherstockes of women in England.

Philo. Their **Netherstockes** in like maner are   2550
Netherstocks   either of Silk **Iarnsey**, **Worsted**, **Crewell**, or at
of Iarnsey   least of as fine **Yarne**, **Threed**, or **Cloath** as is
or silke.   possible to be had, yea, they are not ashamed to
                weare hose of all kinde of changeable collours, as
                greene, red, white, russet, tawnie, and els what   2555
                not: which wanton light collours, no sober chaste
                christian can hardly, without suspition of light-
                nesse, at any time weare: but what so euer is a
                deformity or shame to others, is an ornament to
                them that be past all shame. Then these delicate   2560
Corked shoes   hosen must be cunningly knit, and curiously
Pinsnets,   indented in euery point, with **quirkes, clockes,**
pantoffles,   **open seame,** and euery thing els accordingly:
& such like   whereto they haue **Corked shoes, Pinsnets, Pan-**
for women.   **toffles, and Slippers:** some of black Veluet, some   2565
                of white, some of green, // and some of yellow: G4ᵛ
                some of Spanish leather, and some of English
                stitched with silke and imbrodered with golde
The   and siluer all ouer the foot, with other gewgawes
innumerable   innumerable: All which if I should take vpon me   2570
fashiõs,   to expresse, I might as easily number the sandes
of womens   of the sea, the starres in the Skie, or the grasse
attire.   vpon the earth, so infinite and innumerable be
                their abuses. For were I neuer so expert an
                Arithmetician, I were neuer able to recompt the   2575
                one halfe of them, the Deuill brocheth so many
                newe fashions euery day. Wherefore to their Au-
                thor I leaue them, not omitting to tell you (as an

G4ᵛ. PH: *Costly perfumes in England.*

2580 **interim**, by the way) of a certaine kinde of sweet
Pride vsed amongest the Gentlemen and Gentlewomen in **England**.

    Spud. I haue learned out of the booke of
God, that all Pride is stinking before the face of
God: wherfore I greatly desire to know what
2585 **abortiue Miscreant** this may be, for it is some
portenteous mishapen monster, I am fully
perswaded.

Pride
stinking
before the
face of God.

Muske Ciuet and sweet powder in England.

2590   **Philo.** Is not this a sweet Pride, to haue
Ciuet, Muske, sweete powders, fragrant Pomanders, odorous perfumes, and such like, whereof
the smell may be felt and perceiued, not onely all
ouer the house, or place where they be present,
2595 but also a stones cast off almost, yea, the bed
wherein they haue laid their delicate bodies, the
places where they haue sate, the clothes &
thinges which they haue touched shall smell a
week, a moneth and more after they be gone.
2600 But the Prophet **Esayas** telleth them, in stead of
their **Pomanders, Muskes, Ciuetes, Balmes,
sweet odours** and **Perfumes**, they shall haue
stench and horrour in the nethermost hel. Let
them take heed to it and amend their wicked
2605 liues in time. And in the Summer time whilest
flowers be greene and fragrant, ye shall not haue
any Gentlewoman almost, no nor yet any Droye
or Puzsle in the Country, but they will cary in
their hands Nosgayes and Posies of flowers to
2610 smell at, and which is more, two or three sticked
in their breasts before, for what cause I cannot
tell, except it be to allure their amorous Paramours to catch at them, and to smell at their
breastes, whereby I doubt not but they get many
2615 a slabbering kisse, and peraduenture more friendship besides, they know what I meane. //

The hauing of
Ciuet, Muske,
or other
perfumes a
sweet kinde
of pride.
Esa.cap.3.

Nosegaies, &
Posies of
flowers worne
and caried
abroad.

Beware the
Spanish
pippe

The curious
smelles
obnubilate
the spirites,
and darken
the sences.

Spud. You will be thought very straight laced   H1
to speak against these things, for I haue hard it
said that sweet smelles do corroborate the sences,
comfort the spirites, and recreate both the body   2620
and mind of man greatly, do they not so?

Philo. They are so farre from comforting the
braine, or reuiuing the spirits of man, that as
mistes and exhalations which euaporate from
these earthly bodies, and are drawne vp by the   2625
attractiue power of the Sun, Moone and starres,
do obscure and darken the beames of the Sunne.
So these (in a maner) palpable odours, fumes,

Sweet smels
of Muskes,
Ciuet, & such
like annoy
the spirits.

vapours, and smelles of Musks, Ciuets, Poman-
ders, Perfumes, Balmes, and such like ascending   2630
to the braine, doe rather darken and obscure the
spirites and sences, then either lighten thẽ, or
comfort them any maner of way. But howsoeuer
it falleth out, sure I am, they are ensignes of
Pride, allurements to sin, and prouocations to   2635
vice. After al this, when they haue attired themselues thus, in the midst of their pride, it is a
world to consider their coynesse in gestures, their

The vain
gestures &
coynes of
womẽ in
the midst of
their peacock
feathers

minsednes in words and speeches, their gingerlynesse in tripping on toes like young Goates, their   2640
demure nicitie, and babishnesse, and withall their
haughty stomacks, and more then **Cyclopicall**
countenances: their fingers must be decked with

Fingers
clogged with
rings.
Womens
trinkets,
Sweeted
gloues.
Looking
glasses
the deuils
spectacles.

gold, siluer and precious stones: their wristes
with bracelets, and armelets of gold, and other   2645
costly iewels, their hands couered with their
sweet washed gloues, imbrodered with gold, siluer, and what not, and to such abhomination it
is grown, as they must haue their looking glasses
caried with them wheresoeuer they go: And good   2650
reason, for els how could they see the deuill in
them? For no doubt they are the deuils specta-

H1. PH: *Sweete smelles hurtfull.*

cles, to allure vs to pride, and consequently to
destruction for euer.

2655   **Spud.** The Deuill could neuer haue found out
a more pestilent euill than this, for hereby man
beholding his face, and being naturally giuen to
flatter himselfe too much, is easily drawne to
thinke well of himselfe: and yet no man seeth the
2660   true proportion of his face, but a counterfeit
effigy and false image thereof in the glasse,
which the Deuill suffereth him to see, that thereby he may rise into pride, and offend the diuine   Looking
Maiesty. Therefore may these looking glasses be   glasses the
2665   called the Deuils bellowes, wherewith he bloweth   Deuils
the blast of pride into our heartes: and those that   bellowes.
looke in them, may be said to looke in the Deu-
ils Arse, whilest he infuseth the venemous //
H1ᵛ   winde of Pride into their soules.

2670   ## Scarffes and Maskes in England.

Phil. Then must they haue their Silke Scarffes
cast about their faces, and fluttering in the wind
with great tassels at euery end, either of Golde,
siluer or silke. But I knowe wherefore they will
2675   say, they weare these scarffes, namely, to keep
them from sunburning. But I would aske these   A question
Nicelings one question, wherin if they can re-   to scarffe
solue me, then I will say as they say, that scarffes wearers.
are necessarie, and not flagges of pride. Can that
2680   thing which is most glorious and faire of it selfe,
make any thing foule or ill fauoured? the Sunne
is a most glorious and faire creature, and therefore can not make them fouler then they are of
their owne nature. From whence then it is that
2685   the Sunne burneth them, and altereth their
Orient collour into worser hue? The cause there-

---

of proceedeth from their owne **genuine** corruption and naturall **prauitie.** For no more is their
fowlnesse to be ascribed to the splendent beames
of the Sunne, then the stench of a dead Carkasse   2690
may be sayd to proceed of the Sunne, and not
rather of it owne corruption and filthinesse. They
busie themselues in preseruing the beautie of
their bodies, which lasteth but for a time, and in
time is cause of it owne corruption, and which in   2695
effect is nothing els but putrification it selfe, and
a dunghill couered with white and red: but for
the beauty of the soule they care nothing at all.

Visours or
inuisories
of Veluet,
to ride
abroad in.

When they vse to ride abroad they haue
Masks & visors made of veluet (or in my iudg-   2700
ment they may rather be called inuisories) wherwith they couer all their faces, hauing holes made
in them against their eyes, wherout they looke.
So that if a man that knew not their guise before, should chaunce to meet one of them, he   2705
would thinke he met a monster or a Deuil, for

Sues
volutabris
versantur.

face he can shew none, but two broad holes a-
gainst their eyes, with glasses in them. Thus they
prophane the name of God, and liue in all kind
of voluptuousnes and pleasure, worse then euer   2710
did the Heathen.

Spud. What thinke you, are not the inuenters
and first finders out of these new toyes & deuillish deuices in great danger, and partakers with
them of euill committed?   2715

Philo. It can not be, but the Inuentors of
these new toyes, are in great danger before God,
as they who shal render accomptes // to God,   H2

The first
finders and
inuenters of
new fashions,

not only for the inuention of them, but also for
the euil committed by them. For whosoeuer is   2720
authour of any euill, must needs answere for the
euill. And surely the authors of these newfangles,

H2. PH: *A Caueat for Artificers.*

are worthy to be cannonized saints, when the
yeare of **Iubilie** commeth (I meane Saintes of
2725   Sathan) for what deed so flagitious, what attempt
so daungerous, or what fact so hainous, which
with **alacritie** is not **plausiblie** committed for the
maintenance of these Deuillish toyes and deuices? And albeit that the persons themselues
2730   who offend this way shall dy in their sinnes, their
owne bloud being poured vpon their owne heads,
yet the authors of these new toyes where through
they offended, shall bee guilty of their deaths, &
surely answer for their destruction in the day of
2735   the Lord.

       Spud. But say they, If I make them not, an-
other will, and it is as good for me to make them
as another, and it is my liuing, wherefore I am
discharged of blame if I make them, being com-
2740   maunded with sweat of my face, and with trauell
and paine to get my liuing?

       Philo. We are commanded indeed to get our
liuing with the sweate of our face, but how? Not
in doing those thinges which are euil of them-
2745   selues, and also draw and entice others to euill,
but in things lawful and honest, and which induce to godlines. And to say, others will make
them if they do not, no more excuseth them of
offence before God, then for a Murtherer or a
2750   theefe to say, if I had not robbed or killed this
man, another would, dischargeth him from the
penalty of the law, or guilt of the fact. Is it lawfull for vs to do euill, because others doe it? Or
doth the wickednes of another deliuer vs from
2755   blame, if we commit the same offence? No, nothing lesse. Wherefore, let Taylors, and artificers
beware, how they eyther inuent or make these
new deuises and deuilish fashions euery day: &
being requested to make them, if they perceiue
2760   them to tend to vice, & to allure to sin, let them
refuse them in the name of God, more tēdering

Marginal notes:

are culpable
of all the euil
that cōmeth
by them

A vaine
excuse.

We are boūd
to get our
liuing in wel
doing, not in
euil doing.

A caueat to
artificers that
inuent new
fashions.

A caueat for
Tailours and
Artificers.

the saluation of many, then the priuate commodity of themselues alone, which thing if euery
one would doe, he should deliuer his owne soule,
and support an infinite number from falling into   2765
the gulfe of sinne, and so in short time these new
toyes, fond deuices, and childish bableries (newe
fashions I should say) would soone vanish away,
and come to naught: which God grant may come
to passe. //   2770

The meane attire of both
Heathen and other

H2ᵛ

Women in olde time.

Spud. Did the women of the former world
attire themselues in such sort, as these women   2775
doe?

Phi. The women of the former age you may
be sure neuer apparelled themselues like one of
these: But least you should thinke, that the godly
only liued thus austerely, you shall heare how   2780
little the very **Heathen** and **Barbarian** women
haue, and do at this present esteeme of apparel,
as **Stuperius** witnesseth, whose wordes are these,
speaking of the **Egyptian** women: **Vestimenta
sciunt nec noua pristinis mutare, verum semper**   2785
**his in cultibus gaudent perpetuo tempore con-
gredi, quascunque gentes hunc per orbem visi-
tent.** Which may be thus turned into English
verse.

> *The Egiptian Matrones neuer vse, their*
> *   fashions of attire to change:*   2790
> *But euer keep one form to chuse, although*
> *   they visite nations strange.*

And as writers do affirme, all the women there,
indifferently goe with their haire hanging downe,
with a broad hat vpon their heads and other at-

H2ᵛ. PH: *Womens habite in other countries.*

2795   tire as plaine as the rest, so farre are these people
from pride, and hunting after straunge fashions,
as our women do. The women of **Affrica** are
witnessed by the same **Stuperius**, and others to
be so far from affecting of strange fashions, or
2800   curiosity in apparell, that they cloth themselues
in a maner all ouer **Ferinis pellibus, with beastes
skinnes,** furres and such like. And this they think
so rich attire, as they vse it altogether, when they
celebrate their festiuall solemne dayes, or when
2805   they goe abroade to bee seene. The **Brasilian**
women esteeme so little of apparell also, as they
rather choose to goe naked (their secrete partes
onely being couered) then they would be thought
to bee proude, or desirous of such vanity. The
2810   **Cantabrian** women likewise, with many other
doe the same. In high **Germanie** the women vse
in effect one kind of apparell or habite, without
any difference at all, nothing like other Nations,
delighting in newfangles: yea, the wiues there,
2815   are so farre from pride, that they will not disdaine to carie all their housholde stuffe, and
other supellectiles about with them vppon their
backes, in time of necessity. Their Maides and
Virgins goe very plaine, with kertchers onely on
2820   their heades, their haire hanging downe behind
in token of Virginity. Thus you see euery nation
H3   // how barbarous soeuer, are much inferiour to
the people of **England** in pride and excesse of
apparell: and yet these examples I alleadge not, to
2825   the end I would wish all others to vse the same,
or the very like sauage kind of habite: but to
shew how far they bee from pride, and how
much the other be wedded to the same. And as
for the vertuous and godly Christian women,
2830   from the beginning of the world, they haue so

The maners of
other nations
in attire,

H3. PH: *Brutish attire not commendable*

little cared for the vaine glorie of apparel and so
little or rather nothing at all, were they ac-
quainted therewith, as they hunted for nothing

els so much, as for the ornaments of the minde,
as **Wisedome, continencie, chastity, and true**   2835
godlinesse, thinking the same beautie sufficient.
They counted it great shame to cloath their bodies with sumptuous apparell, and their mindes to
be naked, and voyd of true vertue. So, if these
women would seeke after the beauty of the mind,   2840
they would not affect apparell so much: for if
they be faire in body already, then neede they
not gorgeous apparell to make them fairer: and if
they bee deformed in body, it is not the apparell
that can make them fairer. And either their   2845
beauty consisteth in them, or in their apparel: if
in them then not in the apparell, and so it is
meere foolery to weare it. And if in apparell, then
not in them, and so can not the garments make
them fair, whome God and Nature hath made   2850
otherwise. Wherefore, looke in what shape, forme,
or condition euery one is created by God, let him
content himselfe with the same without any alteration or change, with praise to his Creator.

    Spud. They hold, (notwithstanding) that it is   2855
the pride of the heart, which God so much hat-
eth and detesteth.

    Philo. It is very true that God punisheth the

pride of the hart with eternall damnation (if they
repent not) for he will bee serued and obeyed,   2860
eyther with the whole man, or els with none.
Then if he punish pride of the heart with euerlasting damnation, hee must needs in iustice
punish the pride of apparel with the like, being

both ioyned in one **predicament** of sinne: and   2865
the pride of apparell much more hurting before
the world then the other. Also, it is manifest,
that the pride of apparell riseth first frō the corruption of the hart, as the effectes from the cause,

2870   the fruit from the root of the tree: then if the
        pride of the heart, which notwithstanding it
        hurteth not outwardly, but is secrete betwixt God
        and himselfe, be damnable in it owne nature be-
        fore God, then must it needs be, that the pride //
H3ᵛ   of apparell (which sheweth it selfe to the worlde,
        both offensiue to God, and hurtfull to man, and
        which also is the fruit of the pride of the heart,
        and throweth almost as many as beholde it, at
        least, as many as follow it, into the deepe Dun-
2880   gion of hell) is much more pernicious and dam-
        nable then the other.

            Spud. Hath the Lord plagued this sinne of
        pride, with any notable plague or punishment,
        euer from the beginning of the worlde vnto this
2885   day, or hath he passed it ouer as a thing of small
        importance?

Punishments of pride in all ages.
Philo.

        Most fearfull plagues and dreadfull iudgments of
2890   God haue in all ages bene poured vpon them
        that offended herein, as all histories both holy
        and prophane do beare record. For proofe where-
        of, I will giue you a tast but of a few, whereby
        may appeare how wonderfully the Lord in all
2895   ages, times, kindreds, & peoples, hath punished
        those that through pride (like wicked runnagats,
        and backsliders from God) haue rebelled against   Examples
        his Maiestie. The deuill, who before was an An-   of Gods
        gel in heauen, arrogating to himself the imperiall punishments
2900   throne of the maiestie of God, was cast down in-   executed
        to the lake of hel burning with fire and sulphur   vpon thē
        for euer. **Adam** desiring to be a God (for the   that offended
        serpent told him he should be as God, knowing   in pride
        both good and euill) was for the sin of pride   in all ages.

H3ᵛ. PH: *Punishments for pride.*

thrown down to the bottom of hel, and not only   2905
he, but all his posterity to the end of the world.
The hoste of **Core, Dathan** and **Abiram,** for
their exceeding pride, in stirring vp mutinies and
rebellions against their lawful Magistrate, were
swallowed vp quicke into hell, the earth opening   2910
her mouth and deuouring them, with all their
complices whatsoeuer. The people of **Babylon** intending to build a tower, whose top shuld reach
the heauens, thinking that if God should drowne
the world again with water, they would be sure   2915
ynough on the toppe of their high turrets: yea,
they intended to sit with God himselfe (if need
were) were all confounded, and a diuers **language**
put into euery mans mouth, that none knew
what other spake. And thus wer they forced to   2920
leaue their building, and dispersed themselues
abroad vpon the face of the earth, and hereof
sprang the first diuersity of languages in the
world. Wherefore, when we heare any language
spoken that we know not, it may be a **memoran-**   2925
dum vnto vs, to // put vs in minde of our pride,   H4
which was the cause thereof.

A
memorandum.

    Goliah the great Gyant, the huge **Cyclops,**
and sworne enemy to the children of **Israell,** for
his pride against the Lord, was slaine by **Dauid**   2930
the faithfull seruant of the Lord.

Antiochus.

    Antiochus intending to ouerthrowe and sacke
Ierusalem, to spoyle the **Sanctuarie** and **Temple**
of the Lord, and to kill the people of God, was
for his pride ouerturned in his chariote, riding   2935
thitherward, his belly bursting, and filthy wormes
crawling out most lothsomly, and in fine, began
so to stinke and smell, as neither his seruantes
nor hee himselfe could abide his owne sauour,

H4. PH: *Proud Kings punished.*

2940 and thus ended his life in great misery and wretchednes.

Nabuchadnezar, was for his pride cast out of his kingdom, and forced to eat grasse with wild beasts in the wildernesse.

Nebuchodo-
nosor.Dan.4.

2945 King Saule, for his Pride and disobedience, was deposed of his Principality and Kingly regiment, and in the end slue himselfe on mount Gelboe most desperately.

King Saule.

Sodoma and Gomorra, were both destroyed
2950 with fire and Brimstone from heauen for their sinne of Pride and contempt of the Lord.

All the world in the dayes of Noah was drowned with an vniuersall deluge for pride and contumacy of heart.

2955 King Ezekiah, for his pride in shewing to the Ambassadors of the king of Babylon, all his treasure (for hee sent messengers vnto him with giftes and letters congratulatorie, reioycing for the recouery of his health) lost all his iewels,
2960 treasures and riches, with his sonnes also, being transported captiues into Babylon.

2.Reg.20.

King Dauid for his pride in numbring the people contrary to the wil of God, was grieuously punished, & three score and ten thousand of his
2965 people slaine with a grieuous pestilence for the same.

2.Samuel.1.c
24.vers.15.

King Pharao for his pride against the Lord (for he thought him selfe a God vpon the earth, and therefore asked hee Moyses in derision, who
2970 is the Lord?) was drowned in the red Sea with all his hoaste. The proud Pharisie iustifying himselfe, for his pride was reprooued of the Lord, and reiected. King Herode for attyring himselfe in sumptuous aray, and not ascribing glory to the
2975 Lord, was striken dead, by an Angell, and wormes consumed his flesh immediately. All these, with infinite millions moe in all ages, haue perished through pride, and therefore let not this

The proud
pharisie
King Herode

people thinke // that they shall escape vnpunished, who drinke vp pride, as it were sweet   2980
wine, feed vpon it, as vpon dilicious meates, and
wallow in it, as filthy Swine doe in the myre.
Will the Lord punish his peculiar people and
elect vessels, and let them goe free? Wherefore I
would wish them to be warned, for it is a terrible   2985
Gods plagues
are prepared
if wee repent
not
thing to fall into the hands of God, who is a
consuming fire, and a fearfull God. His **Bowe** is
bent, his **arrowes of iudgement** are drawne to the
heade, his fire is kindeled, his wrath is gone out,
and ready to bee poured vpon the contemners of   2990
his lawes. Tempt not the Lord any longer, prouoke not his wrath, **exasperate** not his iudgmẽts
towards thee. For as mercy procedeth from him,
so doth Iustice also: and be sure of it, he payeth
home at the last. For as in mercy he suffereth no   2995
good deed to be vnrewarded, so in his iust iudgment there is no wickednesse without repentance
which he leaueth vnpunished. And yet notwithstanding, their wickednes and pride is such as
stinketh before the face of God, and maketh the   3000
enemies to blaspheme, and speake euill of the
wayes of the Lord: for say they, the men of **Eng-**
Our
newfangles
& toyes
are occasions
why al
nations
mocke &
flout vs.
land are wicked, and dissolute in all their waies,
which easilie appeareth by their apparel, and
newfangled fashions euery day inuented. The   3005
beastly Epicures, the Drunkards, and Swilboules
vpon their Ale-benches, when their heads are in-
toxicate with new wine and strong drinke, will
not sticke to belch forth, and say that the inhabitants of **England** go brauely in apparell changing   3010
fashions euery day for no cause so much, as to
delight the eyes of theyr whorish mates withall,
and to inamour the mindes of their fleshlie Paramours. Thus be this people a laughing stocke to

3015 al the world for their pride, a slaunder to the
word of God, and to their profession, **scandalles**
to their brethren, a dishonour and reproch to the
lord, and very **Caterpillers** to themselues, in
wasting and consuming their goods and treasures,
3020 vpon vanities and trifles.

The dayly exercises of the Women of England.

Spud.
I perceiue these are nice Dames, I pray you what
3025 exercises follow they for the most part being thus
clothed in their robes, and how doe they spend
the time? For I stand in doubt they scarse spend
it wel.

  Philo. You need not to doubt. For they spend
I1 the time verie wel // I warrant you, and to their
own contentments. For some of them lie in bed
(I will not say with whome) till nine or ten of
the clocke euery morning, then being rouzed
foorth of their dennes, they are two or three
3035 houres in putting on of their robes, which done,
they goe to dinner, where no delicates eyther of
wines or meates are wanting. Then their bodies
being satisfied, and their heades prettily mizzeled
with wine, they walke abroad for a time, or els
3040 conferre with their familiars (as women you
knowe are talkatiue ynough, and can chat like
Pies) all the world knoweth it. Thus some spend
the day till supper time, and then the night, as
before. Other some spend the greatest part of the
3045 day in sitting at the dore, to shew their braueries,
to make knowne their beauties, to beholde the
passengers by, to view the coast, to see fashions,
and to acquaint themselues with the brauest fellowes, for if not for these causes, I see no other
3050 causes why they should sit at their doores, from

I1. PH: *Handbaskets cloakes to sinne.*

gentlewomen
of London,

morning till noone (as many do) from Noon to
night, thus vainly spending their golden dayes in
filthy idlenesse and sin. Againe, othersome being
weary of that exercise, take occasion (about vrgent affaires, you must suppose) to walke into the   3055
towne, & least any thing might be gathered, but
that they goe about serious matters indeed they
take their baskets in their hands, or vnder their

**Handbaskets
cloakes
to sin**

armes, vnder which pretence pretie conceits are
practized, and yet may no man say blacke is their   3060
eye. But if all other waies faile them, yet haue
they one which be sure will speed.

  Spud. What way is that, I pray you declare
vnto me?

Gardens in Englande.   3065

Philo.

Seeing you are so desirous to know, I will tel
you. In the fieldes and **Suburbes** of the Cities
they haue Gardens, either palled, or walled round
about very high, with their Harbers, and bowers   3070
fit for the purpose. And least they might be espied in these open places, they haue their ban-

**Gardens in
the fields no
better then
the stewes.**

quetting houses with **Galleries, Turrets,** & what
not els therein sumptuously erected: wherin they
may (and doubtlesse do) many of them play the   3075
filthy persons. And for that their Gardens are
locked, some of them haue three or foure keyes a
peece, whereof one they keep for themselues, the
other their **Paramours** haue to goe in before
them, least happely they might be // perceiued,   I1ᵛ
for then were all the sport dasht. Then to these
Gardens they repair when they list, with a bas-
ket & a boy, where they meeting their sweet
harts, receiue their wished desires. These gardens
are excellent places, and for the purpose, for if   3085

I1ᵛ. PH: *Gardens places of Bawdrie.*

they can speake with their dearlings no where els, Gardens places of baudry
yet there they may be sure to meet them, and to
receiue the guerdon of their paines, they knowe
what I meane. But I wish them to amend for fear
3090 of Gods heauy wrath in the day of vengeance.

    Spud. Why? do you condemne the vse of
Gardens and garden houses then altogether?

    Phil. No: nothing lesse. For I know they bee
very healthfull, comfortable, and wholsome for
3095 mans body, and such thinges, as the vse whereof Euery thing abused, is not to be remooued, but the abuse to be taken away only.
can we not lacke. But I condemne these abuses,
these corruptions, and enormities there vsed, and
I pray God they may be reformed. There is nothing so good but it may be abused, yet I am not
3100 precise, that I would haue the thing remooued
for the abuse, but the abuse to be taken away,
whereby the thing it selfe is made worse. Nor I
speake not against the good and godly women,
for I know there be a great number, & the Lord
3105 increase the number of them, that are chast, wise,
sober, continent, and vertuous matrones, and
voyd of all these corruptions. But against those
light, lewd, and incontinent harlots (as it is well
known there be too many) that run to those
3110 places, as fast as euer did the brothels to the
Stewes. And truly I thinke some of those places
are little better then the Stewes and Brothell
houses were in times paste: I beseech the Lord to
purge them cleane eyther with the Oliue branch
3115 of his mercy, or with the sharpe rod of his iudgement, that this wickednesse may be put away.

    Spud. Are those nice Dames, gentle, sober,
and discreete, or otherwise giuen to chiding,
brawling, and vnquietnesse? For they shew them-
3120 selues abroad (by report) as though butter woulde
not melt in their mouthes.

    Philo. There are some sober, wise, gentle, women good and bad, but the greater
discreet, and vertuous **Matrones**, as any be in all
the world. And there be other some (yea **maior**

number
naught.

numerus) that are neuer well, but when they bee   3125
eyther brawling, scolding, or fighting eyther with
some of their housholde, or some others: and
such Deuilles, as a man were better to be hanged
then to dwell with them. But because I haue //   I2
small experience thereof my selfe, saue only by   3130
the report of them that haue made triall thereof
themselues, I will say no more, committing them
ouer to the Lord, to whom they eyther stande if
they doe well, or fall, if they doe euill.

    Spud. Seeing that by diuine assistance you   3135
haue now finished your discourse of the apparell
of **England**, shew mee (I pray you) what other
abuses be there vsed, for I am perswaded, that
pride the Mother of sinne, is not without her
Daughters semblable to her selfe?   3140

The horrible vice of Whoredome
in England.

Philo.

The horrible vice of Whoredome is there too too

Whoredome
in England
too too rife.

much frequented, to the great dishonour of God,   3145
the prouoking of his iudgementes against them,
the staine and blemish of their profession, the
euill example of al the world, & finally, to their
owne damnation for euer, except they repent.

    Spud. I haue heard them reason thus, that   3150

Vain and
vngodly
reasons
pretending
that
whoredom
is no sin

mutuall coition betwixt man and woman, is not
so much offensiue before God. For do not all
creatures (say they) as well **Reptilia terræ**, as **Vo-**
latilia Cœli, Creeping thinges vppon the earth,
as flying in the aire, and all other creatures in   3155
generall, both small and great, ingender together?
hath not nature and kinde ordayned them so,
and giuen them members proper to that vse?
And doth not the lord (say they) as it were with

I2. PH: *Horrible whoredome in England.*

3160   a **stimule**, or pricke (by his mandate, saying,
Crescite, & multiplicamini, & replete terram:
Increase, multiply, & fill the earth) stir them vp
to the same? Otherwise the world woulde become barren and soone fall to decay: wherefore
3165   they conclude, that Whordome is a badge of
loue, a cognizance of **amitie, a tutch of lustie**
youth, a friendlie daliance, a redintegration of
loue, and an ensigne of good will, rather meritorious than damnable. These with the like bee
3170   their ridiculous reasons, which I haue heard them
many times to alleadge in defence of their carnall
pollutions.

       Philo. Cursed be those mouthes, that thus do
blaspheme the mighty God of **Israell,** and his sa-
3175   cred worde, making the same cloakes to couer
their sinne withall. They are much worser then //
I2ᵛ   **Libertines,** who think all things lawfull, or **Ath-**
eistes, who deny there is any God. The deuils
themselues neuer sinned so horribly, nor erred so
3180   grosly, as these (not Christians, but Dogges) do,
that make whordome a vertue, and meritorious.
But because you shal see their deceptions dis-
played, and their damnable abuses more plainly
discouered, I will reduce you to the first insti-
3185   tution of this godly ordinance of Matrimony.

       The Lord our God hauing created all things,
in heauen, earth, or hell whatsoeuer, created of
euery sexe two, male and female, and last of all
other creatures, he made man after his own like-
3190   nes and similitude, giuing him a woman, made of
a rib of his owne body, to be a companion and
comforter vnto him, and linking them togither in
the honourable state of venerable wedlock, he
blessed them both, saying: **Crescite, multiplica-**
3195   **mini, & replete terram.** *Increase, multiply, and*

Marginal notes:

Oh wicked
Libertines,

Those that
make
whoredom
lawfull
are worser
then Deuils

The first
institution of
matrimony,
Gen.2.
Math.19.
Mark.
Luke 16.
1.Cor 6.
Ephe.5.

I2ᵛ. PH: *Gods curse for whoredome.*

replenish the earth: wherby it is more then apparent, that the Lord, whose name is **Iehouah**, the
mighty God of **Israell**, is the **Authour** of godly

Mariage
instituted for
foure causes.
Matrimonie, Instituting it in the time of mans
innocency in **Paradise**, and that as me semeth for   3200
four causes. First for the auoydance of whor-
dome: Secondly, for the mutuall comfort and
consolation, that the one might haue of the
other, in all aduersities and calamities whatsoeuer: Thirdly, for propagation of children in the   3205
feare of the Lord, that both the world might be

All mutuall
copulation,
except
mariage is
vnlawful.
increased thereby, and the Lord also glorified in
him. And fourthly to be a figure or type of our
spirituall wedlocke, betwixt Christ and his
Church, both militant and triumphant. This con-   3210
gression, and mutual copulation of those, that be
thus ioyned together in the godly state of blessed
Matrimonie, is pure **Virginity**, and allowable before God and man, as an action wherto the Lord
hath promised his blessing through his mercie,   3215
not by our merite, **ex opere operato**, as some
shame not to say. All other goings togither and
coitions are damnable, pestifferous, and execrable. So, now you se, that whereas the Lord saith,
Increase, multiplie, and fill the earth: hee allud-   3220
eth to those that are linked together in the state
of godly Matrimonie and wedlocke, and not otherwise. For, to those that go together after any
other sort, he hath denounced his curse and
wrath for euermore, as his all sauing word bear-   3225
eth record.

And whereas they say, that all creatures vppon the earth do ingender together, I graunt it is
true. But how, **In suo genere**, *in //* *their owne*   I3
kind. There is no creature creeping on the earth,   3230

How al
or flying in the aire, how irrationable soeuer, that

I3. PH: *fidelitie in maried couples.*

doeth so degenerate, as man doth, but keepeth
the same state and order, wherein they were
made at the first, which thing if man did, he
3235   should not commit such abhominable whordome,
and filthy sinne as he doeth. It is said of those
that write **de natura animalium**, that (almost) all
vnreasonable beasts, and flying fowles after they
haue once linked, and vnited themselues togeth-
3240   er, to any one of the same kind, and after they
haue once espoused themselues the one to the
other, they will neuer ioyn themselues after with
any other, till the one be dissolued from the
other by death. And thus they keepe the knot of
3245   matrimony inuiolable to the end. And if any
chance to reuolt, & go together with any other
during the life of his first mate, all the rest of the
same kinde assemble together, as it were in a
counsel or parliament, and eyther kill, or grie-
3250   uously punish the **Adulterer**, or **Adulteresse**,
whether soeuer it be: which law I would God,
were amongst Christians established. By all
which it may appeare, how horrible a sinne
Whoredome is in **Nature**, that the very vnrea-
3255   sonable creatures doe abhorre it.

    The Heathen people who know not God, so
much loth this stinking sin of **Whoredome**, that
some burne them quicke, some hang them on
gibbets, some cut of their heades, some their
3260   armes, legs, and hands, some put out their eyes,
some burne them in the face, some cut off their
noses, some one part of their body, some another, and some with one kind of **torture**, and some
with another, but none leaueth them vnpunished:
3265   so that we are set to schoole to learne our
A.B.C. (like young **Nouices** or children, scarce
crept out of the swadling cloathes) how to punish
whoredome, euen by the vnreasonable creatures,
and by the Heathen people themselues, who are
3270   ignorant of the diuine goodnes.

creatures do
goe together
in their kind.

The
fidelitie of
vnreasonable
creatures
in mariage
one towards
another.

How much the
Heathen haue
detested
whoredome.

Sundry
punishments
of whoredome
amongst the
Heathen

Spud. I pray you rehearse some places out of the word of God wherein this cursed vice of **Whoredome** is forbidden, for my better instruction.

Testimonies out of the word of God wherin whordome is forbid.

Philo. Our Sauiour Christ in the eighth of **Iohn**, speaking to the woman, whom the malicious **Iewes** had apprehended in Adultery, bad her **goe her way, and sinne no more.** If it had not bene a most grieuous sinne, he would neuer haue bid her sin no more. In the fifth of **Mathew** he saith, who so lusteth after a woman in his // heart, hath committed the fact already, and therefore is guilty of death for the same. To the Pharisies, asking him, whether a man might not put away his wife for any occasion? Christ answered, for no cause saue for Whoredome only, inferring that whoredome is so hainous a sinne, as for the perpetration thereof, it shall be lawfull for a man, to deuide himselfe from his owne **Wife, and the Wife** from her **owne Husband.** The Apostle **Paule** saith: **Know you not that your bodies are the members of Christ, shall I then take the members of Christ (saith he) and make thē the members of an whore? God forbid, knowe you not that he who coupleth himself with an Harlot, is become one bodie with her? Flie fornication (saith he) therfore, for euerie other sinne that a man committeth is without the bodie, but who so committeth fornication, sinneth against his owne body.** And in another place, Knowe you not that your bodies are the temples of the holy Ghost, which dwelleth within you? And who so destroyeth the Temple of God him shall God destroy.

Math.5.

Math.19.
Mark.10.
Luke.16.

1.Cor.6

3275

3280
I3ᵛ

3285

3290

3295

3300

In another place he saith: **Be not deceiued, for neither whoremonger, Adulterer, Fornicator,**   3305

I3ᵛ. PH: *Examples against whoredome.*

incestuous person, nor such like shall euer enter
into the kingdome of heauen. Againe, Coniu-
gium honorabile est inter omnes. Mariage is
3310 honourable amongst all men, and the bed vndefiled, but whoremongers and Adulterers God
shall iudge. In the Reuelation of Saint Iohn it is
saide, That they who were not defiled with
women, do wait vpon the Lambe, whether so-
3315 euer he goeth. The Apostle Paule, willeth vs to
be so farre from fornication, that it may not
once be named amongst vs, as becommeth
Saints, with infinite such places, which for breui-
tie I omit, referring you in the old Testament to
3320 these & such places, namely, the 20. of Exodus.
20. of Leuiticus. 22. Deuteronomy. 27. 2.
Kinges. 11. Leuiticus. 18. Exodus. 22, Num. 5.
Eccle. 9. Prouer. 23. Prouer. 7. vers. 24.

Spud. As you haue now prooued by inuinci-
3325 ble testimonies of holy scripture, that whoredome
is forbidden by the Lord: so I pray you shew me
the grieuousnes thereof by some seuere and rare
examples of Gods iust iudgment poured foorth
vpon the same from the beginning.

3330 Examples of whoredom punished
in all ages.

Philo. The whole world was destroyed with   Gen.7.8
I4 water, not any // liuing thing left vpon the earth,
(saue in the Arke of Noah) for the sinne of
3335 Whoredome, Incest and brothelry vsed in those
dayes. Sodoma and Gomorrha, two famous Citties, were consumed with fire and brimstone
from heauen, for the like sinne of Whoredome,   Gene.19.
Adulterie and fornication. The Cittie of the Si-   Gene.24.
3340 chemites, man, woman and childe, were put to
the edge of the sworde, for the rauishing of

I4. PH: *Punishments for Whordome.*

Dina, the daughter of **Iacob**. The Lord also told
Abimelech, that if he did not let goe vntouched
Sara, **Abrahams** wife, both he and all his hous-

Gene.20.
Gene.26.
Gene.18.

hold shall die the death, notwithstanding he did   3345
it ignorantlie. The very same happened to **Isaac**
also. **Iudah** vnderstanding that his daughter in
Lawe was **impregnate**, and great with childe, and
not knowing by whome, commaunded that she
should be burned, without any further delay. Was   3350

2.Reg.16.

not **Absolon**, King **Dauid** his sonne, plagued all
his life, for going in to his Fathers Concubines?
And did not **Achitophel** who gaue counsell so to

Genes 29

doe, hang himselfe? Was not **Ruben** the first
borne sonne of **Iacob**, accursed for going vp to   3355
his fathers bed, and lost he not his byrthright, his
dignity, and primacy ouer his brethren for the
same? Were there not aboue three score and fiue
thousand men slain, for the Adultery done with

Iudg 20.

one **Leuits** wife? Was not King **Dauid** punished   3360
all the dayes of his life, for his Adultery done

2.Reg.13,12.

with **Bersabe**, **Vrias** his wife? Was not his sonne
Ammon for lying with his Sister **Thamar** slaine?

1.Reg.11.

Was not **Salamon** being peruerted with many
Heathen women, cast out of the fauour of God,   3365
notwithstanding, beeing otherwise, the wisest
prince in all the world? **Achab** at the perswasions

3.Reg.21.

of **Iesabell** his cursed wife, falling to Idolatrie,
and worshipping of Idolles and Deuils, suffered
most cruell punishment in this life all his dayes: 3370
besides what hee suffereth nowe, God onely
knoweth? Were not the **Israelite** and **Madian-
itish** woman both slaine for Whoredome by that

Numer 25.

woorthy man **Phinees**, who ranne them both
through their priuy members with his Iauelin or   3375

Iudg 16

sword? Was not **Sampson** brought to a miserable
end, his eyes being both put out, and he made to
bee a laughing stocke to all men, through his too
much fauouring of wanton women? Was not
King **Pharao** woonderfully plagued, for but in-   3380

tending euil in his heart, toward **Sara, Abraham**   Gene.12
his wife? Did not the Lord slay (with a most
grieuous mortalitie) foure and twenty thousande
I4ʳ   of the Israelites in one // day, for whoredome
3385   and adulterie, with the women of the **Moabits**
and **Madianites.**

By these and such like fearfull examples of
the iustice of God, poured vpon these whoremongers and Adulterers, we may learne to know
3390   the grieuousnes of the same, and the punishment
due to al **Whoremongers** and **Fornicators**, either
in this life, or in the life to come, or els in both:
for if the Lorde deferre the punishment of
Whordome in this life, he reserueth it for the
3395   world to come, suffering the wicked to wallow in
their sinne, and to fill vp the measure of their iniquity, that their damnation may be iust. And if
the Lord left not sinne vnpunished, no, not in
his most deare Saints, what he shall do in them,
3400   who dayly crucifie him a new, let the godly iudge.
Spud. Now I am fully perswaded by your inuincible reasons, that there is no sinne greater
before the face of God then Whoredome, wherefore God graunt that all his may auoid it.
3405   **Phil.** You haue said true, for there is no sin
comparable vnto it, for besides that it bringeth
euerlasting damnation to all that liue therein to
the end, without repentance: It also bringeth
these inconueniences, with many moe, **videlicet,**   **What euils**
3410   it dimmeth the sight, it impaireth the hearing, it   **whordome**
infirmeth the sinewes, it weakeneth the ioynts, it   **bringeth to**
exhausteth the marow, consumeth the radicall   **mans body**
moysture and supplement of the body, it riueleth   **in this life.**
the face, appalleth the countenance, it dulleth the
3415   spirits, it hurteth the memory, it weakeneth the
whole body, it bringeth consumption, it causeth

---

vlceration, scab scurffe, blaine, botch, pocks and
byles, it maketh hoare haires, bald pates: induceth olde age, and in fine, bringeth death before
Nature vrge it, malady enforce it, or age con-   3420
straine it.

    Spud. Seeing that Whoredom bringeth such
soure sauce with it, as namely death euerlasting
after this life, and so many discommodities besides in this life, I woonder that men dare com-   3425
mit the same so securely as they do now a dayes?

    Philo. It is so little feared in **England**, that
vntil one hath had two or three Bastardes, they
esteeme him no man (for that they call a mans
deed) in so much that euery scuruy Boy of xii.   3430
xvi. or xx. yeares of age will make no conscience
of it, to haue two or three, peraduenture halfe a
dozen seueral women with child at once and this
exploit being done, he shewes thẽ all a faire paire
of heeles, and away goeth he **pilo velocius,** *as*   3435
round as a ball, (as they say) // into some   K1
straunge place where he is not knowne: where
how hee liueth, let the world iudge, for **Cœlum
non animum mutant, qui trans mare currunt:
Though they chaunge their place of abode yet**   3440
their naughty dispositions they retaine still.
Then hauing estraunged themselues thus for a
small space, they returne againe, not to their
pristine cursed life (I dare say) but to their countrey, and then no man say, blacke is their eie, but   3445
all is wel, and they as good Christians, as those
that suffer them vnpunished.

    Spud. The state and condition of that Coun-
trey is most miserable, if it be true you report, it
were much better, that euery one had his lawfull   3450
wife, and euery woman her lawful husband, as

K1. PH: *Causes of bastardy in England.*

the Apostle commandeth, then thus to be plunged in the filthy sinne of Whoredome.

Philo. That is the onely salue and soueraigne remedy, which the Lord ordayned against Whoredome, that those who haue not the gift of continency might marrie, and so keepe their vessels vndefiled to the Lord. But notwithstanding, in **England** there is ouer great liberty permitted therein: for, little Infantes in swadling Cloutes, are often married by their ambitious Parentes and friendes, when they know neither good nor euill, and this is the **origene** of much wickednes, and directly against the worde of God, and examples of the primitiue age. And besides this, you shal haue euery saucy boy, of ten, fourteene, sixteen, or twenty yeares of age, catch vp a woman and mary her, without any feare of God at all, or respect had, either to her religion, wisdom, integrity of life, or any other vertue, or which is more, without any respect how they may liue together, with sufficient maintenance for their callings and estate. No, no, it maketh no matter for these things, so he haue his pretty pussy to huggle withal, for that is the only thing he desireth. Then build they vp a cottage though but of Elder poales, in euery lane ende almost, where they liue as beggers all their life after. This filleth the land with such store of Beggers, as we call them, that in short time (except some remedy be prouided to preuent the same) it is like to grow to great pouerty & extream misery, which God forbid.

Spud. I can not see how this geare should be holpen.

Philo. What, if a restraint were made, that none (except vpon speciall and vrgent causes) shuld marie before they come to twenty // or

3455
3460
3465
3470
3475
3480
3485
K1ᵛ

Mariage, an antidotary against whordome.

Marying of infants in swadling cloathes.

Euerie boy snacheth vp a woman to wife.

Cottages in euery lane end.

A restraint of mariage.

K1ᵛ. PH: *Remedies to suppresse whoredome.*

foure and twenty yeares, or at least before they be
fourteene or eighteene years olde, would not this
make fewer Beggers, then now there are?   3490

Spud. But if this were established, then
should wee haue moe Bastardes, and of the two,
I had rather wee had many children lawfully be-
got, than many Bastards.

Phil. The occasion of begetting of many Bas-   3495
tards were soone cut off, if either the punishmẽt
which God his law doth allow, or els which good
pollicie hath constituted, were inflicted vpon the
offenders. For, the punishment appointed for
Whoredome now is so light, that they esteeme   3500
not of it, they feare it not, they make but a iest
of it. For what greate thing is it, to goe two or
three dayes in a white sheete, or els in a Cope (a
ridiculous kinde of punishment,) before the Congregation, and that sometimes not past an hower   3505
or two in a day, hauing their vsuall garmentes
vnderneath, as commonly they haue. And truely
I cannot a little admire, nor yet sufficiently
deplore that wickednesse of the **Ecclesiasticall
Magistrates**, in not punishing more grieuously   3510
this horrible sinne of whoredom: for to goe in a
sheet with a white wand in their handes, is but a
plaine mocking of God and of his Lawes. This
impunity (in respect of condigne punishment,
which that vice requireth) doth rather animate &   3515
imbolden them to the act, then fear them from
it. In so much, as I haue heard some miscreants
impudently say, that he is but a beast, that for
such white liuered punishment, would abstaine
from such gallant pastime: but certaine it is that 3520
they, who thinke it such sweet meate here, shall
finde the sauce sowre and bitter inough in hell.
And yet as light, & as easie as this punishment
is, it may be, and is dayly dispensed withall for
money: and this is thought to be the best kind of   3525
punishmẽt to punish them by the purse. Then

How whoredom
may bee
suppressed.

The
punishment
for whordome
ouer remisse.

Whoredome
ought not to
be punished
by the purse.

the which what can be a greater disorder in a
Christian common wealth? Is this any thing els
then to buy and sell the bodies and soules of
3530 Christians for money? Can the Pope himselfe
doe any more then this? Is not this a mainte-
naunce of the Stewes? Yea, so long as this is
vsed, the Stewes shall neuer be out of **Englande.**
Let the Magistrates therefore of the **Ecclesias-**
3535 **ticall Hierarchie** (for to them I speake) take heed
that they be not maintayners of Stewes and
Whoredome, whereof they would so faine be
K2 thought to be suppressers. For this kinde // of
dispensing with Whoredome, Adulterie, and For-
3540 nication for money, and setting of them free à
**culpa & pæna, from the fault it selfe, and
punishment due for the fault,** what is it els then
not onely a maintenance, but also a stirring of
them vppe to commit Whoredome, when for a
3545 little money they may be discharged of all guilt?
And this being certaine, or at least very likelie,
that whosoeuer getteth one with childe, of what
reputation or degree soeuer she bee of, (if he be
single) he shall be forced to marrie her, and thus
3550 for a little peece of money they may both haue a
Bull of dispensation. This being so, who (I say)
will not seeke to aspire as high as he may, and to
deflower (in hope of further gaine) as many as he
can. This siluer punishment is it, that defileth
3555 honest Matrones, polluteth chaste Virgines, and
dishonesteth poore maids, to their vtter shame
and vndooing for euer. I say nothing, how the
money receyued for these dispensations is bestowed, how spent, nor whereunto imployed. The
3560 Lorde for his mercies sake, giue them grace to
punish vice seuerely, as the word of God doth
commaund, and not after their owne sensuall ap-

To dispence
with
whoredom for
money, is a
plain
maintenance
of whordom.

K2. PH: *Due punishments for whoredom.*

petites and licentious lustes, that God may be
glorified, and their consciences discharged at the
great day of the Lord.   3565

Spud. What punishment would you haue inflicted vpon such as commit this horrible kinde
of sinne?

Philo. I would wish that the man or woman
who are certainlie knowne and prooued without   3570
all scruple or doubt, to haue committed the horrible fact of **Whoredome, Adulterie, Incest,** or
Fornication, should either drinke a draught of
Moyses cuppe, that is, taste of present death, as
Gods worde doeth commaund, and good pollicie   3575
allowe, or els, if that be thought too seuere (as in
euill, men will be more mercifull, then the Authour of mercy himselfe, but in goodnesse, farewell
mercy) then would God they might bee **cauterized,** and seared with a hotte Iron vppon the   3580
cheeke, forehead, or some other parte of their
bodie that might bee seene, to the ende that the
Adulterous children of Sathan, might be discerned from the honest and chast Christians. But
(alas) this vice (with the rest) wanteth such due   3585
punishment, as God his word doth commaund to
bee inflicted vppon them. The Magistrates winke
at it, or els as looking through their fingers, they
see it, and will not see it. //

Yea so farre of are some, from suffering con-   K2ᵛ
digne punishment, for this horrible sin, that they
get good maintenance with practising the same.
For you shall haue some, yea many thousands,
that liue vpon nothing els, and yet go cloathed

Gentlewomen like, both in their silkes and Vel-   3595
uets, and otherwise, their fingers clogged with
ringes, their wristes with bracelets and Iewels,

K2ᵛ. PH: *Knowne whores kept openly.*

and their purses full of golde and siluer? And
hereof they make no conscience so their hus-
3600 bands know it not: Or if they doe, some are such
peasants and such **maicocks**, that either they wil
not, or (which is truer) they dare not reprooue
them for it. But and if the husband once reprooue them for their misdemeanor, then they
3605 conspire his death by some meane or other. And
all this commeth to passe, because the punishment thereof is so easie and gentle as it is. And
some both Gentlemen and others (whereof some
I knowe) are so nusled vp herein, that hauing put
3610 away their owne wiues: they keepe whores openly, without any great punishment for it, and hauing bene conuented before the Magistrates, and
there deposed vpon a booke to put away their
whores, haue put them foorth at one doore, &
3615 taken them in at the other. And thus they dally
in their othes with the Lord, and stop the course
of the Lawe with **Rubrum vnguentum**, whereof
they haue store to bestow vpon such wickednes,
but not a peny to giue towards any good purpose.
3620   Wherefore, in the name of God, let al men
that haue put away their honest wiues, be forced
to take them againe, and abandon all whores or
els to taste of the law: & let al whores be cut off
with the sword of iustice. For, as long as this **im-**
3625 **munity** & **impunity** is permitted amongst vs, let
vs neuer look to please God, but rather prouoke
his heauy iudgments against vs. And the reason
is, for that there is no sinne in all the world, but
these whores and whoremasters will gredily com-
3630 mit for inioying of their Whoredome? And Hel,
destruction, and death euerlasting is the guerdon
thereof, and yet men cannot beware of it. The
Lord keep all his children from it, and present
them blamelesse before his tribunall seate, with-
3635 out spot or wrinkle at the great day of the Lord.
      Spud. What notable abuses els haue you

practising of
whordome.

Putting away
honest wiues
and retaining
whores.

Law ought to
be executed
without
partialitie.

seene there frequented: for seeing you haue be-
gunne in part, I pray you describe the whole. //

The Gluttonie and excesse
in England.

Philo.

Dainty fare, gluttony, and gourmandice vsed in Engl.

I haue seene that which griueth me to report.
The people there are maruellously giuen to daintie fare, gluttony, belly cheere & many also to
drunkennesse, and gourmandize.   3645

Spud. That is a manifest argument of good
hospitality, which both is commended in the
word of God, and which I knowe you wil not
reprehend.

Godly hospitality to be commended.

Phil. Godly hospitality is a thing in no wise   3650
woorthy of reprehension, but rather of great
commendation, for many haue receiued Angels
into their houses, at vnawares, by vsing the same:
as **Abraham, Lot, Tobias**, and many others. Yet
if Hospitality flowe ouer into superfluitie and   3655
riotous excesse, it is not tollerable. For now
adayes, if the table be not pestered from the one
end to the other, as thicke as one dish can stand
by another, with delicate meat of sundry sortes,
one cleane different from another, & to euery   3660

Varietie of dishes, and meates with their curious sauces.

dish a seuerall sawce appropriate to his kind, it is
thought there vnworthy the name of a dinner:
yea, so many dishes shal you haue there on the
table at once, as the vnsatiablest **Helluo**, the de-
uouringst **Glutton**, or the greediest **Cormorant**   3665
that euer was, can scarce eate of euery one a little. And these many shall you haue at the first
course, as many at the second, and peraduenture,
mo at the third, besides other sweet iunkets and
delicate confections of spiceries, and I can not   3670

Excesse of

tell what. And to these dainties, al kind of Wines

K3. PH: *Great excesse in delicate fare.*

are not wanting, you may be sure. Oh what nici-
ty, what prodigality is this? what vanitie, what
excesse, riote and superfluity is here? Oh farewel

3675 former world? for I haue heard my father say,
that in his daies one dish or two of good wholsome meat, was thought sufficient for a man of
great worship to dine withall, & if they had three
or foure kindes, it was reputed a sumptuous feast.

3680 A good peece of Beefe was thought then, good
meat and able for the best, but nowe, it is
thought too grosse for their tender stomackes to
disgest: If this be so, I maruell how our forefathers liued, who eat little els but colde meates,

3685 grosse and hard of disgesture? yea, most of them
fed vppon Graine, Corne, rootes, Pulse, Hearbes,
weeds, and such other baggage, and yet liued
longer then we, were healthfuller then we, of
better complexion then we, and much stronger

3690 then we in euery respect, wherefore I cannot per-
K3ᵛ swade my selfe otherwise, but that // our nicenesse and curiousnesse in diet, hath altered our
nature, distempered our bodies, and made vs subiect to millions of diseases, more then euer were

3695 our forefathers subiect vnto, and consequently of
shorter life then they.

Spud. They will aske you againe, wherefore
God made such variety of meates, but to be eaten
of men, what answere giue you to that?

3700 Philo. The Lord our God ordayned indeed,
the vse of meates and drinkes for man to sustaine
the fraile and brittle state of his mortall body for
a time. But he gaue them not vnto him for delight and pleasure onely, but for necessitie and

3705 neede: For as the olde **Adage** saith, **Non viuimus
vt edamus, sed edimus vt viuamus: We liue not
to eate, but we eate to liue**, we must not swill

Sidenotes:

meates.

The austerity
and godly
simplicity of
the former
world in
meates and
drinkes.

The faraginy
or rough
fare of our
forefathers.

Our nice fare
hath altered
our bodies &
changed our
nature.

Medietie to
be obserued
in meates.

K3ᵛ. PH: *How meates bring destruction.*

and ingurgitate so much into our stomackes, as
no more can bee crammed in? The Lorde pro-
uided them that they shoulde bee as meanes to   3710
preserue our bodies for a time whilest we liue

**When
meats and
drinkes are
instruments
of destruction
vnto vs.**

and soiourne in this vaste Wildernesse of the
world, but not that they should be instrumentes
of destruction to vs both of bodie and soule. And
trulie they are no lesse, when they are taken im-   3715
moderately without the feare of God. Besides
that, doeth not the impletion and society of
meates and drinkes prouoke lust: as **Hiero** sayth:
Venter mero estuans spumat in libidinem: The

Genes.24.

bellie inflamed with wine, bursteth foorth into   3720
lust? Doeth not lust bring foorth sinne, and sinne
bring foorth death? The Children of **Israell**, giuing themselues to delicate fare and Gluttonie, fell
to Idolatrie, Sacriledge and Apostasie, worship-

1.Reg 2

ping stockes, stones, and Deuilles, in steed of the   3725
liuing God. The sonnes of **Helie** the Priest, giuing themselues to daintie fare and belly cheare,
fel into such sinne, as the Lord slewe them all,
and their Father also for that he chastised them
not for the same. The children of blessed **Iob** in   3730
middest of all their banquettinges and riot, were
slaine by the Lord, the whole house falling vpon
them, and destroying them most pitifulie. **Bal-**
thazar, King of the **Chaldeans**, in middest of all
his good cheare, sawe a hand, writing vpon the   3735

**Daniel 5
verse.5.25.**

walle these wordes, **Mene, mene, Techel vphar-**
sin: signifying that his kingdome shoulde be tak-
en from him, and so it was, and hee slaine the
same night by the hand of the Lorde. The rich
Glutton in the Gospell, for his riotous feastinges,   3740
and inordinate liuing // was condemned to the   K4

Luke 16

fire of hell. Our Father **Adam** with all his Of-
spring (to the end of the worlde) was condemned

K4. PH: *Small Hospitalitie in England.*

to Hel fire for taking one Apple to satisfie his
3745   gluttonous desire withall. Gluttony was one of
the chiefest **Cannons**, wherewith the Deuill as-   Math.4.
sayled Christ, thinking thereby to batter his
kingdome, and to winne the fielde for euer. Yet
notwithstanding, the grieuousnesse hereof, the
3750   same is thought to be a countenance, and a great
credite to a man in **England**. But true Hospitality consisteth not in many dishes, nor in sundry
sortes of meates (the substance whereof is
chaunged almost into accidentes thorow their
3755   curious **Cookeries**, and **impotionate** slibber-   Wherin
sawces, which rotte their bodies and shorten their   hospitalitie
dayes) but rather in giuing liberally to the poore   consisteth.
and needy members of Iesus Christ, helping
them to meate, drinke, lodging, clothing, and
3760   such other necessaries, whereof they stand in
neede. But such is their hospitality, that the
poore haue the least parte of it. You shall haue
twenty, fourty, sixtie, yea a hundred pound spent
in some one house in banquetting and feasting,
3765   yet the poore shall haue little or nothing: if they
haue any thing, it is but the refuse meate,
scrappes and paringes, such as a Dogge would   The small
scarce eate sometimes, and well if they can get   reliefe of
that too: In steede whereof, nowe and then not a   the poore.
3770   few haue whipping cheare to feed themselues
withall. Yea, it is counted but a small matter for
a man that can scarsly dispende fourty poundes
by the yeare, to bestowe against one time, tenne
or twenty poundes thereof in Spices. And truly
3775   so long and so grieuously hath this excesse of
gluttony and dainty fare surffeted in **England**,
that I feare me, it will spew out many of his
maisters out of doores before it be long. But as
some be ouer largeous and profluous herein, so
3780   other some are spare ynough: for when any
meate is stirring, then locke they vp their gates
that no man may come in. Another sort haue so

Locking vp
of gates whē
meate is
stirring.

many houses, that they visite them not once in
seuen yeares, many **Chimneyes**, but litle smoke,
faire houses, but small Hospitality. And to bee   3785
plaine, there are three **Canckers** which in processe of time will eate vp the whole common

Three
deuouring
cankers.

wealth of **England**, if speedy reformation be not
had: namely dainty fare, gorgious buildings, &
sumptuous apparell, which three deuouring **Can-**   3790
kers, especially, yet not without their cosin ger-
mans do flourish there. God remooue them
thence for his Christs sake. //

    Spud. I had thought that dainty fare and   K4ᵛ
good cheer had both nourished the body perfect-   3795
ly, and also prolonged life greatly, & doth it not
so thinke you?

Who more
subiect to
infirmities
thē they that
fare best.

    Philo. Experience as by my former intima-
tions you may gather, teacheth cleane contrary:
For, who is sicklier then they, that fare delici-   3800
ously euery day? who is corrupter? who belcheth
more? who looketh worse? who is weaker and
febler then they? who hath more filthy choller,
flegme, and putrifaction (together with grosse
humours) then they? And to be briefe, who dy-   3805
eth sooner then they? Doe we not see the poore
man that eateth browne bread (whereof some is
made of Rye, Barley, Peason, Beanes, Oates, and
such other grosse graines) and drinketh small
drinke, yea, sometimes water, feedeth vpon   3810
Milke, Butter, and Cheese, I say, do we not see
such a one healthfuller, stronger, fairer complectioned, and longer liued then the other that fared
daintily euery day? And how shuld it be other-

Eating of
diuers meats
at one time
hurtful.

wise? for will not the eating of diuers and sundry   3815
kindes of meats of contrary operations and qualities (at one meale) ingender distemperance in
body? And the body distempered, wil it not fall

K4ᵛ. PH: *Diuersitie of meats hurtfull.*

3820

into sundry diseases? One meat is hard of disges-
tion, another light, and whilest the meate of hard
disgesture is in concocting, the other meat of
light disgesture doth putrifie and stink, and this
is the very mother of all diseases: one is of this
quality, another of that: one of this operation,

3825

another of that: one kind of meat is good for this
thing, an other is naught for that. Then how can
all these contrarieties and repugnancies agree
together in one body at one and the same time?
will not one contrary impugne his contrary? one

3830

enemie resist another? Then what wise man is he
that will receiue all these enemies into his body
at one time? Doe we not see by experience, that
they that giue themselues to dainty fare & sweet
meates, are neuer in health? doth not their sight

3835

waxe dimme, their eares hard of hearing, their
teeth rotte and fall out? Doeth not their breath
stinke, their stomackes belch foorth filthy humours, & their memory decay? Do not their
Spirites and sences become heauie and dull, by

3840

reason of the filthy vapours and stinking fumes
which rise from their gingered breasts and spiced
stomakes, and fuming vp to the head, mortifie
the vitall spirites, and intellectiue powers, in so
much that the whole body becommeth pursie and

3845

corpulent, yea sometimes decrepite withall, and

L1

full of all filthy corruption. // The Lorde keepe
his chosen from the tasting thereof.

The speedy
decaie of
those that
giue themselues
to daintie fare,

Drunkennesse in England.

Spud. You spake of Drunkennesse, what say

3850

you of that?

Philo. I say, that it is a horrible vice, and too
too much vsed in **England.** Euery Country, Citie, Towne, Village & other places haue aboun-

---

L1. PH: *The beastly vice of drunkennesse*

The beastlie
vice of
drunkennes
frequented
in England.

dance of Alehouses, Tauernes and Innes in them,
which are haunted with Mault-wormes night and   3855
day, that you would woonder to see them. You
shall haue them there sitting at the wine and
Good-ale all the day long, yea, all the night, peraduenture all the week together, so long as any
mony is left, swilling, gulling, and carousing from   3860
one to another, till neuer a one can speake a
ready word. Then when with the Spirite of the
Butterie they are thus possessed, a world it is to
consider their gestures, their countenances and
demeanours, one towards another, and towards   3865
euery one els. How they stutte and stammer,
stagger and reel to and fro, like madmen, some
vomiting, spewing, and disgorging their filthy

The spirit of the
butterie is
drunkennesse
and excesse.

stomackes, other some pissing vnder the boord as
they sit, and which is most horrible, some fall to   3870
swearing, cursing, and banning, interlacing their
speeches with curious tearmes of blasphemie, to
the great dishonour of God, and offence of the
godly hearers.

    Spud. But they will say, that God ordayned   3875
wines and strong drinkes to cheare the heart, and
to sustaine the body withall, therefore it is lawfull
to vse them to that end.

    Philo. Meats (moderately taken by the bless-

The lothsom
qualities of
those that
be drunke.

ing of God) corroborate the body, refresh the   3880
Arteries, and reuiue the Spirits, making them apter, euery member to doe his office, as God hath
appointed them: but being immoderately taken
(as commonly they be) they are instruments of
damnation to the abusers thereof, and nourish   3885
not the body, but corrupt it rather, casting it into

The
transfiguration
of those that
be drunke.

a sea of diseases: besides, a man once drunke
with wine or strong drinke, rather resembleth a
bruite beast, then a christian man: For, do not
his eies begin to stare, and to be red, fiery &   3890
bleared, blubbering foorth seas of teares? Doth
he not froth and fome at the mouth like a Bore?

Doth not his tongue faulter, and stammer in his
mouth? Doeth not his head seeme as heauy as a
3895 Milstone, beeing not able to beare it vp? Are not
L1ᵛ his wittes and spirits, as it were drowned? // Is
not his vnderstanding altogether decayed? Doe
not his handes and all his body tremble, quauer
and shake, as it were with a **quotidian** Feuer? It
3900 casteth him also into a Dropsie, or Plurisie nothing so soone, it infeebleth the Senewes, it weak- The
eneth the natural strength, it corrupteth the discommodities
bloud, it dissolueth the whole man at the length, of drunkennes.
and finally, maketh him forgetfull of himselfe al-
3905 together, so that what hee doeth being drunke,
hee remembreth not beeing sober. The Drunk-
arde in his drunkennesse, killeth his friende, re-
uileth his louer, discloseth secretes, and regardeth
no man: Hee vtterly expelleth all feare of God
3910 out of his minde, all loue of his friends and kinsfolkes, all remembrance of honesty, ciuility and
humanity: so that I wil not fear to call Drunkards
beasts, & no men, and much worse then beasts,
for beastes neuer exceede in any such kind of ex-
3915 cesse or superfluity, but alway **modum adhibent** Drunkards
appetitui: They measure their appetites by the worse then
rule of necessity, which would God we would doe. beasts

Spud. Seeing it is so great an offence before
God, I pray you shew me some testimonies of
3920 the holy scripture against it, for whatsoeuer is
euil, the word of God (I doubt not) reprooueth
the same.

Phil. It seemeth you haue not read holy
scripture very much, for if you had, you should
3925 haue found it, not onely spoke against, but also
throwne downe euen to hel, for proofe whereof,
of infinite places, I will recite a few. The Prophete **Esayas** thundereth out against it, saying, Væ Esay.5.

L1ᵛ. PH: *Drunkards worse then Beasts.*

Testimonies
against
drunkennes,
out of the
worde of God.

qui consurgitis mane ad ebrietatem sectandam.
Wo be to them that rise earlie to follow drunk-　3930
ennes, wallowing therein from morning to
night, vntil they bee set on fire with wine and
strong drinke. Therfore gapeth hell, and open-
eth her mouth wide, that the glorie, multitude
and wealth of them that delight therein, may　3935
goe downe into it, saith the Prophet.

The Prophete Hoseas saith, Fornicatio, vi-

Hoseas c.4

num, & mustum auferent animum. Whoredome, wine, and strong drinke, infatuate the
heart of man.　　　　　　　　　　　　　　　　3940

Ioel.1.

The Prophet Ioel biddeth al Drunkards waile,
saying. Weep and howle you wine bibbers, for
the destruction of wickednesse that shall fall
vpon you.

Habacuck.2

The Prophete Habacuck, soundeth a most　3945
dreadfull alarum, not only to all Drunkards, but
also to al that make them drunken saying, Woe
be to him that giueth his neighbour drinke till
hee // be drunke, that thou maist see his pri-　　L2
uities.　　　　　　　　　　　　　　　　　　　3950

Prouerb c 20

Salamon sayth, Wine maketh a man to be
scorneful, & strong wine maketh a man vnquiet,
who so taketh pleasure in it, shal not be wise. In
another place. Keep not company with wine-
bibbers and riotous persons, for such as be　　3955
Drunkards shall come to beggerie.

Prouerb.23

In the twenty and three of his Prouerbs, he
saith, To whom is woe? To whom is sorrow? To
whome is strife? To whome is murmuring? To
whom are wounds without cause? and to whom　3960
are red eyes? Euen to them that tarie long at the
wine, to them that goe and seeke mixt wine.
And againe, Looke not thou vpon the wine
when it is red, and when it sheweth his collour

L2. PH: *Drunkennesse forbidden.*

3965   in the cuppe, or goeth downe pleasantlie, for in
the end, it will bite like a serpent, and hurt like
a Cockatrice, or Basilicocke, which slea or kill
men with the poison of their sight. Againe, It is
not for Kings to drink Wine, nor for Princes to
3970   drink strong drink. Our Sauiour Christ in the   Prouer 31
Gospell of S. Luke, biddeth vs take heede that
wee be not ouercome with surfetting and Drunk-   Luke.21
ennesse, and cares of this life, least the day of the
Lorde come vpon vs at vnawares.

3975   S. Paule to the Ephesians biddeth beware,
that we be not drunken with wine, wherein is excesse, but to be filled with the Spirit. The same
Apostle in another place, saith: **That neither
Whoremonger, Adulterer, Drunkard, Glutton,**
3980   **riotous person, nor such like shall euer enter
into the Kingdome of heauen.** By these few
places out of many, you may see the vnlawfulnes
of this vice, which is so much frequented.

Spud. Let me intreat you to shew me some
3985   examples withall, whereby I may see, the effects
thereof, and what punishment hath bene shewed
vpon the offenders therein in all ages.

Punishment of Drunkardes.

Philo. Drunkennesse caused **Lot** to commit
3990   **Incest** with his own two Daughters, who got   Genes.19.
them both with child, he not perceiuing it, nei-
ther when they lay downe, nor when they rose   Examples
vp. See how drunkennes assotteth a man, depriu-   against
ing him of all sence, reason and vnderstanding.   drunkennesse.

3995   Drunkennesse caused **Noah** to lie with his
L2ᵛ   priuities bare in his // Tabernacle, in such beastly
sort, as his wicked sonne **Cham** iested and scof-
fed at the same.

Through drunkennes **Holofernes**, that great   Luke 16.

L2ᵛ. PH: *Examples against Drunkennesse.*

and inuincible Monarch of the **Assyrians** was   4000
ouercome by a woman, hauing his head cut from
his shoulders with a Faulchon.

Luke.16   Through Drunkennes King **Herod** was
brought to such idiocy and foolish dotage, that
he caused the head of good **Iohn Baptist** to be   4005
cut off to satisfie the request of a dauncing
Strumpet.

That rich **Epulo** of whom S. **Luke** maketh
Luke.16.   mention was for his drunkennesse and riotous excesse condemned to the fire of hell for euer: with   4010
many moe examples, which for shortnesse I omit.
Now seeing then, that Drunkennesse is both offensiue to God, and bringeth such euils in this
life present: Let vs in the name of God auoid it,
as a most wicked thing and pernicious euill.   4015

How farre   For euery Drunkard is so far estranged from
Drunkards are   himselfe, that as one in an extasie, or rather in a
estranged
from   plaine Phrensie, he may not be saide to be **sui**
themselues.   **animi compos**, *a man of sound wit*, but rather a
very **Bedlem**, or much worse, no Christian, but   4020
an Antichristian, no member of Christ Iesus, but
an Imp of **Sathan**, and a limme of the Deuil.
Wherfore in the name of God, let vs auoid al excesse, imbrace tẽperancy & sobriety, and receiue
so much as may satisfie nature, not the **insatiate**   4025
appetites of our greedy desires. Knowing that
except the Lord blesse our meates and drinks,
What if God   within our bodies, and giue them power and
blesse not   strength, to nourish and feed the same: and our
our meat.
bodies their natural powers euery member to do   4030
his office, and duty, our meats shall lie in our
stomackes stinking, smelling, and rotting like
filthy Carion in all lothsome stinke.

So farre off ought we to be from abusing the
good creatures of God by riot, drunkennesse, or   4035
Giuing of   excesse, that we ought neuer to take a morsell of
thanks before   bread, nor sope of drinke, without humble
meat & after.
thankes giuing to the Lord for the same before.

For we neuer read, that our Sauiour Christ euer
4040 eate, or dranke but he gaue thanks (or as we call
it, said grace) both before the receipt thereof, and
after. This need he not to haue done in respect
of himselfe, but for our example and learning, according to this saying, **Omnis Christi actio, nos-**
4045 **tra est instructio. Euerie action of our Sauiour**
Christ is our example and instruction, to follow
as neere as we are able.

Or if all that hath been sayd heretofore, be
L3 not sufficient to withdraw // vs from this beastly
4050 vice of drunkennesse: yet let vs set before our
eyes this most fearful iudgement of God, executed vpon a sort of drunkards, the storie whereof is
this. The eight day of February **1578,** in the
country of **Swaben,** there were dwelling eight
4055 men, Citizens and citizens sonnes, very riotously
and prodigally giuen, the names of whom, for the
better credit of the story, I haue sette downe, *viz.*
Adam Giebens, George Kepell, Iohn Keisell,
Peter Hersdorse, Iohn Waganaer, Simon Hen-
4060 **rickes, Harman Fron, Iacob Harmans,** all which
would needs goe to the **Tauerne,** vpon the **Sab-**
both day in the morning very early, in contẽpt of
the Lord and his **Sabboth.** And comming to the
house of one **Anthony Hage** an honest godly
4065 man, who keeps a **Tauerne** in the same town,
called for **burnt wine, Sacke, Malmsie, Hip-**
ocrasse, and what not. The Hoste tolde them,
that they should haue none of all these, before
the Diuine seruice and Sermon time were past,
4070 and counselled them to goe heare the sacred
word of God preached. But they (saue **Adam**
Giebens who aduised them to heare the Sermon,
for feare of Gods wrath) denied, saying, that they
loathed that kinde of Exercise. The good Hoste

A most
dreadful
example
of Gods
iudgments
shewed vpon
certain
drunkards,
abusing
the good
creatures
of God.

The propertie
of a good
host.

L3. RT T*he property of a good hoste.*

neither giuing them any wine himselfe, nor suf-   4075
fering any other, went to the **Sermon**, as duty
did bind him: who being gone, they fell to curs-

A caueat for
cursers and
banners.

ing, banning, and swearing, wishing that he
might breake his neck, or euer he came againe
from the sermon, & brusting foorth into these   4080
intemperate speeches, the Deuil break our
neckes, if we depart hence this day, either quicke
or dead, till we haue had some wine. Straight
way the Deuill appeared vnto them, in the like-
nes of a young man, bringing in his hand a Flag-   4085
on of wine, and demaunding of them why they
caroused not, he drank vnto them, saying: Good
fellowes, be merry, for ye shall haue wine
ynough, for you seeme lusty Lads, and I hope
you wil pay me wel, who inconsiderately an-   4090
swered, that they would pay him, or els they

The desperate
securitie of
Drunkards.

would guage their neckes, yea, their bodies and
soules rather then to fayle. Thus they continued
swilling, gulling and carousing so long, as til one
could scarsly see another. At the last the deuil   4095
their Host, told them that they must needes pay
the shotte, whereat their hearts waxed cold. But

The deuils
reward to his
darlings the
drunkards.

the Deuill comforting them, said: Bee of good
cheere, for now must you drinke boyling Leade,
Pitch, and Brimstone with me in the pit of hell   4100
for euermore: Hereupon immediately he made
their eies like flames of fire, and in breadth as //   L3ᵛ
broad as sawcers. Then began they to call for
mercy, but it was too late. And ere they could
call againe for mercie and grace, the Deuill pre-   4105
uented them, brake their neckes asunder, and
threwe most horrible flames of fire, out of their
mouthes. And thus ended these seuen Drunkardes their miserable daies, whose iudgement I
leaue to the Lord.   4110

L3ᵛ. PH: *An example of Gods wrath:*

The other, **Adam Gibens**, who counselled
them before to go hear the sermon, hauing some
sparks of faith in him, was preserued from death,
by the great mercie of God, and greatly repēted
4115   his former life, yelding praise vnto God for his
deliuerance. Thus haue I, **in sempiternam rei
memoriam**, faithfully recorded the storie of these
eight Drunkards, & of their fearful end, taken
out of a Dutch copie printed at **Amsterdam**, and
4120   at **Straesburcht**, for a caueat to al drunkards,
Gluttons and riotous persons throughout the
whole world, that they offend not the Lord in
the like kind of offence.

An other like example of Gods diuine iustice,
4125   shewed vpon two blasphemous Drunkards in **Almaine**, in the towne of **Nekershofene**, chaunced
the fourth day of Iuly **1580**. the trueth whereof is
as followeth. These two drunken Varlets, trauelling by the way, came into an **Inne**, and called
4130   for bread and wine. The Hoste with speed
brought them very good, but they disliking the
wine for the newnesse thereof, commanded better wine to be brought, so in fine they had both
new and old good store. Thus sate they swilling,
4135   and carowsing one to another, til they were both
as drunke as Swine. Then one of them pouring
foorth wine, carowsed to his fellow, the other
pledging him, asked to whome he should drinke,
quoth this **varlet** drinke to God, he hearing that,
4140   poured foorth wine, & dranke to God. This
done, he asked his cōpanion of which wine God
should pledge him, of the new, or of the old. He
answered, of whether thou wilt. Then he taking
the new wine in his hand, filled the cup there-
4145   with, and reaching foorth his arme as high as he
coulde, as though God should haue pledged him
in deede, sayd these words: God, I wold fane
know what wine thou louest best, this new wine
is good ynough, and too good for thee, if thou

The mercy of
god in sauing
of Adam
Gibiens

An example
of Gods
wrath and
seuere iustice
executed vpon
2. Drunkards
in Almaine.

A caueat to
blasphemers,
and contemners
of the maiestie
of God.

hadst sent better, thou shouldest haue had better,   4150
but such as it is take it, pledge mee quickly, and
carrouse it off euery sope, as I haue done to thee,
if not, thou doest me wrong. Hauing thus
stretched foorth his arme, with the cup of wine,
and withall hauing vttered foorth these words,   4155
the lorde // proceedeth in iudgement against   L4
him, causing his arme to stande stedfast and vn-
mooueable, so as he was not able to pul it to
him, nor to steere his body out of the place, and
in this agony he remayned a long time after, his   4160
countenance not changed, but rolling his eyes to
and fro, fearful to behold. And as for breath
there was none perceiued to come foorth of him,
nor yet to speake one word he was not able: and
yet for all that, seemed to euery one to be aliue.   4165
After this the people assayed to remooue him
from that place, but they could not by any
strength. In the end they tyed horses to him, to
drawe him thence, but they could not once steere
him. Then they assayed to burne the house, &   4170
him withall, but no fire would once take hold of
the house: wherefore, when they saw all their
wayes and deuises to be frustrate, perswading
themselues that God had made him a Spectacle
to all Drunkards, they surceased their enterprises   4175
any further, & wished the will of the Lord to be
done. And in this place, and in the same pitifull
case you haue heard, standeth this blasphemous
villain to this day vnremooueable, till it please
the Lord, in the bowels of his mercy to release   4180
him, whose blessed will be fulfilled for euer. The
other drunken beast his companion, they hanged
vpon a gibbet, before the dore of the same house,
as he wel deserued. Thus hath the Lord in al
ages, and at all times, punished this horrible vice   4185
of Drunkennesse, which God grant euery true
Christian man may avoyd, for feare of Gods
vengeance.

Behold the
blasphemy
of this deuil,
and feare.

Oh feareful
iudgment of
god, yet
most iust
punishment.

Couetousnesse in England.

4190 **Spud.**

Shew me, I pray you, the state of that country a
little further: is it a welthy cuntry within it self,
or otherwise poore & bare?

Philo. It is a most famous Iland, and a fertile
4195 Country, abounding with all manner of store, as
well of riches and treasure, as of all thinges els
whatsoeuer: but as the countrey is wealthy and
rich, so are the inhabitantes from the highest to
the lowest, from the Prieste, to the inferiour
4200 sorte, euen all in generall, woonderfully inclined
to **Couetousnes** and **Ambition**, which thing,
whilest they followe, they can neuer be satisfied:
for **Crescit amor nummi, quantum ipsa pecunia
crescit, The loue of money doeth by so much**
4205 **the more increase, by how much more the money it selfe doth increase:** And the nature of a
L4ᵛ couetous man is such, that // **tam deest quod
habet, quam quod non habet: As wel that thing
which he hath, as that which he hath not, is**
4210 **wanting vnto him.** Therefore may a couetous
man well bee compared to hell, which euer gapeth and yawneth for more, and is neuer content
with ynough. For right as hel euer hunteth after
more, so a couetous man drowned in the Quag-
4215 myre of **Auarice**, and plunged in the plash of
Ambition, hauing his **summum voluptatem** reposed in momentary riches, is neuer content with
ynough, but still thirsteth for more, much like to
a man sicke of an ague, who the more he drink-
4220 eth the more he thirsteth, and the more he
drinketh, the more his disease increaseth. Therefore I holde it true, which is writ: **Bursa auari os
est diaboli, The pouch of a rich couetous man,**

The insatiable
desire of a
couetous man.

The purse of
a rich man.

is the mouth of the Deuill, which euer is open
to receiue, but alway shut to giue. 4225

Spud. But they will easily wipe away this
blot: For are wee not bound to prouide for our
selues (say they) our Wiues, our children, our
familie? Doth not the Apostle hold him for an
Infidell or a **Deneger** of the faith, who prouideth 4230
not for his wife and familie? And therfore, herein
we shewe our selues rather good husbandes, carefull and obedient Christians, then couetous or
ambitious persons: This haue I heard them alleadge for themselues. 4235

Philo. Euery Christian man is bound in conscience before God to prouide for his houshold
& famely, but yet so as his immoderate care surpasse not the boundes, nor **transcende** the lim-
ittes of true godlinesse. His chiefest trust and 4240
care is to rest only in the Lorde, who giueth liberally to euery one that asketh of him in verity
and truth, and reprocheth no man, and withall
he is to vse such ordinarie means, as God hath
appointed for the getting of the same. But so 4245
farre from couetousnesse, and from immoderate
care would the Lord haue vs to be, that we ought
not this day to care for to morrow: for (saith he)
sufficient to the day, is the trauell of the same.
After all these things (with a distrustfull and 4250
inordinate care,) doe the Heathen seeke, who
knowe not God, saith our Sauiour Christ but be
you not like to them. And yet I say, as wee are
not to distrust the prouidence of God, or dispaire
for any thing: so are we not to presume, nor yet 4255
to tempt the Lord our God, but to vse such ordinary meanes, as he hath commaunded and appointed to that end and purpose, to get our liuing and maintenance withall. But this // people M1

How far euery man is bound to prouide for his Familie.

Immoderate care for riches reprooued.

M1. PH: *Inclosures in England.*

4260 leauing these godly means, do all run headlong to
couetousnesse & ambition, attempting alwayes,
& assaying al means possible to heap vp riches.
So likewise, **Landlordes** make **merchandize** of
their poore **Tenants**, racking their rents, raising
4265 their **Fines** and **Incomes**, and setting them so
straight vpon the **tenter hookes**, as no man can
liue on them. Besides that, as though this pillage
and pollage, were not rapacious ynough, they
take in, and inclose **commons, Moores, heathes,**
4270 and other common pastures, whereout the poore
commonalty were woont to haue all their prouision and feeding for their cattell, and (which is
more) corne for themselues to liue vpon: all
which are now in most places taken from them,
4275 by those greedy **Puttockes**, to the greate impou-
erishing and vtter beggering of many whole
Townes and **Parishes**, whose tragicall cries and
incessant clamors, haue long since pearced the
Skies, and presented themselues before the Mai-
4280 esty of God, crying: **How long Lord, how long
wilt thou deferre to reuenge this villanie, done
to thy poore Saintes, and silly members vpon
the earth?** Take heed therefore you rich men,
that poll & pill the poore, for the bloud of as
4285 many as miscarry any maner of way, through
your iniurious exactions, biting oppressions, and
indirect dealings, shal be required at your hands,
at the great day of the Lord.

    Cursed is he (sayth our Sauiour Christ) **that**
4290 **offendeth one of these little ones: it were better**
that a Milstone were hanged about his necke,
and he cast into the middest of the sea. Christ
so intirely loueth his poore members vpon earth,
that he imputeth the contumely, which is done
4295 to any one of thẽ, to be done vnto himself, and
will reuenge it, as done to himselfe: Wherfore,
God giue them grace to lay open their inclosures
againe, to let fall their **Rentes, Fines, incomes,**

Landlords
racke their
tenants.

Inclosing
of Commons
frõ the
poore.

Iniurie to
Christ his
members is
iniurie to
Christ.

Inclosures.

and other impositions, whereby God is offended, the poore brethren beggered, and I feare me, the 4300
whole Realm wil be brought to vtter ruine and decay, if this mischiefe be not mette withall and incountred with very shortly. For these Inclosures bee the causes why rich men eate vppe poore men, as beastes doe eate grasse. These I say are 4305
Caterpillers and **deuouring Locustes** that **massacre** the poore, and eate vp the whole Realme, to the destruction of the same: the Lord amend them.

Lawyers ruffle in poore mens riches.

Vpon the other side, the **Lawyers** they ruffle 4310
it out in their **silks, Veluets** and chaines of gold: They build gorgious houses, & stately // Turrets. M1ᵛ
They keepe a Port like mighty Potentates, they haue their bandes and retinues of men attendant vpon them dayly, they purchase Castles and 4315
Towers, lands and Lordships, and what not? And all vpon the polling and pilling of the poore commons. They haue so good consciences, that all is fish that comes to the nette, they refuse nothing that is offered, and what they doe for it, 4320
in preferring theyr poore Clyents causes, the Lord knoweth, and one day they shall finde it: if

Ointment to grease Lawyers in the fist withall.

you haue **argent**, or rather **rubrum vnguentum** I dare not say golde, but red Ointment to grease them in the fist withall, then your sute shall want 4325
no furtherance, but if this liquor be wanting, then farewell Clyent, he may goe shooe the Goose, for any good successe he is like to haue of his matter: without this, **Sheriffes** & Officers will returne Writtes with a **tarde venit**, or with a 4330
non est inuentus, smally to the poore mans profite. But so long as any of this oyntment is dropping, they will beare him in hand, his matter is good and iust, and all to keepe him in vre, till all

---

M1ᵛ. PH: *Polling Lawyers in England.*

4335 bee gone, and then will they tell him his matter
      is naught: and if one aske them why they told
      not their Clients so in the beginning, they will
      answere, I knew not so much at the first, the
      fault is in himself he told me the best but not the
4340 worst. He shewed me not this **Euidence** and that
      Euidence, this **President** and that **President**, this
      Writing and that **Writing**, turning all the fault
      vppon the **suggester**, whereas the whole fault in-
      deed is in himselfe, as his owne conscience can
4345 beare him witnesse. In presence of their Clientes,
      they will be so earnest one with another, as one
      (that knewe not their sleights) would thinke they
      would goe togither by the eares. This is in steed
      of a shooing-horne to drawe on their Clyents
4350 withal: but immediatly after their Clients be
      gone, they laugh in their sleeues to see how pret-
      ily they can fetch in such summes of money, and
      that vnder the pretence of equity and iustice. But
      though they can for a time (**prestigiatorum more**)
4355 like cunning deceiuers, cast a myst before the
      blind world, yet the Lord, who seeth the secrets
      of al harts shal make them manifest to all the
      world, and reward them according to their doings.

          Vpon the other side, **Marchant men**, by their
4360 **marting, chaffering** & **changing**, by their coun-
      terfeit ballances, & vntrue weights, and by their
      surprising of their wares, heap vp infinit treas-
      ures. **Artificers** and **occupiers**, euen all in gener-
M2   all, will not sel their wares // for any reasonable
4365 price, but sweare and teare pitifully, that such a
      thing cost them so much, and such a thing so
      much, whereas they swear as false, as the liuing
      Lord is true: but one day let them be sure, that
      the Lord (who saith, **Thou shalt not sweare at**

The pretensed
excuse of
Lawyers whē
their Clients
haue lost
their plees.

The sleightie
practises of
Lawyers.

The fraudulent
dealing of
Marchant
men.
Artificers.

M2. PH: *What maketh thinges deare.*

all, nor deceiue thy brother in bargaining) will   4370
reuenge this villany done to his Maiestie.

Yea, into such ruinous estate hath Couetousnesse brought that land, that in plenty of all
things, there is scarsitie and dearth of all things.
So that, that which might haue been bought   4375
heretofore, within this twenty, or fourty yeares,
for twenty Shillings, is now worth twenty Nobles, or twenty pounds. That which then was
woorth twenty pounde, is nowe woorth an hundred pounde and more: Whereby the rich men   4380
haue so ballanced their chestes with gold and siluer, as they cracke againe. And to such excesse is
this couetousnes growne, as euery one that hath
money, will not sticke to take his neighbours
house ouer his head, long before his yeares be ex-   4385
pired: Wherby many a poore man, with his wife,
children and whole famely are forced to begge
their bread all the dayes of their liues after. Another sort who flowe in wealth, if a poore man
haue either house or land, they will neuer rest   4390
vntill they haue purchased it, giuing him not the
third part, of that it is worth. Besides al this so
desperately giuen are many, that for the getting
of siluer & gold, they will not sticke to imbrue
their hands, and bathe their armes in the bloud   4395
of their owne Parents and friends most vnnatur-
allie. Other some will not make any conscience
to sweare & forsweare themselues, to lye, dissem-
ble, and deceiue the dearest friendes they haue in
the world. Therefore the Heathen Poet **Virgil**   4400
saide very well, **O sacra auri fames, quid non,
mortalia pectora cogis: O cursed desire of gold,
what mischiefe is it, but thou forcest man to
attempt it, for the loue of thee?** This immoderate thirst of gold and money, bringeth an infin-   4405
it number to shamefull end, as we see dayly,
some are hanged for murthering, some for kill-
ing, some for robbing, some for stealing: some

Great dearth
in plenty of
all things.

Taking of
houses ouer
mens heads.

The desperat
desire of men
to get mony.

Many broght
to ruful end
through
means of

for one thinge, some for another. So that surely
I thinke, the number of men to be greater, **Quos
dira auaritiæ pestis absorpsit, quam quos gladius
vel ensis perforauit.** *whom the pestilence of auarice
hath swallowed vp, then the number of those whom
the sword hath destroyed.* The Lord asswage the
raging heate hereof with the oile of his gracious
mercy, if it be his good pleasure & wil. //

Spud. If I might be so bold, I wold request
you to shew me out of the word of God, wher
this so detestable a vice is reprooued?

Philo. Our sauiour Christ Iesus, the teacher
of all truth, in his Euangelie, the sixth of **Mathew,** saith: **Be not carefull for to morrow day, for
the morrow shall care for it selfe.**

Againe, **Be not carefull for apparell, what
you shall put on, nor for meat what you shall
eat, but seeke you the Kingdome of heauen, and
the righteousnesse therof, and al these things
shal be giuen vnto you.** He charged his Disciples
to bee so farre from couetousnes, as not to cary
two coates with them in their iourneyes, nor yet
any mony in their purses. He told his disciples
another time striuing which of them should bee
the greatest, that he who woulde be the greatest,
must humble himselfe to be seruaunt of all.
When the people would haue aduanced him to
haue been King, he refused it, and hid himselfe.
He telleth vs, **we cannot serue two masters God
and Mammon.** He biddeth vs not to set our
mindes vpon couetousnes, inferring, that where
our riches is, there will our hearts be also. He
saith, it is harder for a rich man (that is, for a
man whose trust is in his riches) to enter into the
**Kingdom of God, then for a Camell to goe
through the eie of a needle.** The Apostle biddeth

Marginal notes:

gold & siluer.

Math.6
Testimonies
out of the
word of God,
against
couetousnes.

Luke,6.

Math.

Line numbers: 4410, 4415, M2v, 4420, 4425, 4430, 4435, 4440

vs if we haue meat, drink, and cloathing, to be   4445
content, for they that will be rich (saith he) fall

1.Tim.6
into diuers temptations and snares of the deuill,
which drowne men in perdition.

Psal.39.
Dauid saith, Man disquieteth himselfe in
vaine, heaping vp riches, and cannot tell who   4450
shal possesse them.

Prouerb.1.
Salomon compareth a couetous man to him
that murdereth, and sheddeth innocent bloud.
Again, Hel and destruction are neuer full, so the
eyes of men can neuer be satisfied. The Apostle   4455
Saint Paule saith, Neither Whoremongers, A-

Prouerb.27.
dulterers, nor couetous persons, nor extortioners, shall euer enter into the Kingdome of
Heauen. And saith further, that the loue of
money is the root of all euill. Christ biddeth vs   4460
to be liberall, and lende to them that haue need,

Math.5
Luke.6.
not looking for any restitution againe, and neuer
to turne our face away from any poore man, and
then the face of the Lord shall not be turned
away from vs. By these few places, it is manifest   4465
how farre from all Couetousnes the Lord would
haue all his children to be.

Spud. Be there any examples in the holy
Scriptures of the // Iustice of God, inflicted vpon   M3
them that haue offended herein.   4470

The
punishment of
couetousnes
shewed by
examples.
Philo. The Scripture is full of such fearfull
examples of the iust iudgments of God, executed
vpon them that haue offended herein. Whereof I
will recite three or foure, for the satisfying of
your minde.   4475

Adam was cast out of Paradise for coueting
that fruite, which was inhibited him to eate.

4.Reg.5.
Gehesie the seruant of Elizeus the Prophet,
was smitten with an incurable leprosie, for that
he, to satisfie his couetous desire, exacted gold,   4480

M3. PH: *Plagues of Couetousnesse*

Siluer, and other rich Garments of **Naaman**, the
King of **Syria** his seruant.

Balaam was reprooued of his Asse for his   Num.22.
couetousnesse, in going to curse the Children of
4485   **Israel**, at the request of King **Balac**, who promised him aboundance of gold and siluer so to doe.

Achab the King, for couetousnesse to haue
poore **Naboth** his Vineyard, slewe him, and dyed
after himselfe, with all his progenie, a shamefull
4490   death.

The sonnes of **Samuel**, were for their insatia-   Samuel 8
ble couetousnes, restrained from euer enioying
their fathers Kingdome.

Iudas for couetousnes of money, sold the Sa-
4495   uiour of the world, and betrayed him to the
Iewes, but afterwarde died a miserable death, his
belly bursting, and his bowels gushing out.

Ananias and **Saphira** his wife, for couetous-   Actes.5.
nesse in concealing parte of the price of their
4500   lands from the Apostles, were both slain, and
dyed a fearfull death.

Achan was stoned to death by the Lord his
commandement for his couetousnesse, for stealing gold, siluer, and iewels at the sacking of **Ier-**
4505   **icho**, and all his goods were burned presently.
Thus you see how for couetousnes of mony, in al
ages, men haue made shipwrack of their consciences, and in the ende by the iust iudgement of
God, haue died fearefull deaths, whose iudg-
4510   ments I leaue to the Lorde.

Spud. Seeing that couetousnes is so wicked a
sinne, and so offensiue both to God and man, &
so pernicious to the soul, I maruell what moou-
eth men to follow the same so much as they doe?

4515   **Philo.** Two things in my iudgement doe
mooue men to affect money so much as they   What make
doe: The one, a feare, least they should fall into   men to affect
pouerty and beggery (oh distrustfull Infidelitie)   money.
the other a desire to be aduanced and promoted

to high dignities and honours // vppon earth.   M3^v
And they see, the world is such, that hee who
hath money ynough, shall be **Rabbied** and **Mais-
tered** at euery word, and withall saluted by the
vaine title of **Gentleman** and **worshipfull**, though
notwithstanding he be a dunghill Gentleman, or   4525
a gentleman of the first head, as they vse to term
them. And to such extreame madnesse is it
grOwne, that now a dayes euery Butcher, shoo-
maker, Tailer, Cobler, and Husband-man, yea,
euery Tinker, Pedler and Swineheard, euery arti-   4530
ficer and other, **Gregarii ordinis**, of the vilest
sort of men that bee, must be called by the vaine
name of Maisters at euery word. But it is certaine, that no wise man will entitle them with
any of these names, **Worshipful** or **maister** (for   4535
they are names and titles of dignity, proper to
the godly wise, for some especiall vertue inherent
in them, either els for their birth or calling, due
vnto them) but such **Titiuillers**, flattering **Parasites**, & glosing **Gnatoes**, as flatter them, expect-   4540
ing some pleasure, or benefite at their hands:
which thing, if they were not blown vp with the
bellowes of Pride, and puffed vp with the winde
of vaineglory, they might easily perceiue. For certaine it is, they doe but mocke and floute them   4545
with these titles, knowing they deserue no lesse.
And therefore as wise men and fearing God, they
should refuse those vainglorious names, remē-
bring the words of our Sauiour Christ, **Be not
called Maister, in token there is but one onely**   4550
true Maister and Lord in heauen: which only
true Maister and Lord, God graunt all other may
follow both in life & name, vntill they come to
be perfect men in Iesus Christ.

Marginal notes:

Euery begger
almost is
called master
at euery word.

Titiuillers
that is
flattering
fellows.

M3^v. PH: *vaine titles of master & worship in* Eng.

4555   **Spud.** The people being so set vpon couetousnesse, as I gather by your speeches they be, is
it possible that they will lend money without vsury, or without some hostage, gage, or pawne? I
think not, For vsury followeth couetousnes, as
4560   the shadow doth the body.

Phil.   Great Vsurie in England.

It is as impossible for a man to borrow money in   Vsury.
England (for the most part) without Vsury, interest and loan, or without some good hostage,
4565   gage, pawne or pledge, as it is for a dead man to
speake with audible voice.

     Spud. I haue heard say, that the Positiue   The positiue
lawes, and statute lawes there, do permit them to   Lawes.
take Vsury, appointing them how much they
4570   shall take for euery pound. //
M4   **Phil.** Although the Statute lawes (for the
auoyding of further inconueniences) do permit
certaine summes of mony to be giuen & taken
ouerplus beyond and aboue the principall, for the
4575   lone of money lent, yet are the Vsurers no more
discharged from the guilt of Vsurie before God
thereby, then the adulterous **Iewes** were from
whoredome, because **Moises** gaue them a **per-
missiue law** for euery one to put away his wife,
4580   that would, for any light offence. And yet the
positiue lawes there giue no liberty to commit   The Lawes
Vsury: but seeing how farre it rageth, least it   of England
should exceed, rage further and ouerflowe the   permit
bankes of all reason and godlinesse (as couetous-   no Vsury
4585   nes is a raging sea, and a bottomlesse pit, neuer
satisfied nor contented) they haue limitted it
within certaine meeres, and boundes (to bridle
the insaciable desires of couetous men) beyonde
the which it is not lawfull for any to goe: But

M4. PH: V*surie vnlawfull.*

this permission of the Lawes argueth not, that it   4590
is lawfull to take Vsury, no more (I say) then the
permission of **Moises** argued that whoredom and
adultery was thẽ lawful and good, because **Moses**
permitted them to put away their wiues, for the
auoiding of greater euils. For as Christ said to   4595
the **Iewes: From the beginning it was not so**: so
say I to these Vsurers, from the beginning it was
not so, nor yet ought to be so.

    Spud. If no interest were permitted, no man
would lend, and then how should the poore doe?   4600
Wherefore the Lawes that permit some small
ouerplus therein, doe very well in mine opinion.

    Philo. The Apostle sayth, **Non faciendum est
malum, vt inde veniat bonum. We must not doe
euill, that good may come of it,** yet the lawes in   4605
permitting certaine reasonable gaine to bee receiued for the loane of money lent, least otherwise the poore should vtterly be distressed (for
without some commodity the rich would not
lend) haue not done much amisse, but if they   4610
had quite cut it off, and not yeelded at all to any
such permission, they had done better. But herein the intent of the law is to be considered:
which was to impale within the Forrest or Parke
of reasonable and conscionable gaine, men who   4615
cared not how much they could extort out of
poore mens handes, for the loane of their money
lent, and not to authorize any man to commit
Vsurie, as though it were lawfull because it is
permitted. Therefore those that say that the   4620
Lawes there doe allow of Vsurie and license men
to commit it freely, doe // slaunder the lawes,   M4ᵛ
and are worthy of reprehension: For though the
lawes say, thou shalt not take aboue two shillings
in the pound, ten pound in a hundred, &c. Do-   4625

**The lawes
permit some
ouerplus but
command
it not.**

eth this prooue that it is lawfull to take so much,
or rather that thou shalt not take more then that?
If I see a man will needes fight with another, &
I hauing authority ouer him, say vnto him, thou
4630 shalt not giue him aboue one or two blows at the
most, doth this proue that I licēse him to giue
him one or two blowes, or rather that he shal not
giue him any at al, or if he do, that he shall not
exceed or passe the bounds of reasonable
4635 measure: So this lawe doth but mittigate the
penalty: for it saith, that the party that taketh but
ten pounde for the vse of an hundred pound los-
eth but the ten pound, not his principall.

    Spud. Then I perceiue, if Vsury be not law-
4640 full by the Lawes of the Realme, then is it not
lawfull by the lawes of God.

    Philo. You may be sure of that. For our Saui-
our Christ willeth vs to be so farre from couetousnesse & Vsury, as he saith, **Giue to him that**
4645 **asketh thee, and from him that wold borrow,**
turn not thy face away. And againe, **Lend of thy**
goods to them, who are not able to pay thee
againe, & thy reward shal be great in heauen. If
we must lend our goods then to them, who are
4650 not able to paye vs againe, no, not so much as
the bare thing lent, where is the Interest, the
Vsurie, the gaine and ouerplus which we fish for
so much? Therefore our Sauiour Christ saith,
Beatius est dare quàm accipere, It is more
4655 blessed to giue then to receiue. In the **22.** of
Exodus.Deut.24.23.Leuit.25.Nehe.5.Ezech.
22.18. and many other places, we are forbidden
to vse any kind of Vsury or Interest, or to receiue
againe any ouerplus, beside the principall, either
4660 in Money, Corne, Wine, Oile, Beasts, Cattell,
Meate, Drink, Cloth, or any thing els whatsoeuer. **Dauid** asked a question of the Lorde,
saying: **Lord, who shal dwel in thy Tabernacle?**
or who shal rest in thy holy hil? Whereto he, or

Forbidding to
outrage in
mischiefe, is
no permissiō
to commit
mischiefe.

Math.5.6.

Luke.6,

The worde of
God against
Vsurie.

Psalme 15

rather the holy Ghost in him, giueth the solution   4665
saying: **Euen he that leadeth an incorrupt life,
and hath not giuen his money vnto Vsurie, nor
taken reward against the innocent, who so doeth
these thinges shal neuer fall.** In the **15.** of **Deut.**
the Lord willeth vs not to craue againe the thing   4670
wee haue lent to our Neighbour, for it is the
Lords free yeare. If it be not lawfull then to aske
againe that which is lent (for it is not the law of
good conscience for thee to exact it, if thou be
abler to forbear // it, then the other is to pay it)   N1

**When it is
not lawful to
aske againe
our goods
lent.**

much lesse is it lawfull for thee to demaund any
Vsury or ouerplus. And for this cause the Lorde
saith, **Let there be no begger amongst you, nor
poore person amongst the Tribes of Israell.**
Thus you see the word of God abandoneth Vsu-   4680
rie, euen to hell, and all writers both diuine and
prophane, yea, the very Heathen people, mooued
onely by the instinct of Nature, and rules of Reason, haue alwaies abhorred it.

Therefore, **Cato** being demaunded what Vsu-   4685
ry was, asked againe, what it was to kill a man?

**Heathen men
against vsury
and interest.**

Making Vsurie **equiualent** with Murther: And
good reason, for he that killeth a man, riddeth
him out of his paines at once, but he that taketh
Vsury, is long in Butchering his pacient, causing   4690
him by little and little to languish, and sucking
out his vitall blood, neuer leaueth him so long as
he feeleth any life in him or any more gaines
comming from him. The Vsurer killeth not one,
but many, both husband, wife, children, seruants   4695

**Vsury equall
with murther**

famelie, and all not sparing anie. And if the
poore man haue not wherwith to pay, aswel the
intrest as the principal, whensoeuer this greedy
cormorant doth demand it: then sute is com-
menced against him, out goe Butterflies and   4700

N1. PH: V*surie equall with murther.*

writtes, as thicke as haile: So the poore man is
apprehended, and brought **coram nobis**, then
presently definitiue sentence proceedeth against
him, compelling him to pay aswel the Vsurie and
4705 loane of the money, as the money lent. But if he
haue not to satisfie, as well the one as the other,
then to **Bocardo** goeth he as round as a Ball,
where he shall be sure to lye, vntill he rot one
peece from another, without satisfaction be
4710 made. O cursed **Caitiue**, no man but a deuill: no
Christian but a cruell **Tartarian** and mercilesse
Turke: Darest thou look vp toward heauen, or
canst thou hope to be saued by the death of
Christ, that sufferest thine owne flesh and bloud,
4715 thine own brethren and sisters in the Lord, and
which is more, the flesh and bloud of Christ
Iesus, vessels of saluation, coheires with him of
his supernall kingdom, adoptiue sonnes of his
grace, and finally, Saints in heauen, to lie and rot
4720 in prison for want of paiment of a little drosse,
which at the day of Doome shal beare witnesse
against thee, gnaw thy flesh like a **Canker**, &
condemne thee for euer? The very stones of the
prison walles shall rise vp against thee, & con-
4725 demne thee for thy cruelty. Is this loue? Is this
charity? Is this to doe to others, as thou wouldest
wish others should do to thee? or rather as thou
N1ᵛ wouldest wish the // Lord to doe vnto thee? Art
thou a good member of the body, which not only
4730 cuttest off thy self from the Vine, as a rotten
branch & void loppe, but also hewest off other
members from the same true Vine, Christ Iesus?
No, no, thou art a member of the deuill, a limme
of Sathan, and a childe of perdition.
4735 We ought not to handle our brethren in such
sort, for any worldly matter whatsoeuer. We

Sute
commēced
against
him that
is not able
to pay aswel
the Vsurie as
the principal.

To prison
with him that
cannot pay
the vsurie.

No mercy in
imprisoning
of poore men
for Vsurie

No crueltie to
be shewed but
mercie, and
compassion
ought to be
extended

N1ᵛ. PH: *The tyranny of vsurers.*

ought to shew mercy, and not cruelty to our
brethren, to remit trespasses and offences, rather
then to exact punishment, referring all reuenge to
him, who saith, **mihi vindictam, & ego retri-**   4740
buam. Vengeance is mine, and I will reward, sa-
ith the Lord. Beleeue me, it grieueth me to heare
(as I walk in the streetes) the pitifull cries and
miserable complaints of poore prisoners in dur-
ance for debt, and like so to continue all their   4745
life, destitute of libertie, meate, drinke (though of
the meanest sorte) and clothing to their backes,
lying in filthy strawe, and stinking litter, worse
then any Dogge, voyd of all charitable consola-
tion, and brotherly comfort in this worlde, wish-   4750
ing and thirsting after death, to set them at liber-
ty, and loose them from their Shackles, Giues,
and Iron bandes. Notwithstanding, these mercilesse Tygers are growne to such barbarous cruel-
tie, that they blush not to say, tush he shall eith-   4755
er pay me the whole, or els he shal ly there til his
heeles rot from his buttockes, and before I will
release him, I wil make Dice of his bones. But
take heed thou Deuill (for I dare not call thee a
Christian) least the lord say to thee, as hee did to   4760
that wicked seruant (who hauing great sommes
forgiuen him, wold not forgiue his brother his
smal debt, but catching him by the throat, said,
pay that thou owest) **Bind him hands and feet,**
and cast him into vtter darknes, where shal be   4765
weeping and gnashing of teeth.

An Vsurer is worse then a Theefe, for the
one stealeth but for need, the other for couetousnes and lucre: the one stealeth, but in the night
commonly, the other dayly and hourely, night   4770
and day, at all times indifferently.

An Vsurer is worse then a **Iew**, for they to
this day, wil not take any vsury of their brethren,
according to the law of God.

They are worse thẽ **Iudas**, for he betrayed   4775

The pitifull
crying of
prisoners
in prison
for debt

A Tygerlyke
tyrannical
saying.

Math.18
Mark 11.

An Vsurer
worse then
a theefe.

An Vsurer
worse then
a Iew.

Christ but once, made restitution, and repented
(though his repentance sprang not of faith, but of
despaire) but these Vsurers betray Christ in his
members dayly and hourely without any remorse
4780   or restitution at all. //

N2   They are worse then hell it selfe, for it
punisheth but onely the wicked and reprobate,
but the Vsurer maketh no difference of any but
punisheth all alike.

4785   They are crueller then Death, for it destroyeth but the body, & goeth no further, but the
Vsurer destroyeth both body and soule for euer.
And to be briefe, the Vsurer is worse then the
Deuil himselfe, for the Deuill plagueth but onely
4790   those that are in his hands, or els those whome
God permitteth him, the Vsurer plagueth not
onely those that are within his iurisdiction already, but euen all other without compassion of
any.

4795   Therefore saith **Ambrose**, if any man commit
Vsurie it is extortion, rauine and pillage, and he
ought to die. **Alphonsus** called Vsury nothing els
then a life of death. **Lycurgus** banished all kinde
of Vsury out of his landes. **Cato** did the same.
4800   **Agessilaus**, Generall of the **Lacedemonians**,
burned the Vsurers books in the open Market
places. **Claudius Vespatianus**, and after him
Alexander Seuerus, made sharpe lawes against
Vsurie, & vtterly extirped the same out of their
4805   dominions, **Aristotle, Plato, Pythagoras**, & generally, al Writers both holy and prophane, haue
sharply inueighed against this deuouring **Canker**
of Vsury, & yet cannot we, that fain would be
called Christians auoyd it. And if it be true, that
4810   I heare say, there be no men so great doers in
this noble facultie & famous science, as the Scriu-

An Vsurer
worse then
Iudas.

vsurers worse
then hel.

An Vsurer
worse then
death.

An Vsurer
worse then
the Deuil.

The sayings
of Godly
Fathers
and Writers
against
vsury.

Vsurers
punished
sundry wayes.

N2. PH: *Scriueners instruments of* V*surie.*

Scriueners
the Deuils
agents to
set forward
vsury

eners be: For it is sayd (and I feare mee too true)
that there are some, to whome is committed an
hundred poundes or two, to some more, to some
lesse, they putting in good sureties to the Owners   4815
for the payment of the same againe, with certaine
allowance for the loane thereof: Then come there
poore men to them, with request to lende them
such a summe of money, and they will recom-
pence them at their owne desires, who making   4820
refusall at the first, as though they had it not (to
whette the mindes of the poore peticioners withall, you must vnderstande) at last they lend them
how much they desire, receiuing of the poore
men what interest & also assurance they list   4825
themselues, both binding them, their lands,
goods and all, with forfeiture thereof, if they faile
of payment. Where note by the way, the Scriuen-
er is the Instrument, whereby the deuill worketh
this laudable worke, rewarding his Vassall with a   4830
good fleece for his labour. For first, he hath a
certain allowance of the master deuil who owes
the mony // for helping him to vent for his   N2ᵛ

The
Scriueners
fleece, or
pittance for
his paines.

Coine. Secondly, he hath a great deale more
Vsurie to himselfe, of him who borroweth the   4835
money, than he alloweth yᵉ owner of the mony.
And thirdly, he hath not the least part for making the writings between them. And thus the
poore man is so intangled and wrapped in on
euerie side, as it is impossible for him, hardly to   4840
get out of the Briers againe, without losse of all
that euer he hath, to the very skinne. Thus the
rich are inriched, the poore beggered, and Christ
Iesus dishonoured euery way. God be merciful
vnto vs.   4845

Great swearing in England:

Spud.

What is the naturall disposition of this people?
Are they not a very godly, religious, and faithful
4850 kind of people? For the saying is, that the worde
of God and good religion flourisheth in that
land, better then in the greatest parte of the
worlde besides. And I am fully perswaded, that
where the word of God is truly preached, and his
4855 Sacraments duly ministred (all which they haue)
there must all things needs prosper and goe forward, wherefore I desire to know your iudgement, whether all these things be so or not.

Philo. The word of God is truly and sincerely
4860 preached there and his sacraments sincerely and
purely ministred, as in any place in all the world
besides, no man can deny it, and all things are
pretily well reformed, according to the prescript
of Gods word, sauing that a few remnants of
4865 superstition do remaine behinde vnremooued,
which I hope in time will be weeded out by the
sickle of Gods word. And as concerning the nature, property and disposition of the people, they
be desirous of **newfangles**, praising things past,
4870 contemning things present, and coueting after
things to come. Ambitious, proud, light, and vn-
stable, ready to be caried away with euery blast of
wind. And whereas you aske me, whether they be
religious: I answere: If religion consist in words
4875 only, then are they very religious, but otherwise
plaine irreligious. They heare the worde of God
seriously, night and day (a blessed exercise
doubtlesse) flocking after sermons from place to
place, euery houre almost: they receiue the Sacra-
4880 ments duly, and they behaue themselues in all
thinges very orderly, to the world. But a great
sort play the Hypocrites herein egregiously, and
vnder this cloake of Christianity and profession

Gods word
flourisheth in
England but
the people are
wicked still.

The natural
disposition
of English
men.

// of the Gospell, they commit all kind of deuil- N3
rie, purchasing to themselues the greater damna- 4885
tion, in that they make the worde of God a viz-
ard or cloak to couer their abhominations withal.
And as for sectes schismes, & sundrie factions,
they want none amongst them. But especially,
Papists, and professors of Papisme, are suffered 4890
with too much lenity amongst them. These sedi-
cious Vipers, and **Pythonicall Hydraes**, eyther
lurke secretly in corners, seducing her Maiesties
subiects, and withdrawing their heartes from
their Soueraignes obedience, or els walke openly, 4895
obseruing an outward **decorum**, and an order as
others do, and thẽ may no man say blacke is
their eye, but they are good protestantes. And if
the worst fall, that they be espied and found ranck
Traitors (as all Papistes be) yet shal they be but 4900
committed to prison, where they liue like young
Princes, fed with all delicate meates, clothed in
sumptuous attire, and flowing in aboundance of
gold and siluer. And no maruell, for euery one is
suffered to come to them that will, and to bring 4905
them what maintenance they list. They haue
their liberty at all times to walke abroad, to sport
and pastime themselues, to play at Cardes, Dice,
Tables, Bowles, and what they will: so that it
were better for them to be in prison then foorth. 4910
Alas, shal we suffer these sworne enemies of
Gods glory, of Christes Gospell, and holy religion, to haue this freedome amongst vs? This
maketh them obstinate, and vnreclaimable: this
hardeneth their hearts, & maketh many a Papist 4915
moe then would be, if due punishment were executed vppon them. But to returne againe to my
former discourse. They are also inconstant, arrogant, vainglorious, hautie minded, and aboue all

Great wickednes cõmitted vnder the cloake of the Gospel.

Papists suffered in Englãd with too much lenitie.

Papists liuing in prison like princes.

Exercises of Papists in Prisons in England

N3. PH: *The libertie of Papistes in England.*

4920   thinges inclined to swearing, in so much, as if
        they speake but three or foure words, yet must
        they needs bee interlaced with a bloudy oath or
        two, to the great dishonour of God, and offence
        of the hearers.

*Great
swearing in
England.*

4925   **Spud.** Why sir? Is it so great a matter to
        sweare? Doth not the word of God say, **Thou
        shalt honour me, and sweare by my name, and
        those that sweare by me shal be commended?**
        These places with the like, me think, doe suffi-
4930   ciently proue that it is lawful to sweare at all
        times, doe they not so?

            Philo. Nothing lesse: For you must vnder-
        stand that there bee two maner of swearings or
        othes, the one godly, the other vngodly: the one
4935   lawful & the other dānable. The godly swearing,
N3ᵛ   or lawfull // oath, is when we be called by the
        magistrates, & those that be of authority, in any
        doubtfull matter, to depose a trueth, and is to be
        done in this order. When any matter of contro-

*When, and
how it is
lawfull to
sweare*

4940   uersie happeneth betwixt man and man, vpon
        any occasion whatsoeuer, and the trueth thereof
        cannot by any means possible bee sifted out,
        otherwise then by an oath: then thou being called
        by the lawfull Magistrate, and commaunded vpon
4945   thy allegeance to confesse what thou knowest,
        thou maist, and oughtest to depose the trueth, by
        the inuocation and obtestation of the name of
        God. And in this doing, thou honourest God.
        But beware that those things which thou swear-
4950   est be true, or els thou makest God a lyer (whose
        name thou callest to witnes) thou desirest him to
        poure his wrath vpon thee, thou periurest thy

*The daunger
of a false oth*

        selfe, and purchasest eternall damnation. The
        other vngodly and damnable kinde of swearing, is
4955   when we take in vaine, abuse, and blaspheme the

A wicked
kind of
swearing.

sacred name of God in our ordinary talke, for
euery light trifle. This kind of swearing is neuer
at any time vpon no occasion to be vsed, but the
counsell of our Sauiour Christ is herein to be
obeyed, who saith: **Sweare not at all, neither by**   4960
heauen, for it is his seat, neither by the earth,
for it is his footstoole: neither by Ierusalem, for
it is the citty of the great King: neither shalt
thou sweare by an haire of thine heade, because
thou canst not make one haire white or blacke: 4965
But let your communication be yea, yea: nay,
nay: that is, **yea in heart, and yea in mouth, nay**
in heart, and nay in mouth, for whatsoeuer is
more then this commeth of euill, that is, **of the**
deuill, saith our Sauiour Christ.   4970

　　Spud. I perceiue by your reasons, that swearing is a thing more dangerous then it is taken to
be, and therefore not to be suffered in a Christian common wealth.

Sundry kinds
of othes with
their effectes.

　　Philo. A true oath is dangerous, a false oath   4975
is damnable, and no othe is sure. To sweare be-
fore a lawful Iudge, or otherwise priuately for the
appeasing of controuersies, calling the name of
God to witnesse in trueth and verity, is an honour, and a true seruice done to the Lord: for in   4980
these cases the Apostle biddeth that an oath may
make an end of all controuersies and troubles.
But the other kinde of swearing in priuate and
familiar talke, is most damnable, and therefore
saith **Salomon, A man that is giuen to much**   4985
swearing shall be filled with iniquity, and the
plague of God shall neuer goe from his house.

Swearing
taken for a
vertue
in Englād

And yet notwithstanding this, it is vsed // and   N4
taken there for a vertue. So that he that can lash
out the bloudiest othes, is counted the brauest   4990
fellow: For (say they) it is a signe of a couragious

N4. PH: *The horrible vice of swearing in England.*

hart, of a valiant stomack, and of a **generosious
heroicall, and puissant mind**. And who either for
feare of Gods iudgments will not, or for want of
4995   practise cannot rappe out othes at euery worde,
he is counted a Dastarde, a Coward, an Asse a
Pesant, a Clowne, a Patch, an effeminate person,
and what not that is euill. By continual vse
whereof, it is grown to this perfection, that at
5000   euery other word, you shall heare either Wound-
es, bloud, sides, Heart, nailes, Foote, or some
other part of Christes blessed bodie, sworne by
yea, sometimes no part thereof shall be left vntorne of these bloudy Villaines. And to sweare by
5005   God at euery word, by the World, by S. **Iohn**, by
S. **Marie**, S. **Anne**, by Bread, and Salt, by the
Fire, or by any other Creature, they think it
nothing blame worthy. But I giue all bloudie
Swearers (who crucifie the Lord of life a fresh, as
5010   the Apostle saith, as much as is in their power,
and are as guilty of his death, passion, and
bloudshedding, as euer was **Iudas** that betrayed
him, or the cursed **Iewes** that crucified him) to
vnderstand, that to sweare by God at euerie
5015   worde, is the greatest oth that can be. For in
swearing by God, thou swearest by God the
Father, by God the Sonne, and by God the holy
Ghost, and by all the whole diuine nature, power, Deity, and essence. When thou swearest by
5020   Gods heart, thou swearest by his mysticall wisedome. When thou swearest by his bloud, thou
swearest by his life. When thou swearest by his
feete, thou swearest by his humanity. When thou
swearest by his armes, thou swearest by his pow-
5025   er. Whẽ thou swearest by his finger or tongue,
thou swearest by the holy Spirit. Whẽ thou
swearest by his nosethrels, thou swearest by his
holy inspirations. When thou swearest by his
eyes, thou swearest by his prouidence. Therefore,
5030   learne this, and beware of swearing you bloudy

Not lawful
to sweare by
any creature.

How
dangerous it
is to swear by
any thing.

Butchers, least God destroy you in his wrath.
And if you sweare by the world, by S. **Iohn,**
Marie, Anne, Bread, Salt, Fire, or any other
Creature that euer God made, whatsoeuer it be,

To swear by
any creature
is Idolatrie.

little or much, it is horrible Idolatrie, and dam-   5035
nable in it selfe. For if it were lawfull to sweare
at each worde for euery trifle, yet it were better
to sweare by God in a true matter, then by any
creature whatsoeuer: Because, that which a man
sweareth by, he maketh (as it were) his God of   5040
it, calling it to witnes, that, that thing which //   N4ᵛ
he speaketh is true. All which things duly considered, I am fully perswaded that it were better
for one to kill a man (not that murther is lawfull,
God forbid) then to sweare an oath: And yet   5045

False
swearers for
mony in
England

swearing is of such small moment in **England,** as
I heare say (and I feare me too true) there are
many that for money will not sticke to sweare
any thing though neuer so false, & are wel
ynough known, and discerned from others by the   5050
name of Iurers: they may be called Libertines or
Atheists, nay plain reprobates concerning the
faith, and very deuils incarnate. Were there euer
any deuilles that would abdicate and abandon
themselues to eternall damnation for mony: as   5055
these villaines doe sell their bodies and soules to
eternall destruction for filthy drosse and mucke
of the world? Shal we suffer this villany to be
done to our God, and not to punish it? God
grant there may some law be enacted for the sup-   5060
pression of the same. For now no man by any

A law for
swearers.

law (in force) may rebuke a man for swearing,
though he teare the Lords bodie, & blaspheme
both heauen & earth neuer so much. The Magis-
trates can not compell them to keepe silence, for   5065
if they doe, they will be ready to lay their

N4ᵛ. PH: *False swearers for money in* **England.**

Daggers on their faces. So that by this impunity,
this horrible vice of swearing is suffered still to
remaine without all controlement, to the great
5070   dishonour of God, and nourishing of vice?

Spud. What kind of punishment would you
haue appointed for these notorious bloudy
swearers.

Philo. I wold wish (if it pleased God) that it
5075   were made death: For we read in the lawe of   Punishment
God, that whosoeuer blasphemed the Lord, was   due for
presently stoned to death, without all remorse,   swearers.
which law Iudiciall standeth in force to the
worldes end. And ought not we to be as zealous
5080   for the glory of God, as the people were then?
Or if this be iudged too seuere, I would wish
they might haue a peece of their tongues cut off,
or loose some ioint: If that be too extreame, to
be seared in the foreheade or cheeke with a hotte
5085   Iron, ingrauen with some posie, that they might
be knowne and auoided. Or if this be too strict
that they might bee banished their natiue Countrey, committed to perpetuall prison, or els to be
whipped: or at least forfaite for euery oath, a cer-
5090   taine summe of money and to be committed to
Ward, till the money be paide. If any of these
godly Institutions were executed seuerely, I doubt
not, but all cursed swearing would vanish away
O1   like a smoke. Then should // God be glorified,
5095   and our consciences kept clean against the great
and fearefull day of the Lord appeare.

Spud. If swearing and blaspheming of Gods
name be so hainous a sinne, it is likely, that God
hath plagued the vsers thereof with some notable
5100   punishment in all ages, wherof I pray you shew
me some examples?

O1. PH: *Examples against swearing.*

Philo. I could shew most straunge and fearfull iudgementes of God executed vpon these
cursed kind of Swearers in all ages: but for breui-
ty sake, one or two shal suffice. There was a cer-   5105
tain yong man dwelling in **Lincolneshire** in **England**, (whose tragicall discourse I my selfe penned
about two yeares agoe in verse, referring you to
the said booke for the further declaration thereof)
who was always a filthy swearer: his common   5110

oath was by **Gods bloud**. The Lord willing his
conuersion, chastised him with sicknes many
times to leaue the same, and mooued others, euer
to admonish him of his wickednesse: but all
chastismentes and louing corrections of the Lord,   5115
all friendly admonitions and exhortation of
others, he vtterly contemned, still perseuering in
his bloudy kinde of swearing. Then the Lord
seeing that nothing would preuaile to win him,
arrested him with his **Sargeant Death**, who with   5120
speed laid holde on him, and cast him vpon his
death-bed, where he languished a greate while in

extream misery, not forgetting to spew out his
old vomite of Swearing. At the last, the people
perceiuing his ende to approch, caused the bell to   5125
tolle. Who hearing the Bell tolle for him, russhed
vp in his bed very vehemently, saying, **Gods**

bloud hee shall not haue me yet: with that his
blood gushed out, some at his toes endes, some
at his fingers endes, some at his wristes, some at   5130
his nose and mouth, some at one ioint of his
body, some at another, neuer ceasing till all the
bloud in his body was streamed foorth: And thus
ended this bloodie Swearer his cursed life, whose
Iudgment I leaue to the Lord.   5135

There was also another, whome I knew my
selfe for a dozen or sixteen yeares togither,
dwelling in **Cheshire**, in a towne called **Congleton**, whose vsuall and common oath was euer
to sweare, by **Gods Armes**: But in the ende his   5140

arme being hurt by a knife, could neuer be
healed by no kind of meanes, but still ranckled
and festered from day to day, and at the last so
rotted, as it fell away by peace meale, and he

5145   himself through anguish and paine thereof, died
O1ᵛ   // shortly after. Thus the Lord God plagued both
the one & the other, in the same things wherin
they had offended, that the punnishment might
bee like to the offence. For as the one offended

5150   through swearing by his bloud, so the Lord punished him with bloud. And as the other offended
in swearing by his armes, so the Lorde plagued
him in his arme also. As hee punished the riche
Glutton in hell by the tongue, for that he had

5155   offended in the same, by tasting of delicate
meates. There was also a woman in the Cittie of
London in **England**, who comming into a shop
to buy certaine Merchandize, forsware her selfe,
and the excrements which naturally should haue

5160   discended downward, came foorth at her mouth,
and she died miserablie. With infinit the like
examples of Gods wrath and heauy iudgements,
executed vpon this wicked brood of Swearers,
which if I had time and leasure, I could rehearse.

5165   But contenting my selfe to haue sayd thus much,
I will proceede to other matters, no lesse needfull
to be handled.

Spud. Hauing (by the grace of Christ) heth-
erto spoken of sundry abuses of that country, let

5170   vs proceed a little farther. How doe they sanctifie
and keep the Sabboth day there? In godly Christian exercises, or els in prophane pastimes and
pleasures?

The fearfull
death of
an other
swearer

The example
of a woman
forswearing
her selfe.

O1ᵛ. PH: *The vse of the Sabboth in England.*

The maner of sanctifying the Sabboth
in England: 5175

Philo.

The Sabboth day, of some is well obserued, as
namely, in hearing the blessed worde of God
read, preached, and interpreted, in priuate and
publique Prayers, in singing of godlie Psalmes, in   5180
celebrating the Sacramentes, and in collecting for
the poore and indigent, which are the true vses
and endes, whereto the Sabboth was ordayned.
But other some spend the Sabboth day (for the
most part) in frequenting of bawdy Stage plaies   5185
and Enterludes, in maintayning Lordes of mis-
rule (for so they call a certain kinde of plaie
which they vse) in Maie games, Church Ales,
Feastes, and Wakesses: In Pyping, Dauncing,
Dycing, Carding, Bowling, Tennisse playing: In   5190
Beare bayting, Cockfighting, Hawking, hunting,
and such like. In keeping of Faires, and Markets
on the Sabboth. In keeping of Courts and Leets:
In football playing, and such other deuillish
pastimes: In reading of lasciuious and wanton   5195
bookes, and an infinite number of such // like   O2
practizes, and prophane exercises vsed vpon that
day, wherby the Lorde God is dishonoured, his
Sabboth violated, his Worde neglected, his Sacramentes contemned, and his people merueilously   5200
corrupted, and carried away from true vertue and
godlinesse.

Spud. You will be deemed too too **Stoycall**, if
you should restraine men from these exercises
vpon the Sabboth, for they suppose that, that day   5205
is a day of liberty, and was ordained, and consecrate to that end and purpose, onely to vse what
kinde of exercises they thinke good themselues,
and was it not so?

Prophane
exercises
vpon the
Sabboth day.

O2. PH: T*he prophanation of the Sabboth.*

5210 **Philo.** After that the Lord our God had created the worlde, and all things therein contained
in sixe dayes, in the seuenth day he rested from
all his workes (that is, from creating them, not
from gouerning them) and therefore he com-
5215 maunded that the seuenth day should be kept
holy in all ages to the end of the worlde: then
after that in effect **2000.** yeares, he iterated this
commaundement when he gaue the Law in
Mount **Horeb** to **Moyses,** and in him to all the
5220 Children of **Israell,** saying: Remember (forget it
not) **that thou keepe holie the seuenth day. &c.**
If we must keepe it holy, then must wee not
spende it in such vaine exercises, as please our
selues, but in such godly exercises as he in his
5225 holy word hath commaunded. And in my iudgement, the Lord our God ordayned the seuenth
day to be kept holy, for foure causes especially.
First, to put vs in mind of his wonderfull workmanship, & creation of the world and all other
5230 his creatures besides. Secondly, that his word (the
Church assembling togither) might be preached,
interpreted and expounded, his Sacraments min-
istered sincerely according to the prescript of his
word, and that Suffrages, Orisons and Prayers
5235 both priuate and publique, might be offered to
his excellent Maiesty. Thirdly, for that euery
Christian man might repose himselfe from cor-
porall labour, to the end they might the better
sustain the trauels of the weeke following: and
5240 also to the ende, that all Beastes and cattell,
which the Lorde hath made for mans vse, as
helpes and supportes vnto him in his dayly affaires and businesse, might rest and refresh
themselues, the better to go thorow in their trau-
5245 els afterward. For as the Heathen man knew very
wel, **Sine alterna requie non est durabile quic-
quam. Without some rest or repose, there is not
any thing durable, or able to continue long.** //

When the
Sabboth was
ordained.

Wherefore
the Sabboth
was
instituted.

Fourthly, to the end it might be a **typicall figure**   O2ᵛ
or **signitor** vnto vs, to poynt out (as it were) with   5250
the finger, and to discipher foorth vnto vs that
blessed rest & thrise happy ioy, which the faithfull shal possesse after the day of iudgment in the
kingdome of heauen: wherfore, seeing the Sabboth was instituted for these causes and to these   5255
endes, it is manifest that it was not appointed for
the maintenance of wicked and vngodly pastimes,
and vaine pleasures of the flesh, which God ab-
horreth, and all good men from their hearts, do
lothe and detest.   5260

Punishment
for violating
the Sabboth.

The man of whome we read in the Lawe, for
gathering of a few small stickes, vpon the Sabboth, was stoned to death, by the commandement of God, sounding from the **Theator**, of
Heauen. Then if he were stoned for gathering a   5265
few stickes vppon the Sabboth day, which in
some cases might be lawfull for necessities sake,
and yet did it but once, what shall they bee, who
all the Sabboth dayes of their life, giue themselues to nothing els, but to wallowe in all kind   5270
of wickednesse and sin, to the great contempt
both of the Lord, and his Sabboth? and though
they haue plaid the lazie **Lurdens** all the weeke
before, yet that day of set purpose, they wil toile

Violaters of
the Sabboth.

and labour, in contempt of the Lord and his   5275
Sabboth. But let thẽ be sure, as he that gathered
stickes vpon the Sabboth, was stoned for his contempt of the same, so shall they be stoned, yea
grinded to peeces for their contempt of the Lord
in his Sabboth.   5280

The Iewes
verie precise
in keeping

The **Iewes** are very strict in keping their Sab-
boths, in so much as they will not dresse their
meates and drinks vpon the same day, but set it
on the Tables the day before. They goe not

5285 aboue two miles vpon the Sabboth day, they suffer not the body of any Fellon or malefactor to
hang vpon the gallowes vpon the Sabboth day,
with legions of such like superstitions. And
which is most strange, if any of them fall into

5290 any daunger, they will not suffer any to labour
for their deliuery vpon that day, for violating
their Sabboth. So it chaunced that a certaine **Iew**
being in **England**, by chaunce fell into a priuy
vppon one of their Sabboth dayes, and the people

5295 endeuouring to help him forth, he forbad them
to labour about him vpon the Sabboth day,
choosing rather to dye in that filthy stinking
place (as by the other morning he was dead indeed) then to break or violate the Lords Sabboth.

5300 Wherein, as I do acknowledge they are but too
supersticious, and ouershoot the marke, so we are

O3 therin // plaine contemptuous and negligent,
shooting short of the marke altogither. Yet I am
not so straight laced, that I wold haue no kind of

5305 worke done vppon that day, if present necessity
of the thing require it, (for Christ hath taught vs,
**The Sabboth was made for man, not man for
the Sabboth**) but not for euery light trifle, which
may as well be done other dayes as vpon that

5310 day. And although the day it selfe, in respect of
the nature and propertie thereof, be no better
then another day (for there is no difference of
dayes, except we wil become **Temporizers**, all
times being alike good) yet because the Lord our

5315 God hath commaunded it to be sanctified and
kept holy to himself, let vs (like obedient and
obsequious Children) submit our selues to so
louing a Father, for els we spit against heauen,
we striue against the streame, and we contemne

5320 him in his ordinances. But (perchaunce) you will

the Sabboth.

No worke to
be done vpon
the Sabboth,
except
necessity
inforce it

O3. PH: *The true vse of the Sabboth.*

aske me whether the true vse of the Sabboth
consist in outwarde abstaining from bodily labour
and trauell? I answere no: the true vse of the
Sabboth (for Christians are not bound onely to
the Ceremony of the day) consisteth, as I haue   5325
said, in hearing the word of God truly preached,
thereby to learne and to doe his will,in receauing

Wherein the the Sacraments (as seals of his grace towards vs)
true vse of rightly administred, in vsing publike and priuate
the Sabboth prayer, in thankesgiuing to God for all his bene-   5330
consisteth. fites, in singing of godly Psalmes and other spirituall exercises and meditations, in collecting for
the poore, in doing of good works: and briefly, in
the true obedience of the inward man. And yet
notwithstanding, we must abstaine from the one,   5335
to attend vpon the other: that is, we must re-
fraine from al bodily labours, to the end that we
may the better be resiant about these spirituall
exercises vpon the Sabboth day. This is the true
vse and end of the Lorde his Sabboth, who   5340
graunt that we may rest in him for euer.

    Spud. Hauing shewed the true vse of the
Sabboth, let vs goe forward to speake of those
abuses particularly, whereby the Sabboth of the
Lord is prophaned. And first, to begin with   5345
Stage-plaies and Enterludes: what is your opinion of them? Are they not good examples to
youth to fray them from sinne?

Stage-playes and Enterludes,
with their wickednes.   5350

Philo. Al **Stage-playes**, **Enterludes**, and **Comme-**
dies, are eyther of diuine or prophane matter: If
they be of diuine // matter, then are they most   O3ᵛ
intollerable, or rather **Sacrilegious**, for that the
blessed word of God, is to be handled reuerently,   5355

O3ᵛ. PH: *Stageplaies and Enterludes.*

grauely, and sagely, with veneration to the glorious Maiesty of God, which shineth therein, and
not scoffingly, floutingly, and iybingly, as it is
vpon Stages in Playes and Enterludes, without
5360 any reuerence, worship, or honour at all done to
the same: For it is most certaine, the word of our
Saluation, the price of Christ his bloud, and the
merites of his passion, were not giuen to be de-
rided, and iested at, or to be mixt & enterlaced
5365 with bawdry, scurrility, wanton shewes, and vn-
comely gestures, as is vsed (euery man knoweth)
in these Playes and Enterludes, vppon Stages and
scaffoldes, made for that purpose. In the first of
Iohn we are taught, **that the word is God, and**
5370 **God is the word.** Wherefore, whosoeuer abuseth
this Word of our God on Stages, in Playes and
Enterludes, abuseth the Maiesty of God in the
same, maketh a mocking stocke of him, and pur-
chaseth to himselfe eternall damnation. And no
5375 maruell, for the sacred word of God, and God
himselfe, is neuer to bee thought of, or once to
be named, but with great feare, reuerence, &
obedience to the same. All the holy company of
Heauen, Angels, Archangeles, Cherubins, Sera-
5380 **phins, and all other Seraphicall powers whatso-**
euer, yea, the Deuils themselues (as Saint **Iames**
sayth) doe tremble and quake at the naming of
God, and at the presence of his wrath: and doe
these Mockers and flouters of his Maiesty, these
5385 dissembling Hypocrites, & flattering **Gnatoes**
think to escape vnpunished? Beware therfore you
masking Plaiers, you **painted Sepulchres,** you
double dealing **Ambodexters,** be warned betimes,
& like good **Computists,** cast your accomptes be-
5390 fore what will be the reward thereof in the end,
least God destroy you in his wrath: abuse God
no more, corrupt his people no longer with your
dregges, and intermingle not his blessed word
with such prophane vanities. For at any hand it

The deriding
of the worde
of God in
stageplaies.

Reuerence to
the maiestie
of God due.

A warning
to players.

Not lawful to
intermixt

diuinity with
scurrility.

is not lawfull, to mixt **scurrilitie** with **diuinitie**,   5395
nor **Diuinity** with **scurrility**.

Theopompus mingled **Moyses** lawe with his
writinges, and therefore the Lord stroke him
mad.

Theodictes began the same practise, but the   5400
Lorde stroke him blinde for it. With many others, who attempting the like deuises, were all ouerthrowne, and died miserablie: Besides, what is
their iudgement in the other world, the Lorde
onlie knoweth. Vpon the // other side, if their   O4
Playes be of prophane matters, then tende they

What if
plaies be
of prophane
matter.

to the dishonor of God, and nourishing of vice:
both which are damnable. So that whether they
bee the one or the other, they are quite contrary
to the worde of grace, and sucked out of the   5410
deuils Teates, to nourish vs in Idolatrie, Heathenrie, and sinne. And therefore, they carrying the
note & brand of Gods curse vpon their backes,
which waie soeuer they goe, are to be hissed out
of all Christian Kingdomes, if they will haue   5415
Christ to dwell amongst them.

Spud. Are you able to shew, that euer any
good men from the beginning, haue disliked
playes and Enterludes?

Phil. Not only the word of God doth ouer-   5420
throw them adiudging them, & the practisers of
thẽ to Hell, but also all holy **Counsels** and **Syn-**

The Word
of God all
Writers,
Counsels
& Fathers
against Plaies
& Enterludes.

odes, both generall, Nationall, and Prouincial, togither, with al Writers both diuine and prophane,
euer since the beginning haue disallowed them,   5425
& writ (almost) whole volumes against them.

The learned Father **Tertullian** in his booke
de speculo sayth, that Playes were consecrate to
that false Idoll **Bacchus**, for that he is said to
haue found out, and inuented strong drinke.   5430

O4. PH: *stage playes condemned.*

Augustinus de ciuit. Dei, saith, that Playes were ordained by the Deuil, and consecrate to Heathen Gods, to draw vs from Christianity to Idolatry & Gentilisme. And in another place,

5435 **Pecunias Histrionibus dare, vitium est immane, non virtus.** To giue mony to players, is a grieuous sinne, and no vertue.

Chrysostom, calleth those Playes, **festa Sathani**, *feasts of the deuill.*

5440 **Lactantius**, an ancient learned Father saith: **Histrionum impudissimi gestus, nihil aliud nisi libidinem mouent.** The shamelesse gestures of Players, serue to nothing so much as to mooue the flesh to lust and vncleannesse. And therefore

5445 in the **30.** Counsell of **Carthage**, and in the Sinode of **Laodicea:** It was decreed that no Christian man or woman shoulde resorte to Playes and Enterludes, where is nothing but Blasphemy, Scurrility and Whoredome maintained.

5450 **Scipio** seeing the **Romanes** bent to erect Theaters and places for Playes dehorted them from it with most prudent reasons, and forcible arguments.

Valerius maximus saith, Playes were neuer

5455 brought vp, **sine regni rubore. Without shame to the Country.**

Aristotle debarreth youth of accesse to Plaies

O4ᵛ and Enterludes, // least they seeking to quench the thirst of **Venus**, do quench it with a pottle of

5460 fire.

Augustus banished **Ouid**, for making bookes of Loue, **Enterludes**, and such other amorous trumperie.

Constantius, ordayned that no Player, shuld

5465 be admitted to the Table of the Lord. Then, seeing that Playes were inuented by the deuill,

Sidenotes:

Wherefore plaies were ordained.

Concil 30. Cartha.cap,11. Sinod. Laodicea. Cap.54

Writers both diuine & prophane against plaies and Enterludes.

The endes of plaies and Enterludes.

practized by the **Heathen Gentiles**, and dedicated to their false Idols, gods and goddesses, as the
House, Stage, and Apparell to **Venus**: the Mu-
sicke to **Appollo**: the penning to **Minerua** & the   5470
Muses: the action and pronunciation, to **Mercu-
rie**, and the rest: It is more then manifest, that
they are no fit exercises for Christian men to follow. But if there were no euil in them, saue this,
namely, that the arguments of Tragedies is, **An-**   5475
ger, Wrath, immunity, Cruelty, iniurie, incest,
murther, and such like: The persons or Actors,
are **Gods, Goddesses, Furies, Fiendes, Hags,**

The
arguments
of tragedies.

Kings, Queens, or **Potentates**. Of Commedies,
the matter and ground, is **Loue, Bawdrie, Co-**   5480
sonage, Flatterie, Whoredome, Adulterie: The

The ground
of Comedies

persons or Agents, **Whoores, queanes, baudes,**
scullions, knaues, curtizans, lecherous old men,
amorous young men, with such like of infinite
variety. If, I say, there were nothing els but this,   5485
it were sufficient to withdraw a good Christian
from the vsing of thẽ. For so often, as they goe
to those houses where Players frequent, they goe
to **Venus Pallace**, and **Sathans Sinagogue**, to

Theaters
and Curtains
Venus
Pallaces.

worship Deuils and betray Christ Iesus.   5490

Spud. But notwithstanding, I haue heard
some holde opinion that they be as good as
Sermons, and that many a good example may be
learned out of them?

No plaies
cõparable
to the word
of God.

Philo. Oh blasphemy intollerable: Are filthy   5495
Playes and baudy Enterludes comparable to the
word of God, the food of life, and life it selfe? It
is all one, as if they had said, **Baudrie, Heathen-**
rie, Paganrie, Scurrility, and **Deuilrie** it selfe, is
equall with the worde of God. Or that the Deuill   5500
is equiualent with the Lord.

The Lord our God hath ordained his blessed
word, and made it the ordinarie meane of our
saluation: the deuill hath inferred the other, as
the ordinarie meane of our destruction, and will   5505

they yet compare the one with the other? If he
be accursed that calleth light darknes, and darke-
nesse light, trueth falshood, and falshood truth:
sweet sowre, and sowre sweet, then à **fortiori**,

P1 hee is accursed that // sayth, that Playes and
Enterludes be equiualent with Sermons. Besides
this, there is no mischiefe which these Playes
maintaine not. For, doe they not nourish Idlenesse? and **otia dant vitia. Idlenesse doth minis-**

5515 **ter vice.** Doe they not draw the people from
hearing the word of God, from godly Lectures
and Sermons? For you shall haue them flocke
thither thicke and three folde, when the Church
of God shall be bare and emptie. And those that

5520 will neuer come at Sermons will flowe thither
apace. The reason is, for that the number of
Christ his elect is but few, and the number of the
reprobate is many: the way that leadeth to life is
narrow, and fewe tread that path: the way that

5525 leadeth to death is broad, and many find it. This
sheweth, they are not of God, who refuse to
heare his word (for he that is of God, heareth
God his word, saith our Sauiour Christ) but of
the Deuill, whose exercises they goe to visite. Do

5530 they not maintaine Bawdry, insinuat foolery, &
renue the remembrance of Heathen Idolatrie?
Doe they not induce to whoredome and vncleannesse? Nay, are they not rather plaine deuourers
of maidenly Virginity and chastity? For proofe

5535 whereof, but marke the flocking and running to
Theaters and Curtens, dayly & hourely, night
and day, time and tyde, to see Playes and Enterludes, where such wanton gestures, such bawdy
speeches, such laughing and flearing, such kissing

5540 and bussing, such clipping and culling, such
wincking and glauncing of wanton eies, and the

*He is cursed
that saith,
plaies &
Enterludes are
comparable
to sermons.*

*Wherfore so
manie flocke
to see plaies
& enterludes.*

*The fruites of
Theaters and
plaies.*

P1. PH: *The fruites of Players.*

The goodly
demeanours
vsed at plaies
& Enterludes

The goodly
examples of
plaies and
Enterludes.

What things
are to be
learned
at plaies.

Theaters,
Schooles or
Seminaries
of pseudo-
christianitie,

like is vsed, as is woonderfull to beholde. Then
these goodly **Pageants** being ended, euery mate
sortes to his mate, euery one brings another
homeward of their way very friendly, and in their   5545
secret conclaues (couertly) they play the **Sodomits**, or worse. And these be the fruits of plaies
and Enterludes for the most part. And whereas
you say, there are good examples to be learned in
them: truely so there are: if you wil learn fals-   5550
hood: if you wil learn cosonage: if you wil learne
to deceiue: if you will learne to playe the hypo-
crit: to cog, to lie and falsify, if you will learne to
iest, laugh and fleere, to grinne, to nodde, and
mowe: if you will learne to play the Vice, to   5555
sweare, teare and blaspheme both heauen and
earth: If you will learne to become a Baud, vncleane, and to diuirginate Maides, to defloure
honest Wiues: If you will learne to murther, slay,
kill, picke, steale, rob, and roue: If you will learne   5560
to rebell against Princes, to commit Treason, to
consume treasures, to practise idlenesse, to sing
and talk // of bawdie loue and **Venerie**: If you   P1ᵛ
will learne to deride, scoffe, mocke and floute, to
flatter and smooth: If you will learne to play the   5565
Whoremaister, the Glutton, Drunkard or inces-
tuous person: If you will learne to become proud,
hautie and arrogant: and finally, if you will learne
to contemne God and all his lawes, to care
neither for heauen nor Hell, and to commit all   5570
kind of sinne & mischiefe, you need to goe to no
other schoole, for all these good examples may
you see painted before your eyes in **Enterludes &
Plaies**. Wherefore, that man who giueth money
for the maintenance of them, must needes in-   5575
curre the ineuitable sentence of eternall damna-

P1ᵛ. PH: *Theaters, Schooles of mischiefe.*

tion except he repent. For the Apostle biddeth vs
beware least we communicate with other mens
sinnes, and this their doeing, is not onely to
5580   communicate with other mens sinnes, and to
maintaine euill, to the destruction of themselues
and many others, but also a supporting of a great
sort of idle Lubbers, and laizie **Lurdens**, who
sucke vp and deuour the good **Honey**, where-
5585   upon the good **Bees** should liue.

    Therfore, I beseech al **Players, Founders** and
maintainers of **Playes** and **Enterludes** in the
bowels of Iesus Christ, as they tender the saluation of their soules, & others, to leaue off that
5590   cursed kind of life, and giue themselues to such
honest exercises, and godly mysteries, as God
hath commanded them in his worde to get their
liuinges withall: For who will call him a wise
man that playeth the part of a foole and a Vice?
5595   Who can call him a Christian, who playeth the
part of a Deuill, the sworne enemy of Christ?
Who can call him a iust man, that playeth the
parte of a dissembling Hypocrite? And to be
briefe, who can call him a straight dealing man,
5600   who playeth a Cosoners part? And so of all the
rest. Away therefore with this so infamous an
Arte: for, goe they neuer so braue, yet are they
counted and taken but for beggers. And is it not
true? Liue they not vpon begging of euery one
5605   that comes? And are they not taken by the
Lawes of the realme, for Rogues & Vagabonds?
(I speake of such as trauell the Countries, with
Playes and **Enterludes**, making an occupation of
it) and ought so to be punished, if they had their
5610   desertes. But hoping that they will be warned
now at the last, I will say no more of them, beseeching them to consider what a fearfull thing it
is to fall into the handes of God, and to prouoke
his wrath and heauie displeasure against them-

A diuine
premunire

What it is to
communicat
with other
mens sinnes.

An
exhortatiõ
to plaiers.

The
ignominy due
to players.

Players
liue vpon
begging.

Plaiers
counted
Rogues
by the lawes
of the realme

selues and // others. Which the Lord of his   P2
mercy turne from vs.

    Spud. Of what sorte be the other kinde of
Playes, which you call **Lordes of Misrule?** For
me thinke, the very name it selfe importeth some
euill.   5620

Lordes of Misrule in England.
Philo.

The name indeed is odious both to God and
good men, & such as the very Heathen people
would haue blushed at, once to haue named   5625
amongst them. And if the name importeth some
euil, as you say, then what may the thing it self
be, iudge you. But because you desire to know
the maner of them, I will shew you, as haue
seene them practized my selfe.   5630

    First, all the wilde heads of the Parish, flock-
ing togither, chuse them a graund Captaine (of
mischiefe) whome they innoble with the title of
my **Lord of misrule,** and him they crowne with
great solemnitie, and adopt for their king. This   5635
King annoynted, chooseth foorth twentie, fourtie,
three score, or a hundred lustie Guttes, like to
himselfe, to waite vpon his Lordly Maiesty, and
to guarde his noble person. Then euery one of
these his men, he inuesteth with his **Liueries** of   5640
Greene, Yellow, or some other light wanton collour. And as though that were not (bawdy) gaw-
dy ynough, I should say, they bedecke themselues
with Scarffes, Ribbons and Laces, hanged all
ouer with golde Ringes, precious stones, and   5645
other Iewels: this done, they tie about either
legge twentie or fourtie belles, with rich handkerchiefes in their handes, and sometimes laide a
crosse ouer their shoulders and neckes, borrowed

P2. PH: T*he order of the Lord of* M*isrule.*

5650 for the most part of their pretie **Mopsies**, and
louing **Bessies**, for bussing them in the darke.
Thus all things set in order, then haue they their
Hobby horses, their Dragons and other Antiques, The rablemēt
togither, with their baudie **Pipers**, and thunder- of the Deuils
5655 ing **Drummers**, to strike vp the **Deuils Daunce** guard,
withall: Then martch this Heathen company to-
wards the Church and Church-yarde, their
Pypers pyping, their Drummers thundering, their
stumpes dauncing, their belles iyngling, their
5660 handkercheefes fluttering about their heades like
madde men, their Hobbie horses, and other The behauior
monsters skirmishing amongst the throng: and in of the Deuils
this sorte they goe to the Church (though the band in the
Minister be at Prayer or Preaching) dauncing and tēple of God.
P2ᵛ // swinging their handkerchiefes ouer their
heades in the Church like Deuils incarnate, with
such a confused noise, that no man can heare his
owne voyce. Then the foolish people they looke,
they stare, they laugh, they fleere, and mount
5670 vpon formes and pewes, to see these goodly pag- Receptacles
eants solemnized in this sort. Then after this, in the
about the Church they goe againe and againe, Cemiteries or
and so foorth into the Church yard, where they Churchyards
haue commonly their Sommer haules, their Bow- for the deuils
5675 ers, Arbours, and banquetting houses set vp, agents.
wherein they feast, banquet, and daunce all that
day, and (peraduenture) all that night too. And
thus these terrestriall **furies** spend the Sabboth
day.
5680 Then for the further innobling of this honorable **Lurdane** (Lord I should say) they haue
also certaine papers, wherein is painted some
babblerie or other, of **Imagerie** worke, and these
they call my **Lord of Misrules badges**, or Cog- My Lorde of

---

Misrules
cognizances.

Wearing
my Lord of
misrules
badges.

Sacrifice
brought to
this filthy
Idol, my Lord
of misrule.

nizances. These they giue to euery one that will   5685
giue thẽ mony for them, to maintain them in
this their **Heathenrie, Deuilrie, Whoredome,
Dronkennesse, Pride**, and what not els? And
who will not shew himselfe **buxome** to them, and
giue money for these the Deuils **Cognizances**,   5690
they shall be mocked, and flouted shamefullie.
Yea, and many times carried vpon a Cowlstaffe,
and diued ouer head and eares in water, or otherwise most horriblie abused. And so assotted are
some, that they not onely giue them money, to   5695
maintaine their abhomination withall, but also
weare their Badges and Cognizances in their hats
or cappes openly. But let them take heed, for
these are the Badges, seales, Brandes and Cognizances of the Deuill, whereby he knoweth his   5700
seruants and vassals, from the Children of God.
And so long as they weare them, **Sub vexillo diaboli militant contra Dominum & legem suam**,
they fight vnder the Banner and Standerde of the
Deuill against Christ Iesus and all his lawes. An-   5705
other sort of fantasticall fooles, bring to these
helhoundes (the Lorde of Misrule & his complices) some bread: some good Ale, some new
Cheese some olde cheese, some Custardes, some
Cracknels, some Cakes, some Flaunes, some   5710
Tartes, some Creame, some Meat, some one
thing, some another: but if they knewe, that as
often as they bringe any, to the maintenance of
these execrable pastimes, they offer Sacrifice to
the Deuill and **Sathanas**, they would repent, and   5715
withdrawe their handes, which God graunt they
may.

   Spud. This is a horrible prophanation of the
Sabboth (the // Lord knoweth) & more pestilent   P3

P3. PH: T*he order of Maie-games.*

5720   then pestilence it selfe, but what? Be there any
abuses in their Maie-games like vnto these?

The maner of Maie-games in England.

Philo.

5725   As many as in the other. The order of them is
thus. Against Maie day, Whitsunday, or some
other time of the yeare, euery Parish, Towne,
and village, assemble themselues together, both
men, women and children, olde and young, euen

5730   all indifferently: and either going all togither, or
diuiding themselues into companies, they goe
some to the woods, and groues, some to the hils
and mountaines, some to one place, some to another, where they spende all the night in pleasant

5735   pastimes, and in the morning they returne bringing with them Birch boughes, and branches of
trees, to deck their assemblies withall. And no
maruell, for there is a great Lord present
amongst them, as Superintendent and Lord ouer

5740   their pastimes and sportes: namely, **Sathan**
Prince of **Hell**: But their chiefest iewel they bring
from thence is the **Maie-poale**, which they bring
home with great veneration, as thus: They haue
twentie, or fourtie yoake of Oxen, euery Oxe

5745   hauing a sweete Nosegaie of flowers tyed on the
tip of his hornes, and these Oxen drawe home
this Maie-poale (this stinking Idoll rather) which
is couered all ouer with Flowers and Hearbes,
bound round about with strings from the top to

5750   the bottome, and sometimes painted with variable collours, with two or three hundred men,
women and children following it, with great deuotion. And thus being reared vp, with handkerchiefes and flagges streaming on the top, they

5755   strawe the ground round about, bind green
boughes about it, set vp Summer Haules, Bowers, and Arbours hard by it. And then fal they to

The order of their maie games

A great Lord present in games, as superinten- dent thereof.

The maner of bringing home their maie poles

banquet and feast, to leape and daunce about it,
as the Heathen people did, at the dedication of
their Idolles, whereof this is a perfect patterne, or   5760
rather the thing it selfe. I haue heard it crediblie
reported (and that **viua voce**) by men of great
grauity, credite, and reputation, that of fourtie,
threescore, or a hundred Maides, going to the
wood ouernight, there haue scarcely the third   5765
part of them returned home againe vndefiled.

These be the fruites, which these cursed pastimes bring foorth. Assuredly, I thinke neither
Iewes, nor Turkes, Saracens, nor // Pagans, nor   P3ᵛ
any other people how wicked, or barbarous so-   5770
euer, haue euer vsed such diuillish exercises as
these: nay, they wold haue bene ashamed, once
to haue named them, much lesse to haue vsed
them. Yet we that wold be Christians, think
them not amisse. The Lord forgiue vs, and re-   5775
mooue them farre from vs.

Spud. What is the maner of their Church-
Ales, which you say they vse, for they seeme vncouth and strange to mine eares?

The maner of Church-ales   5780
in England:
Philo.

The manner of them is thus. In certaine townes
where drunken **Bacchus** beares swaie, against
Christmas & Easter, Whitsunday, or some other   5785
time, the Churchwardens (for so they call thẽ) of
euery Parish, with the consent of the whole Parish, prouide halfe a score or twenty quarters of
Mault, whereof some they buy of the Church
stocke, and some is giuen them of the Parish-   5790
ioners themselues, euery one conferring some-
what, according to his ability, which Mault being

*Maie poales a
patterne of
the Heathen
Idols.*

*The fruit of
maie games.*

*The maner of
Church-ales
in England*

---

made into very strong Ale or Beere, is set to sale,
eyther in the Church, or in some other place as-
5795   signed to that purpose. Then when this **Nippita-**
tum, this **Huffecappe,** (as they call it) and this
Nectar of life, is set abroach, well is he that can
get the soonest to it, and spend the most at it,
for he that sitteth the closest to it, and spendes
5800   the most at it, hee is counted the godliest man of
all the rest, and most in Gods fauour, because it
is spent vppon his Church forsooth: But who either for want cannot, or otherwise for feare of
Gods wrath wil not stick to it, he is counted one
5805   destitute, both of Vertue and Godlinesse. In so
much, as you shall haue many poore men, make
hard shift for money to spende thereat. And
good reason for being put into this **Corban**, they
are perswaded it is meritorious, and a good ser-
5810   uice to God. In this kinde of practise, they continue sixe weekes, a quarter of a yeare, yea, halfe
a yeare togither, swilling and gulling, night &
day, til they be as drunke as Swine, & as mad as
March Hares.
5815   **Spud.** Seeing they haue so good vtterance, it
should seem they haue good gaines. But I pray
you, how do they bestow that money which is
got thereby?
        Philo. Oh well I warrant you, if all be true
5820   which they say: for they repaire their **Churches**
P4   and **Chappels** with it: they buy // bookes for seruice, **Cuppes,** for the celebration of the **Sacra-**
ment, Surplesses for **Sir Iohn,** and such other
necessaries. And they maintaine other extraordi-
5825   narie charges, in their Parishes besides. These be
their golden reasons, these be their faire excuses,
& these be their pretensed allegations, whereby
they blind the world, and conueigh themselues

The filthiest beast the godliest man.

How the money is spent which is got by Church-ales.

P4. PH: *Church-ale money bestowed.*

away inuisibly in a Cloud. But if they dance thus
in a Net, no doubt they will be espied.   5830

For if it were so, that they bestowed it as
they say, do they think that the Lord wil haue
his house builded with Drunkennesse, gluttonie,
and such like abhomination? Must we doe euill,
that good may come of it? Must we build this   5835
house of Lime and Stone, with the desolation
and vtter ouerthrowe of his spirituall house purchased with the precious bloud of our sauiour
Iesus Christ? But who seeth not, that they bestow this money vpon nothing lesse, then in   5840
building and repairing of Churches and Oratories? For in most places, lie they not like Swine
coates? Their windowes rent, their doores broken, their walles fallen downe, their roofe all
bare, and what not out of order? Who seeth not   5845
the booke of God rent, ragged, and all betorne,
yea, couered in dust, so as this **Epitaphe** may be
writ with ones finger vpon it, **Ecce nunc in pul-
uere dormio. Alas, beholde I sleepe in dust, and
obliuion**, not once scarce looked vpon, much   5850
lesse read on, and least of all preached vpon. And
on the other side, who seeth not, (this I speake
but to a friend, I pray you say nothing,) in the
meane time their owne houses and Mansion
places are curiously built, and sumptuously   5855
adorned: Which plainely argueth, that they rather
bestowe this drunken got money, vpon prophane
vses, and their owne priuate affaires, then vpon
the house of Prayer, or the temple of God: And
yet this their doing is well liked of, and no man   5860
may say, **Domine, cur ita facis?** For why? They
doe all thinges well, and according to good order,
as they say. And when time commeth, like good
accomptants, they make their accompts as please
themselues.   5865

Spud. Were it not better, & more consonant
to the trueth, that euery one contributed some-

Wil the
lord haue
his house
built with
maintenance
of euill.

The decay of
Churches,
which are
lacerate,
rent & torne.

Sumptuous-
nesse of
their owne
mansions.

what, according to his ability, to the maintenance
of Temples and Churches, then thus to main-
5870   taine them by drunken Church-ales, as you say
they doe?

  Phil. It were much better: & so we read, the
P4ᵛ   Fathers of the old // Testament, euerie one after
his abilitie, did impart somewhat, to the building
5875   of the Tabernacle, which **Moses** erected to the
Lord. So, as in the end, there was such aboundance of all thinges, as the Artificers, consulting
with **Moises**, were glad to request the people, to
stay their liberality, for they had more then they
5880   knew what to doe withall. These people made no
drunken Church-Ales to build their house of
Prayer withall, notwithstanding, their importable
charges, and intollerable costes. But as their zeale Our zeale
was feruent, and very commendable in bringing waxen cold
5885   to the Church, so our zeale is more then frozen & frozen, in
and blameworthy, in detracting from the Church: respect of the
and bestowing it vpon Whoredome, drunken- zeale of the
nesse, Gluttonie, Pride, and such like abhomina- former world
tions, God amend it.

5890   **Spud.** How do they solemnize their feasts,
and Wakesses there and what order doe they obserue in them?

The maner of keeping of
Wakesses, and
5895   *Feastes in England.*
Philo.
This is their order therein: Euerie towne, parish,
and village, some at one time of the yeare, some
at another (but so that euery one keeps his prop-
5900   er day assigned, and appropriate to it selfe, which Saturitie in
they call their Wake day) vseth to make great feastes and
preparation, and prouision for good cheare. To Wakesses.

P4ᵛ. PH: *keeping of Wakesses in England.*

the which all their friendes and Kinsfolkes farre
and neere, are inuited, where is such gluttonie,
such Dronkennes, such fulnesse and impletion   5905
vsed, as the like was neuer seene. In so much, as
the poore men that beare the charges of these
feastes and Wakesses, are the poorer, and keep

**The great
charges of
Wakesses.**

the worser houses the whole yeare after. And no
maruell, for many spend more at one of these   5910
Wakesses, then in al the whole yeare besides.
This makes many a one to thripple and pinch, to
runne into debt and daunger, and finally, brings
many a one to vtter ruine and decay.

Spud. Would you not haue one friend to vis-   5915
ite another, at certaine times of the yeare?

**Against
Wakes and
feastes.**

Philo. I disallow it not, but much commende
it. But why at one prefixed day, more then at another (except businesse vrged it?) why should one
and the same day continue for euer, or be dis-   5920
tinct from other daies, by the name of a Wake
day? Why shuld // there be more excesse of   Q1
meats and drinks at that day, then at any other?
Why should they abstaine from bodily labour
two or three dayes after, peraduenture the whole   5925
weeke, spending it in drunkennesse, Whordome,
gluttony, and other filthy **Sodomiticall** Exercises.

Spud. Seeing you allowe of one friend to visite another, would you not haue them to **congratulate** their comming with some good cheare?   5930

Philo. Yes trulie, but I allow not of such ex-

**Whereto
wakesses and
feasts do
verie aptly
tend.**

cesse of riot and superfluity, as is there vsed. I
thinke it conuenient for one friende to visite another at some times, as opportunity and occasion
shall bee offered, but wherefore should the whole   5935
Towne, parish, Village and Country keepe one
and the same day, and make such gluttonous
feasts as they doe? And therfore, in my opinion,

Q1. PH: *The fruites of Wakesses.*

5940

they are to no ende, except it be to draw
Whores, Theeues, and Verlettes togither, to
maintaine Whoredome, bawdry, gluttony, drunkennes, theft, murther, swearing and all kinde of
mischiefe and abhomination. For, these be the
endes whereto these feastes, and Wakesses doe

5945

tend, as far as euer I could learne, & the best
fruits that they bring foorth.

Spud. From whence sprang these feasts &
Wakesses first of al, can you tell?

Philo. I cannot tell, except from the Pagans

5950

and Heathen people, who when they were assembled together, and had offered sacrifices to
their false goddes and blockish Idols, made feasts
and banquets togither before them, in honour
and reuerence of them, and so appoynted the

5955

same yearely to be obserued in a memoriall of
them for euer. But whence soeuer they had their
original, certaine it is, the Deuill was the father
of them, seeking thereby to drowne vs in perdition and destructtion of body and soule, which

5960

God remooue farre from vs.

Spud. As I remember, you spake of dauncing
before, inferring that the Sabboth was greatly
prophaned thereby: whereof I pray you shew me
your iudgement.

*From whence
these annuall
feasts and
stationary
Wakesses
had their
beginning.*

5965

The horrible vice of pestifferous dancing in England.

Philo.

Dancing as it is vsed (or rather abused) in these
dayes, is an **introduction** to all kind of Whore-

Q1ᵛ

dome, a preparatiue to wantonnes, // a prouoca-
tiue to vncleannes, and an entrance to all kind of
leaudnesse, rather then a pleasant exercise to the
minde, or a wholsome practise for the body (as

Q1ᵛ. PH: *Dauncing in England.*

some would haue it:) And yet notwithstanding,
in **England**, both men, women, and children, are   5975
so skilfull in this laudable science, as they may be
thought nothing inferiour to **Cinœdus**, that **prostitute Ribald**, nor yet to **Sardanapalus**, that effeminate Varlet. Yea, they are not ashamed to

**Schooles of
Dauncing
erected.**

erect schooles of dauncing, thinking it an orna-   5980
ment to their children, to bee expert in this noble
science of Heathen Deuilrie: and yet this people
forsooth, glory of their Christianity and integrity
of life. Indeed, **verbo tenus Christiani vocitentur**, But, **vita & moribus, Ethnicis & paganis**   5985
**deteriores reperientur. From the mouth out-
ward, they may be saide to be good Christians,
but in life and maners, farre worser then the
Heathen or Pagans.** Whereof, if they repent not
and amend, **it shal be easier for the land of Sod-**   5990
**oma & Gomorra, at the day of Iudgment, then
for them.**

 Spud. I haue heard it sayd that dauncing is
both a recreation for the mind, & also an exercise for the body, very wholsome, and not only   5995
that, but also a meane wherby loue is acquired.

**Dauncing a
pleasure to
them that
delight in
vanities.**

 Philo. I will not much deny, but being vsed
in a meane, in time and place conuenient, it is a
certaine solace or recreation to the mindes of
such as take pleasure in such vanities, but it is no   6000
good reason to say, some men take pleasure in a
thing, **ergo**, it is good, but the contrary is rather
true: For this is a **maxime**, that whatsoeuer a carnall man with vncircumcised heart, either desireth or taketh pleasure in, is most abhominable   6005
and wicked before God. As on the other side,
what the spirituall man, **regenerate** and borne
anew in Christ, by the direction of God his
Spirit, desireth or taketh delight in, is good, and
according to the will of God. And seeing mans   6010
nature is too prone of it self to sinne, it hath no
need of allurementes and enticementes to sinne,

(as Dauncing is) but rather of restraintes and in-
hibitions to stay him from the same, which are
6015   not there to be found. For what clipping, what
culling, what kissing and bussing, what smouching & slabbering one of another? what filthy
groping & vnclean handling is not practised
euery where in these dauncings? Yea, the very
6020   deed and action it selfe, which I will not name
for offending chaste eares, shall bee purtrayed
and shadowed foorth in their bawdy gestures of
Q2   one to // another. All which, whether they blow
vp **Venus** coale, or not, who is so blind that
6025   seeth not? Wherefore, let them not think that it
is any recreation (which word is **abusiuelie** vsed
to expresse the ioyes, or delights of the minde,
which signifieth a making againe of that, which
before was made) to the mind of a good Chris-
6030   tian, but rather a corrasiue most sharp and nip-
ping. For seeing that it is euill in it selfe, it is not
a thing wherein a Christian mans heart may take
any pleasure or comfort.

     The only **Summum bonum**, wherein a true
6035   Christians heart is recreated and comforted, is
the meditation of the passion of Iesus Christ, the
effusion of his blood, the remission of sinnes,
and the contemplation of the ineffable ioyes and
beatitudes after this life, prepared for the faithful
6040   in the bloud of Iesus Christ. This is the only
thing wherein a Christian man ought to reioyce,
and take delight in, all other pleasures and delights of this life set apart, as **amarulent** and bitter, bringing foorth fruit to eternal destruction,
6045   but the other to eternall life. And whereas they
conclude, that it is a wholsome exercise for the
body, the contrary is most true, for I haue
knowne diuers, that by the immoderate vse

What
allurements
to sin, be
in dauncing,

Dauncing no
recreation,
but a corasiue
to a good
Christian.

The onely
thing wherin
a good
Christian
doth delight,

Dauncing no
wholsom
exercise for
the bodie.

thereof, haue in short time become **decrepit** and
lame, so remayning to their dying day. Some   6050
haue broke their legs with skipping, leaping,
turning & vauting, and some haue come by one
hurt, some by another, but neuer any came from
thence without some parte of his minde broken
and lame, such a wholsome exercise it is. But say   6055
they, it induceth loue, so I say also, but what
loue? truly a lustfull loue, a **venerous** loue? a concupiscentious, bawdy & beastial loue, such as

What loue
dauncing
procureth.

proceedeth from the stincking pump and loth-
some sinck of carnall affection, & fleshlie appe-   6060
tite, and not such as distilleth from the bowels of
the heart, ingenerate by the Spirite of God.
Wherefore, I exhort them in the bowels of Iesus
Christ to eschue not onely from euill, but also
from all appearance of euill, as the Apostle will-   6065
eth them, proceeding from one vertue to another,
vntill they growe to bee perfect men in Christ
Iesus, knowing that we must giue accomptes at
the day of Iudgment of euery minute and iot of

We must
render
accounts
for time
here lent vs.

time that is lent vs in this life, from the first day   6070
of our birth to the last houre of our death: for
there is nothing more precious, then time, which
is giuen vs to glorifie God in, by good workes,
and not to spend in luxurious exercises after our
owne fantasies and delights. //   6075

Spud. But I haue heard them affirme, that   Q2ᵛ
dauncing is probable by the word of God: for
(say they) did not the women come foorth of all

1.Sam.18.

the citties of **Israell** to meet King **Saule** and also
King **Dauid** (returning from the slaughter of **Go-**   6080
liah) with Psalteries, Fluits, Tabrets, Cymballes
and other musicall Instrumentes, dauncing and
leaping before them? Did not the **Israelites** hau-

Exod.15.

ing passed ouer the red sea, bring foorth their

Q2ᵛ. PH: T*estimonies in the behalfe of dancing.*

6085 Instruments, and daunced for ioy of their deliuerance? Againe, did they not daunce before the
golden Calf, which they had made in **Horeb** or   Exod.32.
Sinai? Did not King **Dauid** dance before the Ark   2.Sam.6.
of the Lord? Did not the daughter of **Iephthah**
6090 daunce with Tabret and Harpe at the returne of   Iudg.11
her father from the field? Did not the women of
the **Israelits** dance comming to visite good **Iud-**
ith? Did not the Damosell daunce before King
Herode? Did not Christ blame the people for   Math.14
6095 their not dauncing, when he sayd, **We haue**
pyped vnto you, but you haue not daunced?
Saith not **Salomon: There is a time to weep, and**   Luke.7
a time to laugh, a time to mourne, and a time   Eccle.3
to daunce? And doth not the Prophet **Dauid** in
6100 many places of his Psalmes commende and commaund dauncing, and playing vpon instrumentes
of Musicke? Wherefore (for this they conclude)
seeing these holy Fathers (whereof some were
guided by the instinct of Gods Spirite) haue not
6105 onely taught it in doctrine, but also expressed it
in their examples of life, who may open his
mouth once to speake against it.

    Philo. The Fathers as they were men, had
their errours, and erred as men: for **Hominis est**
6110 **errare, decipi & labi: It is naturall for man to**   No mã
erre, to be deceiued, & to slide from the trueth.   without
Therfore the Apostle saith: **Follow me in all**   errours both
things as I followe Christ, but to the intent that   in life and
they, who pretende the examples of the Fathers,   doctrine.
6115 and Scriptures falsly wrested, to maintaine their
deuillish dauncings withall, may see their owne
impiety and ignoraunce discouered, I will com-
pendiously set downe the true sence and meaning
of euery place, as they haue cited them particu-
6120 larly. For the first, wheras they say, that the
women came foorth in daunces, with Timbrels
and instruments of ioy to meet **Dauid** and **Saule**,
I aske them for what cause they did so? Was it   1 Samu 18

The first
piller of
dauncing
ouerthrowne.

for wantonnes, or for very ioy of heart, for their
victory gotten against the **Philistins**, their sworne   6125
enemies? Was it in praise of God, or to stirre vp
filthy lust in themselues, or for nicenesse onely,
as our daunces be? Did men // and women   Q3
daunce together, as is now vsed to be done: or
rather was it not done amongst women only? for   6130
so saith the Text. **The women came foorth, &c.**
But admit it were neither so, nor so, wil they
conclude a generall rule of a particular example?
It is no good reason to say, such & such did so,
therefore it is good, or we may doe so: but all   6135
things are to be poised in the ballaunce of holy
scripture, and therby to be allowed or disallowed,
according to the meaning of the holy Ghost, who
is onely to be heard and obeyed in his worde.

No good
cõsequẽt
to say others
did so, ergo,
it is good,
or we may
do the like.

The **Israelitish** women hearing of the fame of   6140
Dauid, and how he had killed their deadly enemy **Goliah,** came foorth to meet him, playing
vpon instruments, dauncing, and singing songs of
ioy and thankesgiuing to the Lord their God,
who had giuen them victorie, and deliuered them   6145
from the deadly hostilitie of him, who sought
their destruction euery way. Nowe, what maketh
this for our leud, wanton, nice, and **vbiquitarie**

The differẽce
between the
dances of our
Forefathers,
and ours.

dauncings (for so I may call them, because they
be vsed euery where) let the godly iudge. Who   6150
seeth not rather that this example (let **Cerberus**
and al other Helhoundes barke what they list to
the contrary) clean ouerthroweth them. Theirs
was a godly kind of dauncing in praise of God:
ours a lustfull baudy kind of dauncing, in praise   6155
of our selues: theirs to shew their inward ioy of
mind for the blessing of God bestowed vpon
them: ours to shew our actiuity, agilitie, and curi-

Q3. PH: E*uill examples not to be followed.*

ous nicitie, and to procure lustfull loue, and such
6160   like wickednes infinite.

But to their second allegation: The children   Their second
(they say) of **Israell** danced, being deliuered out   piller shaken.
of the seruitude of **Pharao**, and hauing passed
ouer the red Sea: I graunt they did so: and good
6165   cause they had so to do: For were they not deliuered and set free from three great calamities and
extream miseries at once? First, from the seruile
bondage of **Egypt**, from the sword of **Pharao**,
who pursued the Rereward of their Hoste, and
6170   from the daungers of the sea, their enemies being
ouerwhelmed in the same?

For these great and inestimable benefites, and
blessings receiued at the handes of God, they
played vpon Instrumentes of Musicke, leaped,
6175   daunced, and sang godly songes vnto the Lord,
shewing by these outward gestures, the inward
ioy of their heartes and mindes. Now, what con-
duceth this to the allowance of our luxurious
dauncings? Is it not directly against them? They
Q3ᵛ   daunced // for ioy in thankesgiuing to God, we
for vaineglorie: they for loue to God, we for loue
of our selues: they to shew the interiour ioy of
the mind, for Gods blessings bestowed vpon
them, we to shew our **concinnity**, dexterity, and
6185   vaine curiosity in the same: they to stir vp, and
make themselues the apter to praise God: we to
stirre vp carnall appetites and fleshly motions:
they to shewe their humilitie before God, and
wee to shew our pride, both before God and the
6190   world. But howsoeuer it be, sure I am, their
Dauncing was not like ours, consisting in **Measures, capers, Quauers**, and I cannot tell what, for
they had no such leasure in **Egypt**, to learn such

Q3ᵛ. PH: *The Israelites Daunces.*

The dauncing
of our
forfathers
may not
be called a
dancing,
but rather
a godly
triũphing,
& reioycing
in heart
for ioy.

vaine curiosity in that baudy Schoole, for making
of Bricke and Tiles. And notwithstanding, it is   6195
ambiguous, whether they may be called a dauncing
or not, at least not like ours, but rather a
certaine kind of modest leaping, skipping, or
mouing of the body, to expresse the ioy of the
mind, in praise of God, as the man did, who   6200
being healed by the power of our Sauiour Christ,
walked in the Temple, leaping, skipping, and
praising God.

We neuer read, that they euer daunced, but
when some woonderfull great blessing of God   6205
was bestowed vpon them, and therefore they
made not a common practise of it, or a dayly occupation, as it were, much lesse set vp Schools of
it, and frequented nothing els night nor day,
Sabboth day nor other as we doe.   6210

Their third
reason
examined.

But to the third reason: The **Israelites** danced
before the Calf in **Horeb**. And what then? They
made a golden Calfe, and adored it, may we
therefore do the like? They committed Idolatry
there, therefore is Idolatry good, because they   6215
committed it? **Adam** disobeyed God, and obeyed
the Deuill: Is obedience therefore to the Deuil
good, because he did so?

Therefore, we must not take heed, what man
hath done heretofore, but what God hath com-   6220
manded in his worde to be done, and that follow,
euen to the death. But to be short, as it is a
friuolous reason to say, because they committed
Idolatry, therefore may we doe the like: So it is
no lesse ridiculous to say, because they daunced, 6225
therfore we may doe the same: For as it is not
lawfull to commit Idolatrie because they did so,
so is it not lawfull to daunce, because they
daunced.

So that if this place conferre any thing for   6230
dauncing, it inferreth that wee must neuer daunce,

Q4 but before a golden Calfe, as // they did: but I
thinke by this time, they are ashamed of their
dances: Therefore, of this place I need to say no
6235 more, giuing them to note, that this their dauncing, in respect of the end thereof, was farre different from ours: for they daunced in honour of
their Idol, we cleane contrarie, though neither
the one nor the other be at any hand lawfull.

6240 Their fourth reason. Did not **Dauid** daunce
before the Ark, say they? Verie true: and this Their fourth
place (as the rest before) refelleth their customa- reason.
rie Dauncinges of men and women together most
excellentlie. For **Dauid** daunced himselfe alone,
6245 without either woman, or musicall Instrument, to
effeminate the minde. And this dauncing of
Dauid was no vsuall thing, nor frequented euery
day but that one time, and that in praise of God,
for the deliuerance of the Arke of God his Tes-
6250 tament, out of the handes of the Infidels and
Heathen people: The ioy of this holy Prophete
was so vehement, for this great blessing of God
(such a feruent zeale hee did beare to the trueth)
that he burst forth into outward shew of the
6255 same, the more to induce others to praise God
also. Would God we would Daunce as **Dauid**
daunced heere, for the deliuery of his alsauing
Woorde out of the handes of the **Italian Philis-**
tine, and Arch-enemy of al trueth, the Pope of
6260 **Rome**, for in this respect I would make one my
selfe to Daunce, to leape, to skippe, to triumph,
and reioice, as **Dauid** did before the Arke. By
this I trust, any indifferent man seeth that by this Why Dauid
place they gaine as much for the maintenance of daunced
6265 their leude lasciuious Dauncinges, and Baudy before the
Chorusses, as they did by the former places, that Ark.

Q4. PH: *Dauncing reprooued.*

is, iust nothing at all, which they may put in
their eyes, and see neuer the worse.

Their fift
reason
examined.

Their fift reason. Did not **Iephthah** his
daughter meet her father, when he came from   6270
warre, dauncing before him, and playing vpon instruments of musicke. **Iephthah** going foorth to
warre against the **Amonits**, promised the Lord
(making a rash vow) that if it wold please his
maiestie, to giue him victorie ouer his enemies,   6275
he would sacrifice the first liuing thing that
should meet him from his house: it pleased God
that his sole daughter & heire, hearing of her
fathers prosperous return (as the maner of the
Country was) ran foorth to meete her father,   6280
playing vpon instrumentes, in praise of God, and
Dauncing before him for ioye. Nowe, what
prooueth // this for their Daunces? Truly it   Q4ᵛ
ouerthroweth them, if it be well considered: For

Wherefore
and how
the daughter
of Iephtha
danced

first, we read that she did this but once, we   6285
dayly: she in praise of God, we in praise of our
selues: she for ioy of her Fathers good successe,
we to stirre vp filthy and vncleane motions: she
with a Virginall grauity: we with a wanton leuity:
she in comely maner, we in baudie gesture. And   6290
moreouer, this sheweth, that women are to
daunce by themselues (if they will needes daunce)
and men by themselues, for so importeth the
text, making no mention of any other her **Col-**
leagues or **Companions** dauncing with her.   6295

Their sixt
Reason.

The sixt reason: Did not the **Israelitish**
women daunce before **Iudith**, comming to visite
her? I grant they did so: the story is thus.

Holofernes, opposing himselfe against the **Is-**
raelites, the chosen people of God, and intending   6300
to ouerthrow them, and to blotte out their remembrance for euer from vnder heauen, assem-

Q4ᵛ. PH: *How dauncing is vnlawfull.*

bled a huge power, and besieged them on euery
side. The **Israelites**, seeing themselues compassed

6305   about, & in great daunger on each side, suborned
good **Iudith**, a vertuous godly woman (for without some stratageme, or pollicy wrought, it was
vnpossible for them in the eyes of the worlde to
haue escaped) to repaire to **Holofernes**, and by

6310   some meanes or other to worke his destruction:
who guided by the hand of God, attempted the
thing and brought it happily to passe. For she
cut off his head with his owne Faulchone, wrapping his body in the Canapie, wherin he lay

6315   sleeping, possest as he was with the Spirite of
drunkennesse: This done, the women of **Israel**
came togither, and went to visite this woorthy
woman, and to congratulate her prosperous successe, with Instruments of Musick, singing of

6320   godly songs, and dauncing for ioy, in honour and
praise to God, for this great victorie obtained.
Now, who seeth not, that these women sang,
daunced and played vpon Instrumentes in praise
of God, and not for any other leudnesse or wan-

6325   tonnesse, as commonly the world doth now adayes. This also ouerthroweth the dauncings of
men and women togither in one company. For
though there was an infinite number of people
by, yet the Text saith, there daunced none but

6330   onely Women, which plainly argueth the vnlawfulnesse of it in respect of men and women togither. And this beeing but a particular fact of a
sort of simple Women, shall we draw it into
example of life, and think it lawfull or good, be-

6335   cause they did practise it? It was a custome in
those daies, when God had bestowed any //

R1   notable blessing vpon his people from his heaue-
enly Consistory, the people in honour, praise and

Side notes:

Iudith cutteth
of the head of
Holofernes.

The
vnlawfulnes
of dauncing
of men
and women
togither

R1. PH: *Dauncing stirreth vp lust.*

thanksgiuing to God for it, woulde play vpon
their instruments, sing godly songes, daunce,   6340
leape, skip, and triumph, shewing foorth the ioy
of their mindes, with their thankfulnesse to God,
by all exteriour gestures that they could deuise.
Which kind of thankfull dauncing, or spiritual
reioysing, wold God, we would follow, leauing all   6345
other wanton dauncing to their father the deuil.

Their seuenth
reason,

Their seuenth reason: Did not (quoth they)
the Damosel dance before King **Herod,** when the
head of **Iohn Baptist** was cut off? She daunced
indeed: And heerein they may see the fruite of   6350
dauncing, what goodnesse it bringeth: For, was
not this the cause of the beheading of **Iohn** the
Baptist? See whether Dauncing stirreth not vp

Dauncing
stirreth vp
lust.

lust, and inflameth not the mind. For, if **Herode**
with seeing her daunce, was so inflamed in her   6355
loue, and rauished in her behauiour that he
promised her, to giue her whatsoeuer she wold
desire, though it were halfe of his Empire or
kingdome, what would hee haue been, if he had
danced with her? and what are those that dance   6360
with them hand in hand, cheeke by cheeke, with
bussing and kissing, slabbering and smearing,
most beastly to behold? In so much, as I haue
heard many impudently say, that they haue chosen their Wiues, and wiues their husbandes by   6365
dauncing: which plainely prooueth the wickednesse of it.

Their eight
reason.
Luke 7.

Their eight reason: Did not Christ rebuke
the people for not dauncing, saying: **We haue
piped vnto you, but you haue not daunced.**   6370
They may as wel conclude, that Christ in this
place was a Pyper or a Minstrell, as that he allowed of dauncing, or reprooued them, for not
exercising the same. This is a **Metaphoricall**
kinde of speech, wherein our Sauiour Christ,   6375
goeth about to reprooue and checke the stiffe-
neckednesse, the rebellion, and pertinacious con-

tumacy of the Scribes and Pharisies, who were
neither moued to receiue the glad tydings of the
6380 Gospel by the austerity of **Iohn** the **Baptist**, who
came preaching vnto thẽ the doctrine of repentance, in mourning sort: neither yet at the
preaching of our Sauiour himself, breaking vnto
them that pure **Ambrosia**, that **Cœlestiall Manna**,
6385 the word of life in ioyfull and gladsome manner.

Iohn the **Baptist**, he pyped vnto them, that
is, he preached vnto them, austerity of life, to
mourne for their sinnes, to repent, to fast, pray,
and such like. //

R1ᵛ   Our Sauiour Christ, he pyped, that is
preached vnto them the glad and comfortable
tydings of the Gospel: yet at neither of these
kinds of preachings they were any whit mooued,
either to imbrace Christ or his Gospell. Where-
6395 fore, he sharply rebuked them, by a similitude of
foolish children sitting in the Market place, and
piping vnto them that would not dance. This is
the true vndoubted sence of this place: which,
whether it ouerthrowe not all kind of lewd
6400 dauncing (at least maketh nothing for them)
allowing a certaine kinde of Spirituall dauncing,
and reioycing of the heart vnto God (that I may
suspende my owne iudgement) let wise men
determine.

6405   Their ninth reason: Saith not **Salomon: There
is a time to weepe, and a time to laugh: a time
to mourne, and a time to daunce?** This place is
directly against their vsuall kinde of dauncing.
For, sayth not the Text, **there is a time**, meaning
6410 sometime, now and then, as the **Israelites** did in
praise of God, when any notable thing happened
vnto them, and not euery day and houre, as wee
doe, making an occupation of it, neuer leauing it,

The more thẽ
obdurat
hardnesse of
the Iewes.

Their ninth
reason.
Eccle,3.

R1ᵛ. PH: *Salomons Spirituall dauncing.*

Salomō
meaneth a
certain kind
of a spiritual
dācing or
reioysing of
the heart.

vntil it leaue vs. But what and if **Salomon** speaketh here of a certaine kinde of spiritual daunc-   6415
ing and reioysing of the hart in praise to God?
This is easily gathered, by the circumstances of
the place, but specially by the sentence precedent
(viz. **There is a time to mourn, & a time to
daunce, &c.**) that is, a time to mourne for our   6420
sins, and a time to daunce or reioyce for the
vnspeakable treasures purchased vnto vs by the
death and passion of Iesus Christ. How much
this place maketh for defence of their **noctur-
nall, diuturnall, wanton, lewde, and lasciuious**   6425
dauncinges (if it bee censured in the imparciall
ballaunce of true iudgement) all the world may
see and iudge. And now to drawe to an end, I

Their vltimū
refugium

wil come vnto their **vltimum refugium**, that is:
Doeth not **Dauid** both commende, and also   6430
commaunde dauncing and playing vpon Instru-
ments in diuers of his Psalmes. In all those
places, the Prophete speaketh of a certaine kind
of spirituall dancing and reioycing of the heart in
the Lord, for his graces and benefits in mercy   6435
bestowed vpon vs. This is the true kind of

Why our feet
wer giuen vs.

dauncing, which the worde of God doeth allowe
of in any place, and not that we should trip like
Goates, skippe like Does, and leap like madde
men. For, to that end our feete were not giuen   6440
vs, but rather to represent the Image of God in
vs, to keepe company // with the Aungels, and to   R2
glorifie our heauenly Father through good workes.

    Spud. Doe you condemne all kinde of daunc-
ing then, as wicked and prophane?   6445

    Philo. All leud, wanton and lasciuious daunc-
ing in publique assemblies and conuenticles without respect, either of sex, kind, time, place, person, or any thing els, by the warrant of the word

---

R2. PH: *What dauncing is condemned.*

6450   of God, I do vtterly condemne: But that kind of
        dancing which is vsed to praise and laud the
        name of God withall (as were the daunces of the
        people of the former world) either priuatelie or
        publiquely is at no hand to be disallowed, but

What
dauncing is
condemned
by the
woord
of God.

6455   rather to be greatly commended. Or if it be vsed
        for mans comfort, recreation, and godly pleasure
        priuately (euery sexe distinct by themselues)
        whether with musicke, or otherwise, it can not be
        but a very tollerable exercise, being vsed moder-
6460   ately, and in the feare of God. And thus, though
        I condemne all filthy, luxurious, and vncleane
        dauncing, yet I condemne not all kinde of daunc-
        ing generally. For certaine it is, the exercise it
        selfe, in it owne nature and quality (though to

6465   some it is lawfull, to other some vnlawfull in di-
        uers respectes) is both auncient and general, hau-
        ing beene vsed euer in all ages, as well of the
        Godly, as of the wicked, almost from the begin-
        ning. Wherefore, when I condemne the same in
6470   some, my meaning is, in respect of the manifold
        abuses thereof. And in my iudgment, as it is vsed
        nowadayes, an Occupation being made of it, and
        a continuall exercise, without any difference or
        respect had eyther to time, person, sexe, or place,
6475   in publique assemblies, and great meetings of
        people, with such beastlie slabberings, kissinges,
        and smouchinges, with other filthy gestures and
        misdemeanours therein accustomed, it is as vn-
        possible to be vsed without doing of infinite hurt,
6480   as it is for a naked man to lie in the middest of
        a hotte glowing fire, and not to burne. But these
        abuses with other the like (as there bee legions
        moe in it) being cutte off from the exercise it
        selfe, the thinge it selfe remaineth more tollerable

6485   in some respectes. Or els, if our Daunces tended,
        as I haue said, to the setting foorth of God his
        glorie (as the Daunces vsed in former ages did)
        to drawe others to Pietie and Sanctitie of life,

and to the praise and reioysing in God, to recreate the minde oppressed with some great toyle or   6490
labour, taken in true vertue & Godlines, I wold
not (being done in the fear of God, // men by   R2ᵛ

Why men
should
dance by
thẽselues,
and women by
thẽselues.

themselues, and women by themselues, for els it
is not possible to be without sinne) much gainstand it. But I see the contrary is euery where   6495
vsed to the great dishonour of God, and corruption of good maners, which God amend.

    Spud. And wherefore would you haue men to
daunce by themselues, and women by them-
selues?   6500

    Philo. Because otherwise it prouoketh lust,
and stirreth vp concupiscence, and the fire of lust
once conceiued (by some irruption or other)
bursteth foorth into open action of Whoredome
and Fornication. And therefore a certaine godlie   6505
Father sayd well: **Omnis saltus in chorea, est
saltus in profundũ Cloacæ, Euery leap or skip in
daunce, is a leap toward hel.** Yet notwithstanding, in **England** it is counted a vertue, & an
ornament to man, yea, and the only way to at-   6510
taine to promotion and aduancement, as experi-
ence teacheth.

    Spud. Notwithstanding, for my further in-
struction, I pray you shew me what Fathers and
Councelles haue iuged of it, and what they haue   6515
writ and decreed against it?

    Philo. If I should shew all the inuectiues of
Fathers, all the decrees of Councels, and all the
places of holy Scripture against the same, I
should neuer make an end: Wherefore, of many   6520

Testimonies
of Fathers,

I will select a few, hoping that they wil suffice
any reasonable man.

R2ᵛ. PH: *Men and women daunce asunder.*

Sirach saith: Frequent not the company of a
woman that is a singer or a dauncer, neither hear
6525 her, least thou be entrapped in her craftinesse.

Chrysostome delating vpon **Mathew**, saith:
In euery daunce the Deuill daunceth by for company, though not visible to the eye, yet sensible
to the mind.

6530 **Theophilus** writing vpon **Marke**, the sixt
chapter, saith: **Mira collusio saltat per illam Diabolus. This is a woonderfull deceit, for the
Deuill daunceth among them for company.**

Augustine, writing vpon the thirtie and two
6535 Psalme, saith: **It is better to digge all the Sabboth day then to daunce.**

Erasmus in his book, **de contemptu mundi,**
sayth: Whose mind is so wel disposed, so stable,
or wel setled, which these wanton dances with
6540 swinging of armes, kicking of legs, playing vpon
Instrumẽts and such like, would not ouercome
and corrupt. Wherefore (saith he,) as thou desirest thine owne credite, and welfare, eschewe these
scabbed and scuruie company of Dauncers. //

R3 **Lodouicus Viues**, saith: Amongest all pleasures, dauncing and voluptuousnesse is the kingdome of **Venus**, and the Empire of **Cupid**: wherfore, saith he: it were better for thee to stay at
home, & to breake either a legge or an arme of
6550 thy bodie: then to breake the legges and armes of
the mind & soule, as thou doest in filthy scuruy
dauncings. And as in all feastes and Pastimes,
Dauncing is the last so it is the extreame of all
other vice. And againe, there were (saith he)
6555 from farre countries, certaine men brought into
our partes of the worlde, who when they saw
men daunce, ran away, merueilously affraid, crying out, and thinking them to haue bin mad.

Councelles,
and writers
against
dauncing.
Eccle.13,

Math.4.

Dauncers
thought to be
mad men,

R3. PH: **D**auncing a world of sinne.

And no maruell, for who seeing them leap like
Squirrils, skippe, like **Hinds**, and trippe like   6560
Goates as they doe, if he neuer saw any before,
wold not thinke them either mad, or els possest
with some Furie.

Bullinger.
 Bullinger, paraphrasting vpon **Mathew 14.**
sayth: After feasting, swilling, and gulling, com-   6565
meth Dauncing, the root of all filthinesse and
vncleannesse.

 Maister **Caluin**, writing vpon **Iob. Serm.8.**
Caluin.
Cap.12. calleth Dauncing the cheefe mischiefe of
all mischiefes: saying, there be such vnchaste ges-   6570
tures in it, as are nothing els, but inticementes to
whoredome.

 Marlorate vpon **Mathew**, saith: Whosoeuer
hath any care eyther of honesty, sobriety, or
grauitie, haue long since bad **adieu** to all filthy   6575
dauncing.

 No man (saith a certaine Heathen Writer) if
he be sober daunceth, except he be mad.

 Salustius, commending **Sempronia** that re-
Salustius.
nowned Whore, for many goodly gifts, con-   6580
demneth her for her ouer great skil in dauncing:
concluding, that dauncing is the instrument of
lechery.

Cicero.
 Cicero saith: A good man would not daunce
in open assemblies, though he might by it get in-   6585
finite treasure.

 The Councel of **Laodicea** decreed, that it
should not be lawful for any Christian to daunce
at mariages or at any solemne feast.

 In another Councell it was enacted, that no   6590
man should dance at any marriage, nor yet at any
other time.

 The Emperour **Iustinian** decreed, that for no
respect in feastes or assemblies, there should be
any dauncing, for feare of corrupting the behold-   6595
ers, and inticing men to sinne.

 Thus you may see, both Scripture, Councels,

R3ᵛ and Fathers, // holy and prophane, Heathen and
other, euen all in generall, haue detested and ab-

6600 horred this filthy dauncing, as the **quagmire** or
puddle of all abhomination, and therefore, it is
no exercise for any Christians to follow: For it
stirreth vp the motions of the flesh, it induceth
lust, it inferreth Baudry, affoordeth ribaldry,

6605 maintaineth wantonnesse, & ministreth oyle to
the stinking lampe of deceitfull Pride: & **in
summa,** nourisheth a world of wickednes and sin.

Spud. Now that the wickednes of it, is so
manifestly shewed, that no man can deny it, I

6610 pray you shewe me who inuented this noble science, or from whence it sprang.

Philo. Hereof, there be sundry and diuers
opinions: for some hold an opinion (& very likely) that it sprang from the Heathen Idolatrous

6615 Pagans, & Infidels, who hauing offered vp their
Sacrifices and oblations to their false Gods, in
reuerence of them, and for ioy of their so doing,
vsed to daunce, leap, and skip before them. And
this may be prooued by the **Israelits** themselues,

6620 who hauing seen & learned the same practise in
Egypt, feared not to imitate the like in the wild-
ernes of **Horeb.** Some again, suppose that **Pyrrhus** one of **Sybils** Priestes, deuised it in **Creet.**
Others holde that the Priests of **Mars,** who in

6625 **Rome** were had in greate estimation for their
dexterity in dauncing, inuented it. Others thinke
that one **Hiero** a **Truculent** and bloudy Tyrant in
Sicilia, who to set vp his tyrannie the more, inhibited the people to speake one to another, for

6630 feare of insurrections & commotions in his kingdome, was the occasion of the inuenting thereof:
for when the **Sicilians** sawe that they might not
vnder payne of death one speake to another, they

All Writers
both holy &
prophane
against
dancing.

Dancing a
world of sin.

Who inuented
dauncing and
from whome
it sprang

A supposal
who inuēted
dauncing.

R3ᵛ. PH: *Who inuented* D*auncing.*

inuented dauncing, to expresse the inward meaning & intentions of the mind, by outward beckes   6635
& exteriour gestures of the body, which vse afterward grew into custom, & now into nature. But
whatsoeuer men say of it, or from whĕce soeuer
it sprãg, S. **Chrysostome** saith plainly (to whom
I willingly subscribe) that it sprãg from the teates   6640
of the Deuils breast, from whence all mischiefe
els doth flow. Therefore, to conclude, if of the
Egges of a **Cockatrice**, may be made good meat

Vnpossible   for man to eate, & if of the Web of a **Spider**,
that dancing   can be made good cloath for mans body to   6645
should be   weare, then may dancing be good, & an exercise
good.   fit for a Christian man to follow, but not els.
Wherfore, God of his mercy remooue it far from
vs.

    Spud. What say you to Musick, is it not a   6650
laudable science? //   R4

Of Musicke in England:
and how it allureth
to vanitie.

Philo.   6655
I say of Musicke, as **Plato, Aristotle, Galen,** and
many others haue said of it, that it is very ill for
young heades, for a certaine kinde of smooth
sweetnesse in it, alluring the hearers to a certaine

A comparison   kind of **effeminacie**, & **pusillanimitie**, much like   6660
betwixt   vnto Honey: for as Honey & such other sweete
honey and   thinges receiued into the stomacke, doeth delight
musicke.   at the first, but afterwarde maketh the stomacke
queasie, and vnable to receiue meate of hard dis-
gesture. So sweet Musicke, at the first delighteth   6665
the eares, but afterward corrupteth and depraueth
the mind, making it queasie, and inclined to all
licentiousnesse of life whatsoeuer. And right as

R4. PH: *Hurt by Musicke.*

good edges are not sharpened (but dulled) by
6670   whetting vppon soft Stones: So good wittes by
hearing of softe Musicke, are rather dulled then
sharpened, and made apt to all **Wantonnesse** and
Sinne. And hereof is it that Writers affirme
Sappho to haue bene expert in Musicke, and
6675   therefore Whorish.

Wits dulled
by musicke.

  Tirus Maximus saith, **The bringing in of**
Musicke was a cup of poison to all the world.

Authors of
the bringing
in of musick.

  Clytomachus, if he euer heard any talking of
Loue, or playing of **Musicall Instrumentes**,
6680   would run his way and bidde them farewell.

  Plutarchus complayneth of Musicke, and
sayth, **that it doeth rather feminine the minde,**
as prickes vnto vice, then conduce to godlines as
spurres vnto vertue.

6685   **Pithagoras** condemneth them for fooles, and
bequeathes them a Cloake-bagge, that measure
Musicke by sound and eare. Thus you heare the
iudgement of the wise concerning Musicke, nowe
iudge thereof as you list your selfe.

6690   **Spud.** I haue heard it said, (and I thought it
very true) that Musicke doeth delight both man
and beast, reuiueth the Spirits, comforteth the
heart and maketh it apter and readier to the seruice of God.

6695   **Phil.** I graunt Musicke is a good gift of God,
and that it delighteth both man & beast, reuiueth the spirits, comforteth the hart and maketh it
apter to serue God, and therfore did **Dauid** both

Musicke the
good gift
of God.

R4ᵛ vse // Musicke himselfe, and also commend the
6700   vse of it to his posterity, (and being vsed to that
end, for mans priuate recreation, Musicke is very
laudable.) But being vsed in publike assemblies,
and priuat conuenticles, as a Directorie to filthy
dauncing, through the sweet harmony and smooth

Of musick
in publike
assemblies,
and conuenticles.

R4ᵛ. PH: *How musicke is tollerable.*

melody thereof, it estrangeth the minde, stirreth   6705
vp filthy lust, womannisheth the mind, rauisheth
the heart, inflameth concupiscẽce, & bringeth in
vncleannes. But if Musick were vsed openly (as I
haue said) to the praise & glory of God, as our

How musick
were
tollerable
and good

Fathers vsed it, and as was intended by it at the   6710
first, or priuately in a mans secret chamber or
house, for his own solace & comfort, to driue
away the fantasies of idle thoughts, to mitigate
care, sorrow, and such other perturbations and
passions of the minde (the only endes whereto   6715
true Musicke tends) it were very commendable &
lawful. If Musicke were thus vsed, it would comfort man woonderfully, & mooue his heart to
serue God the better: but being vsed as it is, it
corrupteth good minds, maketh them woman-   6720
nish, and inclined to all kind of whordome and
vncleannes.

   Spud. What say you then of Musitions and
Minstrels, who liue only vpon the same art?

   Philo. I think that al good minstrels, sober,   6725
& chast musitions, (speaking of such drunken

The scarsity
of good
Musitions and
Minstrels.

sockets, & baudy **Parasites** as raunge the Countries, riming & singing of vnclean, corrupt and
filthy songs in tauernes, Alehouses, Innes, &
other publike assemblies) may dance the wilde   6730
Moris through a needles eye. For how should
they beare chast minds, seeing that their exercise
is the pathway to all Baudry & filthines? There is
no ship so laden with merchandize, as their
heads are pestred with al kind of baudy songs,   6735

The
marchandize of
Minstrels, and
Musitions.

filthy Ballades and scuruy rymes, seruing for euery purpose and for euery company.

   For proofe whereof, who bee baudier knaues
then they? Who vncleaner then they? Who more
licentious, and looser minded then they? Who   6740
more incontinent then they? And brieflie, who
more inclined to all kinde of insolency and leud-
nes then they? Wherfore, if you would haue your

sonne soft, womannish, vncleane, smooth mouth-
6745   ed, affected to baudry, scurrility, filthy rimes, and
vnseemly talking: briefly, if you wold haue him,
as it were transnatured into a woman, or worse,
& inclined to all kind of whordome and abhomination, set him to dancing schoole, & to learne
6750   Musicke, and then shall you not faile of your
S1   purpose. And if you would haue your // daughter
whorish, baudy and vncleane, and a filthy speak-
er, & such like, bring her vp in musicke and
dauncing, & my life for yours, you haue wonne
6755   the goale. And yet notwithstanding, it were better (in respect of the accompt of the world) to be
a **Piper** or a **baudy Minstrel**, then a **diuine**, for
the one is loued for his **Ribauldry**, the other
hated for his grauity, wisdome, & sobriety. Euery
6760   Towne, citie, and country, is full of these **Minstrels** to pipe vp a daunce to the Deuill, but of
good **Diuines**, so few there be, that small skil in
Arithmeticke will suffice to number them.
But some of them will reply and say, what
6765   sir? we haue licences from Iustices of the Peace
to **Pipe**, and vse our **Minstrelsie** to our best commoditie? Cursed be those licences, which license
any man to get his liuing with the destruction of
many thousands. But haue you a license from the
6770   Arch-Iustice Christ Iesus? If you haue so, you
may be glad, if you haue not (for the word of
God is against your vngodly exercises, and condemneth them to hell) then may you as **Rogues,
extrauagantes,** & **Straglers**, be arrested of the
6775   high Iustice Christ Iesus, notwithstanding your
pretensed **Licenses** of earthly men. Then who
shall stand betwixt you and the Iustice of God at
the day of iudgment? who shall excuse you, for
drawing so many thousands to hell? Shal the Ius-

The
wickednes of
Musitions and
Minstrels.

How to haue
children
learned in all
wickednes.

The scarcitie
of Diuines.

Licences
granted to
Musitions &
Minstrels to
exercise their
mystery or
facultie of
mischiefe.

S1. PH: *Licences for Minstrels.*

No licences
to do hurte
withall are to
be graunted

tices of peace? shal their Licenses? Oh no. It wil   6780
not goe for payment at that day: For, neither
ought they to graunt any licenses to any to do
hurt withall, neither (if they would) ought any to
take them.

Giue ouer therefore your occupations, you **Pi-**   6785
pers, you **Fidlers,** you **Minstrels,** and you **Musi-**
tions, you **Drummers,** you **Tabretters** you **Flu-**
ters, & al other of that wicked brood, for the

A Caueat to
Musitions,
Minstrels &
all others of
that stampe.

bloud of al those whom you draw to destruction
through your wicked example and intising al-   6790
lurements, shall be poured vpon your heades, at
the day of Iudgment: but hereof ynough, & per-
chance more then wil please their daintie
humours.

Spud. Is it not lawful vpon the Sabboth day   6795
to play at Dice, Cards, Tables, Boules, Tennise,
& such other pleasant exercises, wherein man
taketh pleasure and delight?

Cardes, Dice, Tables, Tennise,
Boules, and other ex-   6800
Phil.   *ercises, vsed vnlawfully in* **E**ngland.

These be no exercises for any Christian man to
follow any day at al, much lesse vpon the Sabboth day, which the Lord wold haue // to be   S1ᵛ

Exercises
vnlawful
vpon the
Sabboth day.

consecrate to himself & to be spent in holy and   6805
godly exercises, according to his wil. As for
Cards, dice, tables, boules, tennisse, and such
like, they are **Furta officiosa,** a certain kind of
smooth, deceiptfull & sleighty **theft,** whereby
many a one is spoyled of all that euer he hath,   6810

Furta
officiosa.

somtimes of his life withal, yea, of body and
soule for euer: And yet (more is the pity) these
be the only exercises vsed in euery mans house, al
the yeare through: but especially in Christmas

S1ᵛ. PH: *All wicked games vsed in Christmasse.*

6815   time there is nothing els vsed but **Cards, Dice,**
    Tables, masking, mumming, bouling, & such
    like fooleries. And the reason is, for that they
    thinke they haue a Commission & prerogatiue
    that time, to do what they list, & to follow what
6820   vanity they will. But (alas) do they thinke that
    they ar priuiledged at that time to do euil? the
    holier the time is (if one time were holier then
    another, as it is not) the holier ought their exer-
    cises to be. Can time dispence with thẽ, or giue
6825   thẽ liberty to sin? No, no: **the soule which sin-**
    neth shal die, at what time soeuer it offendeth.
    But what will they say? Is it not Christmas? must
    we not be merry? Trueth it is, we ought both
    then, & at all times besides to be merie in the
6830   Lord, but not otherwise, not to swill and gull in
    more then will suffice nature, nor to lauish forth
    more at that time, then at any other times. But
    the true celebration of the feast of **Christmas** is,
    to **meditate** (and as it were to **ruminate** in the
6835   secrete cogitations of our mindes) vpon the incar-
    nation and birth of Iesus Christ, God and man:
    not only at that time, but all the times and daies
    of our life, & to shew our selues thankful to his
    blessed maiesty for the same. Notwithstanding,
6840   who knoweth not, that more mischief is that
    time committed then in all the yeare besides?
    what **masking** and **mumming,** wherby robbery,
    whoredome, and sometime murther is com-
    mitted: what **Dicing** and **Carding,** what eating &
6845   drinking, what banquetting and feasting is then
    vsed, more then in all the yeare besides? to the
    great dishonour of God, and impouerishing of
    the Realme.

       Spud. Is it not lawfull for one Christian to
6850   play with another at any kind of game, or to win
    his money, if he can?

       Phil. To play at **Tables, cards, Dice, Boules,**
    or the like (though a good Christian man wil not

Marginal notes:

All wicked games vsed in Christmas time.

No time priuiledgeth a man to sin.

The true keeping of Christmas.

Wickednes in Christmas.

Vnlawful for one christian to plaie with another to win his money.

so idly, and vainly spend his golden dayes) one
Christian with another, for their priuate recrea-   6855
tions, after some oppresion of studie, to driue
away fantasies, or melancholy passions, & such
like, I doubt not, but they may, vsing it moderately // with intermission, and in the feare of   S2
God? But to play for lucre of Gaine, and for de-   6860
sire only of his brothers substance (rather then
for any other cause) it is not at any hand lawfull,
nor to be suffered.

  For as it is not lawful to rob, steal, & purloin
by deceit, or sleight so is it not lawfull to get thy   6865
Gaming brothers goods from him, by carding, dicing, tab-
worse then ling, bowling, or any other kind of theft, for
open theft. these Games are no better: nay, worser then open
theft, for open theft euery man can beware of,
but this being a crafty politick theft, & cõmonly   6870
done vnder pretence of friendship, few or none at
al can beware of it. The Commandement saith,
Thou shalt not couet nor desire any thing that
belongeth to thy neighbour. Now, it is manifest,
that those that play for money, not only couet   6875
their Brothers money, but also vse craft, falshood,
and deceit, to winne the same.

  The Apostle forbiddeth vs to vse deceit in
bargaining, in buying, or selling: Much lesse then
ought we to vse deceit in gaming.   6880

  Our Sauiour Christ biddeth euery man, doe
A rule to to another, as hee wold another shuld do vnto
restrain him. Which rule, if it were duly obserued, were
vnlawful sufficient to withdraw men both from all kinde
gaming. of gaming, & also from al kind of vniust dealing: 6885
For, as thou woldest not that another man shuld
win thy mony, so thou oughtest not to desire the
winning of his: for thou must do as thou woldest
be done by.

S2. PH: *Gaming houses.*

6890   **Spud.** If gaming for money be so vnlawfull,
wherfore are there gaming houses, & places appointed for maintenance of the same?

Phil. That excuseth not the fault, but **aggrau-
ateth** it rather. And truly great pitie it is, that
6895   these Brothel houses (for so I call all gaming   Gaming
houses) are suffered as they be. For, are they not   houses,
the very **Seminaries** and **nurseries** of all kind of   with their
abhomination, whatsoeuer heart can thinke, or   wickednes.
tongue expresse? And therefore, I maruell that
6900   those, who keepe and maintaine these gaming
houses, can neuer haue light hearts, or once look
vp towards heauen, that not only suffer this
manifest theft in their houses (for gaming is no
better) but also maintain and vphold the same.

6905   The Apostle saith: Not only they that do
euil, **digni sunt morte, Are worthy of death,** but
also, **qui cõsentiunt facientibus, those who consent to them that doe it.** Call to minde then
what euilles come of this wicked exercise I be-
6910   seech you. For doth not swearing, tearing, and
blaspheming the name of God? Doeth not stinking Whoredome, Theft, Robbery, Deceit, Fraud,
S2ᵛ   Cosonage, fighting, // Quarrelling, & sometime
murder? Doth not Pride, rapine, drunkennes,
6915   beggery: and in fine, a shameful end follow it, as
the shadow doth follow the body? Wherfore, I
wil not doubt to call these **Gaming houses** the
slaughter houses, the **shambles,** or **Blockhouses
of the Deuil,** wherein he buthereth Christian
6920   mens soules infinite wayes, God knoweth, the
Lord suppresse them.

Spud. Were there euer any lawes made
against the inordinate abuse hereof, or haue the   Lawes and
godly in any age misliked it?   sanctions

S2ᵛ. PH: *Lawes against Gaming.*

divulgate
against
gaming.

Phil. In all ages & times, both the godly   6925
sober Christians haue detested it, and wholsome
lawes haue been published against it.

Octauius Augustus, was greatly reproched of
the Writers of his time, for his great delight in
gaming, notwithstanding, his manifolde vertues   6930
besides.

Cicero obiected to **Marcus Antonius,** his often gaming, as a note of infamie vnto him.

The infamie
purchased by
gaming.

The noble **Lacedemonians** sent their Ambassadors to **Corinth,** to conclude a peace, who   6935
cōming thither, & finding the people playing at
Dice and Cardes, & vnthriftie games, returned
back againe (**infecta pace**) their peace vncon-
cluded, saying: **It should neuer bee reported,**
that they would ioine in league with Dice play-   6940
ers and Gamesters. The same **Lacedemonians**
sent to **Demetrius,** in derision of his Dice playing, a paire of Dice of gold.

Sir **Thomas Eliot** (that worthy Knight) in his
booke of Gouernance, asketh: **Who wil not**   6945
thinke him a light man, of smal credit, disso-
lute, remisse, and vaine, that is a Dice player or
Gamester?

Publius saith, **Quantò peritior est Aleator in**
sua arte, tanto nequior est & vita & moribus.   6950
How much cunninger a man is in gaming, and
Diceplaying, so much corrupter he is both in
life & maners. *Iustinian* made a law that none
should play at Dice, nor Cardes for no cause,
neither priuately nor openly.   6955

Alexander Seuerus, banished al gamesters out
of his dominions. And if any were found playing,
their goods wer confiscate, and they counted as
mad men euer after, neuer trusted, nor esteemed
of any.   6960

Lodouicus, ordeined that all Gamesters
should depart out of his land, for feare of corrupting of others.

King **Richard** the second, forbad al kind of
6965   gaming, & namely dice playing. King **Henrie** the
fourth ordained, that euery dice player shuld be
imprisoned six dayes, for euery seuerall time he
offended in gaming. //

S3   King **Edward** the fourth ordained, who so
6970   kept gaming houses, shuld suffer imprisonmẽt
three yeeres, & forfeit twenty pound, & the players to be imprisoned two yeares, and forfeit ten
pound.

King **Henry** the seuenth ordained, that euery
6975   Diceplayer shuld be imprisoned all aday, & the
keeper of the dicing house, to forfeit for euery
offence sixe shillings eight pence, and to be
bound by **Recognizaunce** to good behauiour.

King **Henry** the eight ordained, that euery
6980   one that kept dicing houses, should forfeit fourty
shillings, and the players to forfeite sixe shillings
eight pence: with many other good lawes and
statutes, set foorth against this raging abuse of
gaming, which, least I might seeme tedious, I
6985   omit, beseeching the Lorde to root vp, & supplant these, & al other stumbling blocks in his
church & common wealth.

Spud. As I remember, in the Catalogue of
abuses before, you sayd, the Sabboth day was
6990   prophaned by Bear-baiting, Cockfighting, hawking, hunting, keeping of Faires, Courts, & Markets vpon the said day. Is it not lawful then to
follow these exercises vpon the Sabboth day
neither?

*Punishment
for gaming*

*The penaltie
for those that
keep gaming
houses.*

S3. PH: *Punishment for gaming*

Bear-baiting, and other exercises, vsed vnlawfully
vpon the Sabboth day in England.

Phil.

These Heathnish exercises vpon the Sabboth day,
which the Lord would haue consecrated to his
seruice, for the glory of his name, & our spirituall cōfort, are not in any respect tollerable, or to
be suffered. For the bayting of a Beare, besides
that it is a filthy, stinking, & lothsome game, is
it not a perillous exercise? wherin a man is in
danger of his life euery minute of an houre?
which thing though it were not so, yet what
exercise is this meete for any Christian? what
Christian heart can take pleasure to see one
poore beast to rent, teare, and kill another, and
all for his foolish pleasure? And although they be
bloudy beasts to mankind, & seeke his destruction, yet we are not to abuse them, for his sake
who made them, & whose creatures they are. For
notwithstanding that they be euill to vs, and
thirst after our bloud, yet are they good creatures
in their owne nature and kind, and made to set

**No creature
to be abused**

foorth the glory, power, and magnificence of our
God, and for our vse, & therfore for his sake we
ought not to abuse them. It is a common saying
amōgst al men, borrowed // from the French:
Qui aime Iean, aime son chien, that is. **Loue
me, loue my Dog**: So loue God, loue his
creatures.

If any should abuse but the Dog of another
mans, would not he who oweth the Dog, think

**God is
abused, when
his creatures
are misused.**

that the abuse done to his dog **resulteth** to himselfe? And shal we abuse the creatures of God,
yea, take pleasure in abusing them, & yet think
that the contumely done to them, redoundeth

6995

7000

7005

7010

7015

7020
S3ᵛ

7025

7030

S3ᵛ. PH: *A woful crie at* Paris *garden.*

not to him who made them? But admit it were
graunted that it were lawful to abuse the good
creatures of God, yet is it not lawful for vs to
spend our **golden yeares** in such idle & vaine
7035 exercises dayly & hourly as we doe. And some,
who take themselues for no small **fooles**, are so
far assotted, that they will not stick to keep a
dozen or a score of great Mastiues, to their no
small charges, for the maintenance of this goodly
7040 game (forsooth) and will not make any bones of
twenty, fourty, yea an hundred pound at once to
hazard at a beyt: with fight Dog, fight Beare, the
Deuil part al. And to be plaine, I think the Deuil
is master of the game, Bearward and al. A goodly
7045 pastime (forsooth) worthy of commendation, &
wel fitting these Gentlemen of such reputation.
But how much the Lord is offended for the prophanation of his Sabboth by such vnsauory exercises, his heauenly Maiesty of late hath reueiled,
7050 pouring foorth his heauy wrath, his fearful iudgment, and dreadfull vengeance vppon the beholders of these vanities, as hereafter followeth.

Keeping of
Mastiues and
bandogs.

A fearfull example of God his
iudgment vpon the
7055 *Prophaners of the Sabboth day.*

Vpon the thirteenth day of **Ianuary**, being the
Sabboth day, **Anno.1583.** there resorted an infinite number of people men, women, and children,
of each sort to those infamous places, where
7060 these wicked exercises are vsually practised (for
they haue their **Courts, Gardens,** and **Yards** for
the same purpose) & being al come together, and
mounted aloft vpon their **Scaffolds,** and **galleries,**
and in middest of all their iolitie and pastime, al
7065 the whole building (not one sticke standing) fell
downe with a most woonderful and fearfull confusion. So, that either two or three hundred men,
women & children (whereof seuen were killed

dead) were some wounded, some lamed, and othersome bruised and crushed, almost to death.   7070
Some had their brains dasht out, some their
heads al to quasht, some their legges broken,
some their armes, some their backes, some their
// shoulders, some one hurt, some another: so,   S4
that you should haue heard a wofull crie, euen   7075
pearcing the Skies, parentes bewayling their children: Children their louing parents: wiues their
husbands and Husbands their wiues, marueilous
to haue heard. This woful spectacle and heauie
iudgement, pitifull to heare of, but most rufull to   7080
beholde, the Lord sent downe from Heauen, to
shewe vnto the whole world how grieuously he is
offended with those that spend his **Sabboth** in
such wicked exercises, in the meane time leauing
his temple desolate & empty. God graunt all   7085
men may take warning hereby to shun the same,
for fear of like or sharper iudgmẽt to come.

A feareful Iudgment of God,
shewed at the Theaters.

The like iudgment in effect did the Lord shewe   7090
vnto them a litle before, being assembled at their
Theaters, to see their baudy **Enterludes,** and
other fooleries there practised. For he caused the

A woful   earth mightily to shake and quauer, as though al
spectacle.   wold haue fallen downe: whereat the people sore   7095
amazed, some leapt downe from the top of the
Turrets, pinacles, & **towers,** where they stood, to
the groũd, whereby some had their legges broke,
some their armes, some their backs, some hurt
one where, some another where, & many sore   7100
crusht and bruised: but not any, but they went
away sore affraid, & wounded in conscience. And
yet can neither the one, nor the other, fray thẽ

S4. PH: *Cockefighting in England.*

7105 from these deuillish exercises, vntil the Lorde
consume them all in his wrath: which God forbid. The Lord of his mercy, open the eies of the
Magistrates, to pluck downe these places of
abuse, that God may be honored, and their consciences discharged.

7110 **Cockfighting vpon the Sabboth day
in England.**
Besides these exercises, they flock thick & threefold to the **Cockfights**, an exercise nothing to the
rest, where nothing is vsed but swearing, for-
7115 swearing, deceit, fraud, collusion, cosenage,
scolding railing, cōuitious talking, fighting,
brawling, quarrelling, drinking whoring, & which
is worst of al, robbing one another of their
goods, & that not by direct, but indirect means
7120 & attēpts. And yet to blanch and set out these
mischiefs withall (as though they were vertues)
they haue their appointed dayes and set houres,
when these deuilries must be exercised. They
haue houses erected to that purpose, Flags and
7125 Ensignes hanged out, to giue notice of it to
others, and proclamation goes out, to proclaim
the same, to the end that many may come to the
celebration of this solemne feast of mischiefe.

Hauking and hunting vpon the Sabboth day
7130 **in England. //**
S4ᵛ And as for hawking and hunting vppon the Sabboth, it is an exercise vpon that day, no lesse vnlawfull then the other. For no man ought to
spend any day of his life, much lesse euery day,
7135 as many doe in such vaine and idle pastimes.
And therfore, let Gentlemen take heed, for be
sure, accomptes must be giuen at the day of

cockfighting
vpon the
sabboth day.

Appointed
times for
exercise of
deuilries.

Hawking &
hunting vpō
the Sabboth.

No more
libertie
giuen to

one, thē to
another, for
mispending
of their
goods.

Iudgement of euery minute of time, both howe
they haue spent it and in what exercises. And let
them bee sure, no more liberty is giuen them, to   7140
mispend an houre, or one iote of the Lord his
goods, then is giuen to the poorest, and meanest
person that liueth vpon the face of the earth. I
neuer reade of any in the volume of the sacred
Scriptures that was a good man, and a hunter.   7145

No good
Hunters in
scripture.

    Esau, was a great hunter, but a reprobate. **Is-
maell**, a great hunter, but a miscreant. **Nimrod**,
a great Hunter, but yet an abiect, & a vessel of
wrath. This I speake not to condemne Hawking
and hunting altogether, being vsed for recreation   7150
now and then, but against the continual vse
thereof dayly, hourely, weekely, yearely, yea al the
times of their life, without intermission. And
such a felicity haue some in it, as they make it al

Cost
bestowed in
hawkes and
dogs.

their ioy, bestowing more vpō hawks and hounds,   7155
and a sort of idle lubbers to follow them, in one
yeare, then they will giue to the poore members
of Christ Iesus in seuen years, peraduentur in all
the dayes of their life. So long as man in **Paradise** persisted in innocency, all beastes whatso-   7160
euer, were obedient to him, & came and hum-
bled themselues before him. But euer since his

Whē al
beasts were
obediēt
to man and
wherefore
they rebell.

fall, they haue fled from him, and disobeyed him,
because of his sin: that seeing he disobeyed the
Lorde, they againe disobey him. For, so long as   7165
man obeyed God, so long they obeyed him: but
so soon as man disobeyed God, they disobeyed
him, and became enemies to him, as it were
seeking to reuenge that iniurie which man had
done to God, in disobeying his lawes. Wherfore   7170
the cause why all beasts do fly frō vs, & are be-
com enemies vnto vs, is our disobediēce to the
Lord, which we are rather to sorrow for, thē to
hunt after their deaths by the shedding of their
bloud. If necessitie or want of other meats in-   7175
forceth vs to seek after their liues, it is lawful to

vse them in the feare of God, with thankes to his
Name: but for our pastimes, and vaine pleasures
sake, we are not in any wise to spoyle or hurt
7180 them.

Is he a Christian man, or not rather a cruel
Tartarian, that delighteth in bloud? Is hee a
Christian, that spendeth all his life in wanton
pleasures, and pleasaunt delightes? Is he a Chris-
T1 tian that // buyeth vp the Corne of the poore,
turning it into bread (as manie do) to feed dogs
for his pleasure? Is he a Christian, that liueth to
the hurt of his neighbour, in treading & breaking
downe his hedges, in casting open his gates, in
7190 trampling of his corne, & otherwise annoying
him, as hunters do? Wherfore God giue thẽ
grace to see to it, & to amend it betimes, ere it
be too late, for they know, **Mora trahit pericu-**
lum, *Delay bringeth daunger.* Let vs not defer to
7195 leaue euil, and to do good, least the wrath of the
Lord be kindled against vs, & consume vs from
the vpper face of the earth.

Markets, Faires, Courtes, and
Leetes vpon the Sabboth

7200 **Spud.** 　　　*day, in* England.
What say you to keeping of Markets, Faires,
Courtes and Leetes vpon the Sabboth day?
Thinke you it is not lawfull to vse the same vpon
that day?
7205 　　**Philo.** No truly: for can we serue God and
the Deuil togither, can we carry to God & ferrie
to the Deuil, can we serue two masters, & neither offend the one, nor displease the other? **Can**
we serue God & Mammon? Can we please God
7210 and the worlde, both at one time? The Lord wil
not be serued by peecemeale, for eyther he wil

Marginal notes:

For pleasure sake only no man ought to abuse anie of the creatures of God

Hurt by hunting to poore men.

Not lawful to keepe Courts Leets Markets, and Faires, vpon the Sabboth day,

---

T1. PH: *Faires on the Sabboth day.*

haue the whole man, or els none. For saith he,
Thou shalt loue the Lord thy God with all thy
soule, with all thy minde, with all thy power,
with all thy strength, and so foorth, or els with   7215
none at all. Then, seeing that we are to giue ouer
our selues, so wholly and totally to the seruice of
God: all the dayes of our life, but especially vpon
the Sabboth day, being consecrate to that end,
we may not intermeddle with these prophane   7220
exercises vpon that day. For, it is more then
manifest that these Faires, Markets, Courts, &
Leetes vpon the Sabboth day, are not only a hin-
drance vnto vs, in the seruice of God, & an
abuse of the Sabboth, but also leade vs the path-   7225
way to hell. For what cousonage is not there
practised? What falshood, deceit, and fraud is not
there exercised? what dissimulation in bargaining? What setting foorth counterfeit & deceiuable wares is not there vsed? What lying, swear-   7230
ing, forswearing, drunkennesse, whordom, theft,
& sometimes murther, either there, or by the
way thither, is not euery where committed? In
Courts & Leets, what enuy, malice and hatred is
nourished? What Expostulation, rayling scolding,   7235
periuring, & reperiuring is maintained? What
oppression of the poore? what fauouring of the
rich? what iniustice, and indirect // dealing?   T1ᵛ
What bribing, deceiuing, what polling & pilling
is there practised? It wold make a Christian heart   7240
to bleed in beholding it. And yet notwithstanding, we must haue these goodly **Pageants** played
vpon the Sabboth day (in a **wanion**) because
there are no mo dayes in the week. And hereby
it commeth to passe that the Sabboth is pro-   7245
phaned, Gods word contemned, his Commande-
ments disanulled, his **Sacraments conculcate,** his

Abuse of the
Sabboth by
Faires and
Markets

The euill in
Faires and
Markets.

The euils
in Courts
and leets
practised.

ordinances neglected, & in **summa**, his bloud
trode vnder feet, and all mischief maintained.

7250   **Playing at Footbal vpon the**

              Sabboth and other dayes

Spud.   *in England.*

Is the playing at Football, reading of merry
bookes, and such like delectations, a violation or
7255   **prophanation** of the sabboth day?

     Philo. Any exercise, which withdraweth vs
from godlinesse, eyther vpon the Sabboth day, or
any other day els, is wicked & to be forbidden.
Now, who is so grosly blind, that seeth not, that
7260   these aforesaid exercises not only withdraw vs
from godlines and vertue but also hale and allure
vs to wickednes and sin: for as concerning Footeball playing, I protest vnto you, it may rather bee
called a friendly kind of fight, then a play or rec-
7265   reation. A bloudy and murthering practise, then
a fellowly sport or pastime. For, doth not euery
one ly in wayt for his aduersary, seeking to ouerthrow him, and to picke him on his nose, though
it be vpon hard stones, in ditch or dale, in valley
7270   or hole, or what place soeuer it be, he careth not,
so hee may haue him downe. And he that can
serue the most of this fashion he is counted the
only fellow, & who but he? So that by this
means, sometimes their necks are broken, some-
7275   tymes their backes, somtimes their legs, sometime their armes, somtime one part thrust out of
ioint, somtime another sometimes their noses
gush out with blood, sometimes their eyes start
out of their heads, & sometimes hurt in one
7280   place, somtimes in another. But who so euer
scapeth away the best, goeth not **scotfree**, but is
either sore crushed and bruised, so as he dyeth of
it, or els scapeth very hardly: And no maruel, for
they haue sleights to meet one betwixt two, to
7285   dash him against the heart with their elbowes, to

Playing at
footbal.

Football a
friendly kind
of fight.

Hurt by Foot
ball playing.

hit him vnder the short ribbes with their griped
fists, and with their knees to catch him vpon the
hip, and to picke him on his necke, with an hundred such murdering deuises: and hereof groweth
enuy, malice, rancour, chollour, hatred displeas-   7290
Football   **ur, enmity,** and what not els? // And sometimes,   T2
playing a   **fighting, brawling, contention, quarrel picking,**
murthering   **murther, homicide, and great effusion of bloud,**
plaie.   as experience dayly teacheth. Is this murthering
play now an exercise for the Sabboth day? Is this   7295
a Christian dealing, for one brother to maime
and hurt another, and that vpon prepensed malice, or set purpose? Is this to doe to another, as
we would wish another to doe to vs. God make
vs more carefull ouer the bodies of our brethren.   7300

Reading of wicked bookes in E*ngland.*

Reading of   And as for reading of wicked bookes, they are vt-
wicked   terly vnlawful, not only to be read, but once to be
bookes.   named, and that not only vpon the Saboth day,
but also vpon any other day, as which tend to the   7305
dishonor of God, deprauation of good manners,
and corruption of Christian soules. For as corrupt
meats doe annoy the stomacke, and infect the
The euil   body, so the reading of wicked and vngodly
comming by   bookes (which are to the mind, as meate is to the   7310
reading   body) infect the soule, and corrupt the minde,
euil books.   hayling it to destruction, if the great mercy of
God be not present.
And yet notwithstanding, whosoeuer will set
pen to paper now a dayes, how vnhonest soeuer,   7315
or vnseemly of Christian eares, his argument be,
is permited to goe forward, and his work **plausi-**
bly receiued, friendly **licensed,** and gladly **im-**
printed, without any prohibition or contradiction
at all: wherby it is grown to this issue, that books   7320

T2. PH: *Reading of wicked Bookes*

and **pamphlets** of **scurrility** and **bawdry** are better
esteemed and more vendible, then the godliest
and sagest books that be: But if it be a godly
treatise, reproouing vice and teaching vertue,
7325   away with it, for no man almost, though they
make a flourish of vertue & godlines, will buy it,
nor (which is lesse) so much as once touch it.
This maketh the Bible, that blessed book of
God, to be so litle estemed. That renowmed
7330   **Book of Martyrs**, made by that famous Father,
and excellent Instrument in God his Church,
Maister **Iohn Foxe**, so little to be accepted, and
all other good Bookes little or nothing reuerenced, whilest other toyes, fantasies, and bable-
7335   ries, whereof the world is ful, are suffred to be
printed. These prophane **Scheduls, sacrilegious
Libels,** and **Hethnicall pamphlets** of toyes and
bableries, (the Authours whereof may challenge
no small reward at the hands of the deuil for in-
7340   uẽting the same) corrupt mens mindes, peruert
good wits, allure to Bawdry, induce to whor-
T2ᵛ   dome, // suppresse vertue & erect vice: which
thing how shuld it be otherwise, for are they not
inuented & excogitate by **Belzebub**, written by
7345   **Lucifer**, licensed by **Pluto**, printed by **Cerberus**,
& set abroch to sale by the **infernal Furies** themselues, to the poysoning of the whole world? But
let the inuenters, the Licensers, the Printers, &
the sellers of these vaine toyes and more then
7350   **Hethnical impieties** take heed, for the bloud of
al those which perish or take hurt through these
wicked books, shall be poured vpon their heads
at the day of iudgment, and be required at their
hands.
7355   **Spud.** I pray you how might all these enor-

The hurt
that wicked
bookes bring

---

mities, & abuses be reformed? For, it is to small
purpose to shew the abuses, except you shew
withall how they might be amended.

Philo. By putting in practise & executing
those good lawes, and godly statutes, which haue   7360
been heretofore, & dayly are set forth and established, as God be thanked, there are many: the
want of the due execution wherof, is the cause of
all these mischiefs, which both rage and raigne
amongst vs.   7365

Spud. What is the cause why these lawes are
not executed, as they ought to be?

Philo. Truly I cannot tell, except it be thorow
the negligence and corruption of the inferiour
Magistrates: or els perhaps (which thing happen-   7370
eth now & then) for mony they are bought out,
disfranchized, and **dispensed** withal, for as the
saying is, **Pecunia omnia potest. Money can do
all things.** And yet notwithstanding, shall it be
done inuisibly in a **cloud** (vnder **benedicite** I   7375
speak it) the Prince being borne in hand that the
same are duly executed. This fault is the corruption of those that are put in trust to see them
executed (as I haue told you) and notwithstand-
ing do not.   7380

Spud. This is a great abuse doubtlesse, and
worthy of great punishment.

Philo. It is so truly, for if they be good lawes,
tending to the glorie of God, the publike weale
of the Cuntrey, and correction of vice, it is great   7385
pity that mony shuld buy thẽ out. For what is
that els, but to sell vertue for lucre: Godlines for
drosse, yea, mens souls for corruptible money?
Therfore, those that sel them, are not onely traitors to God, to their Prince & country, but are   7390
also the Deuils marchants, to ferry the bodies
and soules of Christians as much as lieth in thẽ,
ouer the sea of this world to the **Stigian** floud of

Why the
lawes are not
executed as
they ought
to be.

T3   hel, burning // with fire and brimston for euer.
7395   And those that buy them are Traitors to God,
        their Prince & cuntry also. For if the lawes were
        at the first good (as God be praised the most of
        the lawes in Englãd be) why should they be
        bought out for money, and if they were euill why
7400   were they published, but had rather bene buried
        in the womb of their mother, before they had
        euer seene the light. And why were lawes consti-
        tute, but to be executed? Els it were as good to
        haue no lawes at all (the people liuing orderly) as
7405   to haue good lawes, and them not executed.

        The Prince ordeining a law, may lawfully re-
        peale & annul the same again, vpon special
        causes and considerations, but no inferiour Mag-
        istrate or subiect whatsoeuer, may stop the course
7410   of any lawe made by the prince, without daunger
        of damnation to his soule, as the word of God
        beareth witnesse. And therefore, woe be to those
        men, that wil not execute the sentence of the
        law, being so godly, and so Christian as they bee
7415   in England, vpon malefactors and offenders.
        Verily, they are as guilty of their bloud before
        God, as euer was Iudas of the death of Christ
        Iesus.

        Spud. Seeing it is so, that all flesh hath cor-
7420   rupted his way before the face of God, and that
        there is such abhomination amongst thẽ, I am
        perswaded that the daie of Iudgment is not far
        off. For when iniquitie shall haue filled vp his
        measure, then shall the end of all things appeare,
7425   as Christ witnesseth in his Euangely.

        Philo. The day of the Lord can not be far of,
        that is most certain: For what wonderfull strange
        miracles, fearful signes, and dreadful tokens hath
        he sent of late dayes, as Preachers & foretellers

They that buy
or sel lawes
for mony are
traitors to
God.

None may stai
the course of
the lawes, but
the prince.

The wonderful
signes and

T3. PH: *Lawes not executed.*

tokens which
the Lord hath
sent to warne
vs of the day
of iudgment

of his wrath due vnto vs, for our impenitencie &   7430
wickednes of life? Hath he not caused the earth
to tremble and quake? the same earth to remooue
from place to place? the seas and waters to roare,
swell and burst out and ouerflow their banks, to
the destruction of many thousands? Hath he not   7435
caused the Elements and Skies, to send foorth
flashing fire? To raine downe Wheat, a wonderfull thing as euer was hard, & the like? Hath he
not caused wonderful Eclipses in the Sun &
Moone, with most dreadful Coniunctions of   7440
Stars, & Planets, as the like this thousand yeares,
hath not been seene or heard of? Haue not the
clouds distilled down aboundāce of rain & sho-
ures with all kind of vnseasonable weather, to the
destroying (almost) of al things vpon the earth?   7445
Haue we not seen Comets, blasing stars, // firy   T3ᵛ
Drakes, men fighting in the aire, most fearfull to
behold? Hath not dame **Nature** her selfe denied
vnto vs her operation, in sending forth **abortiues**,
vntimely births, vgglesom **Monsters**, and fearfull   7450
mishapen creatures both in man & beast. So,
that it seemeth, all the creatures of God are an-
gry with vs, and threaten vs with destruction, and
yet are we nothing at al amended: (alas) what
shal become of vs? Remēber we not there is a   7455
God that shal iudge vs righteously? that there is
a Deuil, who shal torment vs after this life
vnspeakably, if we repent not? At that day, the
wicked shal find that there is a materiall Hell, a
place of all kinds of tortures, wherin they shal   7460
bee punished in fire and Brimstone, amongst the
terrible company of vgglesome deuils world without ende, how light soeuer they make account of
it in this world. For some such ther be, that
when they heare mention of hel, or of the paines   7465

T3ᵛ. PH: *Gods warnings, late shewed.*

therof in the other world, they make a mock of
it, thinking they be but metaphoricall speaches,
only spoken to terrifie vs withall, and not otherwise. But certaine it is, as there is a God, that
7470   will rewarde his children, so there is a Deuill that
will **remunerate** his seruaunts: And as there is a
Heauen, a materiall place of perfect ioy prepared
for the Godly, so there is a Hell, a materiall   A materiall
place of punishment for the wicked and repro-   hel after
7475   bate, prepared for the Deuill and his Angels, or   this life.
els the word of God is in no wise to be credited:
which blasphemie, once to think of, God keep all
his children from.

    Spud. But they will easily auoyd this, for they
7480   say, it is written **At what time so euer a sinner
doth repent him of his sinne, I will put all his
wickednes out of my remembrance, saith the
Lord.** So that if they may haue three words at
the last, they wil wish no more. What think you
7485   of these fellowes?

    Philo. I think them no men but deuils, no
Christiãs, but worse then either **Turks** or **Iewes,**
or any other **infidels** whatsoeuer, and more to be
auoyded then the poyson of a **Serpent**: for the
7490   one slayeth but the body, but the other both
body and soule for euer. Wherfore, let euery
good christian man take heed of thẽ, & auoid
thẽ. For it is truly said, **cum bonis bonus eris, &
cum peruersis peruerteris,** *with the good thou*
7495   *shalt learn good, but with the wicked thou shalt be
peruerted.*

    Spud. Do you think then, that, that cannot
be a true repentãce which is deferred to the last
gaspe?

7500   **Philo.** No truly: For true repentance must
T4   spring out of a liuely // faith, with an inward

T4. PH: *Who are true repentantes.*

No true
repentance
which is
deferred to
the last
gaspe.

Two maner of
repentãces
a false
repentance,
and a true
repentance.

Euery light
affection
is no true
repentance.

lothing, & detesting of sin. But this deferred repentance springeth not of faith, but rather of the
feare of death which he seeth imminent before
his eyes, of the grief & tediousnes of paine, of   7505
the horrour of hell, & feare of God his **ineuitable**
iudgmẽt, which he knoweth now he must needes
abide: & therfore, this can be no true repentance:
For, there are two maner of repentances, the one
a true repentãce to life, the other a false repen-   7510
tance to death: as we may see by **Iudas**, who is
said to haue repẽted, & which is more to haue
confessed his fault, & which is most of all, to
haue made restitution, & yet was it a false repentance: and why? because it sprang not out of true   7515
faith, but as before. **Peter repented & wept bit-**
terly, and was saued therby, though he neither
made confession, nor satisfaction, & why? because it sprang of a true and liuely faith. So these
fellowes may say they repent, but except it be a   7520
true repentance springing of faith, it can serue
them no more to life, then the pretenced repentãce of **Iudas** did serue him to saluation. Let
them beware, for **Cain** repented, yet is he condemned. **Esau** did repent, yet is he condemned.   7525
Antiochus did repent, yet is he condẽned. **Iudas**
did repent, yet is he condemned, with infinit mo,
and why so? because their prolõged repentance
sprang not of faith, & of an inward hatred vnto
sin, &c. Thus they may see, that euery light af-   7530
fection, is no true repentance: and that it is not
ynough to say at the last, **I repent, I repent,** for
vnles it be a true repentance indeed, it is worth
nothing. But in deed if it were so, that man had
liberum arbitrium, *free wil and power of himself,*   7535
to repent truly when he wold, and that God had
promised in his worde to accept of that repentance, it were another matter. But repentance is,
donum Dei, *the gift of God,* **de sursum veniens á**
patre luminum, *comming from aboue, from the*   7540

father of light: and therefore it is not in our
powers to repent when we will: **It is the Lorde**
that giueth the gift, when, where, and to whom
it shal please him: and of him are we to craue it
7545   incessantly, by faithfull prayer, and not otherwise
to presume of our owne repentance, when indeed
we haue nothing lesse, then a true repentance.

Spud. Then thus much I gather by your
wordes, that as true repentance (which is a cer-
7550   taine inward griefe, and sorrow of hearte, conceiued for our sinnes, with a hatred and loathing
of the same) serueth to saluation through the
mercie of God in Christe: so fained repentance
saueth not from perdition. And therfore, we
T4ᵛ   must // repent dayly and hourly, and not to deferre our repentance to the last gaspe, as many
do, then which nothing is more perillous.

Philo. True it is, for may not he be called a
great foole, that by deferring and prolonging of
7560   repentance to the last gasp (as they say) will
hazard his body & soule to eternal damnation for
euer? Wheras by dayly repentance he may assure
himselfe, both of the fauour of God, & of life
euerlasting (by faith) in the mercy of God,
7565   through the most precious bloud of his dear
Sonne, Iesus Christ, our alone sauiour and Re-
deemer, to whom be praise for euer.

Spud. Now must I needs say, as the wise
King **Salomon** said, **all things are vaine and**
7570   **transitorie, and that nothing is permanent vnder**
the Sunne: The works of men are vnperfect, and
lead to destruction, their exercises are vaine, and
wicked altogether. Wherefore, I setting apart all
the vanities of this life, will from henceforth con-
7575   secrate my selfe wholly to the seruice of my God,
and to follow him in his word, which only is per-

All thinges
are vaine and
vanity it self.

T4ᵛ. PH: *A Christian Protestation.*

manent, and leadeth vnto life. And I most hartily
thank the Lord my God for your good company
this day, and for your graue instructions, promis-
ing by the assistance of God his grace, to follow   7580
and obey them to my possible power, all the
dayes of my life.

    Philo. God giue you grace so to do, and
euery Christian man els, and to auoyd all the
vanities, and deceiuable pleasures of this life, for   7585
certainly they leade the path to eternall destruction both of body and soule for euer, to as many
as obey them. For, it is vnpossible to wallow in
the delights and pleasures of this world, & to liue
in ioy for euer in the kingdome of heauen. And   7590
thus we hauing spent the day, and also ended our
iourney: we must now depart, beseeching God
that we may both meete againe in the Kingdome
of heauen, there to raigne and liue with him for
euer, through Iesus Christ our Lord. To whome   7595
with the Father, and the holy Spirite be all honour and glorie for euermore. Amen.

FINIS.

God haue the praise, both now
and alwaies. *Amen.*   7600

**The ioyes of
this life,
tread the path
to death.**

Commentary

Variant readings which are found in more than one of the first three editions have been quoted from the latest edition.

14 **Philip Stubs, Gent.** The author is not styled a gentleman O1–O3.

16.0 **[Publisher's Device]** McKerrow identifies this device as belonging to Richard Jones (*Devices*, fig. 283; cf. figure 7); the title-pages O1–O3 read in its place: "MATH.3.ver.2. **Repent, for the kingdome of God is at hande. LVKE. 13.ver.5. I say vnto you, except you repent you shall all perish.**" (cf. figures 1–6).

20–21 **To ... England** O1–O3 were dedicated to Philip Howard, Earl of Arundel. This choice of patron is extraordinary. Howard lived a profligate court life before converting to Catholicism in the early 1580s, and was arrested as a recusant in 1585. Even more startling is Stubbes's comment in *The Second part* (1583), again dedicated to the Earl, that the *Abuses* met with Howard's "not onely acceptation, but also most bountifull remuneration" (sig. A4). Extracts from Stubbes's dedication to Howard are included in Appendix I (Passage A).

27–32 **Right ... creatures** Gen. 1:1–2:3.

31–32 **that ... creatures** i.e., that God might be glorified in man, more than in all of his other creations (cf. 54–55).

32–37 **And ... creature** *Fiat/fiant* is the verb in Gen. 1:3, 6, 14; *faciamus* in Gen. 1:26. This passage echoes the Geneva sidenote to Gen. 1:26: "God cõmanded the water and the earth, to brĩg forthe other creatures: but of man he saith, Let vs make: signifying, yᵗ God taketh counsel with his wisdome & vertue, purposing to make an excellent worke aboue all the rest of his creacion".

42–48 **what Creature ... mind** cf. Aristotle, *De Partibus Animalium* (trans. Ogle, 4.10).

47 **respect** consider, take into account.

48–50 **And ... only man** 1 John 2:25.

51–53 & preferred ... apart,) Ps. 8:5.

54–55 in him, & by him i.e., in man, and by man.

56 integrity uncorrupted condition.

61–63 Which ... prayer Exod. 25:8.

67 conferred contributed.

69 purple purple cloth.

    skarlet rich worsted cloth available in many colors. Cloth dyed the color of
    scarlet, which is probably what Stubbes describes here, was the most expen-
    sive: "The use of crimson scarlet [in England] was early limited to the use
    of the royal family, noblemen, and civil officials" (Linthicum, *Costume*, 88).

    ornaments furnishings of the Church and its worship.

70 haire haircloth, or more generally, any kind of coarse fabric.

73–74 his ... Christ Heb. 9:11.

79 chiefe ... builder Heb. 11:10.

81–82 the ... Mite Mark 12:41–44; Luke 21:1–4.

84 effect ... affect accomplished results ... inward disposition.

85 talents (1) an ancient denomination of money; (2) the powers of mind or
    body viewed as divinely entrusted to a person for use and improvement;
    Matt. 25:14–30, Luke 19:12–26. Stubbes applies the parable at 95–103.

86 simply without addition.

87 straite computist strict or exacting accountant.

89–90 who ... sworde i.e., who actually commits the murder.

97–98 vnprofitable seruaunt Luke 17:10.

105–6 palpable ... schoole i.e., manifest rudeness of language rendering true
    wisdom impossible, anticipating subsequent allusions to "the rudenesse of
    my pen" (123–24) and "my rude speaches" (155–56).

109 semblable such-like.

113 plausible approving.

114 collected compiled; O1–O3 read "published", but the revision is apt, as
    many passages are heavily indebted to previously printed works (cf. pp. 22–
    27).

116–17 whose ... tutched i.e., the only ones who will resent his criticisms are
    those who know themselves most at fault (Tilley, *Proverbs*, H700).

120 stomackes dispositions, tempers.

    countenances displays of feeling.

127 infatigable indefatigable, untiring.

132 most meetest most meet; double superlatives were common (Abbott, *Gram-
    mar*, 11).

140 ripe fit for curative treatment.

141–42 **in generall** without exception.

142 **Silkes ... Sattens** This litany of fabrics repeated in the opening chapters echoes statutes and proclamations limiting the use of these materials to those of station and wealth.

Veluets Damasks The frequency with which items in a list are not punctuated suggests that the consistent use of commas was not considered essential.

145 **frequented** practiced habitually.

147 **all** any whatever.

160 **estates** conditions in general.

166 **I.F. ... Book** Much of the prefatory material printed O1–O3 was deleted in Q1 (cf. Appendix I, Passages B–D). Perhaps the most significant omission is the "Preface to the Reader", in which Stubbes asserts that his book reprehends not the thing itself (theaters, dancing, rich apparel), but its abuse.

168 **store** provide.

174 **Laurell palle** cloak or mantle made of laurel. This is an unusual image, the poet using the word "laurel" attributively in the sense of "cloak of honor".

178 **mickle** great.

194 **SPVDEVS. PHILOPONVS.** The names derive from the Greek, and mean "earnest student" and "lover of hard work" respectively; cf. p. 24.

200.1–3 **Flying ... lyer** Tilley, *Proverbs*, F44.

211–16 **Trulie ... indifferently** Interpreting this speech as autobiographical, and assuming that he began his travels at the age of twenty-one, Furnivall speculates that Stubbes was born in 1555 (*Abuses*, ed. Furnivall, 2:50, n. 2).

213 **after** i.e., afterwards, later.

214 **Anglia** This is the only place in Q1 where England is referred to in Latin; in O1–O3, proper names other than those of the two protagonists were usually spelled in reverse and Latinized (i.e., "Ailgna").

222.2 **chargeable** costly, expensive.

225 **trauell** both "travel" and "labor" (travail) may be implicit.

229 **to ... selfe** to subject or habituate myself.

230 **nurture** moral training and discipline.

231 **ciuill** well-bred, refined.

232 **countries** counties, districts (i.e., within England); since Philoponus is supposed to have travelled into England from his own native land it seems likely that the modern sense is intended at 235.

233 **commodities** conveniences.

236–39 **For ... abroad** Tilley, *Proverbs*, N274.

239 **bruit** wanting in reason or understanding.

245–50 **for ... graue** A similar saying is attributed to Aristotle by Diogenes Laertius: "Being asked how the educated differ from the uneducated, 'As much,' he said, 'as the living from the dead'" (*Philosophers*, trans. Hicks, 5.19).

248 **science** knowledge.

253–54 **(vntill ... iourney) vse** The Q1 punctuation has been emended (cf. collation) since missing, reversed, or misplaced parentheses O1–O3 were usually corrected in a subsequent edition, a practice which suggests that these usages were considered not merely variant, but wrong.

260–62 **Comes ... Chariot** Publilius Syrus, *Sententiae*, ed. Duff and Duff, line 116 (in other eds. 104); Tilley, *Proverbs*, C559.

265 **dispute** Despite Spudeus's deference, the assumption is that there will be differences of opinion; O1–O3 read "combate".

267 **Ciuilian** authority on the Civil Law; the opposition is not between country and city but uneducated and learned.

267.2 **scandal** offense.

272 **filed** neatly elaborated.

281 **famous** reputable.

290 **magnanimitie** lofty courage, fortitude.

291–92 **complexion** bodily constitution.

294–98 **This ... especially?** Question marks are used to mark both interrogatory and exclamatory statements.

295–96 **either else** or else.

296 **meerlie** entirely.

303–4 **corrupt** O1–O2 read "abrupte", meaning "broken away from restraint".

304 **peruerse** wicked.

313 **nature: and** This colon perhaps emphasizes the third of the causes of human sin as the worst; a comma was printed here O1–O3.

  intestine inward, innate.

316–25 **But ... father** The language of the New Testament is woven throughout this exhortation to good works; specific allusions are traced below.

316–17 **But ... creatures** 2 Cor. 5:17.

317–19 **created ... in** Eph. 2:10.

319–21 **we ... light** Rom. 13:12.

321–22 **to walk ... life** Rom. 6:4.

322–23 **and to ... speaketh** Phil. 2:12.

324–25 **And ... father** Matt. 5:16.

332 **Tara tantara** words imitating the sound of a trumpet.

333–35 **Arise ... workes** recurrent biblical belief; cf. Rev. 20:12.

343–44 **Vnusquisque ... burthen** Gal. 6:5 (Tilley, *Proverbs*, B725, earliest example dated 1600).

344–46 **Anima ... die?** Ezek. 18:20; cf. also Ezek. 18:4.

348–49 **hath ... destruction** i.e., has given up to wickedness and death, alluding to Rom. 1:28.

349 **destinate** destined.

353–54 **scintillula ... grace** Reminiscent of Boethius, *The Consolation of Philosophy*: "Jam tibi ex hac minima scintillula vitalis calor illuxerit" (1 pr. 6; PL 63.654), or in English, "presently out of this tiny spark your vital warmth will glow again" (trans. Tester). Cf. "sparks of faith" at 4113.

355–56 **members ... bodie** New Testament metaphor for Christ's church (Rom. 12:4–5; 1 Cor. 12:27).

360–68 **If ... perfection?** cf. 1 Cor. 12:12–26.

366–68 **his ... his** its ... its; "his" represents the genitive of "it" as well as "he" (Abbott, *Grammar*, 228).

368 **integritie** original perfect state.

369–70 **considerately** carefully, deliberately.

372 **defection** falling away from religion and virtue, apostasy.

378–79 **And ... time** Gal. 6:10.

380–82 **To ... another** cf. Rom. 12:15–16: "Reioyce with them that reioyce, & wepe with them that wepe. Be of like affection one towards another"; in every edition Stubbes omits the reference to rejoicing and focuses the reader's attention exclusively on shared sorrow.

384–88 **Ortus ... part** Plato, *Epistles*, ed. Bury, 9.358A.

386 **challengeth** lays claim to.

387 **friends** relatives, kinsfolk.

388 **optimo iure** "by the highest duty".

    vendicate assert a claim to; the earliest example recorded in *OED* of "vindicate" used in this sense is dated 1725, suggesting that the Q1 variant (cf. collation) is a printer's error.

399 **intestine** inward.

402 **frequented** practiced, used habitually.

408 **describe** O1 reads "cipher foorth", meaning "express" or "delineate"; "cipher" was replaced O2–O3 with the synonym "discipher".

411 **competent** suitable, sufficient.

    comprehend include, comprise.

419 **lethal** mortal.

419–36 **But ... other** Paul explains in his letter to the Romans that salvation depends entirely upon faith and the grace of God (cf. Rom. 9:15–16).

422–24 **Vae . . . iudged** Stubbes attributes this quotation in *A Motiue to Good Workes* to St. Bernard (sig. O3), perhaps thinking of the explication of Isaiah 64:6 found in the sermon *In Festo Omnium Sanctorum* (PL 183. 459C). The passage is in fact found in Guillelmus, *Expositio in Epistolam ad Romanos*: "Sed vae quantaecunque justitiae hominis, si remota misericordia judicetur" (PL 180.582B).

451 **in it** in its; common form of the possessive pronoun (Abbott, *Grammar*, 228).

453 **the wise man** i.e., Jesus son of Sirach, author of the book of Ecclesiasticus.

454–55 **Initium . . . euilles** Tilley, *Proverbs*, P578. A conflation of Sir. 10:13 (variously verse 14 or 15), "For pride is the original of sinne", and 1 Tim. 6:10, "For the desire of money is the roote of all euil". These verses are juxtaposed in Augustine, *In Epistolam Joannis* 8.6, PL 35.2039.

459 **ingenerate** engendered.

460–61 **Matercula . . . mischief** metaphor usually associated with idleness rather than pride (Tilley, *Proverbs*, I13).

462–63 **flagicious** heinous, villainous.

464 **venterous** dangerous, risky.

468 **successe** issue, upshot.

476–83 **For . . . sinne** Horace, *Ars Poetica* 180–81: "Less vividly is the mind stirred by what finds entrance through the ears than by what is brought before the trusty eyes" (trans. Fairclough); the passage is quoted in Latin in the preface to O1 (cf. Appendix I–B, 24–25).

478 **opposite to** in front of.

482 **obiect to** presented or exposed to.

   exemplary example; not a rare or foreign usage, and so probably printed in contrasting type O3–Q1 for emphasis.

490 **contemneth** despises, scorns.

492–94 **whose . . . woman** Isa. 64:6; the Geneva sidenote reads, "our righteousnes, & best vertues are before thee as vile cloutes, or, (as some read) like the menstruous clothes of a woman".

494.1 **Isaias 50** Verses 10–11 warn that those who walk by their own lights "shal lie downe in sorowe".

498–500 **Qui . . . good** Phil. 2:13. The concluding words of the translation, "to doe good", is an amplification of the Latin; the marginal explanation in the 1599 Geneva Bible makes explicit the verse's relevance: "A most sure and grounded argument against pride, for that wee haue nothing in vs praiseworthy, but it commeth of the free gift of God, and is without vs, for we haue no abilitie or power, so much as to will well (much lesse to doe well) but onely of the free mercie of God".

501–2 **Ne ... strength** 1 Cor. 1:29; the last half of the translation, "of his owne power and strength", is another example of amplification.

506 **proper** intrinsic, inherent.

514 **affinitie** relations by marriage.

consanguinitie blood-relations.

516 **sanctimony** religiousness, sanctity.

522 **aperto ore** not printed O1–O2.

527 **race** family, stock.

530 **sort** manner.

544 **Author** originator.

547 **meere** absolutely.

548–51 **(for ... withal.)** Unidentified, but reminiscent of Horace: "the word once let slip flies beyond recall" (*Epistles*, trans. Fairclough, 1.18.71; Tilley, *Proverbs*, W838). Whereas Horace warns against the danger of careless speech, Stubbes suggests that words are quickly dispersed and therefore harmless; the version of the quotation in Latin was not printed O1–O2.

555.1 **Decorum** seemliness, propriety of behavior; this Latin word was adopted into the English language towards the end of the sixteenth century, but the use of contrasting type at 556 and 4896 suggests that Stubbes may still consider it a foreign usage.

557–59 **Doth ... order** 1 Cor. 14:40.

563 **contrare** contrary.

563–68 **For ... Christians?** The book's fictional context slips as Philoponus begins to speak as an Englishman rather than as a traveller to the country.

566 **disguise** disfigure.

572.1–2 **Circes ... pottes** sorceresses in Greek and Latin legend; Gascoigne explains the meaning of the allusion more fully in *A delicate Diet, for daintie-mouthde Droonkardes* (1576): "[the ancient poets] feigned y^t Medea, Circe, and such other coulde Metamorphose & transforme men into Beastes, Byrdes, Plantes, and Flowres: meaning therby, that whosoever is so blinded in sensuality ... shal without doubt transforme him self, or be transformed from a man to a Beast, &c" (464).

573 **shed foorth** poured out.

influence power conceived of as an influx or infusion.

578 **impotionate** poisoned. This is the first of only two examples cited in *OED*, both of which are taken from the *Abuses*; the second is found at 3755 and, as here, was introduced into O2 as a revision. In O1 this passage reads, "hath drunke so deepe of the dregges of this Cup".

585 **Chaldeans** Chaldea was located in biblical times in the southernmost Tigris and Euphrates valley.

Heluetians Helvetia was a European country of Roman times which included a large part of modern-day Switzerland.

586 **Zuitzers** Switzers, inhabitants of Switzerland.

589–90 **This ... withall** cf. "he has a cloak for his knavery" (Tilley, *Proverbs*, C419, first usage dated c. 1633); the image is repeated at 3175–76 and elsewhere.

589 **visour** mask.

590 **own shame** O1–O2 read "Sodometrie"; cf. notes to "**Sodomits**" and "sodometicall" at 5546–47 and 5927.

593–94 **neuer ... alter** This passage was revised from the past to the present tense between O3 and Q1, but the revision was only partially executed, Q1's "altered" (cf. collation) being a remnant of the earlier version; instead of returning to the O3 reading I have emended the passage to complete the process of revision.

596 **Iacobus Stuperius** cf. p. 27.

596–97 **lib. ... habitibus** "the book about the different apparel of our age".

604–9 **Non ... raunge** The last half line of the translation, "or els attire, wherein abroade they raunge" is an amplification; the Latin "quotation" from "Stuperius" at 2784–88 mentions both the customs and attire of Egyptian women.

608 **at all** Without changing the Latin, Stubbes revised "lightly", the reading found O1–O3, to "at all" in Q1.

chop and chaunge alliterative phrase meaning "alter"; Tilley, *Proverbs*, C363.

611 **Cantabrians** ancient warlike tribe of northern Spain.

615 **in effect** in fact.

619–20 **Other ... apparelled** "go" is inferred from the previous sentence.

620 **haire** haircloth, or more generally, any kind of coarse fabric.

622 **hosen** breeches, either with attached or separate stockings.

623 **bandes** collars worn around the neck by men and women; strips of material encircling hats were also called bands (1447) but Stubbes is probably speaking here specifically about collars (cf. 1470–1539).

624 **ciuilest** Probably meaning "most civilized", but Stubbes may have had in mind "best-governed".

626 **brauely** finely, handsomely.

627 **Carzies ... Rugges** woollen cloths produced in England.

629–30 **silkes ... Taffaties** cf. 142n.

629 **Damaskes** "Damask was an expensive silk, partly because of its complicated

weaving . . . partly because of the high import duties imposed upon silks. Its price . . . placed it out of the reach of many persons to whom sumptuary laws allowed its use" (Linthicum, *Costumes*, 120).

Grograins coarse-grained taffeta weaves made of mohair, silk, or worsted.

630 **Taffaties** variant of "taffetas".

634 **strange** unusual, exceptional.

634.2 **curious** particular, difficult to satisfy.

642–43 **shall . . . so?** Exod. 23:2.

645 **shal . . . dy?** Ezek. 18:20.

652 **Sarcenet** thin silk fabric.

653 **Chamlet** "Probably a kind of mohair or, later, camel hair cloth, mixed with wool, silk and cotton, and having a watered appearance" (Cunnington and Cunnington, *Costume*, 213–14).

657–60 **So . . . tollerable** Stubbes probably derives this subtlety from the *Homily against Excess of Apparel* (1563) which teaches that we should "content ourselves with that which God sendeth, whether it be much or little" (*Sermons*, 326); cf. 752–62.

660 **captiuate** enthralled.

662–66 **And . . . them** The preamble to the proclamation issued on 15 June 1574 enforcing statutes of apparel recognizes the economic implications of the growing fashion for foreign goods: "The excess of apparel and the superfluity of unnecessary foreign wares thereto belonging now of late years is grown by sufferance to such an extremity that the manifest decay . . . of a great part of the wealth of the whole realm generally is like to follow" (*TRP*, 2:381).

664–65 **laugh . . . sleeues** i.e., laugh to themselves (Tilley, *Proverbs*, S535).

665–66 **affecting of** showing fondness for.

667–72 **And . . . doe** Some support for this claim is found in a letter to the Company of Merchant Adventurers dated 8 August 1566 which states that "Armenians and other are desirous to barter with us, giving silke for karsies" (Hakluyt, *Voyages*, 3:56–57).

674 **store** sufficient or abundant supply.

679 **comelier then they** O1 reads "as comlie as they".

680–81 **farre . . . say** Tilley, *Proverbs*, D12.

685 **calling** station in life, rank.

686–88 **I . . . calling.** Distinctions of rank are central to Elizabethan statutes and proclamations regulating apparel and are supported in the *Homily against Excess of Apparel* as Scriptural (*Sermons*, 326–27). This speech, however, was heavily revised for O2 and in the original version this sentence concludes in a manner more explicitly critical of excess among all social classes: "yet a meane is to be keept, for, **omne extremum vertitur in vitium**, euery extreme, is turned into vice".

687 **Magistery** magistracy.

695 **offend** transgress.

696–702 **but ... bodies** cf. 1801–49n.

698 **erogate** distributed.

699 **subuention** relief, support.

702 **refection** nourishment of food and drink.

703 **priuate subiectes** i.e., those not holding public office or official position.

707–11 **except ... purpose** The Queen's physicians, officers of her household, and sheriffs of shires, for example, were exempted from the sumptuary proclamation of 12 February 1580 (*TRP*, 2: 459–61).

711–26 **But ... wealth** It is not pride, but an anxiety about the blurring of boundaries of rank, which emerges as the impetus motivating Stubbes to inveigh against the abuse of apparel; that the laws governing apparel were not being strictly obeyed or enforced is a point stressed in the opening remarks to the sumptuary proclamation issued 12 February 1580 (*TRP*, 2: 454–55) and the *Homily against Excess of Apparel* (*Sermons*, 324).

716 **who is noble** probably omitted from Q1 as the result of compositorial eyeskip (cf. collation).

719 **Gentilitie** gentry.

Yeomanrie "Yeomen are those, which ... may dispend of their owne free land in yearelie reuenue, to the summe of fortie shillings sterling ... & with grasing, frequenting of markets, and keeping of seruants ... do come to great welth, in somuch that manie of them are able and doo buie the lands of vnthriftie gentlemen" (Harrison, *Description of England*, 1577, ed. Furnivall, 132–33): Laslett emphasizes the distinction between gentlemen, who had no need to labor for their living, and yeomen, who were "the most successful of those who worked the land" (*World We Have Lost Further Explored*, 43).

724 **seruile** belonging to the serving class or lower orders.

731–36 **I ... ynough** The right of the gentry and magistrates to wear rich clothing is emphasized in the preface to O1 (cf. Appendix I–B, 77–96).

735 **Thraso** name of a braggart soldier in Terence's *Eunuchus*; hence, braggart. O1 reads "fixnet", which presumably means the same thing, but is the only example of the word recorded in *OED*.

indifferẽtly equally, indiscriminately.

738–39 **splendish** make splendid.

741 **Arase** cloth of arras, a rich tapestry fabric.

742 **pendices** canopies? i.e., any structure with a sloping roof.

743–44 **serue … occupations** i.e., are not only of practical use.

744 **decore** decorate, adorn.

766 **diffuse** obscure, vague.

771–77 **When … likenesse** Gen. 1:1–2:3.

771–72 **intellectible** intellective, capable of understanding.

774 **Christ Iesus** synonymous with God's word and wisdom (cf. Prov. 8:22).

781–90 **Then … life** The temptation story is found at Gen. 3; Isa. 14:12–15 describes the pride of Lucifer and his fall from heaven.

781 **maligner** one who regards another with envy.

783 **arrogating** claiming or appropriating without right.

787 **torteous** injurious, harmful.

790–91 **condescending** yielding consent, acquiescing.

799 **contracted** entered into; O1–O3 read "committed".

805.1 **Impudent** shameless, immodest.

816–19 **Thirdly … eyes?** By phrasing his last point as a question Spudeus looks for, and receives, affirmation from his traveling companion.

819 **luxurious** lascivious.

820 **collection** conclusion, deduction.

823 **prickes … eyes** causes of mental irritation.

827 **exercise** accustom; O1–O3 read "excite".

827–28 **contrition … compunction** not rare usages; probably printed in contrasting type O3–Q1 for emphasis.

834 **creatures** creations.

838–39 **decke … sepulchres** Matt. 23:27.

840 **brauerie** finery, fine clothes.

848 **perpetual** O1–O3 read "permanent".

848–49 **patterne … euer** The placement in Q1 of the closing bracket after "for euer" (cf. collation) is almost certainly an error despite the presence of two revisions in this speech that appear authorial: Spudeus is asking if their clothing should be forever a "rule or patterne" to us, not stating in parenthesis that we are forever Adam's posterity (cf. Philoponus's paraphrase of the question at 866–71).

849 **of force** of necessity.

850 **for vs** added Q1.

855–60 **(for … owne)** The conclusion of the parenthesis after "thereof" in Q1 (cf. collation) is another example of a misplaced closing bracket: both biblical citations verify that Adam and Eve could have been dressed in sumptuous clothing if the Lord had so chosen.

855–57 **Domini … thereof** Ps. 24:1.

858–60 **Gold ... owne** Hag. 2:9: "The siluer *is* mine, and the golde *is* mine, saith the Lord of hostes". The concluding phrase seems to derive from the Geneva sidenote: "Therefore when his time cometh, he can make all the treasures of yᵉ worlde to serue his purpose".

862 **pedagogie** discipline, training.

873 **an ... iote** synonyms meaning "the very least amount".

877 **legendes** accounts.

878–79 **censures** judgements, opinions.

882 **mediocritie** moderation, temperance.

884 **inuested** clothed.

885–90 **But ... damnation** At 649–57 Stubbes justifies the use of rich apparel in some foreign countries by arguing that God has made nothing else available to them.

887–88 **proanesse** O1–O3 read "procliuitie".

895–900 **I ... pride** The *Homily against Excess of Apparel* similarly permits a moderate use of rich clothing: "[Almighty God] alloweth us apparel, not only for necessities' sake, but also for an honest comeliness" (*Sermons*, 324–25).

895.2 **reposed** placed.

897–99 **(as ... ragges)** O1 reads: "(as our Papistes, Papists? no, Sorbonists, Sorbonists? no, Atheists, atheists? no, plaine Sathanists do, placing all thier religion in hethen garments, & Romish raggs)".

897 **Sorbonicall Papists** theologians at the Sorbonne.

898 **Romish** Roman Catholic.

905 **scandalles** offenses.

906 **riote** wanton or wasteful living.

919 **splendent** gorgeous, magnificent.

923 **assotted** possessed by stupidity.

930–34 **Then ... Mothes** Matt. 6:19–21.

934–36 **His ... Prophete** Philoponus misquotes Isa. 55:8, "For my thoghts *are* not your thoghts, nether *are* your waies my waies", perhaps conflating it with the conclusion to Rom. 11:33, "how vnsearcheable are his iudgemẽts, & his wayes past finding out!"

937.5 **fairer** The creature of God is necessarily fair; the issue concerns the use of apparel to improve on one's looks; the Q1 reading (cf. collation) is a misprint.

941–47 **For ... good** Gen. 1:26–31.

945 **excellentest** common form of the superlative (Abbott, *Grammar*, 9); cf. 953.

945–46 **whom ... likenesse)** Gen. 1:26.

951 **conuince** convict.

952–56 **who ... before** cf. Ps. 8:5.

956–58 **But ... thus?** The analogy of the potter and the clay recurs in the Bible, but Stubbes's phrasing is suggestive of Rom. 9:20.

959 **better fauoured** of a more attractive appearance.

960–61 **proportion** form, shape.

967–68 **this glory** O1–O3 read "his glory".

969 **hagges** applicable both to men and women.

974 **miscreants** misbelievers, heretics.

974–76 **hath cast ... opinion** i.e., has given up to wickedness and a preconceived [negative] estimation, alluding to Rom. 1:28.

976–77 **bowels** considered the seat of tender emotions (*OED*, sb.^{1} 3b).

980 **refelled** refuted, disproved.

982–84 **Linguas ... fingers** Tilley, *Proverbs*, F239; Latin source unknown.

984–85 **not ... heaven** i.e., we should not contemptuously defy the power of God (Tilley, *Proverbs*, H355).

985 **kicke ... pricke** Acts 9:5; the 1599 Geneva sidenote explains, "This is a prouerbe which is spoken of them that through their owne stubburnesse hurt themselues".

986–87 **For ... fire** Deut. 4:24.

987–89 **and ... sinne** Ps. 11:6.

1000–1 **curiously** handsomely, beautifully.

1001 **plumed ... Pride** cf. "As proud as a peacock" (Tilley, *Proverbs*, P157); feathers are similarly associated with pride at 2524–25 and 2635.4–7.

1002 **contemne** despise, scorn.

1006 **stand with** be consistent or consonant with.

1007 **after** in a manner answering to; O1–O2 read "for".

1008 **externe** external.

1013 **the rather** the more readily.

1022–23 **Vnder ... knowledge** Tilley, *Proverbs*, C476.

1033 **cloutes** clothes, rags.

  ornaments qualities that confer honor.

1034 **roisteth** blusters and swaggers.

1037 **induments** accomplishments, adornments.

1039 **indued ... with** possessed, or not possessed of.

1057 **promptuary** repository.

1062 **Magisterie** magistracy.

1063 **presbyterie** assembly of ministers and ruling elders within a local area constituting the ecclesiastical court below the synod; alternatively, the body of elders of a parish church.

1064–66 **For ... honour** 1 Tim. 5:17.

1072–75 **For . . . Worship?** cf. Juvenal: "What avail your pedigrees? . . . Though you deck your hall from end to end with ancient waxen images, Virtue is the one and only true nobility" (*Satires*, trans. Ramsay, 8.1–20).

1073 **preuayleth** avails, profits.

1073–74 **progenie** parentage, descent.

1075–76 **a . . . Scabberd** cf. Tilley, *Proverbs*, S1048: "A leaden sword in a golden scabbard"; imagery reversed in all editions.

1076–79 **Is . . . lothsomnesse?** Matt. 23:27.

1085 **lustie** insolent, self-confident.

1090.1 **exordiū** beginning.

1091–1105 **Meaning . . . Worshipfull** The logical conclusion of the anecdote, that worthy individuals of low birth who earn a respected position in society better deserve to wear rich clothing than ignoble gentlemen who ignore their responsibilities to the community, is twisted into a fear of pranked-up commoners disguised as virtuous gentry.

1103 **tagge and rag** i.e., "every Tom, Dick, and Harry" (Tilley, *Proverbs*, T10).

1110–11 **summe . . . substance** essence.

1119–20 **by . . . presaged** i.e., predicted by their clothes.

1122–24 **neither . . . other?** i.e., neither a feature of the clothing, nor intrinsic to themselves; Stubbes concludes this tortured argument by returning to the assumption that holiness is not to be found either in the apparel or in the person wearing it.

1124 **Or . . . so** i.e., that both they and their clothing are holy.

1129 **creature** creation.

1129.2 **trimly** cleverly, neatly.

1129.3 **continued** O1–O3 read "contriued".

1132–34 **Therefore . . . all** This remedy is also advanced for gardens (3091–102), dancing (6460–85), and gaming (6852–63). The preface to O1 suggests that the theaters could be similarly reformed, but this position is contradicted in the actual chapter on stage-plays where all forms of theater, whether secular or religious, are condemned. The preface was omitted O2–Q1.

1135 **well seasoned** brought to a state of perfection.

1139–41 **The apparell . . . God** 1 Tim. 4:4.

1147–51 **And . . . also** Stubbes is speaking of those who are not part of the nobility, gentry, or magistracy (cf. 682 ff.).

1152–55 **Sublata . . . fayleth** Walther cites "sublata causa tollitur effectus" as proverbial (*Proverbia*, 30588b), a saying which is also current in English (Tilley, *Proverbs*, C202).

1156–57 **the effect . . . attyre** This line, completing Stubbes's application of the proverb to his argument, was omitted from Q1, probably as a result of eye-skip (cf. collation).

1157 **ingenerate** engendered.

1164 **preposterously** in an inverted order.

1167 **combinate** combined.

1170–76 **For . . . execution** cf. 142n.

1172 **sanctions** laws, decrees.

1181 **better cheape** a better bargain, lower-priced.

1183–84 **as . . . burne** image used at Prov. 6:27 to warn against adultery.

1184–91 **Therfore . . . too** paraphrasing the *Homily against Excess of Apparel*: "Therefore all may not look to wear like apparel, but every one, according to his degree, as God hath placed him. Which, if it were observed, many one doubtless should be compelled to wear a russet-coat, which now ruf-fleth in silks and velvets" (*Sermons*, 326–27).

1188 **ruffle** swagger, bear themselves proudly.

1190–91 **Frize coates** i.e., coats made of coarse woollen fabric.

1195 **kind** gender or kindred.

1198–1200 **Hominis . . . deceiued** Tilley, *Proverbs*, E179.

1201 **affected** aimed at, aspired to.

1212 **Painyms** i.e., paynims (pagans, heathens).

1214 **Clearkes** scholars.

1219–50 **That . . . like** Adapted from the *Homily against Excess of Apparel* (*Sermons*, 333); Stubbes incorporates the example of the wife of Philo from an earlier page (*Sermons*, 331) and makes some of the examples, which in the sermon are all specific to women, applicable to both sexes.

1220–21 **Democrates** Democritus of Abdera, b. 460–457 B.C.E.

1223 **tempered** mingled, blended.

1225–28 **Sophocles . . . follie** Source of anecdote unknown.

1228–32 **Socrates . . . life** cf. Plato, *The Republic*, Book 5, concerning the feasibility of training women in the gymnasium to be guardians of the state: "The women of the guardians, then, must strip, since they will be clothed with virtue as a garment" (trans. Shorey, 457A).

1235 **Philo** Philon of Larissa (160/59–c. 80 B.C.E.), Cicero's mentor.

1239 **Dionisius** probably Dionysius I (c. 430–367 B.C.E.), tyrant of Syracuse, who had an important political connection with Sparta.

1241–42 **Lacedemonians** inhabitants of Sparta.

1244–46 **King . . . cloutes** Taken from Cato's oration to the Romans as recorded by Livy: "In the memory of our forefathers Pyrrhus, through his agent Cineas, tried to corrupt with gifts the minds of our men and women as well. Not yet had the Oppian law been passed to curb female extravagance, yet not one woman took his gifts" (trans. Sage, 34.4.6).

1244 **King Pirrhus** Pyrrhus (319–272 B.C.E.), King of Epirus, who invaded Italy in the early part of the third century B.C.E.

1246 **menstruous cloutes** rags defiled with menstrual blood (cf. 493–94).

1249 **conditions** personal qualities, morals.

1250–57 **Diogenes ... more** Diogenes Laertius notes that, "He was the first, say some, to fold his cloak because he was obliged to sleep in it as well ... He had written to some one to try and procure a cottage for him. When this man was a long time about it, he took for his abode the tub in the Metroön" (*Philosophers*, trans. Hicks, 6.22–23).

1250 **Diogenes** Diogenes of Sinope, c. 400–c. 325 B.C.E.

1253 **pompous** magnificent.

1254 **resiant** resident; O1–O3 print the synonym "cōmorant".

1257–85 **A ... kingdome** philosopher and source unidentified.

1258 **adressed himself** made his way.

1262–69 **The ... reuerence** This run-on sentence construction, invariant O1–Q1, conveys a sense of haste.

1263 **lighten** descend, alight [upon him].

1268 **plausiblie** with approval.

1285–1300 **I ... ornamentes** Diogenes Laertius tells this story of both Aristippus (dates uncertain) and Diogenes of Sinope (*Philosophers*, trans. Hicks, 2.75 and 6.32).

1290 **Tinsell** rich material made of silk or wool interwoven with gold or silver thread.

1296 **glistering** sparkling, glittering.

1299 **spitting ... heauen** cf. 984–85n.

1312–13 **peculiar people** i.e., God's own chosen people (see Titus 2:14).

1316–19 **What ... beastes?** Gen. 3:21.

1317.1 **Probation** proof, demonstrative evidence.

1323–27 **What ... Leather?** Reference to the mantle of Elias (Elijah) is found at 1 Kings 19:13, 19, and his girdle is mentioned as an identifying feature at 2 Kings 1:8.

1327–28 **Elizeus ... same?** When Elijah ascended to heaven in a whirlwind, Elizeus (Elisha) tore his own clothes and picked up the mantle of his mentor (2 Kings 2:11–15).

1328–34 **And ... house?** 1 Sam. 9:18.

1336–39 **The ... Wildernesse?** Neh. 9:21.

1339–42 **Was ... loynes?** Matt. 3:4, Mark 1:6.

1342 **succinctorie** succinctorium, a band or scarf embroidered with an Agnus Dei, worn pendant from the girdle by the Pope on certain occasions.

1342–47 **Peter ... apparell** This episode is recounted four times in the New Testament, but while it is usually a woman who first recognizes Peter, it is the others gathered around who identify him by his speech; cf. Mark 14:69–70.

1347–51 **The ... skinnes** Heb. 11:37; the next four lines elaborate on this verse.

1356–59 **did ... wouen?** John 19:23.

1360–62 **which ... thought** If "Stuperius" is not a deliberate fiction, the similarity of expression between this passage and 593–96 suggests this detail may derive from the same book.

1360 **which fashions** i.e., coats without seams; this style is referred to in the singular at 1357–58, but the latter plural form is invariant O1–Q1.

1363 **curious** elaborately or beautifully wrought.

1365–67 **Nitimur ... denied** vs Ovid, *Amores*, ed. Showerman, 3.4.17; Tilley, *Proverbs*, F585.

1367–83 **We ... expresse** derivative of the *Homily against Excess of Apparel* (*Sermons*, 327).

1369 **mediocrity** moderation, temperance.

1372 **presses** large cupboards.

1373 **coffers** chests.

1380 **one cut** Slashes of varying length were cut into clothing so that the material underneath, often of a contrasting color, could show through.
  laced trimmed with lace.

1381 **one of golde ... siluer** i.e., one of cloth of gold, another of cloth of silver: "One to three pounds a yard, depending on its elaborateness, was the price of cloth of gold. Cloth of silver was slightly less expensive" (Linthicum, *Costume*, 114). The use of these materials was prohibited in the proclamation issued 12 February 1580 to those who were under the degree of baron or baroness (*TRP*, 2:458–59).

1387 **degrees** successive steps or stages.

1389 **borne ... hande** assured me, but with the suggestion that Spudeus is sceptical about the truth of what he has been told (Tilley, *Proverbs*, H94); Stubbes uses the phrase at 7376 when he speaks of the prince being deluded to believe that the laws of the country are enforced.

1391–92 **impertinent ... vagaries** irrelevant and unprofitable digressions.

1398–1400 **Your ... them** This passage is phrased differently in O1: "Your request seemeth both intricate, and harde, considering there bee **Tot tantae**

maeryadaes inuentionum, So manie, and so fonde fashions, and inuentions of Apparell euerie day". Heavy revision led to the division of the sentence into two sentence fragments (cf. collation); as it seems likely that this punctuation is corrupt, the author's manuscript revisions perhaps being misread by the compositor as a new sentence, I have returned to the original punctuation.

1399 **Meryades** myriads, vast numbers.

1402–3 **pro ... mea** "to the best of my ability". O1–O3 print a fuller Latin saying: "**Pro virili mea, omnibus neruulis vndique extensis**"; the translation was left unchanged when the Latin was revised for Q1.

1408 **vse** wear.

sharpe ... crowne i.e., the crown of the hat tapers towards the top. The first example cited in *OED* of the word "crown" used in this sense is dated 1678 (sb. 20), but at 1414–15 there is no doubt that he is describing various shapes of hat rather than the positions in which hats are worn on the crown of the head.

1409 **pearking vp** sticking up.

speare or shaft spire.

1412 **fantasies** whims, caprices.

1413–14 **like ... house** i.e., a single merlon between two embrasures.

1415 **bande** hatband.

1419 **to an end** consecutively; O1–O3 read "two daies" instead of "two moneths".

1419–22 **And ... sinne** loosely based on Ps. 78:32–33; Tilley, *Proverbs*, N302: "Nothing is more precious than time".

1423 **stuffe** material.

1425–26 **Sarcenet** thin silk fabric.

1427–31 **These ... besides** not included in O1 which prints, "far fetched, and deare bought you maye bee sure".

1428 **Beuer hattes** literally, hats made out of beaver fur.

xx ... shillings i.e., one pound, a pound and a half, two pounds; in old English currency, there were 240 pence (abbreviated d.) in a pound sterling, and a shilling (abbreviated s.) was worth one-twentieth of a pound, or twelve pence. Some idea of the expense of these hats in real money is suggested by a proclamation regulating London wages issued 3 August 1587 which states that in addition to food and drink the best hatmakers should earn by year £4 13s. 4d., the best shoemakers, tailors, and hosiers £4, the best clothworkers £5, and the best alebrewers, blacksmiths, butchers, and cooks £6 (*TRP*, 2:536–37).

1430 **sort** multitude.

1433 **indifferently** equally, indiscriminately.

1436 **be pinked** i.e., have tiny slits or holes, one-sixteenth to three-fourths of an inch in length, cut into the material, and often arranged in patterns.

cunningly with skillful art.

carued cut (cf. 1655n.).

1437–39 **And ... they haue** The irony perhaps lies in the suggestion that after much wearing the perforations in the hat join together to make a smaller number of larger holes.

1437 **profitable** serviceable, useful.

1439–43 **They ... behold** mentioned only in Q1, but taffeta hats had been popular since the reign of Henry VIII (Linthicum, *Costume*, 231).

1440 **quilted** padded.

imbroydered Embroidery on clothing is presented as a common form of excess among the English (cf. the trimming of ruffs, shirts, and boothose), and it was supposed to signal great wealth or station; the proclamation issued 12 February 1580 prohibits embroidery with silk to be worn by men of lower rank than a baron's son, knight, or gentleman attendant on Her Majesty, or who had been assessed at less than £200, in lands or fees (*TRP*, 2:458).

golde, siluer gold and silver thread.

1441 **of ... sortes** presumably, of several colors.

monsters imaginary animals such as the griffin or centaur.

1441–42 **antiques** antics, monstrous or caricatured representations of animals.

1443 **woonderfull** astonishing.

1444–47 **Besides ... bands** This is an unexpected detail since hatbands made of silk, cypress, gold, and silver, and decorated with pearls and buttons were popular among women as well as men; Linthicum suggests that this passage describes a type of cap with only minimal trimming (*Costume*, 218–19).

1448 **Assie** asinine.

1451 **fantasticall** foppish, capricious.

1454 **peaking** projecting or rising in a peak.

1455 **Cockscombs** caps worn by professional fools.

fooles bables sticks carried by jesters as a mock emblem of office. Stubbes's reluctance to describe feathers in hats as cockscombs sits uneasily with his subsequent description of them as fools' baubles, an inconsistency which results from late authorial revision, O1–O3 reading "as **sternes of Pride**, and **ensignes of vanity**". His use of the word "sternes" in this sense is unique; according to *OED*, he misuses it to mean ensign, or flag.

1458 **aduanced** promoted, but probably also with the suggestion of being physically raised up.

1463 **lightnes** unsteadiness, frivolity.

1464 **fond imaginations** foolish opinions.

plainly absolutely, completely.

conuince convict.

1472 **They ... Ruffes** Huge ruffs are also criticized in the proclamation enforcing statutes of apparel dated 12 February 1580, where Her Majesty's pleasure is that no person should "wear such great and excessive ruffs ... as had not been used before two years past; but that all persons should in modest and comely sort leave off such fond disguised and monstrous manner of attiring themselves" (*TRP*, 2:462).

monstrous both "gigantic" and "unnatural" can be inferred throughout this and the next chapter.

1473 **Cambricke, Holland, Lawn** various types of linen; according to Stow's *Annales*, supplemented by E. Howes in 1615, "[i]n the third yeere of the raigne of queene **Elizabeth,** 1562. beganne the knowledge and wearing of Lawne, and Cambrick, which was then brought into England, by very small quantities, and when the Queene had Ruffes, made thereof, for her owne princely wearing, there was none in England could tell how to starch them, for vntil then all the Kinges and Queenes of ENGLAND wore Fine Holland in Ruffes" (sigs. Dddd1ᵛ–2).

1475 **a quarter ... deep** i.e., the width of the ruff from the edge to where it fastens at the neck; the full ruff would measure over half a yard in diameter.

1478 **their shoulder points** Doublets with detachable sleeves were fastened with ties (points) at the shoulder, but since not all doublets were so fashioned it seems more likely that Stubbes means the points of their shoulders; cf. 2410.

1479 **Pentise** These huge, hanging ruffs remind Philoponus of awnings offering shelter against the weather; O1–O3 read "vaile", also meaning awnings (cf. the similar usage at 2159).

1479–83 **But ... sayles** Although Stubbes kept tinkering with this sentence, he never again achieved the vividness of imagery found in O1: "But if **Aeolus** with his blasts, or **Neptune** with his stormes, chaunce to hit vppon the crasie [damaged] bark of their brused ruffes, then they goe flip flap in the winde like rags flying abroad, and lye vpon their shoulders like the dishcloute of a slutte".

1482 **dishcloutes** dishcloths.

1482–83 **Windmill sayles** canvas sheets attached to the arms of a windmill.

1486.1–2 **arches or pillers** supporting structures; used literally in the sense that supportasses and starch prop up ruffs, and figuratively in that they maintain pride.

1486.8 **Supportasses** cf. 1500–7; an extremely rare usage, the more common term being "supporter".

1488–94 **The ... neckes** The technique of starching became generally known in England with the arrival in 1564 of a starcher from Flanders called Mistress Dinghen van den Plasse (Stow, *Annales*, 1615, sig. Dddd2ᵛ).

1492 **diue** dip.

1494–99 **And ... like** included only in Q1; although colored starch is mentioned in the literature of the period, "white, and very rarely yellow, seems to have prevailed in England, judging from portraits" (Cunnington and Cunnington, *Costume*, 113).

1501 **crested** ribbed.

whipped ouer bound.

1504 **applyed** fastened.

1506 **Bande** collar (i.e., of the shirt); also used, as at 1512 and 1518.4, to refer to either the "falling band" which lay flat on the shoulders or the goffered ruff.

1511 **ordayneth** furnishes, provides.

1512 **chargeable** costly, expensive.

1513–14 **such ... sort?** O1–O3 read, "if they haue, they are better monied then I am?"

1518 **for fayling** just in case.

1518.3 **statelie** both "of imposing proportions" and "befitting a person of high estate".

1522 **wrought** decorated.

silke woorke silk embroidery.

1523–24 **laced ... price** Ruffs were trimmed with different types of openwork lace made of either gold and silver thread, silk, or linen, some ruffs being constructed entirely of lace; bobbin lace and purl lace (cf. 2311n. and 2318n.) were made with gold and silver thread and silk, while cutwork and drawnwork (cf. 2316n.) were expensive embroidered laces worked on linen.

1525 **Vnde** Latin, meaning "whence" (a source being understood); today we might say "the wherewithal". O1–O3 read "**Argent**".

geare rubbish.

1526–30 **for ... rope** i.e., for they will maintain these costly ruffs either by selling or mortgaging their lands, or by stealing the money at the cost of their lives, Shooters Hill, Stangate, and the Salisbury plain being notorious locations for highway robbery. The idea of selling land in these locations may have been intended as a joke, Stubbes assuming that his reader would be able to infer the crime associated with these places; although the passage was reworked in each successive edition, it is similarly obscure in all of them.

1530 **Tyborn** Tyburn, a former place of execution in London for Middlesex criminals.

1530–35 **& in ... Gallowes** only in Q1; fashionable ruffs became increasingly elaborate throughout the reign of Elizabeth I, and this probably refers to the late style of setting ruffs in a series of multiple horizontal pleats.

1532 **lengthes** The precise dimensions of this unit of measurement are uncertain, but Howes notes that ruffs of twelve lengths of material stood "a full quarter of a yearde deepe" and were known in France as "the English Monster" (Stow, *Annales*, 1615, sig. Dddd2ᵛ).

1533 **set** pleated.

1536–39 **The ... vsed** Stubbes returns in these early chapters to the conviction that the excessive wearing of sumptuous (foreign) apparel is responsible for price inflation and widespread poverty; cf. 662–66 with its note, and the parenthetical remark at 1588–92. At 4372–82, Stubbes alternatively explains escalating prices as the consequence of greed.

1541 **all in a manner** very nearly everyone.

1543–44 **Camericke** variant of "cambric".

1551 **wrought** decorated.

1552 **Needle woorke** any kind of work done with a needle, but in this instance embroidery.

1553 **curiously** skilfully, elaborately.

1553–54 **open seame** Arnold suggests that this refers to a decorative seam similar to that found on the top of a coif photographed as fig. 298b in her book *Queen Elizabeth's Wardrobe Unlock'd* (private correspondence); term used in a slightly different sense at 1712 and 2563.

1554 **knackes** trifles, toys.

1555–63 **Insomuch ... is** not in O1.

1556–57 **ten shillings ... fourty** i.e., half a pound, a pound, two pounds; cf. 1428n.

1558 **twenty Nobles** i.e., £6 13s. 4d; the value of these gold coins had settled at six shillings eight pence by 1550.

1560–61 **a crowne** i.e., five shillings, or a quarter of a pound sterling.

1566–67 **or if it doe** i.e., "or if this situation do occur"; O1–O3 read "if they do", referring to "Shirtes".

1568–69 **Si ... attollant** "if they raise their crests and lift up their horns". The phrase appears in Paulinus, *Dissertatio Quarta* (PL 99.557B).

1569–70 **if . . . Pantoffles** i.e., to stand on one's dignity or to affect a superior air (Tilley, *Proverbs*, P43); pantofles were mules with a low wedge heel worn as an overshoe (cf. 1740–72).

1570 **hoise . . . high** i.e., exalt themselves.

1571 **diamond** expensive (?); invariant usage, but none of the *OED* definitions fits this context (cf. 1991).

1573 **nice** unmanly? This adjective carried a wide range of meanings including "delicate" and "wanton"; "unmanly" is suggested as the primary sense in light of Stubbes's preoccupation with men becoming weak and womanish through the use of luxurious clothing.

1575 **daintie** fine, handsome.

1576–1607 **It . . . hower** A similar argument, using much of the same vocabulary, is used to advocate a more austere diet at 3675–96.

1576 **curiositie** excessive care or attention.

1577 **nicenesse** luxury.

1577–78 **transnatureth** changes the nature of.

1578–79 **infirme** physically weak.

1581 **confines** bordering regions; contrasting type O3–Q1 conveys emphasis.

1584–85 **within . . . yeares** i.e., within the last eighty or a hundred years.

1586 **Frize** woollen fabric with a heavy nap on one side.

hosen breeches, with either attached or separate stockings.

1586–87 **huswiues Carzie** Housewife cloth was a middle quality linen cloth intended for family use, and Stubbes is presumably referring to a similar quality woollen cloth.

1593 **streight** tight-fitting, narrow.

1596 **disgest** digest.

1597 **hard** i.e., hard to digest; cf. 3685. O1–O3 read "crude".

1598 **fairer complectioned** of a more robust physical constitution.

1602 **nesher** more delicate and weak.

1603 **hardnesse** hardship.

1606 **extenuate** stretch out; a very rare usage, and *OED* suggests it may have been confused for "extend".

1610–11 **nicenesse . . . curiosity** luxury . . . excessive care (cf. 1576–77).

1613 **fond toyes** foolish trifles.

nice cf. 1573n.

1615 **effeminat** womanish, self-indulgent.

1616 **nice** As the nuances of this word are influenced by context, the Q1 revision of "wanton girls" to "wayrish girles" later in the line is significant.

wayrish Probably "wearish", meaning feeble or delicate, but this spelling is not listed by *OED* as an alternative form; O1 reads "yonge", while O2 and O3 read "wanton".

1617 **puissant ... men** O1–O3 read, "puissant **agentes**, or manly men", "agents" being used in the sense of one who acts or exerts power.

1621 **monstrous** enormous and unnatural; cf. 1472n.

1624 **priuie members** private parts, genitals.

  quilted padded.

1625 **bombasted** i.e., padded with hair, cotton wool, etc.

  sewed i.e., with layers of material and padding sewn together.

1631–36 **Now ... iudge** i.e., the fashionable peascod belly.

1640–41 **gourmandice** gluttony.

1650 **Pudenda** genitals; according to *OED*, the word was not adopted into English from Latin before 1634.

1652 **Bombast** any material used as padding.

1654 **Grograine Chamlet** cf. 629n. and 653n.

1655 **slashed ... pinked** Various methods of decoratively cutting a garment, often allowing a contrasting material underneath to show through; unlike pinking (cf. 1436n.), the first four techniques suggest fairly long cuts in the material.

1656 **laced** trimmed with lace.

  all ... lace Instead of cutwork or drawnwork, the usual type of lace decorating doublets and gowns was a straight-edged braid or openwork bobbin lace constructed of many threads twisted and knotted together and sewn flat onto the material; any of these various types of trim, however, could be implicit in the ambiguous term "costly lace".

1657–58 **stand vpon** discourse upon at length.

1658 **particularlie** one by one, individually.

1663 **Hosen** breeches, with either attached or separate stockings; also called "hose".

1667–68 **French ... Venetians** styles discussed below.

1668–76 **The ... knees** The length and shape of French hose, also known as trunk hose, could vary considerably; what distinguishes them from other breeches is that they have either canions (1675) or stockings sewn on as extensions (Cunnington and Cunnington, *Costume*, 114–16).

1671 **sidenesse** length.

1673–74 **(being ... side)** The closing bracket is not in O2–Q1 but since the tendency is to use brackets in pairs, I have assumed a printer's error and emended the text in accordance with O1.

1674 **side** long.

1674–75 **some ... out** Both of these styles of French hose were usually decorated with strips of material, or "panes", running the length of the breech,
either sewn onto the garment or cut into the top layer of material; the material underneath was visible and could be pulled through, or "drawn out".

1675 **ornaments** decorations, embellishments.
   Canions tight knee-length extensions sewn to trunk hose, and worn with separate stockings.

1676 **adioyned** joined on.

1677 **Gallie hosen** also known as galligaskins; the origin of the word is uncertain, but it may be an attributive use of "galley", denoting sailors' clothing.
Like Venetians (1680), these knee-length breeches were worn with separate
stockings.

1679 **gardes** "A guard was a band or border placed on a garment for ornament.
The material of guards was, of course, different from that of the garment
which they ornamented; usually also, the colours contrasted" (Linthicum,
Costume, 150); cf. 1872 and 2453–55.
   laide downe trimmed or embroidered; the more common construction was
   "layd on" (cf. 1683).

1679–80 **either hose** i.e., each leg of the breeches, as in "a pair of hose".

1680 **Venetian hosen** The precise difference between these and gally hosen is
unclear, but whereas Venetians were both voluminous or narrow, gally hos-
en were usually baggy (Cunnington and Cunnington, *Costume*, 121–22).

1682 **finely** admirably, excellently; used ironically.

1683 **poyntes** ribbons or laces usually finished with metal tags.

1684 **rowes** streaks or stripes; O1–O3 read "rewes of lace".

1688 **Seruingman ... them** invariant shift from singular to plural subject.

1689 **condition** social rank or position.
   stick hesitate.

1690 **these kinde** The plural form of the demonstrative adjective was commonly
used with "kind" followed by a plural substantive.

1691 **sutable** matching (i.e., in color or style).

1694 **ten shillinges** i.e., half a pound.

1694–95 **Marke price** 13s. 4d, or two-thirds of a pound.

1695–96 **after ... rate** at a corresponding price.

1698–99 **of one paire** on one pair.

1699–1700 **Breeches ... neither** The clause following the parenthesis was added
in O2 but the preceding punctuation was never accordingly adapted; assuming an oversight, I have emended the full-stop found in Q1 after
"Breeches" to a colon (cf. collation).

1701 This ... euer The first "as" of the relative construction was sometimes omitted (Abbott, *Grammar*, 276).

woonderfull i.e., such as to excite astonishment.

1702 Rodde of Iustice O1–O3 read "Sworde of Iustice" and may originally have been an allusion to Ps. 7:12.

1703–4 with ... confuted The narrative construct falters as Stubbes forgets that he is supposed to be writing spoken dialogue; cf. 2291–93.

1705 Nether Stockins stockings. The only example of this rare expression cited in *OED* is dated 1591, the more common word being "netherstocks" in its various forms (cf. 1707); since this section was not set off with a chapter heading O1–O3 this term only appears Q1. The catchword to sig. E4 reads "Nether", which suggests that "**Costly**" was a late revision to the title.

1708 not of cloth The Cunningtons maintain that English hose before about 1530 were not knitted, but made of cloth and sewn with a seam (*Costume*, 37); Thirsk, however, argues that knitting was probably "a peasant handicraft ... which leaves no trace in our records because it had nothing attractive to offer to merchants in national or international trade" ("Folly," 53).

1709 Iarnsey used attributively for fine worsted from Jersey.

Worsted yarn made of long staple wool combed parallel and closely twisted. According to Howes, worsted stockings were not made in England before 1564, when an apprentice named William Rider borrowed and copied a pair belonging to an Italian merchant: "Within few yeeres after, began the plentuous making both of Gersey, and Wollen stockings, & so in short space they waxed common" (Stow, *Annales*, 1615, sig. Dddd2ᵛ).

1710 Crewell slackly twisted worsted yarn.

1712 curiously elaborately.

open seame shaping seam running down the back of the leg. Arnold suggests the design may have been similar to the open stitch pattern seen on the stockings in which Eleanora of Toledo was buried in 1562 (private correspondence; cf. Arnold, *Queen Elizabeth's Wardrobe Unlock'd*, figs. 301, 301a).

1713 quirkes and clockes ornamental patterns worked on the side of a stocking.

1715–25 And ... more It seems likely, in light of the yearly London wages set out in the proclamation of 3 August 1587 (cf. 1428n.) that this is an overstatement: "Stubb's [sic] exaggerations obscure what for economic historians must be one of the most significant features of this flourishing industry, namely that many different kinds of stockings were made to suit all purses and purposes" (Thirsk, "Folly," 59).

1716 impudent insolency shameless pride.

outrage extravagance, excessive luxury.

1722 **royal** valued at this time at approximately twelve shillings.

1732 **exceed** pass the bounds of propriety. O1–O3 print "rage", meaning to reach a high degree of intensity; the same substitution was made at 2510.

1740 **Corked ... England** Many chapter titles original to Q1, including this one, were incorporated without altering the format of the printer's copy to allow for an initial ornamental letter in the text which follows; it is unclear whether this was an oversight or a deliberate decision to conserve page space.

Corked shooes any shoes made with cork soles.

1741 **To** in addition to, besides.

1742 **Pinsnets** This style apparently became obsolete after 1600 and no contemporary description is available; Stubbes seems to imply that pinsnets, also known as pinsons, are similar, or at least related, to pantofles.

Pantoffles cf. 1569–70n.

1743 **two inches or more** O1–O3 read "a finger or two".

1747 **razed ... cut** i.e., decoratively slashed.

1748 **laid on** trimmed, embroidered.

1754 **abroad** out of doors.

1755.2 **slippers** precise sense uncertain (cf. 2565). According to the Cunningtons, these "may possibly be represented by a close-fitting shoe with a long narrow tongue, which extended up the front of the ankle" (*Costume*, 128), perhaps describing the light shoe worn inside pantofles; Linthicum argues that slippers denote slip-on shoes in general and can be used as synonymous with pantofles (*Costume*, 264).

1756 **faine** forced, obliged.

1757 **spurne** kick.

1760 **nicenesse** luxury, indulgence; the idea is that men wear these shoes in order to be fashionable (cf. 1775–78).

1762–69 **For ... same** Joseph Hall alludes to pantofles in *Virgidemiae* (1597), writing that men "tread on corked stilts a prisoners pace" (ed. Davenport, 4.6.11).

1763 **easie** conducive to ease, comfortable.

1765–67 **Againe ... ground** pantofles were usually shorter than the length of the inner shoe (Linthicum, *Costume*, 252); O1 reads "on" instead of "from" the ground.

1766 **whereas** seeing that.

1778 **commoditie** advantage, benefit.

1782–83 **collours ... collours** colors ... collars.

1784–85 **Mandilians** These short jackets had open side seams, and the fashion was to wear them turned through ninety degrees, with the sleeves hanging down at the back and front.

1792 **some . . . all** This detail, not in Q1 (cf. collation), was probably omitted as a result of compositorial eye-skip.

1792–93 **pleated . . . gathered** i.e., the material at the back is either gathered into the seam which runs across the shoulders or formed into short pleats and stitched onto an underlying piece of fabric (cf. 2470–72); see Arnold, *Patterns of Fashion*, 98–100, 118–19.

1792 **creasted** ribbed.

1796–97 **good . . . foule** Tilley, *Proverbs*, D89.

1796 **prouision** foresight.

1797–1801 **But . . . doe** Augustine, *Epistolarum* 93.12.50, PL 33.345; 185.9.35, PL 33.808–809. Stubbes uses the argument again in *A Motiue to Good Workes* (sig. K4), there citing Augustine as his source.

1800 **Presses** large cupboards.

Wardrobes rooms in which clothing was kept.

1801–49 **Doe . . . besides** Stubbes is unusual here in advocating charity for the homeless. As Linda Woodbridge documents in *Vagrancy, Homelessness, and English Renaissance Literature* (Urbana, IL: University of Illinois Press, 2001), Elizabethan Poor Laws distinguished between the deserving, settled poor, and undeserving vagrants, rending the latter "almost nonhuman" (13–14, see 1–37, and Appendix A, "Historical Contexts for the Study of Vagrancy and Poverty," 267–84). Compare 696–702, 3478–82, 5605–10.

1805–9 **God . . . withall** Deut. 15:7–11.

1808 **store** plenty, abundance.

1815–16 **messe of pottage** portion of soup.

1817 **cheare** kindly welcome, hospitable entertainment; "whipping cheare", used ironically to mean flogging, is recorded in Tilley (*Proverbs*, W308).

1822 **whereas** where.

1824 **well** Philoponus seems to mean "lucky" or "fortunate", but the first example of this sense of the adjective cited in *OED* is dated 1665 (a. 6b); the usage is invariant.

1827 **nor . . . hide** and also not [covering] to hide.

1831–43 **And . . . miserablie** The same brutal measures are described by Nashe in *Christs Teares Over Jerusalem* (1593): "There were thē in the heate of the sicknes, that thought to purge and clense theyr houses by conueying their infected seruaunts forth by night into the fieldes, which there starued and dyed, for want of reliefe and warme-keeping" (ed. McKerrow, 2:160).

1840 **are . . . down** The reading found O3–Q1, "or layd down", seems corrupt as the reader never learns what happens to the servants after they are taken away; as this sentence was heavily revised after O1, I have emended on the basis of the O2 reading.

1843.1 **Turkish** Although, according to *OED*, this adjective means simply "of the Turks" and is not used as synonymous with "savage" or "barbarous" before 1600, the latter definition is at least glanced at both here and at 1845.

1847–49 **Vnus ... besides** exaggerated form of the proverb "One eyewitness is better than ten earwitnesses" (Tilley, *Proverbs*, E274; Erasmus, *Adagia* 2.6.54).

1850 **excursions** digressions.

1864 **red tawny** two separate colors.

1867–68 **Spanish ... fashions** The Spanish cloak was short and full with a hood; the French cloak was long and full, sometimes reaching to the ankle, and worn fashionably over the left shoulder in such a way that it was kept on only with difficulty; and the Dutch cloak, similar to the mandilian, was waist-length, sleeved, and usually heavily decorated with guards (Linthicum, *Costume*, 193–95). In 1580, presumably referring to the French style, Elizabeth I commanded that "no person shall use or wear such excessive long cloaks, being in common sight monstrous, as now of late are begun to be used, and before two years past hath not been used in this realm" (*TRP*, 2:462).

1869 **girdlestead** waist.

1871 **liker** more like; common form of the comparative adjective before "than" (Abbott, *Grammar*, 6).

gownes loose, flowing robes, often lined with fur, worn both for warmth and for ceremonial purposes.

1871–80 **Then ... lined** In O1 this passage reads, "These clokes must be garded, laced, & thorowly faced: and somtimes so lyned".

1871 **garded** trimmed.

1872 **gards** cf. 1679n.

1872–73 **laced ... silke** cf. 1656n. Decorative lace made of gold or silver could be as expensive as Stubbes suggests; Earnshaw notes that such trimming was "moved from one dress or doublet to another, and inventoried under jewellery" (*Lace*, 24).

1875 **skirtes** borders; cf. 2308.

1877 **Bables** baubles; cheap, showy ornaments.

1877–78 **Bugles** tube-shaped glass beads, usually black; bugles as a form of trim were prohibited in 1580 to men under the station of baron's son, knight or gentleman in attendance on Her Majesty, who were not in possession of £200, in lands and fees (*TRP*, 2:190, 458).

1879 **faced** trimmed with another material.

1880 **withall** in addition, moreover.

1880–81 **standeth ... much** costs almost as much; this expression usually takes an indirect object, but cf. 1910–11.

1883–84 **hanged ... tassels** i.e., held on to the shoulders with tagged laces and clasps.

1890–91 **of our sauiour** O1–O3 read "at the hands of our **Proconsul** & chiefe **Prouost**".

1892–94 **but ... poyson** Spudeus's metaphor is unclear, as one would expect new fashions to be hammered, rather than sucked, out of a forge; O1–O2 read "drawen". It is possible that Stubbes may have had in mind the action of a bellows (cf. 2664–69, and the similar image at 591–92).

1894 **confusion** ruin; O1 reads "destruction".

1896 **Boothose** stockings worn over netherstocks to protect them from dirt.

1901 **this** i.e., this fine cloth.

1903 **wrought** decorated, embroidered; cf. the trimming of ruffs and shirts (1522, 1551–53).

1905 **clogged** encumbered, filled up.

1906 **Antiques** antics, monstrous or caricatured representations of animals.

1910–11 **to stand some in** some to cost; cf. 1880–81n.

1913–14 **so long ... waste** Stubbes is presumably referring to boothose that would be turned over the tops of the boots.

1915 **reasonable ... shirte** It is not unusual to find an adjective used as an adverb (Abbott, *Grammar*, 1).

1921 **gewgawes** trifles, ornaments.

1922 **blaunched** whitened, perhaps as a consequence of the silver and gold embroidery? or possibly "perverted"? (cf. *OED*, a. 1 and 5); invariant usage.

1923 **gazing** that look or stare curiously.

1924 **vertiginy** vertigo, giddiness.

1925 **phantasticall** foppish, capricious.

1929–36 **To ... goodly** Stubbes's complaint echoes the proclamation enforcing statutes of apparel dated 15 June 1574: "None shall wear spurs, swords, rapiers, daggers ... gilt, silvered, or damasked: except knights and barons' sons, and others of higher degree or place, and gentlemen in ordinary office attendant upon the Queen's majesty's person" (*TRP*, 2:384); this directive appears as early as 1562 and was repeated in the sumptuary proclamation of 1580 (*TRP*, 2:458).

1930–37 **with ... prid** not in O1.

1930.3 **damasked** ornamented with inlayed designs in gold or silver.

1931 **Angell golde** twenty-two carat gold.

argented ouer covered with silver; the verbal form is not recorded in *OED* (but see "silver" v. 1).

1932 **both ... without** presumably referring to a cup hilt which envelops the hand.

1935 **Vernished** coated with varnish.

1942 **appale** make pale with fear; related to the modern verb "appal".

1944 **Martialist** military man, warrior.

1948 **auaileable** serviceable, profitable.

1959–60 **Redde ... stewardship** Luke 16:2.

1965 **discouered** disclosed, revealed.

guises fashions, styles.

1971 **prest** eager, keen.

1974 **à crepundiis** "from a child's rattle", hence, "from childhood". *ILS* attests to this saying as an inscription in the ancient world (I.1183); cf. St. Jerome, *Epistola* 108.3, PL 22.879.

1978 **counteruaile** reciprocate.

1979 **supply** compensate for.

1983–84 **but ... trust** This invariant punctuation is meaningful but not logical; the brackets suggest irony.

1983 **munificencie** munificence, generosity.

1988 **corrasiue** corrosive, annoyance.

stomackes This word, like "breasts" or "hearts", designated the inward seat of passion and emotions; "tender stomackes", however, is perhaps used ironically to mean "mild dispositions".

1988–89 **tender ... minds** O1–O3 read "hautie stomackes ... tēder breasts".

1989 **nippitatum** strong, high-quality liquor or ale, nippitate; Stubbes is perhaps suggesting that his criticisms will act on women like strong alcohol, making them belligerent and defiant.

1991 **diamond** brilliant, shining (?). This invariant usage is the second of only two examples cited in *OED* (sb. 8c); cf. 1571.

1993–94 **for ... obliuion** Job vii.21.

1996 **Penitentiaries** persons under the direction of a confessor, penitents.

1999 **purpose** discourse, conversation.

2000–1 **Collouring ... England** not in O1–O3; an initial ornamental letter was incorporated into Q1 to mark the new chapter, but the speech prefix "Philo." was not repeated.

2002–3 **The ... faces** The German merchant Samuel Kiechel visited England in 1585 and offers a contrasting report: "Item, the women there are charming, and by nature so mighty pretty, as I have scarcely ever beheld, for they do

not falsify, paint or bedaub them-selves as in Italy or other places" (translated from the German by Rye, *England as Seen by Foreigners*, 89–90).

2003 **Liquors** liquids.

2005 **decored** adorned, embellished.

2008 **indignation** wrath, anger.

2008–9 **at ... tremble** Jer. 10:10, but similar phrases are found elsewhere in the
Bible.

2009–11 **at ... away** 2 Pet. 3:10–12.

2013–14 **he is ... God** Exod. 20:5, which actually reads "zelotes".

2016–25 **If ... them?** This analogy is from Cyprian's treatise, *De Habitu Virginum* ¶15, PL 4.455A. Stubbes quotes further from this treatise at 2077–
98. Augustine quotes this passage from Cyprian in *De Doctrina Christiana*
4.21.49, PL 34.113.

2017–18 **Cobbler** clumsy workman, botcher.

2025–42 **Doe ... word** A similar line of reasoning is used to condemn rich
clothing at 936–56. This passage echoes Tertullian's attack on women and
cosmetics in *De Cultu Feminarum* 2.5, PL 1.1321A: "To them, I suppose,
the plastic skill of God is displeasing! In their own persons, I suppose, they
convict, they censure, the Artificer of all things! For censure they do when
they amend, when they add to, [His work]" (trans. Thelwall, 320–21).

2029 **slibbersauces** messy, repulsive concoctions; O1–O2 print "sibbersawces".

2029–30 **these ... intentions** i.e., to make themselves appear more beautiful.

2036 **them** themselves.

2048–50 **they ... repent** Isa. 8:14–15.

2054 **denounce** proclaim, pronounce.

2055–59 **Depart ... creation** Matt. 25:12, 41.

2064–68 **But ... confections** Elizabethan cosmetics and lotions included such
ingredients as ceruse (white lead), turpentine, and sublimate of mercury.

2065 **simples** single uncompounded substances, serving as ingredients in a
mixture.

2067 **artificially** skilfully, cleverly.

tempered mixed, blended.

2068 **condiments** An invariant and apparently unique usage synonymous with
"confections", meaning mixtures or compounds; these words were also paired
O1–O3 in the chapter on gluttony, but "condimentes" was revised in Q1 to
"iunkets" (cf. 3669).

2070 **amiable** lovely.

2073 **Fathers** Church Fathers, early Christian writers.

2077–85 **S. Cyprian ... blacke** *De Habitu Virginum* ¶16, PL 4.455B. The bibli-

cal verse cited is Matt. 5:36; Jesus uses these words to warn against swearing, not face-painting, but the verse as appropriated by Cyprian demonstrates the extent to which women dare to challenge the word and power
of the Lord. Augustine quotes this passage in *De Doctrina Christiana*
4.21.49, PL 34.113–14.

2077 **S. Cyprian** Thascius Caecilianus Cyprianus (200–258), Bishop of Carthage
and Church Father.

2080 **corrupted** spoiled.

2081 **brothell** prostitute.

2085–98 **In . . . hell** Diples, a vertical series of marginal commas, drew the reader's attention in O1 to this injunction against face-painting.

2085–93 **In . . . creatures** Cyprian, *De Habitu Virginum* ¶17, PL 4.456A. This
is Stubbes's only quotation from Cyprian's attack on women who paint
their faces and dye their hair that does not appear in Augustine, *De Doctrina Christiana*.

2093–98 **Againe . . . hell** Cyprian, *De Habitu Virginum* ¶16, PL 4.456A, quoted
by Augustine, *De Doctrina Christiana* 4.21.49, PL 34.114.

2098–108 **Saint . . . lesse?** Ambrose, *De Virginibus* 1.6.28, PL 16.196C–197A,
quoted by Augustine, *De Doctrina Christiana* 4.21.50, PL 34.114.

2098 **Saint Ambrose** c. 339–97, Bishop of Milan and Christian theologian.

2103 **change** exchange.

2108–11 **Can . . . fayrer?** brackets introduced Q1. Although the parenthetical
statement grammatically ends at "filthie", the placement of the closing
bracket has not been emended as the parenthesis characterizes the artificial
means by which women think to make themselves more fair as both filthy
and cursed; a similar rhetorical use of parenthesis is found at 1981–87.

2112 **inuections** invectives.

2113 **grounded** strongly founded.

moe more in number.

Augustine St. Augustine of Hippo (354–430).

2114 **Hierome** St. Jerome (c. 342–420), biblical scholar and translator of the
Bible into the Vulgate.

Chrysostom St. John Chrysostom (c. 347–407), Bishop of Constantinople.

Gregorie Pope Gregory I (c. 540–604).

Caluin John Calvin (1509–1564), French theologian and reformer.

2114–15 **Peter Martir** martyr, saint (1205–1252), Inquisitor for North Italy
under Pope Gregory IX.

2115 **Gualter** Rodolph Walther (1518–1586), Swiss Protestant theologian.

2117–18 **those . . . collouring** i.e., those . . . [actions of] painting and coloring.

2117 **brothellous** whorish.

2120–21 **Pauca ... sufficient** Tilley, *Proverbs*, W781. The lack of punctuation in
   Q1 to separate the Latin from its translation is another example of the
   omission of punctuation which coincides with a line break.

2125–38 **And ... chaunge** not in O1.

2128–29 **orient** lustrous, brilliant.

2130–35 **Then ... other?** Matt. 6:30.

2140–41 **the Sunne ... glorie** 1 Cor. 15:41.

2149 **tricking** arranging, trimming.

   laying out arranging, ordering.

2150 **of force** necessarily, unavoidably.

2150–51 **frizled** curled in small, crisp curls.

2151 **crisped** closely and stiffly curled.

   a worlde a wonder; an abbreviated version of the expression "it is a world"
   found at 2637–38.

2151–52 **on ... borders** Norris argues that this phrase means "braids of hair encircling the head" (3:736), an interpretation supported neither by *OED* nor
   surviving pictorial evidence; Stubbes is perhaps describing the shape of the
   masses of curls which curve in "borders" around the women's faces, using
   "wreathes" to mean "twisted bands" in much the same way as at 2160 and
   2163.1.

2153–54 **And ... what** Stubbes refers to the practice of rolling either smooth or
   curled hair back from the forehead over a pad or wire structure around
   which the hair is wrapped and shaped, the face sometimes being further
   framed with a fringe of tight curls.

2153.1–4 **SN Simia ... insignia** "An ape will always be an ape, though it wear
   decorations of gold" (Walther, *Proverbia* 29635b; Erasmus, *Adagia* 1.7.11);
   Tilley, *Proverbs*, S451: "Silk and satin make not a gentleman" (cf. 2448.1–
   2).

2155 **grim ... sterne** formidable and threatening in appearance.

2156 **matrones** This usage is significant since married women had only very recently begun to wear their hair uncovered (de Courtais, *Headdress and
   Hairstyles*, 49).

2157 **bolstered haire** i.e, natural hair arranged over "sausages" of false hair to
   give lift and bulk.

   crested arranged in such a way that it resembles the comb, or crest, on a bird's
   head.

2158 **frontiers** foreheads.

2158–60 **hanging ... side** i.e., women's hair, built up on top and to the sides of their heads, reminds him of awnings (cf. note to "pentise" at 1479). "Glasse windowes" probably suggests that the women's faces remain clearly visible from each side. The simile is obscure and potentially misleading as one might see the women's hair falling into, rather than projecting above, their faces, but a similar image is used by Dekker in the *Gull's Hornbook* (1609) to describe men's hairstyles: "having goodly penthouses of hair to over-shadow [the eyes]" (ed. McKerrow, 29).

2160–61 **great ... siluer** Ornamental bands, called upper billiments, curved around the top edge of high dressed hair and were made of precious metals or rich material decorated with jewels: "[They] either formed part of a small cap, caul or band fitting over the coil of hair at the back or [they were] simply the back portion of the French hood complete with the black velvet hanging flap" (de Courtais, *Headdress and Hairstyles*, 52).

2161–62 **applyed** fastened.

2162–70 **And ... recompt** Jewels were fastened into the hair like brooches, sometimes in such a way as to dangle on the forehead.

2163.2 **circumgiring** encompassing; Stubbes is the only writer cited in *OED* to use the verb in this sense.

2164 **wreathed** shaped as a wreath or band around their faces.

2165 **Bugles** tube-shaped glass beads, usually black; cf. 1877–78n.

Bables showy trinkets, gewgaws.

2166 **Ouches** brooches worn as ornaments.

glasses things (presumably beads) made of glass.

2169–70 **recompt** recount, relate.

2170–73 **But ... godlinesse** 1 Pet. 3:3–4; the Geneva (1599) sidenote explains that Peter "condemneth the riot and excesse of women and setteth foorth their true apparelling such as is precious before God: to wit, the inward and incorruptible which consisteth in a meeke and quiet spirit".

2171 **vanites** variant of "vanities".

2174–76 **The ... them** 1 Cor. 11:15.

2175 **cherish** tend, foster.

2177–78 **laying it forth** decking it out, arraying it; O1–O3 read "laying it out" (cf. 2149, 2180, and 2181.3).

2187 **strange beasts** It is not the animals, but the use to which their hair is put, which Stubbes finds unaccountable.

2188–98 **And ... haire** not in O1.

2191 **nice** Both "wanton" and "difficult to please" could be understood here.

2199 **order** formal array, arrangement.

2204 **chaunging ... accidents** i.e., converting the underlying essence of a thing into its non-essential attributes; Stubbes's complaint is that cosmetic details such as styling and color have become all-important (cf. 3753–54).

2206–8 **So ... same** Hair and head coverings for women are prescribed at 1 Cor. 11:1–15 as important tokens of their obedience and subjection to men.

2209 **made it ... pride** O1 reads, "made (as it were) a **Metamorphosis** of it, making it an ornament of Pride".

2211 **stiffenecked people** Exod. 32:9; Deut. 9:13.

2213 **the straite ... Lord** Matt. 7:14.

2214 **Cisternes** artificial reservoirs.

2216 **confusion** ruin.

2217 **French Hoodes** headdresses "made on a stiff foundation and worn far back", with a strip of material hanging behind which could be flipped up and fastened on top of the women's heads (Cunnington and Cunnington, *Costume*, 74).

2220.1 **Capitall** of the head; according to *OED*, this adjective was not used in the sense of "excellent" or "first-rate" prior to the eighteenth century.

2222 **Hatte** Hats for women, as opposed to caps or hoods, were a relatively new fashion innovation (de Courtais, *Headdress and Hairstyles*, 56).

2223 **Kercher** kerchief. Linthicum notes that "they were worn only by the lower classes" (*Costume*, 162), a point confirmed by the Cunningtons (*Costume*, 197–99); kerchiefs are presumably mentioned because they were worn over the head.

2224–26 **Veluet ... of that** The condensed Q1 version (cf. collation) is likely to have resulted from careless type-setting, the compositor's eye skipping twice within the same sentence.

2227 **fantasies** whims, caprices.
   serpentine cunning, evil.

2229 **sticke** hesitate.

2230–31 **euery Marchants ... Gentlewomen** i.e., all severally. In this period, "every" could take either a singular or plural substantive — here it takes both; the passage is invariant.

2238–39 **run ... another** Tilley, *Proverbs*, B27; "a malo, ad peius" means "from bad to worse".

2239–40 **vntill ... iniquity** Matt. 23:32; the Geneva (1599) sidenote reads: "A prouerbe vsed of the Iewes, which hath this meaning, Goe ye on also & follow your ancestors, that at length your wickednesse may come to the full".

2242.1–3 **Trahit ... voluptas** "each is led by his or her liking" (Vergil, *Eclogue*, trans. Fairclough, 2.65).

2243 **furnish foorth** decorate, embellish.

2244 **Cawles** net caps, lined with expensive material and often set with jewels, covering the hair arranged in a bun at the back of the head.

2246–47 **(for ... worst)** This passage provides good evidence that Stubbes revised the book with only the most recently published version to hand as a printing error in O2 was compounded in subsequent editions. The closing bracket found in O1 was reversed in O2, leading to the inclusion of an extra closing bracket after "Cawles" (2248) in O3; these two brackets were dropped in Q1, but not the original opening bracket.

2252–56 **And ... variety** These caps made of a whitish-grey fur were far less prevalent in this period than they were fifty years earlier (Cunnington and Cunnington, *Costume*, 80); not in O1.

2253–54 **like ... Priestes** i.e., the peaks resemble mitres.

2255 **perriwinckles** wigs (more fully, "periwigs").

Chitterlings ornamental pleatings, frills. A similar usage in *A delicate Diet, for daintiemouthde Droonkardes* (1576) suggests this is probably a passing reference to elaborate ruffs: "we doo not onelye reteyne [foreign defects], but we do so farre exceede them: that of a *Spanish* Codpeece, we make an English footeball ... of a *French* ruffe, an English Chytterling" (Gascoigne, ed. Cunliffe, 2:466).

2255–56 **Apish** foolish, trifling.

2256–59 **Thus ... naughtinesse** perhaps alluding to the parable of the lazy servant, condemned for misusing the money lent to him by his master (Matt. 25:14–30); cf. 84–101.

2259 **naughtinesse** wickedness, depravity.

2261 **decay** downfall, ruin.

2262 **Minions** hussies.

2263 **Sempronians** Sempronia, the wife of D. Junius Brutus (consul 77 B.C.E.), took part in Catiline's conspiracy; her promiscuous character is recorded by Sallust in *The War with Catiline* (ed. Rolfe, 25.1–5).

2269–76 **There ... eie** source unknown.

2271 **Philautoi ... themselues** Erasmus, *Adagia* 1.3.92.

2273 **Margarites** pearls.

2280 **frequented** practiced.

2284 **Humility** O1 reads "chastitie".

2287–88 **Libertines ... Epicures ... Atheists** Stubbes's application of these terms is generalized, the implicit connection being that those who hold these opinions consider themselves exempt from conventional moral and religious obligations and therefore represent the epitome of pride and wickedness; in O1–O3 this sentence concludes, "nor that the wickednesse of them might euer coūterpoyze, with the wickednesse of these people".

2290.2 **Neckerchers** here used as synonymous with ruffs; cf. 2354.

2290.3 **Partlets** articles of dress, sometimes beautifully decorated, used to fill in the décolletage; partlets could be made with a high neck and finished with a frill, a feature which eventually developed into the larger, separate ruff.

2291–92 **no . . . describe it** Stubbes once again overlooks the fact that he is supposed to be writing spoken dialogue; cf. 1703–4.

2294–95 **Hollande . . . Cammericke** types of linen; cf. 1473n.

2300 **streaked** made smooth by rubbing.

2301 **applyed** fastened.

2302 **Supportasses** cf. 1500–7 and 1486.8n.; Arnold in *Patterns of Fashion* describes gowns in which "[a] pair of eyelet holes is worked in the centre back of the stiffened standing collar for a ribbon point to attach a supportasse or underpropper" (122, 118).

2303–10 **beyond . . . wot** As the page heading to sig. G2 suggests, this passage describes two styles of wearing ruffs: a number of "minor" ruffs worn one on top of another, and a single large ruff.

2304 **fetch** contrivance, trick.

2305 **orders** rows.

2305–7 **three . . . another** In portraits one frequently sees two, and sometimes three, narrow ruffs pushed up high against the chin; double ruffs had been forbidden as early as 1562 by royal proclamation (*TRP*, 2:190), but a similar reference to "the three-pild ruffe" appears in the induction to Jonson's *Every Man out of his Humour* (1599, ed. Herford and Simpson, 3:Ind., 111).

2305–6 **degrees** steps, levels.

2306 **gradatim** defined in O1: "placed gradatim, step by step".

2307 **vnder** of less size than.

2308 **skirtes** borders.

2308–9 **are . . . crested** i.e., are pleated and ribbed (crested) with long pleats radiating out from the neck (cf. 1500–1, 2470–71).

2311 **golde . . . lace** Both bobbin lace and purl lace were made of these materials and were used to trim ruffs, but this passage probably alludes to the former, as purl lace is named at 2318; bobbin lace, an openwork lace also used to trim garments such as sleeves, cloaks, and gloves, was made by twisting a number of separate threads around pins on a cushion.

2312 **stately** befitting a person of high estate.

    wrought decorated.

    needle worke any work done with the needle; perhaps a reference to the decorative stitching found in cutwork and drawnwork (cf. 2316n.), but more probably embroidery.

2313 **sparkled** thickly dotted, speckled.

2314–15 **other Antiques** Unlike modern English, "other" is used in this passage to distinguish antics, which are purposely caricatured animal figures, from representations of the sun, moon, and stars; cf. *Macbeth* (4.3.90–91): "All these [vices] are portable, / With other graces weighed".

2316 **open worke** cutwork or drawnwork, two popular types of lace for ruffs: in the former, sections of the material were cut away, whereas in the latter, individual threads were carefully pulled out. The open spaces thus created by either technique were then filled in with decorative needle stitches. The proclamation issued 12 February 1580 prohibited the wearing of "white works, alias cutworks, made beyond the seas" to women of less estate than the daughters of barons, the wives of knights and baron's sons, and those who were married to men assessed in the subsidy book at less than £200 in lands (*TRP*, 2:459).

2317 **close worke** surface embroidery (Earnshaw, *Lace*, 17); the term is not listed in *OED*, and Palliser refers to the same decorative technique as "close embroidery" (*History of Lace*, 14). O1 mentions open work and purl lace, but not close work.

2318 **purled lace** needle lace consisting of tiny loops that could be built up into more elaborate triangles; it edged such garments as collars and ruffs, and was made of gold or silver thread or silk (Earnshaw, *Lace*, 160).

2318.2 **curiositie** elaborate workmanship.

2319–20 **the Ruffe ... selfe** i.e., the decorative trimming has completely overwhelmed the underlying article; cf. the similar criticism at 2204 that "the substance [is changed] into accidents".

2320–21 **Sometimes ... eares** i.e., the ruffs would be pinned to the supportasses underneath, "giv[ing] a tilt up at the back and down in front" (Cunnington and Cunnington, *Costume*, 113).

2321–22 **they ... shoulders** i.e., instead of being fixed onto supportasses, the pleated ruffs extended straight out from the neck.

2324 **deuises** pleasures, inclinations.

2324–27 **Suus ... sweetest** Tilley, *Proverbs*, F65; Erasmus, *Adagia* 3.4.2. The translation given O1–O3 is less literal: "Euery one thinketh his owne wayes best".

2326 **foist** fart.

2327–95 **But ... doe** Not in O1, and Stubbes's source for this supposedly true event is unidentified; John Cooke alludes to the same story in *Tu Quoque*

(1614): "and for pride, the woman that had her Ruffe poak'd by the divell, is but a Puritan to [my sister]" (ed. Berman, 3.319–20).

2331 **27. of Maie. 1582.** It is not unusual to find unabbreviated dates in the *Abuses* punctuated with full-stops; cf. 7057.

2335 **vpon a time** on one occasion, once.

2337 **against** in anticipation of.

2340 **proper** good-looking, comely; cf. 2357.

2343 **laid them out** arranged them.

2345 **in no case** by no means.

2345–46 **curious and dainty** particular, difficult to satisfy.

2347 **set** pleat.

2347.2 **lubricious** lewd, lascivious.

2351 **teare** blaspheme.

　ban curse.

2357 **braue** finely-dressed.

2360 **agonized** subjected to torture.

　pelting chafe violent rage or fury.

2362–63 **(as … stomacks)** cf. Tilley, *Proverbs*, W649: "A woman conceals what she knows not".

2364 **abused** imposed upon, cheated.

2367–68 **contentation** satisfaction.

2368 **looking** looking at, beholding.

2372 **writhed** wrung. This emendation has been introduced as neither "writh" (Q1) nor "writhe" (O2–O3) are listed in *OED* as forms of the verb in the past tense; it seems possible that the O2–Q1 readings derive from a compositorial misreading of a manuscript "ed" for "e".

2374 **vgglesome** horrible, gruesome.

2375–76 **amorous** lovely.

2376 **deformed** disfigured, marred.

2392 **their … glasses** "A pocket looking-glass was the common companion of the fashionables of both sexes at this time. The ladies carried it either in their pockets or hanging at their sides, and sometimes it was inserted in the fan" (Planché, *British Costume*, 284); cf. 2649–54.

2396 **Camilion** chameleon; the spelling used O2–Q1 is not listed in *OED*, but there seems no need to return to the O1 reading "camelion".

2396–97 **As … white** Tilley, *Proverbs*, C222.

2399 **Proteus** sea god in Greek and Roman mythology renowned for his ability to change shape.

2403 **outrage** run riot, go to excess.

2404 **weake brethren** alluding to 1 Cor. 8:9–13, where Paul warns the early Christians not to use their liberty in indifferent matters if their actions may confuse those who are less knowledgeable (the weak brethren), thus leading them into sin.

2405 **offend** cause to stumble or sin.

2406 **Doublets for Women** An extant woman's doublet is described by Arnold in *Patterns of Fashion*: "The doublet has a decidedly masculine appearance and has previously been described as that of a young man. The absence of a linen strip with worked eyelet holes at the waist, to which breeches or trunk-hose would have been attached by points, the slightly curved shape of the centre front, the lacing strips beneath the buttons and buttonholes and the shoulder rolls suggested that this garment might have been worn by a girl or a slim young woman ... the theory was finally confirmed by a small German gouache painting" (107).

2408–9 **buttoned ... breast** The variant Q1 reading, "buttoned vp to the breast" (cf. collation), is almost certainly a mistake as it implies that these garments buttoned up only as far as the breast when doublets and jerkins tended to fasten either visibly or invisibly all the way up the front.

2409 **wings ... pinions** decorative pieces of material, varying in size and shape, sewn around the armhole to cover the seam or ties fastening the sleeve to the main body of the garment.

2410 **shoulder pointes** points of the shoulders; cf. 1478n.

2414 **kind** gender, sex.

2419–22 **It ... also** Deut. 22:5.

2423 **compasse** O1–O3 read "limites and bandes".

2424–28 **Our ... kinde** This criticism of women in men's apparel paraphrases Stephen Gosson's attack on the cross-dressed boy actor printed in *Playes Confuted* (1582): "garments are set downe for signes distinctiue betwene sexe & sexe, to take vnto vs those garments that are manifest signes of another sexe, is to falsifie, forge, and adulterate, contrarie to the expresse rule of the worde of God" (ed. Kinney, sig. E3ᵛ).

2427 **participate ... same** i.e., have some of the qualities of, or a common character with, the other sex.

2428 **adulterate** corrupt, falsify.

2429–31 **Wherefore ... men** Such accusations were commonly levelled at cross-dressed women; William Averell, for example, writes in 1588: "though they be in sexe Women, yet in attire they appeare to be men, and are like **Androgini**, who counterfayting the shape of either kind, are in deede neither, so while they are in condition women, and woulde seeme in apparrell men, they are neither men nor women, but plaine Monsters" (sig. B1ᵛ).

2430–31 **of both kindes** possessing both genders.

2434 **as is incident** as is naturally appertaining; O2–O3 read "as is proper" (sentence not in O1). I have emended the awkward Q1 substitution of "&" for "as" in this phrase as a nonsensical error, despite deliberate revision of the next word but one.

2436–37 **Circes ... Medea** cf. 572.1–2n.

2440–42 **but ... conuersation** Although extravagant attire was worn by both sexes, accusations of sexual profligacy are directed only at women; cf. 2511.1–4.

2441–42 **dissolutenesse** O1–O3 read "venereous [venereal] inclination".

2442 **conuersation** behavior.

2443 **Gownes** originally long robes worn loose over kirtles (described at 2480–84); extended in the second half of the sixteenth century to include fitted dresses.

2448–51 **But ... part** Norris describes this style of trim: "the whole surface of the surcote and underdress is covered with bands of gold lace, about an inch in width, set close in horizontal, perpendicular, and oblique lines" (3:680).

2448.1–2 **Simiae in purpuris** "Apes in purple cloth" (Walther, *Proverbia*, 29635c; Erasmus, *Adagia* 1.7.10).

2449 **layd** trimmed.

2450 **lace** cf. 1656n.

2453 **garded** trimmed.

2453–54 **great ... least** An item in the proclamation enforcing statutes of apparel dated 12 February 1580 would have been applicable by analogy to women's clothing: "no person under the degree of a baron, a knight of the order, one of the Privy Council, [or] a gentleman ... ordinarily attendant upon her majesty's person shall wear any guards of velvet upon any one garment, exceeding in the whole in velvet the breadth of six inches" (*TRP*, 2:461).

2453 **gardes of Veluet** cf. 1679n.

2454–55 **edged ... lace** i.e., the gowns, not the guards, were bordered with lace; cf. the trimming of kirtles at 2482–84.

2459–61 **some with ... tailes** Probably describing false sleeves which attached at the armhole and hung down the skirt behind the bodice sleeves.

2461 **cast ... tailes** i.e., pushed back from the point at which they are fastened to the gown, not draped over the opposite shoulder.

2462–65 **cut ... gallantly** i.e., the outer fabric would be cut at regular intervals and the contrasting material underneath pulled (or "drawne out") through the gaps to form puffs, with ribbons (or sometimes metal tags or jewels) placed between the puffs.

2464 **poynted** adorned with tagged points or laces.

2465 **true . . . knottes** Tilley, *Proverbs*, L571; precisely how these ornamental bows were tied is uncertain, but Ashley notes they were probably constructed out of two intertwined overhand knots (*Book of Knots*, 383).

2465–66 **(for . . . them.)** The full-stop found here O1–O3 was probably lost in Q1 as a result of a line break (cf. collation).

2466 **Capes** By the early seventeenth century this word was synonymous with cloaks, but Stubbes is probably describing a feature resembling a tippet which attached to the gown at the neck and hung loose over the shoulders; cf. *The Taming of the Shrew*, where the tailor describes Katherine's gown as having "a small compassed cape" (ed. Wells and Taylor, 4.3.137).

2468 **fine . . . Taffeta** perhaps describing tuft taffeta which had a pile or nap arranged in stripes (Linthicum, *Costume*, 124).

2469 **fringed about** furnished with a decorative border of strings either loose or gathered into tassels; cf. Arnold, *Patterns of Fashion* (fig. 252).

2470–71 **pleated . . . backe** cf. 1792–93n.; instead of "creasted", O1–O3 read "riueled", also meaning pleated or gathered in small folds.

2473 **Peticoates** underskirts.

2478–79 **of . . . collour** probably describing a shot silk which shows different colors under different aspects, but cf. 2554 where a similar phrase means "in a variety of colors".

2480–81 **Kirtles** With the changing shape and construction of women's dresses in the sixteenth century, kirtles and petticoats both came to describe skirts (Cunnington and Cunnington, *Costume*, 149). Since Stubbes distinguishes between the two garments, it appears he is using the former term in its original sense to describe full-length dresses worn under gowns.

2484–89 **So . . . togither** Samuel Kiechel, a visitor to England in 1585, likewise described the effect of all these layers as ungainly: "[Englishwomen] are somewhat awkward in their style of dress; for they dress in splendid stuffs, and many a one wears three cloth gowns or petticoats, one over the other" (translated from the German in Rye, *England as Seen by Foreigners*, 90).

2485–86 **women . . . themselues** not listed in either Tilley, *Proverbs*, or Dent, *Proverbial Language*, but appearing in a similar form in John Lyly's *Euphues* (1579): "Take from them their perywigges, their paintings, their Iewells, their rowles, their boulstrings, and thou shalt soone perceiue that a woman is the least parte of hir selfe" (ed. Arber, 116); cf. 2319–20n.

2488 **Puppits or Mawmettes** dolls.

2489 **clowtes** cloths, rags.

2491–92 **euery ... Yeoman** Although Philoponus concedes at 715–22 that the yeomanry are permitted to wear rich garments, expensive clothing apparently remains an abuse in members of this farming class who lack sufficient financial income to pay for it. Ironically, however, as Stone's analysis of the Elizabethan aristocracy demonstrates, even noblemen were unable to afford the cost of modern fashions; most notably, the Earl of Arundel, to whom the first three editions of the *Abuses* were dedicated, owed £1203. 7s. 6d. to tailors, mercers, embroiderers, and other tradesmen in 1585 (Stone, "Anatomy," 33).

2492 **Husbandman** farmer.

2493 **Cottager** rural laborer.

2496–97 **a brace ... pounds** two hundred pounds.

2498–99 **quo ... wrong** Tilley, *Proverbs*, H588; the expression derives from Terence: "quo iure quaque iniuria" (*Andria*, ed. Sargeaunt, 214).

2504 **friendes** relatives, kinsfolk.

2507 **pittance** allowance, presumably of money.

2512–16 **For ... measure** Jacob Rathgeb, private secretary to Frederick, Duke of Württemberg, kept a record of their travels in England in 1592, observing that "The women have much more liberty than perhaps in any other place ... for they go dressed out in exceedingly fine clothes, and give all their attention to their ruffs and stuffs, to such a degree indeed, that, as I am informed, many a one does not hesitate to wear velvet in the streets, which is common with them, whilst at home perhaps they have not a piece of dry bread" (*A True and Faithful Narrative*, translated from the German in Rye, *England as Seen by Foreigners*, 7–8).

2516 **braueries** finery, fine clothes.

2517–19 **(worthy ... folly)** not cited in either Tilley, *Proverbs*, or Dent, *Proverbial Language*, but the saying is repeated in the *Second part* (sig. C1ᵛ), and a version of it appears in Painter's *Palace of Pleasure* (1566; ed. Jacobs, 1:46).

2517–18 **inaugured** inaugurated.

2519 **buxome** obedient, compliant.

2520 **prostitute** corrupt, debased.

2523 **surmounting** surpassing, exceeding.

2524–25 **decked ... vanity** cf. 1001n.

2526–48 **This ... dayly** cf. Sir. 30:7–13.

2528 **euent** outcome, issue.

successe result, upshot.

2530 **pittie** tenderness, mildness.

2533 **cockering** indulging, pampering.

2534 **naughtines** wickedness, depravity.

2535–38 **For . . . also** Tilley, *Proverbs*, H687.

2538–41 **So . . . vnbowable** Tilley, *Proverbs*, T632, W27.

2538 **sprig** twig.

  twist branch.

2539 **bowable** bendable, pliable.

2541–44 **If . . . all** Tilley, *Proverbs*, W136.

2545 **bow** incline.

2546 **lore** doctrine, teaching.

2549 **Netherstockes** stockings.

2550–51 **Netherstockes . . . Silk** According to Stow's *Annales* (1615), the first pair of knit silk stockings made in England was presented to the Queen by her silkwoman, Mistress Mountague, in 1560 (sig. Dddd1ᵛ); although their value halved between 1567 and 1582 as they became increasingly common (Thirsk, "Folly," 54), silk stockings remained by law a privilege of those of wealth or birth (*TRP*, 2:459).

2551 **Iarnsey . . . Crewell** worsted yarns; cf. notes to 1709–10.

2553–63 **possible . . . accordingly** O1 reads "possible to be had cunningly knit, and curiously indented, in euery point".

2554 **hose** stockings; used at 1663 ff. to describe breeches.

  changeable variable; cf. 2478–79n.

2556 **wanton** Besides the still current senses of lewd or frivolous, this adjective could also signify bright or lively. Nuances of all these senses are probably suggested here; cf. 5641.

  light frivolous.

2557–58 **lightnesse** lewdness, wantonness.

2561.2 **Pinsnets** cf. 1742n.

2561.3 **pantoffles** mules with a low wedge heel worn as an overshoe.

2562 **indented** embossed? Stubbes may be referring to stockings knit with elaborate raised patterns.

  quirkes, clockes ornamental patterns worked on the side of a stocking.

2563 **open seame** cf. 1712n.

2564 **whereto** besides which.

2565 **Slippers** cf. 1755.2n.

2566–67 **yellow: some** The lack of any punctuation here in Q1 (cf. collation) is unusual and probably represents a compositorial oversight since this long sentence is otherwise punctuated with colons in such a way as to present the reader with a series of related, but distinct, thoughts.

2567 **Spanish leather** cordwain, a type of leather imported from Cordova.

2571–73 **I . . . earth** biblical imagery; cf. Gen. 22:17 and Ps. 72:16.

2579 **interim** interval, interlude.

2585 **abortiue** born prematurely.

    Miscreant *OED* suggests either heretic or villain, but Spudeus is speaking about a thing — a "sweet Pride" or a "mishapen monster" — rather than a person. This invariant usage is an apparently unique example of "miscreant" used in place of "miscreance", meaning abortive growth; it may perhaps result from a compositorial substitution for the neologism "miscreance".

2586 **portenteous** prodigious, monstrous.

2588 **sweet powder** sometimes referring to a perfumed cosmetic made of ground alabaster or starch, but here probably describing a dry perfume consisting of a combination of herbs, spices, and flowers ground in a mortar (Genders, *History of Scent*, 153).

2591–92 **Pomanders** aromatic substances carried in a small box or bag in the hand or pocket, or suspended by a chain from the neck or waist.

2593 **felt** perceived by the sense of smell.

2595 **stones cast** stone's throw; this expression usually describes a short distance, but Stubbes implies exactly the opposite.

2600–3 **But . . . hel** Isa. 3:24 (paraphrased and augmented).

2605.2 **Posies** bouquets, nosegays.

2605.5 **abroad** out of doors.

2607 **Droye** servant, drudge.

2608 **Puzsle** drab, slut; *OED* suggests "pussle" (the spelling found O1–O3) and "puzzle" as alternative forms, but the Q1 reading seems a reasonable, if not previously recognized, variant of "pucelle".

2610–11 **sticked . . . before** i.e., the women fastened the flowers to the front of their dresses; cf. the portrait of "A Lady Unknown" by a follower of Holbein illustrated in Cunnington and Cunnington, *Costume*, fig. 29a.

2613 **to catch at** to snatch at.

2614.2–3 **Spanish pippe** venereal disease; cf. Greene's use of the expression in *The Second Part of Conny-Catching* (1592): "sometimes they catch such a spanish pip, that they haue no more hair on their heads, then on their nailes" (ed. Harrison, 35).

2615 **slabbering** sloppy, slobbering.

2618.1 **curious** delicate.

2618.3 **obnubilate** dim as with a cloud; also printed in the main text O1–O3, but revised in Q1 to "obscure" (2627).

2619 **corroborate** invigorate.

2620 **comfort** refresh.

recreate enliven.

2623–27 **as mistes ... Sunne** cf. Aristotle, *Meteorologica*, trans. Webster, 1.4.

2624 **exhalations** mists, vapors.

2626 **attractiue** absorptive.

2627 **darken ... Sunne.** O1–O3 read, "darken ... the Sunne, not suffering his radiations to disparcle abroad" ("disparcle" meaning "disperse"). The omission constitutes one full line of text in O3, which raises the possibility that the shortened version may derive from compositorial eye-skip, but as it seems equally feasible that Stubbes, after substituting "obscure" for "obnubilate", further decided to trim a wordy sentence, the passage has not been emended; the full-stop after "Sunne" provides added rhetorical emphasis in a manner similar to a colon.

2629.4 **annoy** affect injuriously.

2631 **darken and obscure** O1–O3 read "denigrate, darken and obscure", providing the only example of the verb "denigrate", meaning "darken mentally", listed in *OED*.

2635.2 **gestures** bearing, carriage; Philoponus's point is that the women's modest deportment is hypocritical.

2635.4–7 **womẽ ... feathers** cf. Tilley, *Proverbs*, P157: "As proud as a peacock", and 1001n.

2638 **consider** view.

coynesse modest shyness.

2639 **minsednes** affected delicacy.

2639–40 **gingerlynesse** the quality of moving in a mincing, effeminate way; according to *OED* the reading found O2–Q1, "gingernesse", is spurious and gained currency only as a result of a misprint in O2.

2640 **like ... Goates** proverbially lecherous (Tilley, *Proverbs*, G167).

2641 **nicitie** shyness, coyness.

babishnesse childish silliness, babyishness.

withall in spite of all, notwithstanding.

2642 **haughty stomacks** pride.

Cyclopicall monstrous; *OED* cites this passage as the first of only two examples of the adjective "cyclopical", the more common form being "cyclopic".

2643 **countenances** aspects, appearances.

2643.2 **clogged** encumbered, hampered.

2643.6 **Sweeted** sweetened, scented.

2647 **sweet washed** perfumed.

2649–50 **looking ... go** cf. 2392n.

2652–53 **spectacles** mirrors.

2655–69 **The ... soules** not in O1.

2660 **proportion** form, shape.

2677 **Nicelings** tender, delicate people.

2686 **Orient** glowing, radiant.

2687 **genuine** natural, not acquired.

2688 **naturall prauitie** innate corruption due to original sin.

2689 **splendent** O1–O3 read "**stelliferous**", loosely used of sunbeams to mean "bearing stars".

2697 **a dunghill ... red** Dent, *Proverbial Language*, D645.11.

2699–700 **they haue ... visors** "The wearing of masks during the Elizabethan period had a dual purpose, first to preserve the face in its original cosmetic perfection and, secondly, to provide protection against the sun which was the chief enemy of a fashionable white complexion. The mask was cut in an oval shape with holes for the eyes, and kept in position by a button held in the teeth" (Gunn, *Artificial Face*, 76).

2700–1 **(or ... inuisories)** The word "visor" derives from *vis*, the French word for "face", and Philoponus jokes that since these visors cover the face, making it invisible, they would be better called "invisories", or "no faces"; the word has been coined for the purpose.

2704 **guise** practice, custom.

2707 **shew** behold, view; Stubbes's use of this verb in Q1 in place of "see" (O1–O3) would have been archaic even to his contemporary readers.

2707.1–3 **Sues ... versantur** "pigs wallowing in a hogpool"; 2 Pet. 2:22. The Apostle explains that it would be better never to have known the ways of righteousness than knowing them, to abandon God's word.

2708 **glasses** Earlier commentators such as Norris (3:523) and Macquoid ("Costume," 97) have suggested that the masks literally had pieces of glass set in the eyeholes, but it seems more likely that Stubbes uses this word in a transferred sense to refer to the women's eyes behind the mask.

2714 **deuices** inventions.

2716–22 **It ... euill** The point is elaborated in the *Second part*: "**Mali alicuius author, ipsius mali, & malorum omnium quae ex inde orientur, reus erit coram Deo,** The author of any euill, is not onely giltie before God of the euill committed, but also of all the euill, which springeth of the same" (sig. E8ᵛ); a similar sentiment is found in Ps.-Ambrose, *Sermones* 24.8, PL 17.653C. At Rom. 1:28–32, Paul explains that the wicked, among whom he numbers the "inuenters of euill things", have been cast off by the Lord; cf. 4284–88, 6785–92, and 7347–54.

2724 **yeare of Iubilie** year occurring every fifty years when property reverts to its original owner (Lev. 25:10–13); used here in a figurative sense to signify the final restitution, the day of judgment.

2725–29 **for ... deuices?** Similar vocabulary and construction are used at 462–67 to describe the lengths to which people go to maintain pride.

2725 **flagitious** heinous, villainous.

2727 **plausiblie** with approval.

2730–31 **their owne bloud ... heads** i.e., responsible for their own death (Josh. 2:19 and Acts 18:6).

2739–41 **being ... liuing** Gen. 3:19.

2743–47 **Not ... godlines** paraphrasing Sir. 15:20.

2752–53 **Is ... it?** alluding to Exod. 23:2.

2761 **tẽdering** esteeming, regarding.

2762–63 **commodity** benefit, profit.

2765–66 **support ... sinne** alluding to Acts 20:35.

2767 **bableries** fooleries, trifles; *OED* claims this is a confusion for "baubleries", but Stubbes uses the noun at three points, each time and in all editions without a medial "u" (cf. 5683, 7334–35).

2771–73 **The ... time** not in O1–O3.

2774 **former** primitive.

2775 **sort** manner.

2779–821 **But ... Virginity** elaborating on examples cited at 589–623.

2783 **Stuperius** cf. 596n.

2790 **vse** are wont.

2790–91 **The ... strange** cf. 608–9.

2791 **to chuse** by choice.

2793 **indifferently** equally, indiscriminately.

2799.1 **maners** customs, fashions; O2–O3 read "meannes" (sidenote not in O1).

2801 **in a maner** almost entirely.

2803 **altogether** entirely; they wear these mean clothes for all occasions.

2804 **solemne** set apart for special, usually religious, ceremonies.

2805 **abroade** out of doors.

2811 **high Germanie** southern Germany.

2812 **in effect** in fact.

2813 **difference** diversity.

2817 **supellectiles** furniture; O1–O2 read "trinkettes".

2819 **kertchers** kerchiefs. The Q1 spelling is not recognized by *OED* as a variant of "kerchers", but seems a reasonable alternative, especially since "kerchief" could be spelled with a medial "t".

2820–21 **their haire ... Virginity** alluding to the outmoded tradition of women covering their hair after marriage (de Courtais, *Headdress and Hairstyles*, 49).

2824 **alleadge** cite, quote.

2835 **continencie** continence, self-restraint.

2841 **affect** be drawn to.

2841–43 **for ... fairer** The same reasoning, adopted from Cyprian and Ambrose, was used to discourage women from wearing makeup (2105–8).

2845–51 **And ... otherwise** Stubbes used this logic in the chapter on pride to prove that holiness could be found in either the apparel or the person wearing it, but not in both (1112–24).

2851 **looke in what** in whatever.

2852 **condition** social rank, picking up recurrent concerns about social disorder (cf. 711–26).

2856 **pride ... heart** cf. 486–509.

2860–61 **for he ... none** alluding to Matt. 6:24, where the 1599 Geneva sidenote reads, "God will be worshipped of the whole man"; cf. 7210–12.

2865 **predicament** condition.

2865–67 **and ... other** Stubbes explains why pride of apparel is a worse sin than either pride of the heart or words at 473–83 and 541–54.

2866 **hurting** causing harm or injury.

  before in the opinion or regard of.

2867–81 **Also ... other** Stubbes's argument is consistent insofar as he maintains that pride of apparel is the worst form of pride because it encourages sin in others; at 1147–84, however, the cause of pride of apparel is ascribed to rich clothing rather than, as here, to pride of the heart.

2873 **himselfe** i.e., the person at fault.

2883 **plague** O1–O3 read "torture"; the repetition may be due to compositorial eye-skip to the previous line, but deliberate authorial revision is a possibility.

2887 **Punishments ... ages** not in O1–O3.

2892 **prophane** secular.

2894 **wonderfully** i.e., so as to excite wonder.

2895 **kindreds** clans, tribes.

2896–97 **runnagats ... backsliders** apostates, deserters of the faith.

2898–2902 **The ... euer** Isa. 14:12–15.

2899 **arrogating** claiming or appropriating without right.

2902–6 **Adam ... world** Gen. 3:23–24; Stubbes loosely interprets hell as any place outside of Paradise.

2907 **hoste** multitude, great company; the three men confronted Moses with two hundred and fifty others.

2907–12 **The ... whatsoeuer** Num. 26:9–10; a full account of the event is found at Num. 16:1–33.

2910 **quicke** alive.

2912 **complices** accomplices.

2912–24 **The ... world** Gen. 11:4–9; the city is also known as Babel.

2914–15 **thinking ... water** Gen. 6–8.

2915 **sure** safe from injury or destruction.

2918 **confounded** thrown into confusion and disorder.

2928 **Cyclops** Originally a race of one-eyed giants from ancient Greek mythology, the term is used allusively.

2928–31 **Goliah ... Lord** 1 Sam. 17.

2932–41 **Antiochus ... wretchednes** 2 Macc. 9:12.

2933 **spoyle** plunder, sack.

2937 **in fine** in the end.

2938 **smell** O1–O2 read "swell".

2939 **sauour** smell.

2942–44 **Nabuchadnezar ... wildernesse** Dan. 4:28–34.

2945–48 **King ... desperately** 1 Sam. 13 and 15 give differing accounts of Saul's disobedience of the Lord, but as a result of his fall from favor he loses the battle against the Philistines and falls on his sword on Mount Gilboa.

2946 **Principality** sovereignty.

2946–47 **regiment** office, function.

2949–51 **Sodoma ... Lord** The catalyst to the destruction of these cities was the Canaanites' attempt to rape Lot's two guests who were angels sent by God (Gen. 19:24–25).

2952–54 **All ... heart** Gen. 6–8.

2953 **vniuersall** covering the whole world.

2954 **contumacy** rebellious stubbornness.

2955–61 **King ... Babylon** 2 Kings 20:12–18.

2957 **hee** i.e., Merodach-baladan, King of Babylon.

2962–66 **King ... same** 2 Sam. 24:1–15, 1 Chron. 21:1–14.

2962.1 **2.Samuel.1.c** The relevance of the opening chapter of 2 Samuel in which Saul's death (cf. 2945–48) is reported to David is unclear, but the sidenote is invariant.

2967–71 **King ... hoaste** Exod. 14:21–29.

2968–70 **(for ... Lord?)** Exod. 5:2.

2971 **hoaste** army.

2971 **iustifying** absolving from the penalty of sin.

2971–73 **The ... reiected** Luke 18:10–14.

2972 **reprooued** rejected.

2973–76 **King ... immediately** Acts 12:21–23.

2981–82 **and ... myre** alluding to 2 Pet. 2:22.

2983–84 **Will ... free?** cf. Rom. 11:21.

2984 **elect vessels** image describing the chosen people of God which derives from Paul's discussion of predestination in Rom. 9.

2985–87 **for ... God** Heb. 10:31.

2986–87 **who ... fire** Heb. 12:29; Deut. 4:24.

2987–91 **His ... lawes** biblical language; cf. Lam. 2:3–4, Deut. 32:22–43.

2989 **gone out** no longer contained.

2990 **contemners** scorners, despisers.

2991–93 **Tempt ... thee** Humans are cautioned at Deut. 6:16, Acts 5:9, and elsewhere not to test God's promises of divine retribution.

2992 **exasperate** render more severe.

2993–98 **For ... vnpunished** Exod. 34:6–7.

2994–95 **payeth home** punishes, visits with retribution.

3006 **Epicures** those who give themselves up to sensual pleasure; cf. 2287–88n.
Swilboules drunkards.

3009 **sticke** hesitate.

3010 **brauely** splendidly, in a showy manner.

3012 **mates** lovers, paramours; instead of "whorish mates", O1–O3 read "harlottes".

3013 **fleshlie** given up to bodily lusts.

3014–15 **Thus ... pride** Echoing the *Homily against Excess of Apparel*: "Thus with our fantastical devices we make ourselves laughing-stocks to other nations" (*Sermons*, 329).

3016 **profession** faith, religion.
scandalles discredits to religion.

3018 **Caterpillers** extortioners.

3021–22 **The ... England** This and the next chapter were not printed in O1; all marginal notes were added in O3, apart from one at 3048.1–5 printed in O2.

3021 **exercises** customary practices.

3036 **delicates** delicacies.

3037 **meates** foods.

3038 **prettily** considerably.
mizzeled muddled, made tipsy.

3040 **familiars** intimate friends.

3040–42 (as ... Pies) cf. "To chatter like a pie" and "Women are great talkers" (Tilley, *Proverbs*, P285, W701).

3042 **Pies** magpies.

3045 **braueries** finery, fine clothes.

3047 **passengers by** passers-by.

coast district, neighborhood.

3048 **brauest** most handsome or finely-dressed.

3059 **pretie** ingenious, clever.

conceits tricks.

3060–61 **may ... eye** i.e., no one may find fault with them: Tilley, *Proverbs*, E252.

3062 **speed** prove successful.

3068 **In ... Cities** The Liberties of London had long existed as notorious areas of prostitution and corruption (Mullaney, *Place of the Stage*, 21).

3069 **palled** i.e., paled, enclosed with a fence.

3070 **Harbers** arbors.

3072–73 **banquetting houses** "A 'banquet' was a course of wine, sweetmeats and fruit served after dinner in intimate and informal surroundings, and a banqueting house was designed to provide an appropriate setting ... as a building type it never took on a very precise form" (Colvin, *King's Works*, 30).

3073 **Galleries** Long Galleries — enclosed rooms usually on an upper floor — were a characteristic feature of houses in this period; their precise function is unclear (Gotch, *Early Renaissance Architecture*, 195).

3080 **happely** haply, by chance.

3086 **dearlings** now-obsolete form of "darlings".

3088 **guerdon** reward, recompense. "The guerdon of their paines" is an ambiguous phrase that perhaps implies both "what they deserve" and "what they ask for"; that is, pregnancy as well as sex.

3094 **comfortable** sustaining, refreshing to the bodily faculties.

3098–102 **There ... worse** As the chapter on gardens is original to O2, this passage did not appear in the first edition. Terry Pearson argues that this sentence, typical of notes of moderation expressed elsewhere in the book, rendered the "Preface to the Reader" redundant after O1 ("Composition and Development", 322). Significantly, however, such tolerance is refuted in the chapters on apparel and absent from the chapter on the theaters; cf. 1147–51, and 1132–34n.

3098–99 **There ... abused** Tilley, *Proverbs*, N317.

3100 **precise** excessively strict in the observance of form, scrupulous; another available meaning is "puritanical".

3107–11 **But ... Stewes** Sentence fragments such as this are fairly common in
the *Abuses*; cf. 2622–33.

3108 **light** wanton, unchaste.

3110 **brothels** prostitutes.

3111–13 **And ... paste** Stow writes in 1603 that attempts had been made in
previous reigns to put an end to prostitution in the Liberties (*Survey*, ed.
Kingford, 2:55), but brothels remained part of London life throughout the
sixteenth century (Archer, *Pursuit of Stability*, 211–15; Shugg, "Prostitution," 294).

3113–16 **I ... away** Probably a general allusion to God's justice since the precise
imagery varies in each edition; O3 reads: "I beseeche the Lord to sweepe
them cleane, eyther with the Oliue braunche of his mercy, or with the
broome of his iudgement, that this wickednesse may be done awaie".

3116 **put away** abolished.

3118 **discreete** silent, reserved.

3120 **(by report)** Spudeus could not have personally witnessed the behavior of
Englishwomen, never having been to England.

3120–21 **butter ... mouthes** Tilley, *Proverbs*, B774.

3122.5 **naught** wicked.

3124–25 **maior numerus** "the greater number".

3128–29 **a man ... them** cf. similar warnings at Prov. 25:24 and Prov. 21:9, and
Tilley, *Proverbs*, H130: "Better be half hanged than ill wed".

3129–32 **But ... more** Stubbes was single at the time of the printing of O1–O3,
eventually marrying in 1586.

3135–37 **Seeing ... England** Stubbes has long since completed his discussion of
clothing, but the previous two chapters were late insertions; in O1, this
speech immediately follows the sentence in which Philoponus likens the
English to caterpillers (3014–20).

3139 **pride ... sinne** cf. 454–55n. and 460–61n.

3140 **semblable** like, similar.

3145 **frequented** practiced.

3146 **prouoking ... them** cf. 2991–93 and its note.

3147 **profession** faith, religion.

3151 **coition** uniting, coming together. According to *OED*, "coition" carried only
a non-sexual sense before 1615, which explains why Spudeus adds the adjective "mutuall", meaning intimate, to refer to sexual intercourse; cf. "mutuall copulation" at 3207.1–2 and 3211.

3151.4 **pretending** alleging.

3153 **as well ... as** both ... and.

3153–55 **Reptilia . . . aire** biblical phrasing taken from Gen. 1:20, 24.

3155–56 **in generall** without exception.

3156 **ingender** have sexual intercourse.

3157 **kinde** nature.

ordayned furnished, equipped.

3160 **stimule** goad, stimulus; *OED* interprets this unique usage as an Anglicized form of "stimulus".

3161–62 **Crescite . . . earth** Gen. 1:28.

3163.2 **Libertines** free-thinkers who hold loose opinions about religion; cf. 2287–88n. and 3177.

3165–69 **Whordome . . . damnable** This passage, printed partly in contrasting type O3–Q1, echoes the *Homily against Whoredom and Uncleanness*: "through the customable use thereof, this vice is grown into such an height, that in a manner among many it is counted no sin at all, but rather a pastime, a dalliance, and but a touch of youth: not rebuked, but winked at; not punished, but laughed at" (*Sermons*, 123).

3166 **cognizance** badge, token.

tutch trace, smack.

lustie vigorous, healthy.

3167 **redintegration** restoration, renewal.

3168 **ensigne** sign, token.

3175–76 **cloakes . . . withall** John 15:22.

3184 **discouered** revealed, made known.

reduce you to i.e., recall to your memory.

3186–92 **The . . . him** Woman is created out of Man's rib at Gen. 2:20–24; Stubbes conflates the two creation stories as it is only at Gen. 1:26–27 that humans are described as God's final creation made in His image.

3188 **euery sexe** all sexes.

3188.5–9 **Math.19 . . . Ephe.5** These marginal references, discussed individually below, direct the reader to biblical verses concerning marriage, divorce, or adultery.

3188.5 **Math.19** A reference to Christ's words concerning the lawfulness of divorce at Matt. 19:4–6; Stubbes returns to this teaching at 3283–90.

3188.6 **Mark.** Mark 10:2–9 retells the encounter between Christ and the Pharisees described at Matt. 19:4–6; no chapter number is given O1–Q1.

3188.7 **Luke 16** Luke 16:18.

3188.8 **1.Cor 6** 1 Cor. 6:16.

3188.9 **Ephe.5** Eph. 5:31.

3194–96 **Crescite . . . earth** Gen. 1:28.

3196 **replenish** fill.

3197–98 **the Lord ... Israell** cf. Ps. 83:17–18.

3201 **auoydance** The only feasible definition provided in *OED* is "the action of shunning anything unwelcome", the first recorded usage of which is dated 1610; a closer definition would derive from "avoid" in the sense of "to do away with" or "to put an end to". Cf. the context in which "avoid" appears in the excerpt from *The Book of Common Prayer* quoted in the following note.

3201–10 **First ... triumphant** Part of the wedding service as set out in *The Book of Common Prayer* (1559): "[consider] the causes for which matrimony was ordained. One was, the procreation of children to be brought up in the fear and nurture of the Lord, and praise of God. Secondly, it was ordained for a remedy against sin, and to avoid fornication ... Thirdly, for the mutual society, help, and comfort, that the one ought to have of the other, both in prosperity and adversity" (ed. Booty, 290–91). The fourth cause cited by Philoponus echoes a passage near the end of the service: "in [the state of matrimony] is signified and represented the spiritual marriage and unity betwixt Christ and his Church" (296).

3205–8 **children ... him** A shift in number such as this is not unprecedented (cf. 1687–88), but as the irregularity was introduced in O3, the reading may be in error; this sentence O1–O2 concludes "in them glorified".

3207.2 **copulation** sexual intercourse; this word could also describe non-sexual coupling, which is why Philoponus specifies that he is speaking of "mutuall", or intimate, union.

3207.3–4 **except mariage** i.e., except sex within marriage.

3210 **Church ... triumphant** Stubbes explains in *The Theater of the Popes Monarchie* (1584) that the Church of God is two-fold: "Militant is that, which ... fighteth and warreth dayly against the Diuell, the world & the fleshe. And Triumphant is that, which beeing deliuered out of this life, resteth in eternall glory" (sigs. A3–A3ᵛ). Reformation thought deleted the intermediate stage from the traditional tripartite formulation "Militant here in earth, expectant in paradise, triumphant in heaven", owing to the rejection of the doctrine of purgatory.

3210–11 **congression** sexual intercourse, copulation.

3210–19 **This ... execrable** paraphrasing Heb. 13:4.

3214–16 **as ... merite** cf. the discussion of faith and works at 419–36.

3216 **ex ... operato** "from a deed carried out": the standard scholastic / Roman Catholic phrase describing the working of a sacrament, now in disfavor.

3219 **se** variant spelling of "see".

3224 **sort** manner.

denounced proclaimed, pronounced.

3229–36 **But ... doeth** The assumptions underlying this example from nature are that different social ranks within human society are as sexually incompatible as different species within the animal kingdom, and that unlawful sex occurs between people of unequal social standing.

3229–30 **In ... kind** listed in Trayner, *Latin Maxims and Phrases*, 267.

3230 **kind** genus, species.

3231 **irrationable** irrational, not endowed with reason.

3232 **degenerate** show a falling away from excellence.

3236–45 **It ... end** Pliny, for example, emphasizes the fidelity of doves (*Naturalis Historia* 10.52.104; trans. Holland, 117).

3237 **de ... animalium** "about the natural characteristics of animals".

3238 **vnreasonable** not endowed with reason.

3243 **dissolued** parted, sundered.

3245 **inuiolable** not to be violated; Philoponus seems to confuse this adjective with "inviolate", meaning free from violation (invariant O1–Q1).

3246 **reuolt** change allegiance.

3251 **whether soeuer** whichever of the two.

3254 **the very** i.e., even the.

3256–64 **The ... vnpunished** Recalling a passage from the *Homily against Whoredom and Uncleanness*: "Among the Locrensians, the adulterers had both their eyes thrust out. The Romans, in times past, punished whoredom, sometime by fire, sometime by sword. If any man among the Egyptians had been taken in adultery, the law was that he should openly, in the presence of all the people, be scourged naked with whips, unto the number of a thousand stripes: the woman that was taken with him had her nose cut off ... Among the Arabians, they that were taken in adultery, had their heads stricken from their bodies" (*Sermons*, 137).

3258–59 **some hang ... gibbets** Num. 25:4. This phrasing is unique to the *Homily against Whoredom and Uncleanness*: "God commanded Moses to take all the head rulers and princes of the people, and *to hang them upon gibbets openly, that every man might see them*, because they either committed, or did not punish whoredom" (*Sermons*, 135–36). Stubbes's inclusion of this penalty as one used among the heathen probably results from the close proximity of the passages in the sermon.

3266 **A.B.C.** O1–O3 read "first **rudimentes**".

3271 **rehearse** quote, cite.

3275–78 **Our ... more** John 8:11.

3280–83 **In ... same** Matt. 5:27–28; cf. Lev. 20:10 and Deut. 22:22–24.

3283–90 **To ... Husband** Matt. 19:7–9. The sidenotes further refer the reader to Mark 10:11–12 and Luke 16:18, but although these apostles agree that remarriage is adulterous, they make no exceptions in the case of extramarital affairs.

3285 **put away** divorce.

occasion reason, cause.

3291–300 **The ... body** 1 Cor. 6:15–18.

3300–4 **And ... destroy** 1 Cor. 3:16–17.

3305–8 **In ... heauen** An inaccurate paraphrase of 1 Cor. 6:9–10: "Be not deceiued: nether fornicatours, nor idolaters, nor adulterers, nor wãtons, nor bouggerers, Nor theues, nor couetous, nor drunkards, nor railers, nor extorcioners shal inherite the kingdome of God".

3308–12 **Againe ... iudge** Heb. 13:4.

3312–15 **In ... goeth** Rev. 14:4.

3314–15 **whether soeuer** whithersoever, wherever.

3315–18 **The ... Saints** Eph. 5:3.

3318 **Saints** God's chosen people, Christians.

3320 **such places** "suche like places" (O1–O2).

20. of Exodus Exod. 20:14.

3321 **20. of Leuiticus** Lev. 20:10.

22. Deuteronomy. 27 i.e., Deut. 22:22–24 and Deut. 27:20–23; O1 reads "Deutronomie 22. Deutro.27".

3321–22 **2. Kinges. 11** i.e., 2 Sam. 11, in which chapter Bathsheba, the wife of Uriah, becomes pregnant with David's child, David has Uriah killed, and the two lovers marry.

3322 **Leuiticus. 18** Among other types of sex, Lev. 18:6–18 prohibits incest; this citation is misprinted Leviticus 11 after O1 (cf. collation).

Exodus. 22 Exod. 22:16–17.

Num. 5 Num. 5:11–31 describes the trial by ordeal that a woman must undergo if her husband believes she has had sex with another man.

3323 **Eccle. 9** Sir. 9:3–9.

Prouer. 23 Prov. 23:27–28.

Prouer. 7. vers. 24 This chapter describes how easily young men are drawn from wisdom by prostitutes.

3327 **rare** excellent.

3332–36 **The ... dayes** Gen. 6–8; cf. esp. Gen. 6:2–3.

3335 **brothelry** harlotry, lewdness.

3336–39 **Sodoma ... fornication** Gen. 19:1–25.

3339–42 **The ... Iacob** Gen. 34; the incorrect sidenote reference to "Gene.24." is invariant.

3342–46 **The ... ignorantlie** Gen. 20:1–7.

3345 **shall** O1–O3 read "shoulde".

3346–47 **The ... also** Gen. 26:1–11.

3347–50 **Iudah ... delay** Gen. 38:11–26; cf. p. 26. The incorrect sidenote, "Gene.18.", is invariant.

3348 **impregnate** pregnant.

3350–52 **Was ... Concubines?** Absalom was killed in retreat from battle (2 Sam. 18:9–15), but there is no suggestion that his death represents divine punishment of sexual transgression; the sidenote is a reference to Absalom's encounter with the concubines at 2 Sam. 16:20–22.

3353–54 **And ... himselfe?** Ahithophel hangs himself (2 Sam. 17:23), not because his advice about the concubines was heeded, but because his advice to pursue and kill David was ignored.

3354–58 **Was ... same?** 1 Chron. 5:1; the sidenote cites the account of Reuben's birth at Gen. 29:32.

3357 **dignity** high estimation, honor.

3358–60 **Were ... wife?** Attacked by locals in the city of Gibeah, the Levite's concubine was raped and murdered (Judg. 19:22–28); the next chapter relates how the Israelites declared war on the Benjaminites as a result of this outrage, the dead in total numbering just over 65,000.

3360–62 **Was ... wife?** 2 Sam. 11–12.

3362 **Bersabe** Bathsheba. Some Latin texts have "Bersabee" instead of the "Bethsabee" that is closer to the Hebrew; the form Stubbes uses is invariant.

3362–63 **Was ... slaine?** 2 Sam. 13; the sidenote cites Tamar's reaction to her brother's proposition: "But she answered him, Naye, my brother, do not force me: for no suche thing oght to be done in Israel: commit not this folie".

3364–67 **Was ... world?** The Lord punished Solomon, not because he had sex with foreign women, but because he worshipped other gods as a result (1 Kings 11:1–13); the sidenote, which should read 3 Reg.11, is invariant O1–Q1.

3364 **peruerted** misled from the true faith in God.

3367–72 **Achab ... knoweth?** 1 Kings 21:20–26.

3369 **suffered** The Q1 reading, "suffer" (cf. collation), is a remnant of the version of the sentence printed O1–O3 which opens with the words, "Did not Achab". Assuming another example of incomplete authorial revision, I have emended in keeping with the changes introduced in Q1.

3372–76 **Were . . . sword?** Num. 25:1–15. As in many of these examples, the Israelite man's sin was not sexual intercourse but apostasy prompted by sexual relations with a foreign woman; the quarto variant is probably a printing error (cf. collation).

3374–75 **ranne . . . members** Verse 8 is less sensational than Stubbes suggests: "thrust them bothe through: *to wit*, the man of Israel, and the womā, through her belly".

3376–79 **Was . . . women?** Judg. 16:4–31.

3379–82 **Was . . . wife?** Gen. 12:10–20; the sidenote is incorrectly cited in O1 as "Gene.22".

3382–86 **Did . . . Madianites** Num. 25.

3383 **mortalitie** visitation of plague.

3395–96 **suffering . . . sinne** Echoing 2 Pet. 2:20–22.

3396–97 **to fill . . . iniquity** Alluding to Matt. 23:32; cf. 2239–40n.

3397–400 **And . . . iudge** cf. 2983–84n.

3399 **Saints** chosen people; cf. "elect vessels" and "peculiar people" at 2983–84.

3400 **who . . . new** cf. Heb. 6:4–6.

3405–6 **no . . . it** This statement is qualified O1–O3: "no sinne (almost) comparable vnto it".

3411 **infirmeth** weakens.

3412 **exhausteth** entirely consumes.

3412–13 **radicall moysture** Medieval philosophers believed this was a humor inherent in plants and animals and considered its presence a necessary condition of life.

3413 **supplement** means available to supply a deficiency.
  riueleth wrinkles.

3414 **appalleth** makes pale.
  countenance face.

3416 **consumption** wasting of the body by disease.

3417 **scab** general term for skin disease.
  scurffe skin condition characterized by the separation of branny scales without inflammation.
  blaine inflammatory swelling, pustules.
  botch ulceration, boils.
  pocks pustules.

3418 **byles** variant spelling of "boils".
  hoare grey or greyish white.

3422–23 **Seeing ... it** "Sweet meat must have sour sauce" (Tilley, *Proverbs*, M839).

3426 **securely** confidently, without care or misgiving.

3428 **vntil ... Bastardes** O1–O2 read, "vntil euery one hath two or three Bastards a peece". In O3, perhaps influenced by the singular pronoun "him" at 3429, "euery one" was revised to "one", but "a peece", originally specifying each member of the collective group of Englishmen, was left unaltered. Q1 reprints the O3 version. Assuming the revision to O3 was deliberate, I have made sense of Q1 by deleting the adverb "a peece".

3430 **scuruy** worthless, contemptible.

3433 **seueral** different.

3434–35 **he ... heeles** Tilley, *Proverbs*, H394.

3435–36 **pilo ... ball** Tilley, *Proverbs*, B61; "Pilo" should read "pila", but the reading has not been emended as the grammatical error may be authorial. A more accurate translation would be "faster than a ball". The simile as printed O1–O3 reads, "**Euro volocius** [sic], *as quicke as a Bee*". This Latin phrase derives from Vergil's *Aeneid* (ed. Mackail, 8.223) and means "swifter than the East wind", but the translation offered by the author is proverbial (Tilley, *Proverbs*, B203).

3437 **straunge** situated outside his own area or neighborhood.

3438–41 **Cœlum ... still** Tilley, *Proverbs*, P374 (from Horace, *Epistles*, ed. Fairclough, 1.11.27).

3441 **naughty** wicked.

3444 **pristine** former, original.

3444–45 **countrey** county, district.

3444.1 **Runnagates** runaways.

3449 **if ... report** i.e., if it be true [what] you report; if you report the truth. This elliptic construction is invariant.

3449–52 **it were ... commandeth** 1 Cor. 7:2–3.

3454 **salue** remedy.

3454–58 **That ... Lord** 1 Cor. 7:8–9.

3455.2 **antidotary** antidote.

3458–65 **But ... age** Furnivall documents child marriages in the diocese of Chester from 1561 to 1566 in *Child-Marriages, Divorces, and Ratifications &c*, but Laslett challenges his evidence as unrepresentative (*World We Have Lost Further Explored*, 87–88).

3462 **friendes** relatives, kinsfolk.

3463 **origene** origin, source; this spelling is not recognized by *OED*, but the

form is invariant and seems a feasible rendering of the word from the
Latin.

3464 **directly ... God** A biblical injunction against arranged marriages of children is unknown.

3465–68 **And ... her** Demographic studies suggest this information is inaccurate, England in this period exhibiting what has been termed a "European
marriage pattern", men and women — if marrying at all — marrying on
average at the relatively late ages of 27 and 24 respectively (Hajnal, "European Marriage Patterns," 110).

3467 **catch vp** snatch, lay hold of.

3472 **callings** livelihoods.

3473 **estate** condition with respect to worldly prosperity.

3474 **huggle** hug.

3479 **store** abundance.

   Beggers shortened version of the O3 passage: "Mendicants, or to speak plain-
   lyer, of Beggers". See 1801–49n.

3483 **this geare** these doings or "goings-on".

3484 **holpen** archaic form of the past participle "helped".

3485–90 **What ... are?** The minimum legal age of marriage was twelve for girls
and fourteen for boys; the suggestion that marriage should be postponed
into the early twenties echoes the Church's efforts in 1571 to raise these re-
spective minimum ages to fourteen and sixteen (Thomas, "Age and Authority," 226–27).

3495 **occasion** opportunity.

3496–97 **if ... allow** i.e., death (Deut. 22:21).

3502–7 **For ... haue** Numerous reformers attacked this particular penance as an
insufficient deterrent; John Stockwood, for example, asked in a sermon
preached at Paul's Cross on 24 August 1578 if "a thorne [whoredom] will
be killed wyth spreading a white sheete ouer it, when it rather craueth an
axe?" (sig. D6).

3503 **Cope** a long cloak or cape.

3507–13 **And ... Lawes** not in O1.

3508 **admire** wonder or marvel at.

3514 **condigne** appropriate.

3519 **white liuered** feeble-spirited; the implication is that those responsible for
the penalty are cowardly and incapable of maintaining control.

3520 **gallant** excellent, splendid.

3522 **bitter** O1–O3 print the synonym "stiptick", the earliest figurative usage of
the adjective cited in *OED*.

3523–65 **And ... Lord** not in O1.

3528–31 **Is ... then this?** cf. 3551n.

3540–42 **à culpa ... fault** O2 reads, "**a culpa, rubore, & paena,** *in this worlde, from the falte it self, from the shame, and punishment due for the fault*". The phrase "in this worlde" was not included after O2, and when revising for Q1, Stubbes apparently further decided the shame remains even after the fine has been paid.

3546–54 **And ... can** i.e., it being the case that offenders are pardoned after being forced to marry, fortune-hunters will have sexual intercourse with as many wealthy virgins as possible; the argument is perhaps clearer in O2 where the adverb "thus" (3549) reads "that".

3551 **Bull of dispensation** Philoponus likens this system of fines to the Roman Catholic practice of indulgences, enabled by a bull of Rome, whereby any sin with its attendant penalty could be pardoned for money.

3557–59 **I ... imployed** Corruption in the minor ecclesiastical courts provoked public protest and criticism; Hill explains that these so-called "bawdy courts" were not permitted to exact fines, but that "court fees and money taken in commutation of penance were difficult to distinguish *de facto* from fines", and that such money was sometimes rerouted, as Stubbes insinuates, into private pockets (*Society and Puritanism*, 313).

3560 **them** i.e., Church magistrates.

3571 **all** any whatever.

scruple doubt, uncertainty.

3572 **fact** crime.

3579–80 **cauterized** branded with a hot iron.

3585 **wanteth** is without, lacks.

3587 **vppon them** i.e., upon those who are guilty of the vice; O1–O2 read "therevpon".

3587–88 **winke at it** i.e., turn a blind eye to it.

3587–89 **The ... it.** A description of the judgement of God shown on two adulterers immediately follows in O1–O3; the omission of a transitional sentence and the substitution of "Yea" for "But" at the opening of the next paragraph (3590) indicate that it was a deliberate revision (cf. Appendix I, Passage E).

3588 **looking ... fingers** Tilley, *Proverbs*, F243.

3596 **clogged** encumbered, hampered.

3601 **peasants** term of abuse used as synonymous with meacocks.

maicocks cowards, weaklings.

3603 **and if** if.

3603–5 **But . . . other** Echoing Chrysostom's forty-eighth homily on the Gospel of Saint Matthew: "[Whoredom] makes men not wanton only, but murderous also. Those women at all events, who desire to commit adultery, are prepared even for the slaying of their injured husbands" (*Homilies*, trans. anon., 2:657; *In Matt.* 48.4, PG 58.492). Any potential allusion is probably second-hand since Stubbes's use of this sermon in the chapter on dancing derives from Northbrooke's *Treatise*.

3607–15 **And . . . other** The practice of divorcing wives to live with other women is censured in the *Homily against Whoredom and Uncleanness* as an everyday occurrence (*Sermons*, 132).

3609 **nusled vp** trained.

3612 **conuented** summoned.

3613 **deposed . . . booke** sworn on oath.

3617 **Rubrum vnguentum** "red ointment"; this play on words more explicitly refers to bribery at 4322–25. The actual *rubrum unguentum* was a drying agent.

3624–25 **immunity** undue freedom, licence.

3633–35 **present . . . Lord** Eph. 5:27.

3637 **frequented** practiced.

3639–40 **The . . . England** This chapter and the next were printed in O1 under the heading, "**Gluttonie and** drunkennesse in **Ailg.**".

3644 **belly cheere** feasting, gluttony.

3645 **gourmandize** gluttony.

3646–48 **That . . . God** cf. 1 Pet. 4:9.

3650 **wise** way, manner.

3650–53 **Godly . . . same** Heb. 13:2.

3653 **at vnawares** without being aware.

3654 **Abraham** When the Lord appears to Abraham and Sarah at Gen. 18:1–15 he is not at first recognized; at the end of the visit, Abraham and Sarah are promised a son.

    Lot As a result of Lot's hospitality (Gen. 19), he and his family are saved from the Lord's destruction of Sodom and Gomorrah; cf. 2949–51n.

    Tobias Tobias employed Raphael to show him the way to Media (Tob. 5:4–7); this example is presumably included because it represents another unwitting encounter with an angel.

3657 **pestered** overcrowded.

3659 **meat** food.

3661 **seuerall** particular, distinctive.

    to his kind to its [i.e., the food's] type, variety.

3661.4 **curious** dainty, delicate.

3664 **Helluo** glutton.

3665 **Cormorant** insatiably greedy person.

3669 **iunkets** cakes or other sweet dishes; O1–O3 read "condimentes".

3670 **confections** prepared dishes used as a relish or a dainty.

spiceries spices.

3675–96 **for ... they** Stubbes attributes the increasingly frail constitution of the English to luxurious clothing at 1576–607; William Harrison claims in his *Description of Britaine and England* (1577) that this taste for delicacies developed within his own lifetime (ed. Furnivall, 144).

3681 **able** suitable, fit.

3683 **disgest** variant of "digest". O1–O3 explain that delicate diets have led to an inability to digest ordinary food: "For if they should (their stomacks being so queasie as they bee, and so vnable to concoct it) they might happely euacuate the same agayne, as other filthie excrementes, crude, and indigest, their bodies receiuing no nourishment thereby, or els it might lye stincking in their stomackes, as dirt in a filthie Sinck or Priuie".

3684 **eat** recognized form of the verb in the past tense.

3685.1 **faraginy** Anglicized form of the ablative of "farrago" (Latin), meaning a mixture, esp. of various types of grain used to feed cattle (not listed in *OED*, but cf. "farrage"); invariant usage.

3687 **baggage** rubbish.

3689 **complexion** bodily constitution.

3691–92 **nicenesse** delicacy, luxury.

3692 **curiousnesse** delicacy.

3693 **distempered** rendered unhealthy or diseased.

3700–3 **The ... time** Gen. 9:3.

3702 **brittle** mortal, perishable.

3705–7 **For ... to liue** Tilley, *Proverbs*, E50; Ps-Cicero uses the saying in the *Rhetorica ad Herennium*: "Esse oportet ut vivas, non vivere ut edas" (ed. Caplan, 4.28.39), and Quintilian quotes it as an example of antithesis (*Institutio Oratoria*, ed. Butler, 9.3.85).

3705.1 **Medietie** moderation.

3708 **ingurgitate** gorge.

3717 **impletion** fullness.

3718 **Hiero** i.e., Hieronymus, or Jerome.

3718–21 **as ... lust?** In fact quoting Gratian's paraphrase of Jerome (*Decretum* Distinctio 35.5, PL 187.196C); for the original passage, cf. Jerome, *Epistola* 69.9, PL 22.663.

3722–26 **The ... God** Exod. 32:6–8; the incorrect sidenote, "Genes.24.", is invariant.

3725 **stockes, stones** i.e., gods of wood and stone, idols.

3726–30 **The ... same** Eli's sons made a practice of confiscating food intended as sacrifices to the Lord, and for this contempt Eli's household was destroyed (1 Sam. 4:12–18).

3730–33 **The ... pitifulie** Job 1:18–19; Job's children were killed to test their father, not because their banquet in itself was sinful.

3733–39 **Balthazar ... Lorde** Dan. 5; verses 22–23 explain that it is not strictly Belshazzar's gluttony that is punished, but his pride and idolatry in eating and drinking from the temple vessels.

3736–37 **Mene ... vpharsin** "This is the interpretacion of the thing, MENE, God hathe nōbred thy kingdome, and hathe finished it: TEKEL, thou art wayed in the balance, and art founde to light. PERES, thy kingdome is diuided, and giuen to the Medes and Persians" (Dan. 5:26–28).

3739–42 **The ... hell** Luke 16:19–31.

3742–45 **Our ... withall** Gen. 3:6; cf. 2902–6, where Stubbes interprets the expulsion of humans from the Garden of Eden as punishment for pride.

3745–48 **Gluttony ... euer** Matt. 4:2–4.

3750 **countenance** apparently synonymous with "credite", but the nearest recognized sense is estimation, or repute in the world.

3751–61 **But ... neede** This definition accords with traditional ideals of hospitality lamented as characteristic of a bygone age (Heal, "The Idea of Hospitality," 66–67); Stubbes complains further about the decay of hospitality in *A Motiue to Good Workes* (sigs. K1–K4). Cf. 1801–49n.

3753–54 **substance ... accidentes** cf. 2204n.

3755 **Cookeries** cooking practices.
   impotionate poisoned; cf. 578n.

3762–71 **You ... withall** cf. 1814–21.

3772 **dispende** expend.

3773 **bestowe** spend, lay out.

3774–78 **And ... long** This concern is well founded since, as Stone describes, extravagant entertainment was one of the chief causes of ruin among the Elizabethan nobility ("Anatomy," 7).

3779 **largeous** liberal, bountiful.
   profluous profluent, flowing.

3784 **many ... smoke** Tilley, *Proverbs*, C348.

3798–846 **Experience ... corruption** Similar dangers are catalogued more concisely in the *Homily against Gluttony and Drunkenness* (*Sermons*, 318).

3800–1 **fare . . . euery day** Luke 16:19.

3801 **corrupter** more lacking a sound physical condition.

3803 **choller** bile.

3804 **putrifaction** ulceration or gangrene.

grosse thick.

3805 **humours** bodily fluids indicative of disease; cf. "filthy humours" at 3837–38.

3808 **Peason** peas.

3809–10 **small drinke** i.e., a mildly alcoholic beverage.

3812–13 **fairer complectioned** of a better physical constitution; the modern sense of "complexion" could also be intended.

3817 **distemperance** bodily disorder, sickness.

3821 **concocting** digesting.

3827 **repugnancies** contradictions; O1–O3 print the synonym "**discrepances**".

3829 **impugne** resist, oppose.

3841 **gingered** permeated with ginger, presumably through excessive indulgence.

spiced seasoned with spices.

3842 **mortifie** neutralize the value or destroy the activity of.

3843 **vitall spirites** fluids or substances thought to permeate the blood and organs, and considered necessary to maintain the body's normal operations.

3844 **pursie** fat.

3855 **Mault-wormes** those who love malt-liquor, drunkards.

3860 **gulling** guzzling.

carousing drinking health and success by draining full bumpers of alcohol.

3862–63 **the Spirite . . . Butterie** cf. 3869.1–4.

3864 **consider** view.

gestures bearing, deportment.

countenances behavior, demeanors.

3866 **stutte** stutter.

3867 **stagger . . . madmen** Ps. 107:27.

3869 **other some** O1–O3 add by way of apology for the subsequent indelicacy, "(Honor sit auribus)", meaning, "let honor be to your ears".

boord table.

3872 **curious** elaborate.

3875–77 **God . . . withall** Ps. 104:15.

3880 **corroborate** invigorate.

3881 **Arteries** Since there is no blood in the arteries after death, medieval writers believed that they held the vital spirit (cf. 3843n.).

3898 **tremble** O2–O3 print the synonym "**Euibrate**", the earliest usage of the verb cited in *OED*.

quauer O1 prints "quiuer".

3899 **quotidian** daily.

3900 **Dropsie** disease characterized by abnormal fluid retention.

Plurisie disease characterized by pain in the chest or side, fever, and loss of appetite.

3903 **dissolueth** weakens, enfeebles.

at the length in the long run.

3908 **discloseth secretes** Erasmus, *Adagia* 2.1.55: "What is in the heart of the sober man is in the mouth of the drunkard" ("Quod in animo sobrii, id est in lingua ebrii").

3915–17 **modum . . . necessity** not listed in Tilley, *Proverbs*, or Dent, *Proverbial Language*, nor included in the *Adagia*; the Latin more precisely reads "They put a limit on their appetite".

3927–36 **The . . . Prophet** Isa. 5:11–14; Stubbes quotes in Latin only the first half of verse 11.

3937–40 **The . . . man** different translation of Hos. 4:11.

3939 **infatuate** render foolish.

3941–44 **The . . . you** The first chapter of Joel is a call to people from all walks of life, including drunkards at verse 5, to mourn the plague devastating the country; the Q1 sidenote, "Ioel.2.", is probably a misprint (cf. collation).

3942 **wine bibbers** drunkards.

3943 **destruction of wickednesse** O1–Q1 read "wickednesse of destruction", a reading which probably results from inadvertent word transposition.

3945–50 **The . . . priuities** Hab. 2:15–16.

3951–53 **Salamon . . . wise** Prov. 20:1.

3953–56 **In . . . beggerie** Prov. 23:20–21.

3957–67 **In . . . Cockatrice** Stubbes is probably quoting this version of Prov. 23:29–32 from either the Geneva Bible or the *Homily against Gluttony and Drunkenness* (*Sermons*, 319) as other available Bibles read "stingeth as / like an adder" in place of "hurt like a Cockatrice".

3959 **murmuring** grumbling, complaining.

3967 **Cockatrice, or Basilicocke** basilisk.

3968–70 **Againe . . . strong drink** Prov. 31:4.

3970–74 **Our . . . vnawares** Luke 21:34.

3974 **at vnawares** unexpectedly, suddenly.

3975–77 **S. Paule . . . Spirit** Eph. 5:18; a sidenote citing "Ephe.5" was printed O1–O2.

3977–81 **The . . . heauen** 1 Cor. 6:9–10; cf. Stubbes's alternative use of the same verses at 3305–8.

3989–93 **Drunkennesse ... vp** Gen. 19:30–38.

3993 **assotteth** makes a fool of.

3995–98 **Drunkennesse ... same** Gen. 9:21–22.

3996 **Tabernacle** tent, hut.

3997 **Cham** i.e., Ham.

3999–4002 **Through ... Faulchon** Judith 13; the incorrect sidenote, "Luke.16", is not in O1–O2.

4002 **Faulchon** curved broad sword with an edge on the convex side.

4003–7 **Through ... Strumpet** Matt. 14:6–12; Mark 6:21–29. Salome is granted her request in the midst of Herod's birthday celebrations, but there is no explicit mention of Herod being incapacitated with drink; the sidenote is wrong O1–Q1.

4008 **Epulo** carouser, feaster.

4008–10 **That ... euer** Luke 16:19–31.

4016–17 **estranged ... himselfe** put beside himself, maddened.

4016–20 **For ... Bedlem** Echoing the *Homily against Gluttony and Drunkenness*: "And no less truly the mind is also annoyed by surfeiting banquets: for sometimes men are stricken with phrensy of mind, and are brought in like manner to mere madness; some wax so brutish and blockish, that they become altogether void of understanding" (*Sermons*, 320).

4017 **extasie** stupor.

4018 **Phrensie** alternative spelling of "frenzy".

4020 **Bedlem** i.e., an inmate of Bethlehem Hospital, a madman.

4022 **Imp of Sathan** child of Satan.

limme ... Deuil agent of Satan.

4026–33 **Knowing ... stinke** These lines paraphrase the *Homily against Gluttony and Drunkenness*: "For except God bless our meats, and give them strength to feed us: again, except God give strength to nature to digest, so that we may take profit by them, either shall we filthily vomit them up again, or else shall they lie stinking in our bodies, as in a loathsome sink or channel, and so diversely infect the whole body" (*Sermons*, 318).

4033 **stinke** This reading at first seems suspicious given the evidence of Stubbes's source text, the proximity of "stinking" in the previous line, and the fact that O1–O2 read "sincke". I have not emended, however, as this change coincided with the substitution of "all" in place of the indefinite article in the same line — a combination which suggests that this variant might represent deliberate revision instead of an error of transmission.

4035 **creatures** creations.

4037 **sope** small amount, sup.

4041 receipt taking in at the mouth.

4044–46 Omnis ... instruction This traditional axiom (often quoted, for instance, by Thomas Aquinas) could be put to various rhetorical use. Stubbes quotes it in *A Motiue to Good Workes* to show that we are not to follow Christ's deeds to the letter: "Therefore it is true, *omnis Christi actio, nostra est instructio, non imitatio*, euery action of Christ is our instruction, but not a president to follow in euery thing" (sig. M5ᵛ).

4048–123 Or ... offence This story is not in O1; sidenotes were added for the printing of O3. The same account, slightly less developed, appears in Stephen Bateman, *The Doome warning all men to the Iudgemente* (1581, sig. Cc6). Bateman does not mention that one of the eight men was saved, a detail which suggests that his book was not Stubbes's immediate source. John Charlewood entered a work on the Stationers' Register on 26 June 1579 entitled "A ballad of vjj dronkardes whome the evill spirit procured to Death at Ravenspurgh in Swaben" (Arber, *Company of Stationers*, 2:354); this ballad, no longer extant and possibly never printed, may have provided the source material for both Stubbes and Bateman.

4052 sort company, group.

4054 Swaben i.e., Swabia, a former German duchy occupying a region now covered by the state of Baden-Württemberg and part of Bavaria.

4065 keeps O3 reads "kepte" in place of the Q1 reading "keep" (cf. collation). Substituting "keep" for "kepte" is an unusual error for a compositor to make since the two words are not graphically similar and the change is ungrammatical. It seems equally unlikely, however, that the Q1 reading represents deliberate revision. "Keep" may derive from a compositorial misreading of "keeps". The possibility that Stubbes revised "kepte" to "keeps" is supported by his presentation of the story as a factual recent incident ("keeps" implying that Hage is even now still tending bar in Swaben), and the use of the present tense to conclude the next anecdote (4177–81).

4065.1 propertie character, nature.

4066 burnt wine i.e., distilled wine, brandy (from the Dutch *brandewijn*).

Sacke white wines imported from Spain and the Canaries.

Malmsie strong sweet wine.

4066–67 Hipocrasse cordial made of wine flavored with spices.

4074 Exercise public worship.

4079 or euer before ever; "ever" added for emphasis.

4080 brusting recognized variant of "bursting".

4092 guage offer as a forfeit.

4092.1 desperate reckless.

4092.2 **securitie** culpable absence of anxiety.

4096–97 **pay the shotte** pay the bill (Tilley, *Proverbs*, S398).

4098.3 **darlings** favorites, minions.

4106 **brake** recognized variant of "broke".

4113 **sparks of faith** cf. 353–54, and note.

4116–17 **in ... memoriam** "in eternal memory of the matter".

4120 **Straesburcht** i.e., Strasburg.

4124–28 **An ... followeth** This account is not in O1; sidenotes were added for the printing of O3. It probably repeats the material found in a pamphlet licenced to John Charlewood on 22 August 1581 entitled *The wrath of GOD in the punishmente of Twoo Drunckardes at Nekers Hofen in Almayne* (Arber, *Company of Stationers*, 2:400); this work, if ever printed, is not extant. A ballad with the similar title, "Th[e] example of GODs wrath ouer ij drunkardes at Nekershofen", was licenced to Edward White on 1 August 1586 (Arber, *Company of Stationers*, 2:451), but again, no copy survives.

4125–26 **Almaine** Germany.

4126 **Nekershofene** The precise location is uncertain, but it presumably lay along the Neckar, a river in Baden-Württemberg which is one of the chief tributaries of the Rhine; "Neckarhofen" is today an area of Mannheim. The name is printed "**Nekershofewe**" in the three editions in which it appears. Inferring a minim error (manuscript "n" misread as "w" when O2 was set up from a revised copy of O1), the name has been emended to correspond with the entries in the Stationers' Register (cf. collation).

4128 **Varlets** knaves, rogues.

4129 **by the way** along the road.

4134 **good store** in abundance.

4136 **as drunke as Swine** Tilley, *Proverbs*, S1042; O2–O3 read "as dronke as Rattes".

4138 **pledging** drinking in response to.

4141.3 **contemners** scorners, despisers.

4143 **whether** whichever of the two.

4156 **L4** One of the few Q1 pages without a page heading.

4159 **steere** variant of "stir", meaning move or shift.

4175 **surceased** gave up, abandoned.

4180 **the bowels ... mercy** i.e., his mercy or compassion.

4195 **store** necessaries.

4200 **in generall** without exception.

4203–6 **Crescit ... increase** Tilley, *Proverbs*, M1144, M1287 (from Juvenal, *Satires*, ed. Ramsay, 14.139).

4207–10 **tam ... him** Publilius Syrus, *Sententiae*, ed. Duff and Duff, 694; Tilley dates the proverb from 1657 (*Proverbs*, M88).

4210–13 **Therefore ... ynough** Prov. 27:20.

4213 **right as** i.e., just as.

4215 **plash** puddle.

4216 **summum voluptatem** "greatest pleasure".

4219–21 **who ... increaseth** O1–O2 read, "who the more he drinketh, the more he thirsteth: the more he thirsteth, the more he drinketh: the more he drinketh, the more his disease increaseth". The middle phrase may have been lost as a result of compositorial eye-skip, but the insertion of the conjunction "and" raises the possibility that the sentence was deliberately shortened.

4222–24 **Bursa ... Deuill** neither biblical nor listed in Tilley, *Proverbs*; Dent, *Proverbial Language*; or Erasmus, *Adagia*.

4225 **alway** always.

4229–31 **Doth ... familie?** 1 Tim. 5:8.

4230 **Deneger** one who denies; *OED* suggests this may be a compositor's error for "deneyer", but the word is probably coined from the Latin verb "denegare", meaning "to deny".

4239 **transcende** exceed; this word was in common use, and so probably printed in contrasting type O3–Q1 for emphasis.

4240–43 **His ... man** James 1:5.

4243 **withall** moreover, in addition.

4244 **ordinarie** orderly.

4245–53 **But ... them** Matt. 6:31–34.

4255 **presume** aspire presumptuously.

4255–56 **nor ... God** cf. 2991–93n.

4261 **alwayes** i.e., all ways; previously printed as two separate words.

4263–67 **So ... them** Population growth and rising food prices had increased the value of arable land, leading many landlords to maximize property income (Lachmann, *From Manor to Markets*, 120–21). Freeholders and some copyholders were protected from rent increases by either common or customary law, but leaseholders could be evicted once their contracts expired or given shorter-term leases with higher rents and fines; tenants without any formal contract could be evicted almost immediately (Kerridge, *Agrarian Problems*, 87).

4263 **make ... of** traffic in.

4264 **racking ... rents** Stubbes complains of rents raised unreasonably high, but rack-rents, in theory at least, could also be lowered (Kerridge, *Agrarian Problems*, 46).

4265 **Fines ... Incomes** sums of money paid to the landlord at the beginning of the tenancy and with any change in the lease. Stubbes enlarges on this subject in the *Second part*: "though [the tenant] pay neuer so great an annuall rent, yet must he pay at his entrance a fine, or (as they call it) an income of ten pound, twenty pound, forty pound, threescore pound, an hundred pound, whereas in truth the purchase thereof is hardly woorth so much" (sig. E4ᵛ).

4266 **straight** severely, oppressively.

4265–66 **setting ... hookes** i.e., putting them in a position of such strain and difficulty (figurative usage); a tenterhook refers to a wooden frame on which cloth or leather is stretched.

4267–77 **Besides ... Parishes** Landlords who forcibly enclosed land without adequate recompense to the local population caused serious social tension in areas such as the Midlands (Thirsk, "Tudor Enclosures," 68–69), and it seems undeniable that enclosure in some parts of the country for subsistence tenants without strong legal claims to their land "proved catastrophic, a descent into landlessness" (Lachmann, *From Manor to Market*, 108). This image of the profit-hungry landlord is perhaps over-simplified, however, as land in many parts of England was peaceably enclosed throughout the sixteenth century by landlords and tenants who agreed it led to an increased productivity (Palliser, *Age of Elizabeth*, 208).

4267–68 **pillage and pollage** extortion.

4271 **commonalty** general body of the community, common people.

4272 **cattell** livestock.

4273 **corne** grain.

4275 **Puttockes** said of those having attributes of birds of prey.

4280–83 **How ... earth?** alluding to Rev. 6:10, and through it to Ps. 13:1.

4282 **silly** deserving of pity or compassion.

4284 **poll & pill** ruin through extortion.

4287 **required ... hands** O1–O3 read "powred vpon your heddes".

4289–92 **Cursed ... sea** Matt. 18:6; Mark 9:42; Luke 17:1–2.

4290 **offendeth** wrongs, sins against.

4294 **imputeth** attributes by vicarious substitution.

4294–96 **he ... to himselfe** Matt. 25:45.

4310–11 **ruffle it out** bear themselves proudly or arrogantly.

4313 **Port** grand style of living.

4319 **all ... nette** i.e., they turn everything to account (Tilley, *Proverbs*, A136).

4323 **argent** silver coin, money.

4324–25 **grease ... fist** Tilley, *Proverbs*, M397.

4327–28 **he ... Goose** i.e., he may as well expend unnecessary labor (Tilley, *Proverbs*, G354).

4329–32 **without ... profite** This form of corruption is clarified in the *Second part*: "The shirifs, bailifs, and other officers also, I would wish, for fees, for bribes, for friendship and rewards, not to returne a **Tarde venit**, or a **Non est inuentus**, when they either haue sent the partie word to auoid couertly, or else looking through their fingers see him, & wil not see him, forcing herby the poore plaintife to lose not only his great & importable charges in the lawe, but also peraduenture his whole right of that which he sueth for" (sig. C8).

4330 **tarde venit** "came late" (legalese).

4331 **non ... inuentus** "[T]he Sheriff's Return to a Writ, when the Defendant is *Not to be found* in his *Bailiwick*" (Jacob, sig. 6S2); more legal jargon.

4333 **beare ... hand** assure him (Tilley, *Proverbs*, H94).

4334 **in vre** i.e., pursuing his case.

4336 **naught** worthless, of no value.

4338.1 **pretensed** pretended, alleged.

4343 **suggester** one who brings a charge against another.

4344 **himselfe** i.e., the lawyer.

4347 **sleights** cunning tricks, stratagems.

4348 **goe ... eares** i.e., be at odds with one another (Tilley, *Proverbs*, E23).

4349 **shooing-horne** shoe-horn.

4351 **laugh ... sleeues** i.e., laugh to themselves (Tilley, *Proverbs*, S535).

4351–52 **pretily** cleverly, ingeniously.

4354 **prestigiatorum more** "in the manner of a cheat". O1 reads "**prestigiatorum instar**", an indifferent revision that has no impact on the sense of the passage.

4355–56 **cast ... world** i.e., obscure the (mental) vision of any onlooker and thus get away with their deceit (Tilley, *Proverbs*, M1017).

4360 **marting** bargaining, business dealing.

   chaffering trading, bartering.

   changing money exchanging.

4362 **surprising** overpricing.

4363 **occupiers** traders, merchants.

4365 **teare** i.e., tear the name of God, blaspheme.

4369–70 **(who ... bargaining)** Perhaps a conflation of 1 Thess. 4:6 and Matt. 5:34; John Jewel similarly relates deceitful speech to cheating business methods in his sermon on 1 Thess. 4:6: "If thou speak more than is true, if thou take more than thy ware is worth, thy conscience knoweth it is none of thine" ("Thessalonians," trans. Ayre, 2:850).

4372–82 **Yea ... againe** Stubbes previously blamed poverty and price inflation on clothing expenditure; cf. 1536–39n.

4377–78 **twenty Shillings ... twenty Nobles** i.e., one pound ... £6 13s. 4d.

4381 **ballanced** heaped up, ballasted.

4382–86 **And ... expired** Stubbes returns to this injustice in the *Second part* (sig. E7); Harrison describes a situation in which farmers are forced to renew their leases eight or ten years before they expire as customary (*Description of England*, 1577, ed. Furnivall, 241).

4397 **make ... conscience** scruple.

4401–4 **O ... thee?** Vergil, *Aeneid*, ed. Mackail, 3.56–57.

4410–14 **Quos ... destroyed** source unidentified, but cf. Alan of Lille, *Anticlaudianus* 9.8, PL 210.573–74.

4420–28 **Our ... you** Matt. 6:31–34.

4421 **Euangelie** Gospel record.

4422 **carefull** anxious, concerned.

to ... day the day after today, tomorrow.

4428–31 **He ... purses** Luke 9:3; the incorrect sidenote reference to "Luke.6" is invariant.

4431–34 **He ... all** Matt. 23:11; the sidenote O1–O3 reads "Matt.9".

4435–36 **When ... himselfe** John 6:15.

4437–38 **He ... Mammon** Matt. 6:24; Tilley, *Proverbs*, G253.

4438 **Mammon** Aramaic word for "riches" found in the Greek text of the Bible and retained in the Vulgate, used as a proper name for the devil of covetousness.

4438–40 **He ... also** Matt. 6:19–21.

4440–44 **He ... needle** Matt. 19:24; Mark 10:25; Luke 18:25.

4444–48 **The ... perdition** condensed rendering of 1 Tim. 6:8–9.

4449–51 **Dauid ... them** Ps. 34:6.

4452–53 **Salomon ... bloud** Prov. 1:19.

4454–55 **Again ... satisfied** Prov. 27:20.

4455–59 **The Apostle ... Heauen** 1 Cor. 6:9–10.

4459–60 **And ... euill** 1 Tim. 6:10.

4460–65 **Christ ... vs** Luke 6:35.

4476–77 **Adam ... eate** Gen. 3, cited elsewhere as evidence of God's punishment for pride (2902–6) and gluttony (3742–45).

4477 **inhibited** forbidden, prohibited.

4478–82 **Gehesie ... seruant** 2 Kings 5:20–27.

4483–86 **Balaam ... doe** Num. 22:21–35; Balaam was rebuked by his mule, not

for covetousness, but for beating it when it refused to walk past the angel
standing invisible in front of them in the road.

4487–90 **Achab ... death** 1 Kings 21–22.

4491–93 **The ... Kingdome** 1 Sam. 8; the Lord reluctantly conceded to the
wish of the elders of Israel to dispossess Samuel's sons, taking the request
as a personal affront (verse 7).

4492 **restrained** forbidden, prohibited; O1–O3 read "deteined", a usage original
to Stubbes.

4494–97 **Iudas ... out** Acts 1:18.

4498–501 **Ananias ... death** Acts 5:1–10.

4502–5 **Achan ... presently** Josh. 7:18–26.

4505 **presently** immediately, instantly.

4507 **made ... of** brought to total ruin; 1 Tim. 1:18–19.

4516 **affect** seek to obtain.

4521–23 **And ... word** Matt. 23:8–10.

4523 **withall** moreover, besides.

4525 **dunghill Gentleman** Dent, *Proverbial Language*, D645.12.

4526 **a gentleman ... head** i.e., an upstart (Tilley, *Proverbs*, G66).

4529 **Husband-man** farmer; the hyphenated form is invariant.

4531 **Gregarii ordinis** "of the common classes".

4538.1 **Titiuillers** name given to devils said to pick up words skipped during
church services, registering them in hell against the offenders; hence scoun-
drels, villains.

4540 **glosing** flattering, fawning.

   Gnatoes people resembling the character Gnatho of Terence; parasites.

4546 **no lesse** anything but.

4549–51 **Be ... heauen** Matt. 23:8–10.

4553–54 **vntill ... Christ** Eph. 4:13.

4554 **perfect** righteous, holy.

4558 **hostage ... pawne** pledge, security.

4559–60 **as ... body** Tilley, *Proverbs*, S263.

4561 **Vsurie** "Usury is a kind of lending of money, or corn, or oil, or wine, or of
any other thing, wherein, upon covenant and bargain, we receive again the
whole principal which we delivered, and somewhat more for the use and
occupying of the same" (Jewel, "Thessalonians," trans. Ayre, 2:851).

4564 **loan** Stubbes refers specifically to the interest paid on a loan, but *OED* defines it as the sum of money loaned at interest; used in the former sense
throughout the chapter (cf. 4705).

4567–68 **Positiue lawes** i.e., laws proceeding from enactment or custom, as
opposed to natural laws.

4571–75 **Although ... lent** This is a misrepresentation of the usury law passed
by Parliament in 1571 which was expressly opposed to all "overplus" except
that exacted by the courts of orphans. The statute, however, distinguished
between loans carrying rates of interest above, and at or below ten per cent
per annum, the former being punished with loss of both the interest and
three times the value of the principal but the latter leading only to the loss
of the interest (*Statutes*, 13 Elizabeth 1, c. 8). Jones argues that these different penalties influenced public views of money-lending, leading to a tolerance of interest rates not perceived to be biting (*God and the Moneylenders*, 144).

4572 **inconueniences** mischiefs, injuries.

4574 **ouerplus** in addition.

4577–80 **then ... offence** An argument summed up in the 1599 Geneva sidenote to Matt. 19:7 in the context of divorce: "Because politike Lawes are
constrained to beare with some things, it followeth not by and by that God
alloweth them".

4579 **put away** divorce.

4580–89 **And ... goe** cf. 4571–75n.

4587 **meeres** boundaries.

4595–96 **For ... not so** Matt. 19:8.

4603–5 **The ... of it** paraphrasing Rom. 3:8.

4609 **commodity** profit, gain.

4614 **impale** confine.

4615 **conscionable** governed by good conscience.

4617 **loane** interest; cf. 4564n.

4628–29 **If ... vnto him** O1–O3 read "If I saye to a man".

4636–38 **for ... principall** This passage has been emended on the evidence of
O1 since the variant printed O2–Q1, "the partie that taketh *aboue* tenne
pounde" (my emphasis), is a misrepresentation of 13 Elizabeth, c. 8, the
salient points of which are discussed at 4571–75n. The mistake may represent confused second thoughts on Stubbes's part, however, as the substitution of "aboue" for "but" is an unusual compositorial error.

4644–48 **Giue ... heauen** passage highlighted in O1 with diples.

4644–46 **Giue ... away** Matt. 5:42; the incorrect sidenote is invariant.

4646–48 **And ... heauen** Luke 6:35.

4653–55 **Therefore ... receiue** Acts 20:35. The Latin was altered for Q1 to
omit the redundant "potius" included O1–O3 (in English, "it is better to
give rather than to receive"); the translation is invariant O1–Q1.

4655–56 **22. of Exodus** Exod. 22:25.

4656 **Deut.24.23** Deut. 24:10–13; Deut. 23:20.

Leuit.25 Lev. 25:35–37.

Nehe.5 Neh. 5:11.

4656–57 Ezech.22.18 Ezek. 22:12; Ezek. 18:7–9.

4662–69 Dauid ... fall Ps. 15:1, 5.

4663 Tabernacle place of abode.

4669–72 In ... yeare Deut. 15:1–2.

4670 craue demand.

4677–79 And ... Israell Deut. 15:7–11.

4682 prophane secular.

4685 Cato Marcus Porcius Cato (234–149 B.C.E.), famous partly for having expelled usurers from Sardinia in 198 B.C.E.; cf. 4799.

4685–86 Therefore ... man? Cicero, *De Officiis*, ed. Miller, 2.25.89.

4697 wherwith the means by which; a similar elliptic construction is found at 4705–6.

4700 Butterflies writs, legal summons; Stubbes likens the writs to swarms of butterflies looking for a place to alight (only example of this sense listed in *OED*).

4701 as thicke as haile Tilley, *Proverbs*, H11.

4702 coram nobis "before us", referring to the court of the King's Bench (legalese).

4705 loane cf. 4564n.

4706 haue ... satisfie i.e., have not the means by which to satisfy.

4707 Bocardo Oxford prison pulled down in 1771, but used of prisons generally.
as round as a Ball i.e., quickly; cf. 3435–36n.

4709 without unless.

4710 Caitiue variant spelling of "caitiff", meaning "villain".

4711 Tartarian Tartar.

4721–23 which ... euer? James 5:3.

4723–25 The ... cruelty Luke 19:40; Dent, *Proverbial Language*, S895.1.

4726–27 Is this ... thee? Luke 6:31; Matt. 7:12.

4728–32 Art ... Iesus? John 15:5–6.

4731 void loppe worthless twig.

4733–34 member ... perdition i.e., follower of Satan; drunkards are similarly described at 4021–22.

4736 sort manner.

4740–41 mihi ... reward Heb. 10:30.

4752 Giues shackles.

4758 I ... bones Creditors were delivered dice after the death of a debtor in prison as the sum of all they were likely to receive; Dent, *Proverbial Language*, D326.11.

4758–66 **But . . . teeth** Matt. 18:23–35. The quotation at 4764–66 is taken from the parable of the marriage feast (Matt. 22:13); the incorrect marginal reference to "Mark xi" is invariant.

4767–87 **An . . . euer** These similes closely follow John Northbrooke's indictment of usurers in *The poore mans garden* (first edition 1571, sigs. LL6–LL6ᵛ). Although Northbrooke's ostensible source, "a boke called sermones discipuli, in the 114. serm[on]", remains unidentified, the passage echoes Ambrose, *De Tobia* 4.12, PL 14.763C–764A, which in translation reads: "[David] considered that Judas himself also should be condemned with this curse, that the usurer should search his substance, because what the proscription of tyrants or the violence of robbers is wont to do, this the wickedness alone of the usurer is accustomed to inflict. The more learned moreover think the devil himself should be compared to a usurer, who destroys the things of the soul and the patrimony of our precious intellect by a kind of lending of iniquity at interest" (trans. Zucker, 30–33).

4767.1–3 **An . . . theefe** This sidenote was omitted from O3 and reinstated in Q1 almost certainly without reference to the manuscript or a printed copy of O1 or O2; cf. pp. 36–40.

4772–74 **An . . . God** Deut. 23:19–20.

4775–78 **They . . . despaire** Matt. 27:3–5.

4792 **iurisdiction** power, control.

4795–97 **Therefore . . . die** *De Bono Mortis* 12.56, PL 14.566B–C; translated by McHugh as "Whoever commits usury or theft is not alive". This example was not printed in *The poore mans garden* prior to the third edition of about 1575 (sig. LL3ᵛ).

4795–805 **Therefore . . . Plato** These classical and other authorities derive from *The poore mans garden* (sigs. LL3ᵛ–LL6).

4796 **rauine** wholesale robbery.

pillage extortion.

4797–98 **Alphonsus . . . death** Alfonso V, King of Aragon (1416–1458). The line is slightly different as quoted by Northbrooke: "**Alphonsus** king of **Aaragon** [sic] was wont to saye, vsury seemeth to mee nothing els then the death of life" (sig. LL5ᵛ).

4798 **Lycurgus** Spartan lawgiver (fl. 825 B.C.E.).

4799 **Cato . . . same** cf. 4685–86n.

4800 **Lacedemonians** Spartans.

4800–2 **Agessilaus . . . places** Agesilaus II, King of Sparta (c. 401–361 B.C.E.). Stubbes condenses Northbrooke's account: "**Agesilaus** Capitayne of the **Lacedemonians**, perswaded **Agis** (who was king before him of the same people) that all reckening bookes of the Vsurers might be burnt. And so entryng their houses, tooke their bookes, and burnt them in the open market place, before the vsurers faces. **Agesilaus** laughinglye at their sorowes, said: That he neuer sawe, *puriorem ignem*, a more purer fire" (sig. LL6).

4802 **Claudius Vespatianus** i.e., Claudius I, Emperor of Rome 9 B.C.E.–54 C.E., and Titus Flavius Vespasian, Emperor 70–79 C.E.; Stubbes misquotes Northbrooke by conflating these authorities into a single person.

4803 **Alexander Seuerus** Marcus Aurelius Severus Alexander, Roman Emperor 222–235 C.E.; according to the *Scriptores Historiae Augustae*, Severus "reduced the interest demanded by money-lenders to the rate of four-per-cent ... [and] permitted [senators] to exact six-per-cent, abrogating, however, the privilege of receiving gifts" (*SHA, Severus Alexander*, trans. Magie, 26.2–4).

4804 **extirped** extirpated, eradicated.

4805 **Aristotle** *Politics*, trans. Jowett, 1258b: "The most hated sort [of wealth-getting], and with the greatest reason, is usury, which makes a gain out of money itself, and not from the natural object of it".

Plato *Laws*, trans. Bury, 742C: "No one shall deposit money with anyone he does not trust, nor lend at interest, since it is permissible for the borrower to refuse entirely to pay back either interest or principal".

Pythagoras This is the only authority not printed in *The poore mans garden* and the reference is not located.

4810 **doers** agents acting on behalf of another.

4811 **facultie** profession.

science occupation, trade.

4811–12 **Scriueners** At first only professional amanuenses, scriveners were by this period arranging loans between parties interested either in putting money out at interest or borrowing on security (Jones, *God and the Moneylenders*, 83); although Stubbes's description of the profession shows an awareness of these more extensive responsibilities, the earliest example cited by *OED* of this sense is dated 1607.

4812–28 **For ... payment** Tawney, citing this passage, concludes that "we find developing also among the scriveners a kind of anticipation of deposit banking. The man who has a surplus of cash leaves it with a scrivener, who pays interest to the depositor and re-lends it at a higher rate" (*Agrarian Problem*, 99); as Jones counters, however, little external supporting evidence is available (*God and the Moneylenders*, 83–84).

4825 **assurance** guarantee.

4831 **fleece** booty.

4832 **owes** owns.

4833 **vent** market or outlet; the same usage is found in the *Second part*: "this is a great prouocation ... to filch & steale ... seing they may haue such good vent for y̆ᵉ same" (sig. F5ᵛ).

4836 **than ... mony** This concluding clause, apparently omitted as the result of eye-skip, is only in O1 (cf. collation).

4839 **intangled** O1–O3 print the synonym "implicate".

4846 **Great ... England** This chapter, excluding Spudeus's final speech (5168–73), is not in O1; the sidenotes are printed O3–Q1.

4849 **faithful** full of Christian faith.

4859 **sincerely** in a proper or correct manner.

4863 **pretily** fairly, passably.

4870 **contemning** scorning, despising.

4871–73 **Ambitious ... wind** Eph. 4:14.

4871 **light** fickle, unsteady.

4877 **exercise** religious observance.

4891–98 **These ... protestantes** The irony of this passage is that O1–O3 were dedicated to the Earl of Arundel, apprehended for recusancy in 1585.

4892 **Pythonicall** *OED* suggests "prophetic", but it seems likely that the intended meaning is "monstrous", with allusion to the serpent fabled in Greek mythology to have been destroyed by Apollo at Delphi.

Hydraes In Greek mythology, this nine-headed serpent grows two heads for each one cut off; the implication is that it is equally difficult to root out the Catholic presence in England.

4896 **decorum** cf. 555.1n.

4909 **Tables** backgammon.

Bowles either carpet-bowling or billiards.

4918 **They** i.e., the English.

4926–27 **Doth ... name** Deut. 6:13.

4932–57 **For ... trifle** This distinction between the godly and ungodly oath is discussed in similar terms in the *Homily against Swearing and Perjury* (*Sermons*, 71–72).

4947 **obtestation** protestation.

4957–58 **neuer ... occasion** Although reversing the intended sense, double negatives such as this result from a desire for emphasis (Abbott 406).

4960–69 **Sweare ... euill** Matt. 5:34–37.

4976 **sure** free from risk.

4980–82 **for ... troubles** Heb. 6:16.

4984 **familiar** common, everyday.

4985–87 **A man ... house** Sir. 23:11.

4992 **valiant stomack** courage, valor.

    generosious not listed in *OED*; this adjective seems to be a unique Anglicized form of "generosus" (Latin), meaning gallant or courageous.

4996 **Dastarde** coward.

4997 **Clowne** peasant, boor.

    Patch fool, dolt.

    effeminate unmanly, weak.

5003–4 **vntorne** not blasphemed; cf. "sweare and teare" at 4365.

5009–10 **who ... saith** Heb. 6:6, where Paul refers to anyone who turns away from God.

5023 **humanity** human condition.

5027 **nosethrels** nostrils.

5028 **inspirations** divine influences.

5051 **Iurers** those who give false witness either against the innocent or in favor of the guilty.

5051–52 **Libertines or Atheists** cf. 2287–88n.

5054 **abdicate** renounce, surrender; the synonym "abandon" was added in O3.

5059–64 **God grant ... much** A law against swearing was enacted in 1623 (21 Jac. 1, c. 20), and the penalty set at one shilling.

5066–67 **lay ... faces** i.e., attack the Magistrates? The phrase is not listed in Tilley, *Proverbs*, Dent, *Proverbial Language*, or the *OED*.

5069 **without all controlement** without any restraint whatever.

5075–79 **For ... end** Lev. 24:16.

5085 **posie** emblem or emblematic device.

5093–94 **vanish ... smoke** Dent, *Proverbial Language*, S576.11.

5095–96 **against ... appeare** i.e., in anticipation of judgment day; this construction is invariant O2–Q1.

5105–35 **There ... Lord** Stubbes apparently wrote a ballad about this event in 1581 called "A fearefull and terrible Example" (cf. 5107–9), but the text is no longer extant; he reused the story later that same year in *Two wunderfull and rare Examples* (cf. pp. 2–3). A similar story features in Stephen Bateman, *The Doome warning all men to the Iudgemente* (1581, sig. Dd4v).

5107 **discourse** narrative, account.

5111 **willing** desiring.

5125 **the bell** i.e., the death-bell.

5142 **ranckled** festered.

5153–56 **As ... meates** Luke 16:19–31.

5155 **tasting** eating.

5156–61 **There ... miserablie** Also related in Stow's *Chronicles* (1580), Anthony

Munday's *A view of sundry Examples* (1580, sig. B3ᵛ), and Stephen Bateman's *The Doome warning all men to the Iudgemente* (1581, sig. Cc4).

5181 **Sacraments** i.e., baptism and Holy Communion.

5184–202 **But ... godlinesse** Complaints about the misuse of the Sabbath were widespread; John Stockwood, for example, avouched in a sermon at Paul's Cross in 1578 "that there is no daye in the weeke, wherin God is so much dishonoured, as on that daye when he shoulde bee best serued" (sigs. D5ᵛ–D6).

5186 **Enterludes** Chambers suggests that this term applies to "any kind of dramatic performance whatever" (*Medieval Stage*, 2:181, 183).

5186–87 **Lordes of misrule** Most often associated with the Christmas revels, Lords of Misrule were elected to preside over other celebrations as well: "His presence [in spring festivals] would appear to be the result of an amalgamation of the burlesque sovereign of the Christmas festivals with the Summer Lord, who used to organize the May game" (Laroque, *Shakespeare's Festive World*, 151). The chapter at 5621–721 makes it clear that Stubbes is referring to Summer Lords.

5187 **plaie** diversion, game.

5188 **Maie games** This term sometimes described morris dances, but 5722–79 clarifies that Stubbes is attacking the whole range of activities associated with Maying customs.

Church Ales These festive gatherings, held in a period when there were no compulsory church rates, were important charity events which raised money for the local parish through the sale of ale and beer; cf. 5780–892.

5189 **Wakesses** i.e., wakes — the double plural form was commonplace; a wake was an annual festival celebrated in honor of the patron saint of the parish church (cf. 5893–5964).

5189.1 **Prophane** irreligious, wicked.

5190 **Carding** card-playing.

Tennisse playing early form of the game ("real tennis"), played in a specially constructed indoor court.

5193 **Leets** annual or semi-annual local courts of record.

5194 **football playing** Elizabethan football should not be confused with either modern-day soccer or rugby; cf. 7250–300 below.

5203 **Stoycall** indifferent to pleasure; this sense was not current before 1577, which may suggest why it is printed in contrasting type in all editions but O2.

5210–16 **After ... worlde** Gen. 2:1–3.

5219 **Mount Horeb** Mount Sinai.

all This is the O1–O2 reading (cf. collation). O3 and Q1 print the variant "call", but the meaning of the sentence is not that God told Moses to call the children of Israel to hear his commandment, but that God gave his law to Moses, and through Moses, to all of the children of Israel. The substitution of "call" for "all" is an error, and it is an error that finds its way into Q1 by way of the printed text of O3.

5220–21 **Remember ... &c** Exod. 20:8.

5233 **sincerely** in a proper or correct manner.

5234 **Suffrages, Orisons** prayers.

5240 **cattell** livestock.

5242 **supportes** O1–O3 read "**adiumentes**", meaning helpers or assistants.

5244 **go ... in** complete; "thorow" = "through".

5245–48 **For ... long** a variant version of Ovid, *Heroides*, ed. Showerman, 4.89: "quod caret alterna requie, durabile non est".

5248 **durable** able to endure toil.

5249 **typicall** emblematic.

5250 **signitor** This word, invariant O1–Q1, was probably coined from the Latin root "signum", meaning mark or token.

5251 **discipher foorth** express, make manifest by outward signs; O1–O3 print the synonym "cipher forthe".

5261–65 **The ... Heauen** Num. 15:32–36.

5264–65 **Theator, of Heauen** i.e., the place from which God's words are publicly presented to the people; this figurative usage is surprising given the vehemence with which Stubbes expresses animosity towards the theater in the next chapter.

5273 **Lurdens** sluggards.

5274 **of set purpose** on purpose.

5279 **grinded** weak form of the verb in the past tense.

5282.2 **precise** strict or scrupulous in religious observance.

5285–87 **they ... day** Stubbes may have picked up this detail from John's account of the Crucifixion, also repeated in the 1559 *Book of Common Prayer* (ed. Booty, 150): "The Iewes then (because it was the Preparation, that the bodies should not remaine vpon the crosse on the Sabbath *day*: for the Sabbath was an high day) besought Pilate that their legs might be broken, and that they might be taken downe" (John 19:31).

5288–99 **And ... Sabboth** not in O1.

5291 **deliuery** rescue, release.

for violating i.e., for fear of violating; this elliptic construction is invariant in the editions the phrase appears.

5292–99 **So ... Sabboth** According to Stow's *Chronicles* (1580), the event dates from about the year 1259 (sig. S3). The words of the Earl of Gloucester included in Holinshed's *Chronicles* (1577) makes explicit the incident's relevance: "christians should doo as much reuerence to their sabboth which is sundaie" (2:254).

5298 **other** following.

5306–8 **(for ... Sabboth)** Mark 2:27.

5313 **Temporizers** people who shape their conduct to conform with views currently in favor; time-servers.

5317 **obsequious** obedient, dutiful.

5318 **spit ... heauen** i.e., contemptuously defy the power of God (Tilley, *Proverbs*, H355).

5319 **striue ... streame** Tilley, *Proverbs*, S927; perhaps deriving from Sir. 4:26.

5332 **exercises** religious observances.

5338 **resiant** settled, occupied.

5342–46 **Hauing ... Enterludes** Sunday playing was discontinued in the city of London at least by 1581 and in the liberties by about 1583 (Chambers, *Elizabethan Stage*, 1:314). As Chambers further notes, however, "both in 1587 and in 1591 the Privy Council had to call the attention of the county justices to the neglect of the regulation" (*Elizabethan Stage*, 1:314–15); cf. 6988–90n.

5344 **particularly** one by one, individually.

5347–48 **Are they ... sinne?** cf. 5491–94n.

5348 **fray** frighten.

5352 **diuine** sacred.

5356 **sagely** in a dignified or solemn manner.

5363 **merites ... passion** i.e., Christ's sacrifice, as the basis on which sinners achieve God's forgiveness.

5368 **scaffoldes** platforms or stages.

5368–70 **In ... word** John 1:1.

5381–83 **Deuils ... wrath** James 2:19.

5387 **masking** hypocritical.
painted Sepulchres Matt. 23:27.

5388 **Ambodexters** obsolete form of "ambidexters", or double-dealers.

5389 **Computists** accountants.

5393.2 **intermixt** intermix, mingle together. This is a rare example of the verb; the verb "mixt" for "mix" (5395) was used somewhat more commonly.

5394–485 **For ... variety** These authorities have been taken from John Northbrooke's *Treatise wherein Dicing, Dauncing, Vaine playes or Enterluds ... are* *reproued* (c. 1577) and Stephen Gosson's *Playes Confuted in Fiue Actions* (c. 1582).

5394–401 **For ... for it** In Northbrooke's *Treatise*, Youth is surprised to learn that Age disapproves of plays since "they play histories out of the scriptures", only to be informed that "Assuredly that is very euill so to doe; to mingle scurrilitie with diuinitie, that is to eate meate with vnwashed hands. Theopompus intermingled a portion of Moses' lawe with his writings, for the whiche God strake him madde: Theodectes began the same practise, and was stricken starke blind" (ed. Collier, 92). The cautionary tales are from Flavius Josephus's *Jewish Antiquities*, ed. Marcus, 12.111–13.

5397 **Theopompus** Athenian comic poet (fl. c. 410–c. 370 B.C.E.).

5400 **Theodictes** Theodectes of Phaselis, tragic poet and rhetorician (c. 375–334 B.C.E.).

5410–12 **sucked ... sinne** In *Playes Confuted*, Gosson claims that "Maygames, Stageplaies, & such like ... were suckt from the Deuilles teate, to Nurce vp Idolatrie" (ed. Kinney, sig. B8).

5422–23 **Counsels ... Synodes** assemblies of ecclesiastics.

5427–34 **The ... Gentilisme** Tertullian and Augustine are cited by Gosson in *Playes Confuted*, the latter authority named only in a marginal note: "Amonge suche Idolatrous spectacles as they sacrificed to their Gods, *Tertullian* affirmeth y^t Playes were consecrated vnto *Bacchus* for the firste findinge out of wine. These Playes were not set vp by the Gentiles of any blinde zeale within themselues, but by the motion of the diuell, as may be prooued by the originall of them in Rome ... [T]he inhabitantes beinge mightelie deuowred with a great plague, the Deuill foreseeing the time whē the plague should cease, taught ye Romanes by the oracles of *Sibilla* to set forth plaies to appease y^e āger of ye Gods, y^t ye pestilence ceasing after this solemnising of their plaies, might nussle thē in idolatrie and wātonnesse euer after" (ed. Kinney, sigs. C1–C1^v).

5427 **Tertullian** Quintus Septimus Florens Tertullianus, Latin Church Father (c. 160–c. 240 C.E.).

5428 **de speculo** i.e., *De Spectaculis* 10, PL 1.642A–644A.

5429 **Bacchus** Greek god of wine.

5431 **Augustinus** St. Augustine of Hippo (354–430 C.E.).

de ciuit. Dei i.e., *De Civitate Dei* 1.32, PL 41.44–45.

5432 **ordained** set up, established.

5434 **Gentilisme** heathenism, paganism.

5434–37 **And ... vertue** Paraphrasing Northbrooke: "Saint Augustine sayth, *Donare quippe res suas histrionibus, vitium est immane, non virtus*: whosoeuer giue their goodes to enterlude and stage players is a great vice and sinne, and not a vertue" (*Treatise*, ed. Collier, 85). The original source is Augustine *Tract. in Joh.* 100.2, PL 35.1891.

5438–39 **Chrysostom ... deuill** Taken from Northbrooke (*Treatise*, ed. Collier, 90); cf. Chrysostom, *In Matt.* 48.3, PG 58.490.

5440–44 **Lactantius ... vncleannesse** Lactantius, *Divinarum Institutionum* 6.20, PL 6.710A. Stubbes gives a variant version of Northbrooke's citation: "Lactantius saith, *Histrionum quoque impudicissimi motus, quid aliud nisi libidines docent et instigant?* those filthie and vnhonest gestures and mouings of enterlude players, what other thing doe they teache than wanton pleasure and stirring of fleshly lusters, vnlawfull appetites and desires, with their bawdie and filthie sayings and counterfeyt doings?" (*Treatise*, ed. Collier, 92).

5440–42 **Lactantius ... mouent** point emphasized in O1 with diples.

5440 **Lactantius** Firmianus Lactantius, Christian orator and apologist (c. 240–c. 320 C.E.).

5444–49 **And ... maintained** Stubbes misquotes Northbrooke who writes: "the godly fathers ... commaunded by councels that none shoulde go or come to playes: as in the third councel of Carthage, and in the synode of Laodicea, it was decreed that no Christians (and especially priests) shoulde come into any place where enterludes and playes are, for that Christians must abstain from such places where blasphemie is commonly vsed" (*Treatise*, ed. Collier, 90). This is followed in the *Treatise* by the words of Chrysostom (5438–39).

5445 **30. ... Carthage** The eleventh canon of the third Synod of Carthage reads: "The sons of the bishops and clergy may not join in secular plays, or witness them" (Hefele, *Councils*, 2:398). The reference to the "30. Counsell" is invariant and may represent confusion on Stubbes's part rather than a printing error; the sidenote, "Concil 30.", was "corrected" to bring it into agreement with the main text, O1–O3 reading "Concilium 3".

5445–46 **Sinode of Laodicea** The fifty-fourth canon of the Synod of Laodicea reads: "The higher and inferior clergy shall not join in witnessing any dramatic performance at weddings or feasts, but before the actors appear they shall rise and go" (Hefele, *Councils*, 2:321).

5450–56 **Scipio ... Country** Taken from *Playes Confuted*: "The noble *Scipio Nasica* perceiuing that the Citie cannot longe endure whose walles stande and manners fall, when hee sawe the whole Senate bent to builde vpp Theaters, and sett out Playes, with earnest persuasion drewe them from it. And *Valerius Maximus* flatlie affirmeth, that they were not brought in to *Rome Sine pacis rubore, without a steine of disgrace to the time of Peace*" (ed. Kinney, sigs.

C2ᵛ–C3). Scipio's opposition to theater is discussed by Augustine in *De Civitate Dei* 1.32, PL 41.44–45.

5450 **Scipio** Scipio Nasica Corculum (fl. 162–154 B.C.E.).

5451–52 **dehorted . . . from** advised . . . against.

5454–56 **Valerius . . . Country** Adapted from Valerius Maximus, *Dictorum Factorumque Memorabilium* 2.4.1.

5454 **Valerius maximus** Roman historian (first century C.E.).

5455 **brought vp** introduced.

5457–60 **Aristotle . . . fire** *Politics*, trans. Jowett, 1336b. The citation is adapted from *Playes Confuted*: "*Aristotle* vtterly forbiddeth yõg men of Plaies till they bee setled in minde & immoueable in affection lest comming to the Stage to fetche Physicke for loue, they quench their heate with a pynte of water and a pottle of fire" (ed. Kinney, sigs. C7–C7ᵛ).

5459 **Venus** sexual desire, lust.

pottle obsolete measure equal to two quarts.

5461 **Augustus** C. Octavius Augustus, Roman emperor (63 B.C.E.–14 C.E.)

Ouid Publius Ovidius Naso, Latin poet (43 B.C.E.–17 C.E.).

5461–63 **Augustus . . . trumperie** Northbrooke briefly mentions that "Ouid was banished by Augustus into Pontus (as it is thought) for making the book of the Craft of Loue" (*Treatise*, ed. Collier, 93); a similar note appears in Gosson's *Schoole of Abuse* (1579, ed. Kinney, sig. A5ᵛ), but Stubbes's use of this pamphlet appears limited to the chapters on dancing and music.

5463 **trumperie** nonsense, rubbish.

5464–65 **Constantius . . . Lord** cf. the *Treatise*: "It was decreed vnder Constantinus, the emperour, that all players of enterludes shoulde be excluded from the Lorde's table" (ed. Collier, 97).

5464 **Constantius** i.e., Flavius Valerius Constantinus, Roman emperor (c. 285–337 C.E.); the name is incorrect O1–Q1.

5465 **the Table of the Lord** i.e., the communion table.

5465–72 **Then . . . rest** Stubbes paraphrases Gosson quoting *De Spectaculis* 10: "*Tertullian* teacheth vs that euery part of the preparation of playes, was dedicated to some heathē god, or goddesse, as the house, stage, apparrell, to *Venus*; the musike, to *Apollo*; the penning, to *Minerua*, and the *Muses*; the pronuntiacion and action to *Mercurie*; he calleth the Theater *Sacrarium Veneris*, *Venus* chappell, by resorting to which we worshippe her" (*Playes Confuted*, ed. Kinney, sig. D7).

5467 **Gentiles** pagans.

5469 **Venus** Roman goddess of love; her connection to the stage is explained at 5489n.

5470 **Minerua** Roman goddess of wisdom.

5471–72 **Mercurie** Roman god of, amongst other things, eloquence.

5475–84 **the ... young men** cf. *Playes Confuted*: "The argumēt of Tragedies is wrath, crueltie, incest, iniurie, murther eyther violent by sworde, or voluntary by poyson. The persons, Gods, Goddesses, furies, fiendes, Kinges, Quenes, and mightie men. The ground worke of *Commedies*, is loue, cosenedge, flatterie, bawderie, slye conueighance of whordome. The persōs, cookes, queanes, knaues, baudes, parasites, courtezannes, lecherouse olde men, amorous yong men" (ed. Kinney, sigs. C5–C5ᵛ). The passage can perhaps be traced to Lactantius: "What of the stage? is it less vile? there comedy discourses of debaucheries and illicit loves, tragedy of incest and parricide" (*Divinarum Institutionum* 6.20, PL 6.710A, trans. Blakeney, chap. 63).

5476 **immunity** undue freedom, licence.

iniurie wrongful action or violation of another's rights.

5477 **persons** characters.

Actors i.e., those with the power to act, doers; cf. "Agents" at 5482.

5478 **Hags** evil spirits in female form, Furies.

5482 **Agents** those who exert power.

queanes harlots, strumpets.

5489 **Venus Pallace** This label derives from Pompey's decision to call his newly-built theater a temple to Venus in order to frustrate the Roman censors (Tertullian, *De Spectaculis* 9–10).

Sathans Sinagogue alluding to Rev. 2:9.

5490.1–2 **Theaters ... Curtains** The Theatre and the Curtain were two of the first playhouses built in London, in 1576 and 1577, respectively.

5491–94 **But ... them?** This was an argument commonly advanced by defenders of the theater. Stubbes himself maintains in his "Preface to the Reader" that "when honest & chast playes, tragedies & enterluds, are vsed to these ends, for the Godly recreatiō of the mind, for the good example of life, for the auoyding of that, which is euill, and learning of that which is good, thā are they very tollerable exercyses". This more moderate attitude flatly contradicts the views expressed here, and the preface was dropped after O1; cf. Appendix I–B.

5501 **equiualent with** equal in excellence or authority to; O1–O3 print the synonymous phrase "equipollent with".

5503 **ordinarie** regular, orderly.

5504 **inferred** conferred, bestowed.

5506–9 **If ... sowre sweet** Isa. 5:20.

5509 à fortiori "so much the more".

5514–15 otia ... vice Tilley, *Proverbs*, I13; Walther, *Proverbia*, 20490.

5515–21 Doe ... apace This complaint dates back to Salvian, the fifth-century presbyter at Marseilles: "spernitur dei templum, ut curratur ad theatrum: ecclesia uacuatur circus impletur" (*De Gubernatione Dei*, ed. Pauly, 6.38).

5516 Lectures Lectures differed from sermons in that they treated of more complex doctrinal issues at greater length (Cragg, *Puritanism*, 210).

5518 thicke ... folde Tilley, *Proverbs*, T100.

5523–25 the way ... find it Matt. 7:13–14.

5527–28 (for ... Christ) John 18:37.

5529 exercises acts of public worship.

5530 insinuat i.e., subtly instil into the spectators' minds.

5534–47 For ... worse Gosson likewise mentions audience behavior in *The Schoole of Abuse* (ed. Kinney, sig. C1ᵛ), a description which relies heavily on Ovid's *Amores* (Zitner, "Gosson, Ovid," 206–8); complaints about licentiousness in the theaters were commonplace, however, and the echoes are probably coincidental.

5537 time ... tyde i.e., at all times.

5539 flearing coarse laughing.

5540 clipping ... culling hugging and cuddling.

5541 wincking significant glancing.

5543 Pageants used in a general sense to mean shows or spectacles; cf. 5670–71.

5544 sortes to pairs up with; precise sense not offered by *OED* (but cf. v.¹ 12a, b).

5546 conclaues private rooms.

5546–47 they ... Sodomits cf. pp. 33–35 and 5927n.

5547 or worse Readers are left to imagine for themselves spectators' activities; it may be a mistake to pin down "the worst" too precisely as its rhetorical power lies in its suggestive indeterminacy (cf. 6746–47).

5548–74 And ... Plaies This passage grows out of a list compiled by Northbrooke (*Treatise*, ed. Collier, 94–95), but, as Ringler warns, the material has little relevance to the Elizabethan stage: "similar lists of subjects are a commonplace of patristic comments on the drama ... Northbrooke got his list of subjects from accounts he had read of third-century Roman spectacles, rather than from his own observation at London theaters in the sixteenth century" ("First Phase," 407 n.15).

5553 cog cheat, deceive.

5555 mowe grimace, make faces.

5560 picke rob, steal.

roue practice piracy.

5565 smooth flatter.

5569.3 Seminaries schools.

5577–79 For ... sinnes 2 John 1:10–11.

5577.2 premunire warning; this sense, not listed in *OED*, probably results from the tendency in medieval Latin to confuse "praemunire", meaning to protect in front, and "praemonere", meaning to warn in advance.

5578 communicate with share, take part in.

5583 sort multitude.

Lubbers louts.

laizie Lurdens O1–O3 read "buzzing dronets"; the only example of "dronets", meaning "drones", cited in *OED* is taken from the "Preface to the Reader" (Appendix I–B, 36).

5586 Founders supporters, maintainers.

5588 bowels considered the seat of mercy and tender emotion.

5591 mysteries professions, callings.

5593–600 For ... part? Barish notes that Richard Baker, writing in 1662, was one of the first defenders of the stage to highlight the inconsistency of identifying an actor with his stage roles: "A Player Acts the part of *Solomon*; but is never the wiser for acting his part: why should he be thought the wickeder for acting the part of *Nero*, or the more blasphemous for acting the part of *Porphyrie?*" (*Theatrum Redevivum*, quoted in Barish, *Antitheatrical Prejudice*, 125–26).

5602 braue finely-dressed; this passage echoes the anxiety about social disorder expressed in the chapters on apparel (cf. 711–26).

5605–10 And ... desertes Acting companies not licensed by two Justices of the Peace and lacking noble patronage were liable to punishment as vagrants under the 1572 "Acte for the punishement of Vacabondes and for Relief of the Poore & Impotent" (Gurr, *Shakespearean Stage*, 27; cf. also Woodbridge, *Vagrancy*, 272–73). First offenders were whipped and then burned through the gristle of the right ear with a hot iron one inch in diameter; if taken again, they were hanged. Cf. 1801–49n.

5606 Rogues vagabonds.

5607 Countries i.e., provinces.

5611–15 beseeching ... others alluding to Heb. 10:30–31.

5617–18 Of ... Misrule? This transitional sentence makes clear the connection in Stubbes's mind between theatrical performances and traditional festival games as different forms of "playing".

5629–30 as haue seene O1–O3 read "as I haue seen"; it is difficult to know if the personal pronoun was deliberately deleted in revision or overlooked, but there seems no need to emend as the sense is clear.

5637 **lustie** arrogant, insolent; other available meanings include "vigorous" and "lustful".

5641 **wanton** cf. 2556n.

5644 **Laces** decorative ties, ribbons.

5648–49 **a crosse** i.e., across; printed as two words O1–Q1.

5653 **Hobby horses** A light frame shaped like a horse is carried by a performer around his waist; the dancer's legs are concealed under a long skirt and short artificial legs at either side complete the illusion of a man riding a horse.

    Dragons The dragon originated in the Saint George's Day celebrations and were subsequently incorporated into the May games (Laroque, *Shakespeare's Festive World*, 110); other traditional morris dance figures include Maid Marian and the friar.

    Antiques clowns, fools.

5653.1 **rablemēt** riotous conduct.

5657 **Church-yarde** hyphenated form used in O1, O3, and Q1.

5659 **stumpes** legs.

5662–68 **and in . . . voyce** Archbishop Grindal prohibited precisely this behavior in his 1571 injunction to the laity at York (*Remains*, ed. Nicholson, 141–42), which suggests that incidents such as Stubbes describes were not unknown.

5663 **sorte** manner.

5669 **fleere** laugh impudently.

5670 **formes** benches.

5670.1 **Receptacles** places to which people retire, in this case, for entertainment and festivity.

5674–75 **Sommer . . . Arbours** Synonyms describing shaded retreats, the sides and roofs of which are constructed out of trees and shrubs.

5675 **banquetting houses** cf. 3072–73 and its note.

5681 **Lurdane** sluggard.

5683 **babblerie** childish foolery (cf. 2767n.).

    Imagerie worke images collectively, probably referring to painted pictures.

5684–85 **Cognizances** devices, emblems.

5689 **buxome** indulgent, obliging.

5692–94 **Yea . . . abused** not in O1–O3. A cowl-staff, or "stang", was a pole supported between the shoulders of two bearers and used to carry burdens; "riding the stang" and water dunkings were popular forms of public humiliation (Brand, *Popular Antiquities*, 2:188–89).

5693 **diued** dipped, submerged.

5694 **assotted** foolish, infatuated.

5702–5 **Sub ... lawes** An ironic rewrite of the formula in the baptismal liturgy: "[this child] shall not be ashamed to confess the faith of Christ crucified, and manfully to fight under his banner against sin, the world, and the devil, and to continue Christ's faithful soldier and servant unto his life's end" (*Book of Common Prayer*, ed. Booty, 275).

5709 **Custardes** open meat or fruit pies covered with broth or milk and thickened with eggs.

5710 **Cracknels** crackers.

Flaunes cheesecakes or modern-style custards.

5713 **any** i.e., any of these foods — meat, cheese, cakes, and so on; O1 reads "any thing".

5725 **order** customary practice.

5726 **Against** in anticipation of.

Whitsunday i.e., the seventh Sunday after Easter.

5726–27 **Against ... yeare** May games were practiced from May Day to late June (Marcus, *Politics of Mirth*, 151).

5726–35 **Against ... pastimes** O1 reads: "Against **May, Whitsonday** or other time, all the yung men and maides, olde men and wiues run gadding ouer night to the woods, groues, hils & mountains, where they spend all the night in plesant pastimes".

5737 **assemblies** gatherings for purposes of social entertainment.

5737–41 **And ... Hell** At 1729–39 the excessive pride of the English in apparel is similarly explained in terms of Satan's malevolent presence.

5750–51 **variable** diverse, various.

5757–60 **And ... Idolles** O1 reads, "And then fall they to daunce about it like as the heathen people did at the dedication of the Idols".

5760 **patterne** copy, likeness.

5761–66 **I ... vndefiled** Christopher Fetherston similarly claims that May games provide unaccustomed opportunity for sexual license (*Dialogue*, 1582, sig. D7ᵛ); Laroque argues that both accounts are based on hearsay, but acknowledges that "May games were not necessarily totally innocent pastoral frolics" (*Shakespeare's Festive World*, 114).

5762 **viua voce** "by word of mouth".

5769 **Saracens** heathens, infidels.

5778–79 **vncouth** unfamiliar.

5786 **Churchwardens** These officials, usually two in number, were chosen annually by the parishioners and were responsible not only for the upkeep of the church and its grounds but also for a whole range of secular duties (Cox, *Churchwardens' Accounts*, 2–5).

5788 **halfe ... quarters** i.e., between eighty and one hundred sixty bushels; a quarter is approximately equal to eight bushels.

5789–92 **whereof ... ability** Despite his disapproval of these festive events, Stubbes's description of parishioners donating to a general fund according to their means anticipates the manner in which he would like to see churches maintained (5866–71) and echoes the account of the construction of the Lord's tabernacle printed in the dedication (61–78).

5789 **buy of** i.e., buy out of.

5793 **set to sale** put on sale.

5796 **Huffecappe** strong ale.

5797 **Nectar** delicious drink.

   is set abroach i.e., when the barrels containing the ale are pierced and left running.

5808 **for ... put** i.e., for the money being put.

   Corban church treasury.

5810–14 **In ... Hares** This extraordinary claim is invariant; other accounts of church-ales more reasonably imply that the holiday lasted a single day (Carew, *Survey*, sig. S4ᵛ; Barnes, "Somerset Churchales," 106–7).

5812 **gulling** guzzling.

5813 **as drunke as Swine** Tilley, *Proverbs*, S1042.

5813–14 **as mad ... Hares** Tilley, *Proverbs*, H148.

5815 **vtterance** sales.

5815–16 **Seeing ... gaines** Church-ales, especially those held at Whitsuntide, were the principal means through which money was raised to support the local parish church (Cox, *Churchwardens' Accounts*, 291).

5823 **Sir Iohn** contemptuous name for a priest.

5827 **pretensed** feigned.

   allegations excuses.

5828–29 **conueigh ... Cloud** Dent, *Proverbial Language*, C443.1.

5829–30 **But ... espied** Tilley, *Proverbs*, N130.

5834–35 **Must ... it?** Rom. 3:8.

5841–42 **Oratories** chapels.

5842–43 **Swine coates** swine-cotes, pigsties.

5846 **betorne** tattered.

5848–50 **Ecce ... obliuion** Echoing Job 7:21; the last two words of the translation are not part of the Latin quotation.

5852–53 **(this ... nothing,)** O1–O3 read, "(this I speake but in waie of **parenthesis**)".

5861 **Domine ... facis?** "O Lord, why do you thus?" This is a conflation of Acts 14:15 and Job 9:12; O1–O3 read "blacke is their eye".

5863–65 **And ... themselues** cf. Luke 16:1–13.

5864 **accomptants** accountants.

5866–71 **Were ... doe?** Richard Carew, defending church-ales in 1602, counters this sort of criticism by observing that parishioners "would sooner depart with 12. pennyworth of ware, then sixepence in coyne, and this shilling they would willingly double, so they might share but some pittance thereof againe. Now in such indifferent matters, to serue their humors, for working them to a good purpose, could breed no maner of scandall" (*Survey*, sig. T2).

5869 **Temples ... Churches** O1–O3 read "Templaries ... Oratories", Stubbes mistakenly using "templaries" as synonymous with "temples".

5872–76 **It ... Lord** A marginal note reading "**Churches are to be maintained by mutuall contribution of euery one after his power**" is included O1–O3.

5872–80 **& so ... withall** Exod. 36:3–6.

5882 **importable** unbearable, unendurable.

5883.3–4 **in respect of** in comparison with.

5891 **order** established practice.

5897–5902 **Euerie ... cheare** Originally celebrated the week after the local saint's day, wakes were supposed to have been limited after the Reformation to the first Sunday in October (Thomas, *Religion*, 66); Heal suggests that it was the reciprocal nature of the event, villages exchanging hospitality, which prevented the adoption of a common date of celebration (*Hospitality*, 361).

5899–5900 **proper** particular.

5900 **and appropriate** i.e., and in a manner specially suited.

5900.1 **Saturitie** repletion.

5905 **fulnesse** excessive indulgence; O1–O3 read "Saturitie".

5908–9 **keep ... houses** i.e., are forced to limit the manner in which they provide for their household and guests.

5912 **thripple** practice small economies.

5913 **daunger** obligation or debt.

5914 **decay** ruin.

5918 **prefixed** fixed in advance; O1–O3 print the synonym "**determinate**".

5927 **Sodomiticall Exercises** Drunkenness and gluttony are bracketed with whoredom as "sodomitical" activities, suggesting that this adjective carries a broad connotative meaning in the sixteenth century, referring not only to issues of sexuality but also to other forms of unrestrained and, in Stubbes's opinion, morally debauched social behavior. Cf. the rhetorically similar passage at 5887–89, where whoredom, drunkenness, gluttony, and pride are described as "abhominations".

5929–30 **congratulate** celebrate.

5933 **conuenient** proper, befitting.

5936 **Country** county, district.

5940 **Verlettes** variant of "varlets".

5951.4 **stationary** fixed; unlike movable festivals such as Easter or harvest-home, wakes were always held on the same day.

5952 **blockish** wooden.

5957 **original** origin, beginning; O1–O3 print the synonym "**exordium**".

5959 **destructtion** spelling not listed in *OED* but emendation unnecessary; O1–O3 print the more usual form, "destruction".

5965–66 **The . . . England** This chapter is dependent on Northbrooke's *Treatise*; affinities between the texts are noted below.

5969 **introduction** preliminary step.

5970 **preparatiue** incentive.

5971 **entrance** beginning; O1–O3 print the synonym "**introite**", *OED*'s only example of this sense.

5976 **science** occupation requiring trained skill.

5977 **Cinœdus** catamite, sodomite (Latin); the accuracy of Stubbes's understanding of the word is in question as he uses it as a proper noun.

5977–78 **prostitute** licentious, abandoned to sensual indulgence.

5978 **Ribald** dissolute, licentious person.

Sardanapalus According to Ctesias' mythical account, the last of the thirty kings of Ninevah; all of these rulers supposedly indulged in luxury and licentiousness but Sardanapalus was the most extreme, dressing in women's clothes and surrounded by concubines in the privacy of his palace. In *The Booke of Wysdome* (1532, repr. c. 1580) his behavior, which Stubbes describes as "effeminate", is ascribed to lechery: "This sinne of Letcherye dyd so poyson the brest of **Sardanapalus**, that all manlye courage was wholye killed in him, and he become so womannish, that he contemned the company of men, only delighted with the fellowship of his Harlots" (sig. G4ᵛ).

5978–79 **effeminate** self-indulgent, unmanly; perhaps also, overly given to women.

5984–85 **Christiani vocitentur** The reading found O1–O2, "Christiani boni vocitentur", more closely represents the translation but I have not emended the quarto passage since "boni" may have been deliberately cut after having been misprinted "booi" in O3; Stubbes's translations do not always precisely reflect the original Latin (cf. 608n. and 5848–50n.).

5984–89 **verbo . . . Pagans** source unidentified, but cf. Augustine, *Contra Faustum* 20.9, PL 42.374.

5986 **deteriores reperientur** O1 reads "**peiores reperiĕtur**", while O2–O3 print "peiores inuenientur". The meaning of the sentence is not affected by any of these substitutions, and the translation is invariant.

5990–92 it . . . them Matt. 11:24.

5998 in a meane with moderation.

6003 a maxime O1–O3 print versions of the phrase, "(basis & fundamentum veritatis) *a ground and foundation of truthe*".

6003–10 For . . . God Rom. 8:5–8.

6004 vncircumcised heart Acts 7:51, Ezek. 44:7, 9; a figurative usage meaning "irreligious", or "not spiritually purified".

6007 regenerate spiritually re-born.

6012 enticementes O1–O3 print the synonym "allections".

6015–16 clipping . . . culling hugging, cuddling (cf. 5540).

6015–25 For . . . not? Compare the similar language used to describe theater audiences at 5534–42. The preface to O1 describes men and women dancing together as an abuse (Appendix I–B, 46–51), and the assertion that people should dance either by themselves or among members of their own sex is one to which Stubbes returns (cf. 6290–95, 6326–32, and the justification of his position at 6498–505). The view that mixed-gender dancing provokes lust and is incompatible with either spiritual rejoicing or mental recreation is stressed by Northbrooke (*Treatise*, ed. Collier, 154–55, 161) and Fetherston (*Dialogue*, sigs. D4–D4ᵛ).

6023–24 blow . . . coale i.e., incite lust.

6027.3 corasiue corrosive, annoyance.

6035 comforted refreshed, invigorated.

6043 amarulent full of bitterness.

6052 vauting obsolete form of "vaulting".

6057 venerous venereal, lustful.

6057–58 concupiscentious lustful.

6059 pump figurative usage deriving from the well of a ship where bilge-water collects.

6060 sinck gathering-place of corruption and vice.

6061 bowels i.e., center, depths.

6062 ingenerate engendered, produced.

6063–66 Wherefore . . . them 1 Thess. 5:22, Phil. 1:8.

6066–68 proceeding . . . Iesus Eph. 4:13.

6068–71 knowing . . . death embellishment of Rom. 14:12.

6071–72 for . . . time Tilley, *Proverbs*, N302.

6072–73 which . . . workes Matt. 5:16.

6074 luxurious unchaste, lecherous.

6075 **fantasies** inclinations, desires.

6076–77 **that ... probable** i.e., that the merits of dancing can be proven; O1–O2 read "prouable" in place of "probable".

6076–107 **But ... it** Northbrooke constructs a similar opportunity to refute Scriptural support for dancing: "Why do you speake so much against dauncing, sithe we haue so many examples in the scriptures of those that were godly, and daunced?" (*Treatise*, ed. Collier, 147). Youth mentions all of the passages listed by Spudeus, omitting only Matthew 14 (Salome dancing before Herod) and Exodus 32 (the Israelites dancing before the golden calf); in the *Treatise*, these examples are cited by Age as proof of the wickedness of dancing.

6078–83 **did ... them?** 1 Sam. 18:6.

6081 **Psalteries** stringed instruments which differ from harps in having the soundboard behind and parallel with the strings.

Fluits obsolete form of "flutes".

Tabrets tabors, small drums.

6083–86 **Did ... deliuerance?** Exod. 15:20–21. The grammatically irregular construction of this sentence, "Did not ... daunced", is invariant.

6086–88 **Againe ... Sinai?** Exod. 32:6.

6088–89 **Did ... Lord?** 2 Sam. 6:5.

6089–91 **Did ... field?** Judg. 11:34.

6091–93 **Did ... Iudith?** Jth. 15:12–13. The marginal note O1–O3 reads "Iudic. 15", an incorrect Latin reference to the book of Judges omitted from Q1.

6093 **Damosell** damsel, girl.

6093–94 **Did ... Herode?** Matt. 14:6.

6094–96 **Did ... daunced?** Luke 7:31–32; Matt. 11:16–17.

6097–99 **Saith ... daunce?** Eccl. 3:4.

6099–102 **And ... Musicke?** cf. Ps. 149:2–3.

6104 **instinct** instigation, prompting.

6109–11 **Hominis ... trueth** Tilley, *Proverbs*, E179.

6112–13 **Therfore ... Christ** 1 Cor. 11:1.

6113–20 **but ... particularly** Northbrooke similarly maintains that advocates of dancing willfully misinterpret the Scriptures: "wheresoeuer you read this worde (daunce) presently you apply it in such sort, as though were ment thereby your filthie dauncings; which is not so if it be diligently considered" (*Treatise*, ed. Collier, 148). Like Philoponus, Age examines and discredits each example put forward in support of dancing.

6114 **pretende** allege as a ground or reason.

6119–20 **particularly** one by one.

6121 **Timbrels** percussion instruments such as tambourines.

6127 **nicenesse** wantonness.

6133.2 **cõsequẽt** consequence, logical inference.

6148 **vbiquitarie** ubiquitous.

6151 **Cerberus** dog in Greek and Latin mythology guarding the gate to Hell.

6152 **barke** O1 reads "alatrate", deriving from the Latin root "allatrare", meaning "to bark".

6158 **actiuity** nimbleness, liveliness.

6158–59 **curious** skillful, expert.

6159 **nicitie** precision of movement? This word, with its overtones of daintiness and control, approaches the sense in which "concinnity" is used at 6184, but no *OED* definition quite captures these nuances of meaning.

6161 **allegation** citation, quotation.

6169 **Rereward** variant of "rearward", used in a transferred sense to describe those at the back of the group.

Hoste large company, multitudes.

6184 **concinnity** skilful harmony of movement.

6185 **curiosity** proficiency, expertise.

6186 **God: we** Colons in this sentence otherwise mark pairs of oppositions but this irregularity has not been emended since it is typical both of the book and of this passage as printed O1–O3.

6187 **motions** impulses, desires.

6191–92 **Measures** *OED* defines "measure" as a dance, but Stubbes refers here to the individual steps of which the dance consists; cf. John Lyly's *Campaspe* (1584): "But let us ... see how well it becomes them to tread the measures in a dance that were wont to set the order for a march" (ed. Hunter, 4.3.36–38).

6192 **capers** leaps into the air.

Quauers eighth notes, presumably implying movements appropriate to a quick rhythm.

6196 **they** i.e., the Israelites' actions.

6200–3 **as ... God** Acts 3:8.

6209 **frequented** practiced; O1–O2 read "frequentyng".

6216–17 **Adam ... Deuill** the temptation story (Gen. 3).

6230 **conferre** O1–O2 read "infer", perhaps explaining the unusual construction of "confer" with "for" instead of "to".

6242 **refelleth** refutes, disproves.

6266 **Chorusses** dances. This sense, not listed in *OED*, derives from the Latin root; the English plural form confirms that Stubbes is using it as an English and not a Latin word (printed in contrasting type O3–Q1).

6273 **Amonits** A biblical race descended from Ben-Ammi, the son of Lot by his younger daughter (Gen. 19:38).

6290 **comely** seemly, decorous.

6301–2 **their remembrance** i.e., remembrance of them.

6304 **compassed** O1–O3 read "circumualled", the only other example of which cited in *OED* is in the verbal form and dated 1623.

6305 **suborned** commissioned in their place.

6313–15 **wrapping ... sleeping** This detail is not biblical; Judith returns to the Israelites with Holofernes' head and the canopy stripped from his bed as proof of her success.

6318 **congratulate** celebrate.

6330–32 **which ... togither** Stubbes's conclusion against dancing O1–O2 is less qualified: "whiche plainly argueth the vnlawfulnesse of it in respect of Man".

6332 **fact** action, deed.

6333 **sort** group.

simple O1–O3 read "imprudent".

6335–38 **It was ... Consistory** A sidenote to this passage in O1 reads, "A custome to daunce in prayse of God". An error in the printing of the next edition transformed the infinitive verb to a noun ("A custome daunce in praise of God"). The O2 sidenote might be interpreted to mean "a customary dance", but it then has little to do with the passage it accompanies: Philoponus is speaking not about a particular dance, but about how people commonly expressed through dance their thanks to God. O3, rather than correcting O2, picks up the mistake and further compounds the error by dropping the words "in praise of". This sidenote was finally omitted in Q1, probably because it no longer corresponded to the main text. These compounded errors indicate strongly that Stubbes tended to revise the *Abuses* with only the most recently published version to hand.

6338 **Consistory** court.

6374 **exercising** practicing, taking part in.

Metaphoricall not a particularly early usage; probably printed in contrasting type O3–Q1 for emphasis.

6382 **sort** manner.

6386–94 **Iohn ... Gospell** enlarging on Luke 7:33–34, with changes.

6391 **comfortable** cheering, encouraging.

6414 **and if** if.

6425 **diuturnall** of long duration.

6426 **censured** judged.

6429 **vltimum refugium** "final refuge".

6440–42 **For . . . Aungels** Chrysostom *In Matt.* 48.3, PG 58.491; the quotation is used by Northbrooke (*Treatise*, ed. Collier, 164).

6442–43 **and to . . . workes** alluding to Matt. 5:16.

6447 **conuenticles** assemblies, meetings.

6448 **kind** gender.

6460–71 **And . . . thereof** Although Stubbes concludes at 6642–49 that dancing should be abolished, this chapter is on the whole in accordance with the goal expressed in the O1 "Preface to the Reader" not to stamp out, but to reform, certain pastimes (see Appendix I–B, 41–55). The marginal note at 6484.1–4 seems out of place as it suggests that dancing is immoral under any circumstances; not in O1–O2, this sidenote may represent second thoughts, or possibly, especially in light of the similarly phrased clause at 6478–79, a non–authorial misinterpretation.

6478 **misdemeanours** Perhaps meaning misconduct, but Stubbes may be referring specifically to the dancers' lewd comportment and physical bearing, a sense not listed in *OED* (but cf. "demeanor" sb. 2).

   accustomed practiced habitually.

6480–81 **as . . . burne** cf. Prov. 6:27.

6484 **more tollerable** O1 reads, more enthusiastically, "very commendable".

6494–95 **gainstand** oppose.

6501–5 **Because . . . Fornication** This conclusion, taken from Northbrooke (*Treatise*, ed. Collier, 160), originates in Rodolph Walther, *Secundum Marcum Homiliae* (51.6, sig. M4ᵛ).

6502 **concupiscence** sexual desire.

6503 **irruption** commonly confused with "eruption", meaning "outbreak".

6505–8 **And . . . hel** quotation unknown. "**Cloacæ**", meaning "sewer", was substituted in Q1 for "**inferni**" without any alteration to the translation.

6523–25 **Sirach . . . craftinesse** Sir. 9:4; the invariant sidenote, "Eccle.13.", seems to derive from Northbrooke's incorrect marginal reference to "Eccle.13, 2" (*Treatise*, ed. Collier, 157).

6526 **delating** variant of "dilating", meaning "enlarging" or "expatiating".

6526–29 **Chrysostome . . . mind** Chrysostom *In Matt.* 48.3, PG 58.491; Stubbes condenses Northbrooke's version of the passage (*Treatise*, ed. Collier, 164–65).

6528 **sensible** evident; O1–O3 print "palpable".

6528.1 **Math.4** citing the arrest of John the Baptist; Northbrooke's sidenote refers the reader to his death at Matt. 14:1–12.

6530–31 **Marke ... chapter** Verses 16–29 repeat the account of the beheading of John the Baptist told in Matthew 14.

6530–33 **Theophilus ... company** Stubbes misquotes the *Treatise*: "Theophilact sayth herevpon: *Mira collusio; saltat per puellam diabolus, &c*. This is a wonderfull collusion; for the deuill daunced by the mayde" (ed. Collier, 159–60). Northbrooke is correct in attributing the quotation to Theophylact, Archbishop of Ochrida (died c. 1107 C.E.), but as the name is incorrect O1–Q1, and the mistake is not likely to have resulted from a printing error, I have not emended it. The Latin is taken from *Argumentum in Evangelium secundum Marcum*, chap. 6 (ed. Oecolampadius, sig. K4ᵛ). Stubbes's translation — which seems conflated with another part of Chrysostom (cf. 6526–29 and note) — should conclude, "for the Devil dances through her". O1–O2 print "**puellam**" in place of "**illam**", or in English, "the girl" instead of "her".

6534–36 **Augustine ... daunce** Augustine, *Enarr. in Ps*. 32.6, PL 36.281.

6534–44 **Augustine ... Dauncers** Paraphrasing Northbrooke's *Treatise*: "Saint Augustine sayth, It is much better to dygge all the whole day, than to daunce (vpon the Sabbaoth daye) ... Erasmus sayth, And when they be wearie of drinking and banketting, then they fall to reuelling and dauncing. Then, whose minde is so well ordered, so sadde, stable, and constant, that these wanton dauncings, the swinging of the armes, the sweet sound of the instruments, and feminine singing, woulde not corrupt, ouercome, and vtterlye molifie? ... therefore, as thou desirest thine owne wealth, looke that thou flee and eschewe this scabbed and scuruie companye of dauncers" (*Treatise*, ed. Collier, 165).

6537 **Erasmus** Desiderius Erasmus, Dutch theologian and humanist (1466?–1536).

in ... mundi Erasmus, *De Contemptu Mundi*, ed. S. Dresden, in *Opera Omnia* V.1 (Amsterdam: North-Holland, 1977), 58.528–32, 60.547–48 (¶7); trans. E. Rummel, in *Collected Works of Erasmus* vol. 66, *Spiritualia*, ed. J. W. O'Malley (Toronto: University of Toronto Press, 1988), 152.

6538 **disposed** governed, controlled.

6545 **Lodouicus Viues** Juan Luis Vives, Spanish scholar (1492–1540).

6545–63 **Lodouicus ... Furie** Stubbes obscures the fact that these words are addressed to women, but otherwise closely reproduces Vives's views as printed in the *Treatise* (ed. Collier, 166–67); Northbrooke is quoting Rychard Hyrde's translation of Vives (*The Instruction of a christen woman*, Book 1, chaps. 13–14, sigs. N2–N4).

6564 **Bullinger** Heinrich Bullinger, Swiss reformer (1504–1575).

paraphrasting paraphrasing.

6564–67 **Bullinger . . . vncleannesse** Taken from Northbrooke (*Treatise*, ed. Collier, 167); the sermon is unidentified, but is not included in Bullinger's *Fiftie godlie and learned sermons* translated by "H. I." in 1577.

6568 **Maister Caluin** John Calvin, French Protestant reformer (1509–1564).

6568–69 **Iob . . . Cap.12** This quotation is from *Sermons* 80, the third on Job 21 (trans. Golding, sig. Cc5). I have not emended the incorrect citation since it is invariant and may be authorial; Northbrooke mistakenly refers to Job 23.

6568–72 **Maister . . . whoredome** Misquoting Northbrooke (*Treatise*, ed. Collier, 169).

6573 **Marlorate** Augustine Marlorat, French Protestant convert and theologian (1506–1563).

6573–76 **Marlorate . . . dauncing** A fairly accurate rendering of Northbrooke (*Treatise*, ed. Collier, 167), but Marlorat is himself citing Calvin (*A Catholike and Ecclesiasticall exposition*, trans. Tymme, sig. Dd5ᵛ).

6574–75 **hath . . . haue** invariant shift in number.

6577 **Heathen Writer** i.e., Cicero, *Pro Murena*, ed. Lord, 6.13.

6577–78 **No . . . mad** Taken from Northbrooke (*Treatise*, ed. Collier, 164), who quotes verbatim from Hyrde's translation of Vives' *Instruction of a christen woman* (sig. N3ᵛ).

6579 **Salustius** i.e., Sallust, Roman historian (86–34 B.C.E.); the passage is from *The War with Catiline* (ed. Rolfe, 25.1–5).

Sempronia Married to D. Junius Brutus (consul 77 B.C.E.), Sempronia took part in Catiline's conspiracy; cf. 2263.

6579–86 **Salustius . . . treasure** cf. Northbrook: "Salust writeth, that Sempronia (a certayne laciuious and vnchast woman) was taught to sing and daunce more elegantlye than became an honest matrone; saying, also, that singing and dauncings are the instruments of lecherie. Cicero sayth, that an honest and good man will not daunce in the market place, although he might by that meanes come to great possessions" (*Treatise*, ed. Collier, 172). Gosson also quotes Sallust's description of Sempronia in *Schoole of Abuse* (ed. Kinney, sigs. A4ᵛ–A5).

6584 **Cicero** highly condensed version of a hypothetical situation posed in *De Officiis*, ed. Miller, 3.24.93.

6587–89 **The . . . feast** canon 53 of the Synod of Laodicea (Hefele, *Councils*, 2:321); cf. 5445–46 and its note.

6587–96 **The . . . sinne** Stubbes condenses Northbrooke's account of these authorities (*Treatise*, ed. Collier, 172).

6590–92 **In ... time** The Council is actually that of Toledo III, can. 23 (589
   C.E.; Isodorus, *Concilia* PL 84.356C–D). Northbrooke cites the "Concilium
   Illerdense" which was held "in the time of Theodoricus the king" (*Treatise*,
   ed. Collier, 172), but this is a mistake.

6593 **Iustinian** Justinian I, East Roman emperor (483–565 C.E.), compiler of the
   Codex though not author of the law quoted.

6593–96 **The ... sinne** Justinian (actually Leo I in the 5th c.) makes no mention
   of dancing, inveighing instead against theatrical performances, gladiatorial
   fighting, and animal baitings on holy days (*Codex*, ed. Krueger, 3.12.9.2,
   law dated 469 C.E.). Stubbes's mistake results from his failure to distinguish
   Northbrooke's amplification of the law from the law itself: "Iustinian, the
   emperour, made a decree, saying: We wyll not haue men giue themselues
   vnto voluptuousnesse; wherefore it shall not be lawfull in the feast dayes to
   vse any dauncings, whether they be for lustes sake, or whether they be done
   for pleasures sake" (*Treatise*, ed. Collier, 172). On the Roman law, see
   Binns, *Intellectual Culture*, chap. 18, esp. 336–38 on the study of law, and
   350–54 on law and the stage.

6599 **in generall** without exception.

6600 **quagmire** The synonym printed O1–O3, "quauemire", was current, but this
   Q1 variant antedates by forty years the earliest figurative usage of the word
   cited in *OED*.

6603 **motions** promptings, desires.

6604 **inferreth** brings on, induces.
   affoordeth promotes; this Old English sense is not recorded by *OED* as current in this period.
   ribaldry debauchery, lasciviousness.

6605–6 **ministreth ... Pride** Tilley, *Proverbs*, O30.

6613–22 **for ... Horeb** Northbrooke attributes this explanation of the origins of
   dancing (*Treatise*, ed. Collier, 167) to Rodolph Walther (*Secundum Marcum
   Homiliae* 51.6, sig. M4ᵛ).

6618–22 **And ... Horeb** Exod. 32:6.

6622–42 **Some ... flow** Taken directly from the *Treatise* (ed. Collier, 146).

6623 **one ... Priestes** Sibylla or the Sibyl is the name of a woman in ancient
   mythology reputed to have powers of prophecy and divination; the term became generic.

6627 **Hiero** Hieron I, tyrant of Syracuse (died 467 B.C.E.). This story is told of
   "a tyrant of Troezen" in Aelian's *Varia Historia* (trans. Wilson, 14.22);
   Abraham Fleming translated *Varia Historia* into English in 1576 as *A registre of Hystories* (cf. sigs. TT4ᵛ–UU1ᵛ).

6627.1 **supposal** hypothesis, conjecture.

6628–29 **inhibited** forbad, prohibited.

6639–42 **S. Chrysostome ... flow** This passage probably derives from *Hom. in Matt.* 6.6–7, PG 57.70, which reads in English: "For it is not God that grants to play, but the devil. At least hear, what was the portion of them that played. 'The people,' it is said, 'sat down to eat and drink, and rose up to play' ... Ask not then of God these things, which thou receivest of the devil" (trans. anon., 1:89). Northbrooke reads: "Saint Chrysostome, an ancient father, sayth that it came first from the deuill; for, when he sawe, (sayth he) that the people had committed idollatrie to the golden calfe, he gaue them this libertie, that they shoulde eate and drinke, and ryse vp to daunce" (*Treatise*, ed. Collier, 146).

6640–41 **sprãg ... breast** cf. 5410–11.

6642–46 **if ... weare** Not in Tilley, *Proverbs*, or Dent, *Proverbial Language*; but a similar analogy was used by Thomas White in his *Sermõ Preached at Pawles Crosse* (1577): "And if you breede Cockatrice egges, of whiche whosoeuer eateth he dieth, and he that treadeth on them, Serpentes come vppe: if you weaue the Spyders webbe, whiche makes no clothe: if the deedes of wickednesse and the workes of robbery be in your hands, well you may looke for health but it is farre from you" (sig. D5).

6643 **Cockatrice** mythological serpent said to kill with its glance.

6656 **Plato** *Republic*, ed. Shorey, 3.411A–B.

Aristotle Aristotle in fact supports the study of music during the formative years: "Enough has been said to show that music has a power of forming the character, and should therefore be introduced into the education of the young" (*Politics*, trans. Jowett, 1340b).

Galen Greek physician (c. 130–c. 200 C.E.). He includes music among activities that corrupt morals: "The habits of the mind are corrupted by the debased use of any of these: of food, of drink, of exercise, of seeing, hearing and, finally, of all music" (*De sanitate tuenda*, trans. Linacre, Book 1, sig. C8).

6667 **queasie** weak, delicate.

6673–75 **And ... Whorish** cf. Gosson: "Sappho was skilfull in Poetrie and sung wel, but she was whorish" (*Schoole*, ed. Kinney, sig. A5).

6673–87 **And ... eare** These citations derive from Gosson's *Schoole of Abuse*; specific borrowings are discussed below.

6674 **Sappho** Greek poetess (fl. 611–592 B.C.E.).

6676 **Tirus Maximus** second century Greek rhetorician and philosopher; the O2–Q1 spelling (cf. collation) probably results from a compositor's error.

6676–77 **Tirus . . . world** Misrepresentation of Gosson: "*Maximus Tyrius* holdeth it for a Maxime, that the bringing of instrumēts to Theaters & plaies, was the first cup that poisoned the common wealth" (*Schoole*, ed. Kinney, sigs. B3–B3ᵛ). The quotation is found in Maximus's twenty-first dissertation: "But the ancient Athenian muse consisted of choirs of boys and men; and the husbandmen being collected in tribes . . . poured forth the extemporaneous song. This muse, however, gradually declining into the art of insatiable grace in the scene and in theatres, became the source to the Athenians of political error" (trans. Taylor, 2:5).

6678 **Clytomachus** celebrated Theban athlete; the Q1 spelling (cf. collation) results from a misprint introduced in O3.

6678–80 **Clytomachus . . . farewell** Paraphrasing Gosson: "*Clitomachus* the wrestler geuen altogether to manly exercise, if hee had hearde any talke of loue, in what cōpany soeuer he had bin, would forsake his seat, & bid them adue" (*Schoole*, ed. Kinney, sigs. B4–B4ᵛ). According to Plutarch, Cleitomachus would leave a party if anyone mentioned sex ("Table-Talk," *Moralia*, ed. Minar et al., 710D–E).

6681 **Plutarchus** Plutarch, Greek biographer and philosopher (c. 46–c. 120 C.E.).

6681–84 **Plutarchus . . . vertue** "On Music," *Moralia*, ed. Einarson and de Lacy, 1136B–C. Stubbes condenses and paraphrases Gosson's citation: "*Plutarch* complaineth, that ignorant men, not knowyng the maiestie of auncient musick, abuse both the eares of the people, and the Arte it selfe: with bringing sweete consortes into Theaters, which rather effeminate the minde, as pricks vnto vice, then procure amendement of manners, as spurres to vertue" (*Schoole*, ed. Kinney, sig. B3).

6682 **feminine** weaken, effeminate; only example of sense cited in *OED*.

6685–87 **Pithagoras . . . eare** Quoted from Gosson almost verbatim (*Schoole*, ed. Kinney, sig. A8). This may be a misrepresentation of Pythagoras's ideas about the music of the spheres which cannot be heard by humans; cf. Maximus's twenty-first dissertation: "If, indeed, we are persuaded by Pythagoras, as it is fit we should, the heavens themselves sing sweetly . . . The beauty of this song is, indeed, known to the gods, but is not perceived by us, through its transcendency and our penury" (trans. Taylor, 2:5–6).

6686 **Cloake-bagge** portmanteau, valise.

6692 **comforteth** strengthens, refreshes.

6698–800 **David . . . posterity** David appoints Asaph and his kindred to sing praises to the Lord at 1 Chron. 16:5–9; this becomes a tradition continued throughout the reign of David's son, Solomon (2 Chron. 7:6).

6703 **conuenticles** assemblies, meetings.

Directorie guide.

6705 **estrangeth** maddens.

6725–31 **I ... eye** Gosson, *Schoole of Abuse*: "If you enquire howe manie suche Poetes and Pipers wee haue in our Age, I am perswaded that euerie one of them may creepe through a ring, or daunce the wilde Morice in a Needles eye" (ed. Kinney, sig. B1).

6727 **sockets** invariant usage, but disparaging sense not recorded in *OED*.

6734 **laden ... merchandize** O1–O3 read "balanced with massie matter", the only example cited in *OED* of "balanced" used to mean "ballasted"; cf. 4381.

6735 **pestred** encumbered.

6744–45 **smooth mouthed** insinuating, flattering.

6746–47 **briefly ... worse** The worst thing Stubbes can imagine a man turning into is a woman — "or worse" points to horrors not yet conceived; cf. 5547n.

6758 **Ribauldry** debauchery; the modern sense of "coarse language" may also be implicit.

6764–67 **But ... commoditie** Musicians were subject to the same regulations as actors under 14 Elizabeth chap. 5 (1572); cf. 5605–10n.

6766–67 **commoditie** advantage, profit.

6774 **extrauagantes** vagrants, vagabonds.

Straglers vagabonds.

6776 **pretensed** feigned, spurious; O1 reads "presented".

6781 **goe ... payment** i.e., be accepted.

6787 **Tabretters** drummers.

6810 **spoyled** robbed.

6814–20 **but ... will** Statutes passed under Henry VII and Henry VIII banning games made an exception of the Christmas season (*Statutes*, 11 Henry VII, chap. 2; 33 Henry VIII, chap. 9, para. 16).

6816 **masking, mumming** entertainments presumably associated with gaming since they were popular at Christmas; Stubbes's claim at 6842–44 that masking encourages robbery, whoredom, and murder probably refers to un-invited visits made by mummers to stately homes, a practice banned by Henry VIII (Laroque, *Shakespeare's Festive World*, 150–51).

6825–26 **the ... offendeth** Ezek. 18:20.

6859–60 **of God?** invariant punctuation.

6860 **lucre of Gaine** acquisition of profits.

6872–74 **The ... neighbour** Exod. 20:17.

6878–80 **The ... gaming** 1 Thess. 4:6; cf. Northbrooke: "If St. Paule forbiddeth

vs to vse deceyte in bargaining and selling, what should we doe in gaming?"
(*Treatise*, ed. Collier, 121).

6881–83 **Our ... him** Matt. 7:12, Luke 6:31.

6897 **Seminaries** places of origin and early development.

6901 **neuer** O1–O3 read "euer"; although the change reverses the intended
meaning, the Q1 variant may represent a deliberate attempt to convey
added emphasis.

6905–8 **The ... it** Rom. 1:31 (variously verse 32); the Latin also quotes Augustine *Enarr. in Ps.* 57.18, PL 36.688.

6914 **rapine** plunder, robbery.

6915 **in fine** in the end.

6915–16 **as ... body?** Tilley, *Proverbs*, S263.

6918 **shambles** slaughter-houses.

Blockhouses apparently synonymous with slaughter-houses (perhaps deriving
from the butcher's block?), but sense not recorded in *OED*.

6923.3 **divulgate** made public, spread abroad.

6928 **Octauius Augustus** Roman emperor (63 B.C.E.–14 C.E.).

6928–31 **Octauius ... besides** cf. Suetonius: "He did not in the least shrink
from a reputation for gaming, and played frankly and openly for recreation
... In the other details of his life it is generally agreed that he was most
temperate and without even the suspicion of any fault" ("Augustus," trans.
Rolfe, 71.1–72.1).

6928–48 **Octauius ... Gamester?** Most of this passage originated in Sir Thomas
Elyot's *The Boke Named the Governour* (1531; ed. Croft, 1:277–79), but the
inclusion of examples such as the reference to Cicero at 6932–33, printed
only in the *Treatise*, indicates that Northbrooke was Stubbes's immediate
source (ed. Collier, 130–32).

6928–82 **Octauius ... pence** These authorities are taken from Northbrooke's
Treatise; cf. below.

6932 **obiected to** brought as a charge against.

Marcus Antonius Roman triumvir (c. 83–30 B.C.E.).

6932–33 **Cicero ... him** *Philippics* 2.23.56.

6934 **Lacedemonians** Spartans.

6934–43 **The ... gold** John of Salisbury, *Policraticus* (1.5). These exempla are
also related in Chaucer's *Pardoner's Tale* (603–28).

6942 **Demetrius** Demetrius I of Macedonia (336–283 B.C.E.).

6944 **Sir Thomas Eliot** English diplomat and scholar (c. 1490–1546).

6944–45 **his ... Gouernance** i.e., *The Boke Named the Governour*, ed. Croft,
1:278–79.

6946 **light** of small account.

6947 **remisse** characterized by a lack of proper restraint.

6949 **Publius** Publilius Syrus, Latin writer of mimes, first century B.C.E.; the misspelled name is invariant.

6949–53 **Publius ... maners** An expansion of Publilius Syrus, *Sententiae*, ed. Duff and Duff, 33; cited in Northbrooke's *Treatise* (ed. Collier, 117).

6953 **Iustinian** Justinian I, East Roman emperor (483–565 C.E.).

6953–55 **Iustinian ... openly** *Codex*, ed. Krueger, 3.43.1.1.

6953–63 **Iustinian ... others** Closely paraphrasing Northbrooke's *Treatise* (ed. Collier, 134).

6956 **Alexander Seuerus** Roman emperor 222–235 C.E.; his laws against gambling are unlocated, but George Whetstone similarly mentions them in *A Mirour for Magestrates* (1584; sig. F1ᵛ).

6961–63 **Lodouicus ... others** Louis IX, King of France (1214–1270) introduced this ban in the ordinance of 1254 as part of a series of moral reforms (Richard, *Saint Louis*, 161).

6964 **King ... second** King of England, 1442–1483.

6964–65 **King ... playing** *Statutes*, 12 Richard II, c. 6.

6964–82 **King ... pence** Stubbes condenses Northbrooke's text (*Treatise*, ed. Collier, 136).

6965–66 **King ... fourth** King of England, 1367–1413.

6965–68 **King ... gaming** *Statutes*, 11 Henry IV, c. 4.

6969 **King ... fourth** King of England, 1442–1483.

6969–73 **King ... pound** *Statutes*, 17 Edward IV, c. 3.

6974 **King ... seuenth** King of England, 1457–1509.

6974–78 **King ... behauiour** *Statutes*, 11 Henry VII, c. 2.

6975 **all aday** i.e., a whole day; O1–O3 print "aday" as two words. Northbrooke's *Treatise* reads "one whole day" (ed. Collier, 136).

6978 **Recognizaunce** legal obligation by which the offender is engaged to observe some condition.

6979 **King ... eight** King of England, 1491–1547.

6979–82 **King ... pence** *Statutes*, 33 Henry VIII, c. 9.

6986 **stumbling blocks** causes of moral stumbling; cf. Rom. 14:13.

6988–90 **As ... Bear-baiting** By 1595, the date of Q1, Thursday had been substituted for Sunday as the regular day for bear-baiting (Chambers, *Elizabethan Stage*, 1:315 n.1, 316). This reform was prompted by the collapse of Paris Garden on 13 January 1583, an event described at 7053–87.

6997 **vpon ... day** Not in O1–O3, suggesting that in 1595 bear-baiting was at least in some places still taking place on Sunday.

7000–1 **which ... seruice** This clause is a good example of the cumulative revision typical of the *Abuses*. O1 reads, "which ye Lord hath cōsecrat to holy vses", the tense of the verb being revised in O2 to "would haue consecrated"; the text is left unchanged in O3, and "his seruice" is substituted for "holy vses" in Q1.

7017 **kind** nature.

7022–23 **Qui ... Dog** Tilley, *Proverbs*, D496.

7026 **oweth** owns.

7027 **resulteth** recoils, rebounds.

7030 **redoundeth** recoils, falls.

7038 **Mastiues** mastiffs; O1 adds, "and bādogs".

7042 **beyt** bait, the action of setting dogs on other animals.

7044 **Bearward** keeper of the bear.

7046 **wel fitting** The more common usage in this period, "wel sittyng", was printed O1–O3.

7049 **reueiled** variant of "revealed".

7053–55 **A ... day** John Field provides a detailed account of this event in *A godly exhortation by occasion of the late judgement of God at Parris garden* (1583), mentioning the names and occupations of the seven casualties, and that the disaster took place during the time of afternoon prayers. Verbal parallels suggest that Stubbes's account is based on this earlier pamphlet: Field, for example, uses the phrase "being now amidest their iolity" (sig. B8, cf. 7064) and describes the wounded as "some hauing theyr legs and armes broken, some theyr backes, theyr bodies beeing sore brused" (sig. C2, cf. 7069–74).

7059 **of each sort** i.e., young and old? This sentence was heavily revised for O3, and this ambiguous remark is probably synonymous with the redundant phrase "both yong and olde" printed O1–O2: "Vppon the thirteene daie of Ianuarie last, beyng the Sabbaoth daie. **Anno. 1583.** the People, Men, Women and Childrē, both yong and olde, an infinite number, flocking to those infamous places ...".

7061 **Courts** courtyards.

7063 **Scaffolds** raised platform for holding spectators.

galleries spaces in which to house spectators; the term was used in a broad sense, but Stubbes clearly has in mind those areas which were raised above ground level. Field uses the word similarly: "This gallery that was double, and compassed the yeard round about, was so shaken at the foundation, (y^t it fell as it were in a moment) flat to the groūd, without post or peece, that was left stāding, so high as the stake whervnto the Beare was tied" (*A godly* *exhortation*, sig. B8). Field specifies that those worst hurt were those who "stood vnder the Galleries on the grounde, vpon whom both the waight of Timbre and people fel" (*A godly exhortation*, sig. C2ᵛ).

7072 **al to quasht** smashed to pieces; O1 reads "all to squasht".

7088–89 **A ... Theaters** The earthquake of 6 April 1580 shook all London; the event is also documented by Thomas Churchyard, *A warning for the wise* (1580), Abraham Fleming, *A Bright Burning Beacon* (1580?), and Arthur Golding, *A discourse vpon the Earthquake* (1580?).

7103 **fray** frighten.

7104–5 **the Lorde ... wrath** Ps. 59.13.

7110–11 **Cockfighting ... England** This chapter title and those which follow are not in O1; most of them specify "vpon the Sabboth day" only in Q1.

7113–14 **nothing ... rest** O1–O3 read "nothing inferiour to the rest", but the phrase as printed in Q1 makes sense as an elided version of the expression "nothing in comparison to the rest" (cf. 1916). This change reverses the relation between cockfights and "the rest", but the tone of the passage remains consistent.

7116 **cōuitious** railing, abusive.

7120 **blanch** palliate, "whitewash".

7137–39 **accomptes ... exercises** Rom. 14:12.

7146 **Esau ... reprobate** Gen. 25:27; Esau is considered wicked because he sold his birthright to his younger brother (Gen. 25:29–34).

7146–47 **Ismaell ... miscreant** Gen. 21:20; God refused to make his covenant with Ishmael, Abraham's illegitimate son (Gen. 17:18–19).

7147–49 **Nimrod ... wrath** Gen. 10:8–9; the Geneva sidenote explains that "His tyrannie came into a p[ro]uerbe as hated bothe of God and man: for he passed not to commit crueltie euē in Gods presēce".

7148 **abiect** outcast.

7148–49 **vessel of wrath** Rom. 9:22.

7156 **sort** group, company.

lubbers louts.

7159–75 **So ... bloud** Animals were alienated from humans after the flood, when God gave them to humankind for food (Gen. 9:2). The misinterpretation may derive from the *Homily against Disobedience and wilful Rebellion*: "And as God would have man to be his obedient subject, so did he make all earthly creatures subject unto man, who kept their due obedience unto man, so long as man remained in his obedience unto God" (*Sermons*, 587).

7179 **spoyle** injure.

7181–82 **or ... Tartarian** O1–O3 print "or not rather a **Pseudo-christian**".

7190 **annoying** harming; O1–O3 print the synonym "**preiudicyng**".

7193–94 **Mora . . . daunger** Tilley, *Proverbs*, D195, Walther, *Proverbia*, n.s. 38321.

7208–9 **Can . . . Mammon?** Matt. 6:24; Luke 16:13.

7212–15 **For . . . strength** Deut. 6:5.

7226–33 **For . . . committed?** "A fairground was a venue for a whole shady world of beggars, cutpurses, charlatans, 'cony-catchers,' prostitutes and pimps, who tended to give it the air of the court of some Beggar-king" (Laroque, *Shakespeare's Festive World*, 166–67).

7229 **counterfeit** made of inferior materials, sham; O1–O3 print the synonym "**fucate**".

7229–30 **deceiuable** deceiptful.

7239 **polling & pilling** extortion and robbery.

7243 **in a wanion** i.e., with a vengeance; "wanion" or "waniand" means "at the time of the waning moon", that is, in an unlucky hour.

7244–49 **And . . . maintained** O1 continues: "**The Lord cut of these with all other sin, both from their soules and thy Sabaoth, that thy name may be glorified, & thy Church truely edified**".

7247 **conculcate** trod under foot, trampled on.

7261 **hale** draw, pull.

7262–66 **for . . . pastime** These games were popularly held on Shrove Tuesday and the sport was as violent as Stubbes suggests, the Essex Assize records, for example, noting the deaths of two players in the winter of 1582 (Emmison, *Disorder*, 226).

7268 **picke** hurl, pitch.

7270 **hole** O1–O3 read "hill".

7274–75 **sometymes . . . backes** This phrase was probably omitted from Q1 as a result of compositorial eye-skip (cf. collation).

7278–79 **start out** burst out.

7283 **scapeth . . . hardly** i.e., recovers with great difficulty.

7284 **sleights** tricks, stratagems.

7286 **short ribbes** lower ribs, not attached to the sternum.
  griped clenched.

7287–88 **with . . . hip** i.e., to strike a blow at his hip with their knees.

7297 **prepensed** premeditated, purposed.

7298–99 **Is . . . to vs** Matt. 7:12; Luke 6:31.

7308 **annoy** injuriously affect.

7317–18 **plausibly** approvingly, with applause.

7330 **Book of Martyrs** The popular title of *Actes and Monuments* (1563); an eight-line poem written by Stubbes in Latin was included at the end of the commendatory material in the fourth edition of 1583 (sig. ¶4).

7332 **Maister . . . Foxe** English martyrologist (1516–1587).

7333–34 **reuerenced** esteemed, respected.

7336 **Scheduls** slips of paper containing writing.

7337 **Libels** short books.

7338 **challenge** demand, lay claim to.

7344 **Belzebub** Eventually coming to designate a devil or Satan himself, this name is mentioned in the Bible at 2 Kings 1:3.

7345 **Pluto** Greek god of the underworld.

7346 **set abroch** published, diffused.

7369 **inferiour** subordinate, lower in rank.

7372 **disfranchized** deprived of their privileges and rights, usually said of people.

7373–74 **Pecunia . . . things** Tilley, *Proverbs*, M1102; O1 reads, "quid non pecunia potest? what is it, but money will bring to passe?".

7375 **done . . . cloud** Dent, *Proverbial Language*, C443.1.
   benedicite blessing.

7384 **publike weale** general good.

7388 **corruptible** perishable, earthly.

7392–93 **as much . . . floud** O1 reads, "as it were in **Charons** boate to the **Stigian** flood".

7393 **Stigian** i.e., of the River Styx, one of the five rivers in Hades, over which the souls of the dead were ferried.

7397 **the most** O1 reads with less reservation "al".

7408–12 **but . . . witnesse** Rom. 13:1–2.

7419–20 **all . . . God** echoing the conditions prompting the flood (Gen. 6:12).

7423–25 **For . . . Euangely** Matt. 24:12–14.

7426 **Philo.** The substitution of the wrong speech prefix in O3 was overlooked for the printing of Q1 (cf. collation).

7426–31 **The . . . life?** Prodigious happenings provided topical subject-matter for pamphlets and are recorded in chronicle histories. As Keith Thomas notes, the English "attached moral importance to such natural occurrences as thunder and lightning, earthquakes, eclipses or comets; even more striking was their capacity for seeing apparitions in the sky of a kind denied to us — galloping horses, dragons or armies in battle" (*Religion and the Decline of Magic*, 89).

7427–28 **wonderfull . . . miracles** O1–O3 read "wonderfull **portents**, straunge miracles". This alteration is suspect, but as there is no strong reason to assume compositorial eye-skip and Q1 makes good sense, I have not returned to the earlier reading.

7429 **Preachers** exhorters, persuaders.

7431–33 **Hath ... to place** Isa. 13:13; perhaps alluding specifically to the earthquake on 6 April 1580.

7432 **remooue** stir, move.

7437–38 **To raine ... like?** This event is described in detail by William Averell in *A wonderfull and straunge newes* (1583, sigs. A8ᵛ–B1).

7438–42 **Hath ... of?** In the continuation of Holinshed's *Chronicles* (1587), Arthur Fleming writes of an astronomer who prompted public concern by predicting that plagues, tempests, and political unrest would result from the conjunction of Saturn and Jupiter on 28 April 1583 (4:511).

7446 **blasing stars** Comets were seen in November 1577 and October 1580.

7446–47 **firy Drakes** fiery meteors.

7447 **men ... aire** Stephen Bateman mentions a similar sighting in *The Doome warning all men to the Iudgemente* (1581, sig. Cc8).

7449 **operation** influence, force.

  abortiues still-born children, premature births.

7450 **vgglesom** horrible, gruesome.

7471 **remunerate** reward.

7475 **prepared ... Angels** Matt. 25:41.

7480–83 **At ... Lord** cf. Ezek. 18:26–28. In this form, it is the first invitatory sentence to Morning Prayer in the 1559 *Book of Common Prayer* (ed. Booty, 49).

7489–91 **for the ... euer** Matt. 10:28.

7493–96 **cum ... peruerted** cf. Prov. 13:20, 2 Sam. 22:27. O1 reads "peruerseris" in place of "peruerteris", or in English, "will have been perverted"; the translation is invariant.

7501 **liuely** living.

7511–16 **as ... before** Matt. 27:3–5.

7516–19 **Peter ... faith** alluding to Peter's denial of Christ (Matt. 26:74–75).

7522 **pretenced** pretended, feigned.

7524–25 **Cain ... condemned** Cain never explicitly repents murdering his brother, crying out against the Lord's curse, "My punishment is greater, then I can beare" (Gen. 4:13); the alternative translation offered in the Geneva sidenote reads, "my sinne is greater then can be pardoned".

7525 **Esau ... condemned** Esau weeps when he learns that Jacob has his birthright and their father's blessing in his place (Gen. 27:37–38).

7526 **Antiochus ... condēned** 2 Macc. 9:11–12.

7526–27 **Iudas ... condemned** cf. 7511–16n.

7528 **prolōged** delayed, postponed.

7530–31 **affection** inclination.

7530–34 **Thus ... nothing** Matt. 7:21.

7538–41 **But ... light** James 1:17.

7542–44 **It is ... please him** common Biblical theme; cf. Rom. 9:15–16.

7555–56 **not to deferre** This is the reading printed O1–O3; Q1 substitutes "did not deferre" (cf. collation).

7569–71 **King ... Sunne** Eccl. 1:2–4; the concluding lines of this sentence (7571–73) appear to be Stubbes's own interpolation.

7599–600 **God ... Amen** not in O1–O3.

Appendix I: Additional Passages

Passages found in one or more of the early versions, but not included as part of Q1, are reprinted below. In each instance the text has been taken from the latest edition in which the passage appears; obvious printing errors have been emended and noted at the bottom of the page but copies of the book have not been collated. A commentary is included after the final passage.

A.

The *Abuses*, dedicated in 1595 to the Magistrates of England, was dedicated O1–O3 to Philip Howard, Earl of Arundel. Passages from the "Epistle Dedicatorie" which were revised in order to accommodate this shift in patronage have been reprinted below; approximately two and a half octavo pages of text following the salutation in O3 have been elided (sigs. A2–A3), the epistle resuming at the top of sig. A3ᵛ (line 121 at the equivalent point in the main text).

A2

To the Right
Honorable, and his singuler good Lorde,
Phillip Earle of Arundell: Phillip
Stubbes, wisheth helth of body & soule, fauour
of God, increase of Godly honour, reward of laudable vertue, and eternall felicitie, in the Heauenly hierarchie by IESVS Christ.
NOBILITAS Patriæ DECVS
[...]

A3ᵛ   After that I had (right honorable) fully perfected this booke, I was
minded, notwithstanding, bothe in regard of the straungenes of the

matter it intreateth of, and also in respect of the rudenesse of my
penne, to haue suppressed it for euer, for diuerse and sundrie causes,
and neuer to haue offred it to the viewe of the World. But notwithstanding, being ouercome by the importunate request, and infatigable   15
desire of my freinds, I graunted to publish the same, as now you see,
is extant.

But, when I had once graũted to imprinte the same, I was in greater doubt than before, fearing, to whome I might dedicat the same so
rude & impolished a worke. And withall I was not ignorant, how hard   20
a thing it is in these daies to finde a Patrone of such books as this,
which shewith to euery one his sin, & discouereth euery Mans wicked
waies, which indeed, the vngodly can not at any hãd abide, but as it
were mad men disgorging their stomacks (Cum in Authorẽ tum
in codicem plenis buccis, & dentibus plusquam caninis ra-   25
bidè feruntur:) they rage, thei fume and raile both against the
AVTHOR and his booke. Thus (vacillante animo) my mind wãdring
too & fro, & resting, as it weare in extasie of despaire, at last I called
to mind your honorable Lordship, whose praises haue pearced the
Skies, & whose laudable vertues ar blowen, not ouer the realme of   30
England onely, but euen to the furthest costs & parts of the world.

All whose vertues, and condigne praises, if I should take vpon mee
to recount, I might as well number the starres in the Sky, or grasse
vpon the Earth.

For, for Godly Wisdome, and zeale to the truth, is not your good   35
Lordship (without offence be it spoken) comparable to the best? For
sobrietie, affabilitie, and gentle curtesie to euerie one, farre excelling
any.

For deuotion and compassion to the poore oppressed, in all places
famous: For Godly fidelitie, to your Soueraigne, loue to the CVN-   40
TREY, and vertues in generall, euerie where most renowmed.

But least I might obscure, your Worthie commendations // with my   A4
vnlearned penne, (litle, or nothing at all, emphaticall) I will rather sur-
cease, than further to proceed hearein, cõtenting my self rather to
haue giuen a shadowe of them, then to haue ciphered them foorth,   45
which indeed are both infinit, and inexplicable.

In consideration (whereof) not withstanding that my Booke be
simpler, baser, and meaner, than that it may (without blushing) present it self to your good Lordship (being far vnworthie of such an honorable Personage) yet according to your accustomed clemencie, I most   50

humbly beseeche your good Lordship to receiue the same into your
honors Patrociny and protection, accepting it as an infallible token of
my faithfull hearte, seruice, and good will towardes your honorable
Lordship: For proofe whereof, would GOD it might once come to
55   passe, that if not otherwise, yet with my humble seruice, I might
shewe foorth the faithfull & euer willing heart I beare in brest to your
good Lordeship, protesting before Heauen and Earth, that though
power want, yet shall fidilitie, and faithfulnes faile neuer.

And because, this my Booke is subiect (my very good Lord) to as
60   many reproches, tauntes and reproofes, as euer was any litle booke
subiect vnto (for that fewe can abyde to heare their sins detected)
therefore I haue had the greater care to commit the same to the guar-
dance & defence of your honour, rather thē to many others, not onely
for that GOD hath made your honour a Lamp of light vnto the
65   world, a mirrour of true nobilitie and a rare Phenix of integritie and
perfection, but also hath made you his substitute, or vicegerent, to reforme vices, punish abuses, and correcte sinne.

And as in mercie he hath giuen you his power & autoritie, so hath
he giuen you a hungrie desire to accomplish the same according to his
70   will: Which zeale in your sacred brest, the LORD increase for euer.

For as your Lordship knoweth, reformation of maners and amendment of life, was neuer more needfull. For, was pride (the chiefest
argument of this Booke) euer so rype? Doe not, both men and women
(for the most part) euery one in generall goe attired in Silkes, Vel-
75   uetes, Damasks, satans, and what not? which are attyre onely for the
A4ᵛ   nobilitie and gentrie, and not for the other at // any hand. Are not
vnlawfull games, Plaies Enterludes, & the like euery where frequented? Is not whordome, couetousnesse, vsurie and the like daylie
practised without all punishment of lawe or execution of iustice?

80   But hereof I nead to say no more, reseruyng the good consideration
as well of these as of the rest, to your Lordships Godly Wisedome.
Beseaching your good Lordship, to pardon my presumtion in speak-
yng thus much, for (Zelus domini hûc adegit me:) the zeale of my
God hath driuen me heather.

85   Thus I ceese to molest your sacred eares any further with my rude
speaches, most humbly beseaching your good Lordship not onely to
admit this my Booke into your honours patronage and protection, but
also to persist, the iust Defender thereof, against the swinishe crew of
railing ZOILVS & flowting MOMVS with their complices of braging

Thrasoes, and barking Phormions to whom it is easier to depraue all   90
things, than to amend any thing themselues. But if I shall perceiue
the same to be accepted of your honour, besides that I shal not care
for a thousand others disliking the same, I shal not onely thinke my
self to haue receiued a sufficient guerdon for my paines & shalbe therby greatly incoraged (if GOD permit) hereafter, to take in hand some   95
memorable thing to your immortall praise, honour and renowm, but
also shal daylie praie to GOD, for your good Lordship long to continue, to his good pleasure and your harts desire, with increase of Godly
honour, reward of laudable vertue, & eternall felicitie in the HEAV-
ENS, by Iesus Christ.   100

Columna gloriæ virtus.

Your Honors to commaund

in the Lorde.

PHILLIP Stubbes.

B.

After the "Epistle Dedicatorie" (line 165), O1 prints:

¶5ᵛ

A PREFACE
TO THE READER.

I thought it conuenient (good **Reader,** who soeuer thou art, yᵗ shalt
read these my poore laboures) to admonish thee (least haply yᵘ might-
5   est take my woords otherwise than I meant them) of this one thing:
That wheras in the processe of this my booke, I haue intreated of cer-
ten exercyses, vsually practised amongest vs, as namely of Playes and
Enterludes, of dauncing, gaming, and such other like: I would not haue
thee so, to take mee, as though my speaches tended, to the ouerthrowe
10   and vtter disliking of all kynd of exercyses in generall: that is nothing
my simple meaning. But the particulare Abuses, which are crept into
euery one of these seuerall exercyses, is the onely thing, which I think
worthie of reprehension.
      For, otherwise (all Abuses cut away) who seeth not, yᵗ some kind of
15   playes, tragedies and enterluds in their own nature, are not onely of
¶6   great anciẽtie, but also very honest and very commendable // exercyses,
being vsed and practised in most Christian common weales, as which
containe matter (such they may be) both of doctrine, erudition, good
example and wholsome instruction? And may be vsed in tyme and place
20   conuenient, as conducible to example of life and reformation of maners.
For such is our grosse & dull nature, that what thing we see opposite
before our eyes, do pearce further, and printe deeper in our harts and
minds, than that thing, which is hard onely with the eares, as **Horace,**
the hethen **Poët** can witnesse. **Segnius irritant animum, dimissa per**
25   **aures, quàm quæ sunt hominum occulis obiecta.** So, that when honest
& chast playes, tragedies, & enterluds, are vsed to these ends, for the
Godly recreatiõ of the mind, for the good example of life, for the
auoyding of that, which is euill, and learning of that which is good, thã
are they very tollerable exercyses. But being vsed (as now commonly
30   they be) to the prophanation of the Lord his sabaoth, to the alluring
and inuegling of the People from the blessed word of God preached, to
Theaters and vnclean assemblies, to ydlenes, vnthriftynes, whordome,
wantõnes, drunkẽnes, and what not? and which is more, when they are

vsed to this end, to maintaine a great sort of ydle Persons, doing
nothing, but playing and loytring, hauing their lyuings of the sweat of   35
other Mens browes, much like vnto dronets deuouring ye sweet honie
of ye poore labouring bees, // than are they exercyses (at no hand) suf-   ¶6^v
ferable.

But being vsed to the ends that I haue said, they are not to be disliked of any sober, and wise Christian.   40

And as concerning dauncing, I wold not haue thee (good **Reader**) to
think that I condemne the exercyse it self altogether, for I know the
wisest Sages and the Godlyest Fathers and Patriarches that euer liued,
haue now and than vsed the same, as **Dauid**, **Salomon**, and many
others: but my woords doo touch & cōcerne the Abuses thereof onely.   45
As being vsed vppon the Sabaoth day, from morning vntill night, in
publique assemblies and frequencies of People, Men & women together,
with pyping, fluting, dromming, and such like inticements to wantonnesse & sin, together with their leapinges, skippings, & other vnchast
gestures, not a few. Being vsed, or rather abused in this sort, I vtterly   50
discommend it.

But vppon the otherside, being vsed in a mans priuat-chamber, or
howse for his Godly solace, and recreation in the feare of GOD, or
otherwise abroade with respect had to the time, place and persons, it is
in no respect to be disalowed.   55

And wheras I speake of gaming, my meaning is not, that it is an
exercise altogether vnlawful. For, I know that one Christian may play
with another, at any kind of Godly, honest, ciuile game, or exercise, for
the mutuall recreation one of the other, so that they be not inflamed
with coueitousnes, // or desire of vnlawfull gaine: for the cōmaundemēt   ¶7
saith, thou shalt not couet: wherfore, if any be voide of these affections,
playing rather for his Godly recreation, than for desire of filthie lucre,
he may vse the same in the feare of God: yet so as the vse therof be not
a let, or hinderance vnto him, to any other Godly exploit.

But, if a man make (as it weare) an occupation of it, spending both   65
his tyme and goods therein, frequenting, gaming howses, bowling allyes,
and such other places, for greedinesse of lucre, to him it is an exercise
altogether discommendable and vnlawfull. Wherfore, as these be exercyses lawfull, to them that know how to vse them in the feare of GOD,
so are they practises at no hand sufferable to them that abuse thē, as I   70
haue shewed. But take away the abuses, the thinges in themselues are
not euill, being vsed as instruments to Godlynes, not made as spurres

vnto vice. There is nothing so good, but it may be abused, yet because
of ye abuses, I am not so strict, that I wold haue the things, themselues
75   remooued, no more than I wold meat and drinke, because it is abused,
vtterly to be taken away.

And wheras also I haue spoken of the excesse in Apparell, and of the
Abuse of the same, as wel in men, as in women generally, I wold not
be so vnderstood, as though my speaches extẽded, to any, either noble,
80   honorable, or worshipful: for, I am so farre from once thinking that any
¶7^v   kind of // sumptuous, or gorgeous attire is not to be worn of any of
them, as I suppose them rather Ornaments in them, than otherwise.

And that they both may, and for some respects, ought to were such
attire (their birthes callings, functions and estats requiring the same) for
85   causes in this my Booke laid downe, as maye appeare, and for the distinction of them from the inferiour sorte, it is prouable both by the
Woord of GOD, Ancient Writers, and common practise of all ages,
People and Nations, from the beginning of the World, to this day.

And therfore, when I speake generally of the excesse of Apparell, my
90   meaning is of the inferiour sorte onely, who for the most parte do farre
surpasse, either noble, honorable, or worshipfull, ruffling in Silks, Veluets, Satens, Damasks, Taffeties, Gold, Siluer, and what not? with their
swoords, daggers, and rapiers guilte, and reguilte, burnished, and costly
ingrauen, with all things els, that any noble, honorable, or worshipfull
95   Man doth, or may weare, so as the one cannot easily be discerned from
the other.

These be the Abuses, that I speake of, these be the euills, that I lament, and these be the persons that my words doo concerne, as the tenure of my Booke consideratly wayed, to any indifferent READER doth
100   purport.

This much I thought good (Gentle **Reader**) to informe thee of, for
¶8   thy better instruction, as // well in these few points, as in all other the
like, whersoeuer they shall chaunce to occurre in my Booke. Beseaching
thee, to construe al things to the best, to beare with the rudenes therof,
105   and to giue the same thy good-woord, and gentle acceptaunce. And
thus in the LORD, I bid thee, farewell.

Thyne to vse in the Lord,

PHILLIP Stubbes.

C.

Before "I. F. In commendation of the Authour and his Book" (line 166),
O2 and O3 print three prefatory poems, the first and third of which are also
included in O1:

PHILIPPVS STV-

B1

BEVS CANDIDO
LECTORI.

Offendit nimia te garrulitate libellus
fortè meus, Lector, miror id ipse nihil.   5
Obsitus est etenim verborũ colluuiõe
plusquam vandalica, rebus & insipidis.
Quare si sapias operam ne perdito posthac
nostra legendo, legas vtiliora, vale.
¶ Idem in Zoilum.   10
ZOILE cum tanta rabie exardescis in omnes,
non aliter rabidus, quàm solet ipse canis:
Dente Theonino rodens alios, calomoque,
incessens hos, qui nil, nocuere tibi:
Vipereã in cunctos vibrans O Zoile linguam,   15
linguam quam inficiunt toxica dira tuam:
Cum Debacchandi finis sit Zoile nullus,
hora quieta tibi nullaque prætereat:
Cum tumeas veluti ventrosus ZOILE bufo,
demiror medius quòd minus ipse crepes.   20
¶ Aliud in eundem.
Dæmones ad tetrum descendat Zoilus antrũ,
hunc lacerent furiæ, Cerborus ore voret.
Imprecor at misero quid pænas, cui satis intus?
dæmona circumfert pectore namque suo.   25
¶ Eiusdem aliud.
Si tibi prolixus nimium liber iste videtur
pauca legas, poterit sic liber esse breuis. //

✣C.B. In commendation
of the Auctors lucubrations.

B1ᵛ

30

You Sages graue with heares so hoare,
attend what you doe heare:
And eke you youthfull gallants all,
marke well and giue good eare.

35
You princely peeres and Senatours,
in sacred breasts imprint:
These saiyngs wise, and prudent eke,
to practize doe not stint.
You Bishoppes, and you prelates all,

40
learne here your flocke to keepe:
You Ministers, and Preachers eke,
to feede your seely sheepe.
You Commons all, whiche doe inioye,
bothe high and lowe degree:

45
Step boldly in amongest the route,
and view with single eye:
This perfect glasse, and mirror pure,
whiche doeth your sinnes descrie:
And sacred precepts doeth prescribe,

50
by name Anatomie.
Approche therefore bothe high and lowe,
this Booke see that thou buye:
And learne thy self by sacred lore,
in vertue for to dye.

55
To God, to Queene, to all men eke,
how thou thy self shouldst frame:
To liue, to dye in vertues lawes,
to win immortall fame. //

B2
Loe here (you readers all) the gaine,

60
whiche you herein maie haue:
Delay not then, giue **Stubbes** the praise,
since freely he it gaue.
Loe here my freende his freendly harte,
whiche he to Countrey beares:

His taken paines to all he sendes,   65
with sighes and tricklyng teares.
In his behalfe I as his freende,
doe humbly of you craue:
His willing minde accept, and giue,
him praise he ought to haue.   70
FINIS.

Τῆς ἀρετῆς ἁεγοῦῆτευχ ῆ
αλδαιαχ.

A.D. In commendation
of the Auctor and his Booke.   75

If mortall man maie challenge praise,
For any thing doen in this life:
Then maie our **Stubbes**, at all assaies,
Inioye the same withouten strife.
Not onely for his Godly zeale,   80
and Christian life accordinglie:
But also for his Booke in sale,
Here present now before thyne eye.
Herein the Abuses of these daies,
As in a glasse thou maiest beholde: 85
Oh buy it then, heare what he saies,
And giue him thankes an hundred folde.

D.

After "I. F. In commendation of the Authour and his Book", O1–O3 print a final prefatory poem:

B3

THE AVTHOR AND

HIS BOOKE.

Now hauing made thee, seely Booke,
and brought thee to this frame:
5   Full loth I am to publishe thee,
least thou impaire my name.
The Booke.
Why so? good Maister, what's the cause,
why you so loth should be,
10   To send me forth into the Worlde,
my fortune for to trye?
The Author
This is the cause, for that I knowe,
the wicked thou wilt moue:
15   And eke because thy ignoraunce
is suche, as fewe can loue.
The Booke.
I doubt not, but all Godly men,
will loue and like me well:
20   And for the other I care not,
in pride although they swell.
The Author.
Thou art also no lesse in thrall,
and subiect euery waie:
25   To MOMVS and to ZOILVS crew,
Who'le dayly at thee bay.
The Booke.
Though MOMVS rage, and ZOILVS carpe:
I feare them not at all,
30   The Lorde my God in whom I trust,
shall cause them soone to fall.

The Author.
Well, sith thou wouldst so faine be gone,
I can thee not withholde:
Adieu therefore, God be thy speede,   35
and blesse thee an hundred folde.
The Booke.
And you also good Maister mine,
God blesse you with his grace:
Preserue you still, and graunt to you,   40
in Heauen a dwelling place.

E.

After line 3589 in the chapter on whoredom, O1–O3 print an account of two adulterers punished by God in London. The sidenotes are included only in O3:

And therefore, the Lorde is forced to take the
sworde into his owne handes, and to execute
punishment himself, because ye Magistrates wil
not do it. For better proofe whereof, marke this
5   straunge and fearefull iudgement of God, shewed
vppon two Adulterous persons in **Munidnol**,
euen the last day in effect, the remembraunce
whereof is yet greene in their heades. //

I1^v There was a man whose name was **W. Rat-**
10   **surb** being certainely knowne to be a notorious

A most dreadfull example of two notorious whoremongers.

Vsurer (and yet pretending alway a singuler zeale
to religion, so that he would seldome times go
without a Bible about him, but see ye iudgements of God vpon them that wil take his word
15   in their mouthes, and yet lyue cleane contrary,
making the worde of God a cloke to couer their
sinne & naughtinesse withall as many do in these
daies) who vpō occasion of businesse visiting
Lewedirb, a place appointed for ye correction of
20   such as be wicked liuers, saw there a famous
Whore but a very proper woman, whome (as is
saide) he knew not, but whether he did, or not,
certain it is, that he procured her deliuery from
thence, bailed her, and hauing put away his owne
25   wife before, kept her in his Chāber, vsing her at
his pleasure. Whilest these two members of the

Whoremongers members of the Deuill.

Deuill were playing the filthie **Sodomites** together in hys chamber, & hauing a litle panne of
coales before them, wherein was a very little fire,

I1. PH: A late exāple for whoredome, in Ailg.
I1^v. PH: Two Adulterers burned in Ailgna.

it pleased God euen in his wrathe, to strike these   30
twoo persones dead in a momente. The woman
falling ouer the panne of coales, was burned, that
all her bowelles gushed out, the man was founde
liyng by, his clothes in some partes being

The punishmẽt
of whordome by
the Lord himself
from heauen.

scorched and burned, and some partes of his   35
body also. But whiche is moste wonderfull, his
arme was burned to the very bone, his Shurt
sleeue, and dublett, not once perished, nor
touched with the fire. Whereby may bee thought,
and not without // great probabilitie of truth,   I2
that it was euen the fire of God his wrathe from
heauen, and not any naturall fire from the Earth.
And in this wonderfull and fearfull manner, were
these cupple founde: which God graunt may be
a **document** or **lesson admonitorie**, to al that   45
heare or read ye same, to auoid the like offence:
and to all Magystrates, an example to see the
same punished with more seueritie, to the glory
of GOD, and their owne discharge.

I2. PH: Knowne Whores kept openly.

F.

A cancelled page (sig. P8) is bound in one of the copies of O1 held at the Bodleian Library, Oxford (Crynes 833). The equivalent position in this edition is after "perish or take hurt" at line 7351. The recto is blank, but a full page of text is printed on the verso; cf. pp. 12–13. The catchword is "they".

P8ᵛ // And which is more, I pray God there be not some vile **Atheists**, & **Nullifidians** amõgst thẽ, who in their harts say **non est Deus**, there is no God at all, and with the filthie swinishe **Epicures** cry out. **Emoi theos tou parou theou to mallon.** that is: giue me yᵉ fruition of these

5 temporall ioyes present, & for the rest that are to come, let God alone: as though indeed they beleeued there were none such. And yᵗ there be some such, their liues showe plaine: for besides all these (with infinit the like **Abuses**.) what colde zeale, what small deuotion, and what frozen affection is their now a dayes to the woord of God?

10 In time of palpable ignorance, I mean, in time of papistrie, when their Temples were stuffed with Idolatrie, supersticion, Imagery and such like: when God was dishonored euerie way, his sacraments prostituted, his blessed woord conculcate, and troden vnder foot, and when they them selues vnderstoode nothing that they heard: then I say, euen

15 then, was there more zeale, feruencie and deuotion to the same, more then **Mahometicall** heathẽrie & **hethnicall** diuilrie then is now to the blessed woord of God, the food of our saluation.

So that it falleth out with them, as it dooth with a man that hauing sore eyes, is not able to abide the bright beames of the Sun. For their

20 liues being wicked, and detestable, //

P8ᵛ. PH: **Atheists and Nullifidians.**

COMMENTARY

Passage A:

2 **singuler** i.e., singularly; commonly used in forms of address to a person of title.

9 **NOBILITAS ... DECVS** "Nobility is the honor of our country".

24 **stomacks** O2 adds "and spewing out the poyson of their maliciouse harts". Since O3's dedicatory epistle was printed from a marked up copy of O1, this revision only appears in O2.

24–26 **Cum ... feruntur** "They are carried away in a rage with puffed-out cheeks and teeth more than dog-like both against the author and against the book". The phraseology is biblical; cf. Job 16:9–10.

31 **costs** regions, districts.

32 **condigne** worthily deserved, merited.

33–34 **I ... Earth** cf. 2571–73n.

42 **commendations** recommendations, commendable features.

43 **emphaticall** suggestive, allusive.

45 **ciphered ... foorth** expressed, portrayed.

46 **inexplicable** inexpressible, indescribable.

52 **Patrociny** patronage, protection.

64–65 **a ... world** cf. Matt. 5:14.

73 **rype** fit for curative treatment.

74 **in generall** without exception.

77–78 **frequented** practiced habitually.

79 **all** any.

83–84 **Zelus ... heather** O1–O2 continue: "knowing, that the Lord hath or-deined you, to himselfe a chosen vessell of honour, to purge his Church of these Abuses, and corruptions, which as in a table are depainted & set foorth in this litle treatise".

89 ZOILVS Greek critic and grammarian; hence, a censorious or malignant critic. MOMVS Greek god of ridicule; hence, a fault-finder.

89–90 **complices ... Phormions** O1–O2 read "complices".

89 **complices** accomplices.

90 **Thrasoes** cf. 735n.

Phormions Athenian admiral sentenced in 428 B.C.E. for embezzlement of public funds; the word is used in a similar context in the *Second part* (sig. A6ᵛ) and in the dedication to *A perfect Pathway to Felicitie* (1610) where Stubbes describes "the poysoned tongues of railing **Phormions** & flouting **Momusses**, to whom all good things are had in disdaine" (sigs. ¶6ᵛ–¶7).

depraue vilify, disparage.

101 **Columna ... virtus** "Virtue is the pillar of glory", a parallel to 9 above, framing the piece.

Passage B:

3 **conuenient** appropriate, suitable.

4 **admonish** inform.

6 **intreated** treated.

7 **exercyses** customary practices.

14–29 **For ... exercyses** This is in sharp contrast to the views expressed in the main text; cf. 5352–416.

15–16 **are ... anciĕtie** i.e., have not only long existed.

20 **conducible** conducive.

21–22 **thing ... pearce** Shifts from singular to plural construction are not unusual in the *Abuses*; cf. 6573–75.

24–25 **Segnius ... obiecta** "Less vividly is the mind stirred by what finds entrance through the ears than by what is brought before the trusty eyes" (a variant paraphrase of Horace, *Ars Poetica*, trans. Fairclough, 180–81); cf. 476–83.

34 **sort** company, group.

35 **loytring** allowing time to pass idly.

36 **dronets** cf. 5583n.

41–45 **And ... onely** cf. 6460–71n.

44 **Dauid, Salomon** cf. 6088–89, 6097–99 and notes.

47 **frequencies** crowds, assemblies.

   Men ... together cf. 6015–25n.

50 **gestures** body movements.

54 **abroade** out of one's house.

56–64 **And ... exploit** cf. the more grudging tolerance of gaming at 6852–63.

58 **ciuile** orderly.

60–61 **for ... couet** Exod. 20:17.

61 **affections** inclinations.

73 **There ... abused** Tilley, *Proverbs*, N317.

74 **strict** rigorous, austere.

85–86 **distinction** distinguishing.

98–99 **tenure** variant of "tenor".

99 **consideratly** carefully, attentively.

   indifferent impartial, unbiased.

Passage C:

1–28 **PHILIPPVS ... breuis** I am grateful to Susan Brock for providing the
  following translation:

PHILLIP STUBBES
to the fair reader.

Perhaps my little book offends you, Reader, with its excessive prating; I don't
wonder at it myself. For it was filled by a swill of words that was more than
vandal-like and by weak subject matter. So, if you are wise, after this don't
waste your effort reading our words, read more useful ones; farewell.

The same against Zoilus.
Zoilus, you are inflamed with a rage against everyone just like a
rabid dog is. Gnashing at some with Theon's tooth and attacking
with the pen these who have done you no harm. Flicking a viper's tongue
at them all, O Zoilus, your tongue which terrible poisons infect.
Zoilus, since there is no limit to your raving and for you no hour
passes quietly, since, Zoilus, you swell up like a pot-bellied bullfrog, I wonder,
standing in the midst of it, that you croak the less.

Another against the same.
Let Zoilus descend to the black cave of the demon, here let the furies
tear him and Cerberus devour him in his jaws. Why do I call down
these torments upon a wretched man who has enough of them
within him? For he carries the demon in his own breast.

Another by the same.
If this book seems too long to you, read just a few words.
Thus the book will seem short.

30 **Auctors** variant of "Author's".
  lucubrations product of nocturnal study and meditation.
31 **heares** variant of "hairs".
33 **eke** also, in addition.
42 **seely** innocent.
43 **Commons** common people.
45 **route** company.
46 **single** honest, sincere.

47 **glasse** mirror.

48 **descrie** disclose, reveal.

53 **learne** teach.

   lore doctrine, teaching.

55–58 **To God ... fame** "learne thy self", is implicit from the previous sentence.

72–73 **[Greek sentence]** Desmond Costa has advised me that this passage, identical in the two editions in which it is printed, has been badly garbled by either the author or the compositor and cannot be translated beyond the first two words which mean "virtue".

76 **challenge** claim.

78 **at all assaies** always.

Passage D:

3 **seely** innocent.

4 **frame** form, shape.

15 **eke** also.

16 **fewe** O1 reads "none".

Passage E:

6 **in Munidnol** i.e., in London. Almost all proper names were spelled backwards and often in Latin O1–O3; O1–O2 read "there".

7 **the last day** yesterday.

   in effect in fact.

9–49 **There ... discharge** Alternative accounts of this event are found in the revised edition of Holinshed's *Chronicles* (1587, 4:504), Stow's *Annales* (1615, sig. Hhhh1), and in a short pamphlet by Samuel Saxey entitled *A straunge and Wonderfull Example of the Iudgement of almighty God, shewed vpon two adulterous persons in London, in the parish of S. Brydes, in Fleetestreete, this thirde of Februarie. 1583* (1583?).

9–10 **W. Ratsurb** i.e., William Bruster.

11 **alway** always.

14–15 **them ... contrary** cf. Ps. 62:4.

16–17 **a cloke ... sinne** John 15:22.

17 **naughtinesse** wickedness, depravity.

17–18 **as ... daies** not in O1–O2.

19 **Lewedirb** i.e., Bridewell, a detention center for prostitutes.

20–21 **a ... woman** Holinshed mentions that her name was Mary Breame.

20 **famous** notorious.

21 **proper** good-looking, beautiful.

24 **put away** sent away, got rid of.

27 **playing ... Sodomites** cf. pp. 33–35 and 5927n.

33 **all ... out** Acts 1:18 (of Judas).

41–42 **the fire ... heauen** 1 Kings 18:38.

44 **these cupple** The plural form of the demonstrative adjective could be used
with reference to a singular noun of multitude.

45 **document** warning, lesson; probably printed in contrasting type for emphasis.
admonitorie warning; "or lesson admonitorie" was added in O2.

49 **discharge** i.e., of their consciences; cf. 7106–9.

Passage F:

2 **Nullifidians** those of no faith or religion.

3–4 **Emoi ... mallon** This sentence is difficult, but Desmond Costa suggests
that with emendation (e.g., "Emoi theos tou parontos theou tou mellontos")
it could be brought into a sense approaching Stubbes's translation: "give me
the god of the present rather than the god of the future". Leslie S. B. Mac-
Coull alternatively suggests reading "theon to mellon": "... as for the future,
it belongs to god".

11 **Imagery** i.e., image-work such as statuary.

13 **conculcate** trod under foot, trampled on.

16 **Mahometicall** Muslim.
hethnicall heathenish.

Appendix II:
Collation and Variant Catchwords

60. his] O1–O3; his his
62. Exodus] *This ed.*; Exodus
93. holdeth] *cor*; holdeth *uncor*
107. feare] O1–O3; fearr
111. amendement, I] O1–O3 *subst*; amendement. I
129. And] O1–O3; *A*nd
151. consideration] O1–O3; considetation
154. God] O1–O3; Cod
186–87. Iustice. A] O1–O3; Iustice, A
228.2. that] O1–O3; That
254. iourney) vse;] O1–O3 *subst*; iourney, vse
272. speeches] O1–O3; specches
317. adopted] *This ed.*; adoapted
342–43. you. Is it not] O1–O3; you, Is it no
B3 PH. charitie] *cor*; charitei *uncor*
388. vendicate] O1–O3 *subst*; vindicate
394. onelie] O1–O3 *subst*; ouelie
407. Philo.] *cor*; Philip. *uncor*
432. damnable] O1–O3; damnabl
465. offensiue] O1–O3; offensine
521–22. progenitors?] O1–O3; progenitors¿
536. gorgeous] O1–O3; georgeous
537.2. apparel] O1–O3 *subst*; a.pparel
565.3. then] O2–O3; them
587. not, I] O1–O3; not. I
594. alter] *This ed.*; altered
648.2. be] O1–O3; bc
653. are] O1–O3; are are
688. calling. The] O2–O3 *subst*; calling The

716. knowe, who is noble, who] O1–O3 *subst*; knowe, who

746. these rich] O1–O3 *subst*; these. rich

763. intreat you] O1–O3 *subst*; intreat yon

772. vnderstanding] O1–O3 *subst*; vnderstanging

848–49. (his posterity) for euer] O1–O3 *subst*; (his posterity for euer)

855–60. (for ... thereof, saith ... owne) yet] O1–O3 *subst*; (for ... thereof) saith
    ... owne: yet

882. mediocritie] O1–O3; mediocritiy

937.5. fairer] O1–O3 *subst*; faire

945. excellentest] O1–O3; ex- // excellentest

C4ᵛ PH. Man] O1–O3 *subst*; Mau

954–56. made (excepting ... creatures) as before.] O2–O3 *subst*; made, excepting
    ... creatures as before)

970. setteth] O1–O3; setteh

996. respect] O1–O3; respcct

D1ᵛ PH. Gentleman] O1–O3; Gentlemau

1057.3–4. worshipped and] O1–O3 *subst*; worshipped. and

1061. respect] O1–O3; rcspect

1087. Gentleman] O1–O3; Gcntleman

1129. and] O1–O3; and and

1129.1. argumẽt] O1–O3; argnmẽt

1156–57. gorgeous attire, the effect ... attyre: but] O1–O3 *subst*; gorgeous attire:
    but

1196. calling?] O1–O3 *subst*; calling

1211. of the] O1–O3; of thc

1215. pestifferous] O1–O3 *subst*; pestiffererous

1230. most] O1–O3 *subst*; moft

1235.1. Vertue] O1–O3; Vertuc

1237. precious] O1–O3 *subst*; prccious

1246–47. opinion] O1–O3; opinon

1262. Court] O1–O3 *subst*; Conrt

1265. apparelled himselfe] O1–O3 *subst*; apparelled, himselfe

1280. in] O1–O3; in in

1290. Tinsell, Aras] O1–O3 *subst*; Tinsell. Aras

1293.3. philosopher] O1–O3 *subst*; philopher

1317.1. Probation,] O1–O3 *subst*; Probation.

1338. their] O1–O3; therr

1358.2. pouertie] O1–O3; pouerttie

1378. winter,] O1–O3 *subst*; winter

1380. whole,] O1–O3; whole

1399. intricate, considering] O1; intricate. Considering

1431. thing] O1–O3 *subst*; lhing

1462. them.] O1–O3 *subst*; them,

1464. imaginations] O1–O3; imagitions

1488. Pride.) The] O3; Pride) The

1514. sort?] O1–O3; sort¿

1540. title on same line as speech prefix] *cor*; title on line above speech prefix *uncor*

1569. attollant, if] O1–O3; attollant if

1600. endure] *This ed.*; undure

1609. past, how] O1–O3; past how

1621. Doublets] O1–O3 *subst*; Doubles

1634. bellies] O1–O3; btllies

1653. their] O1–O3; thcir

1665.2–3. diuers & sundrie] *cor*; di- and sundrie *uncor*

1674. side)] O1 *subst*; side,

1699. Breeches:] *This ed.*; Breeches.

1720. paire of] O1–O3; paire ot

1741.2. pantoffles,] O1–O3 *subst*; pantoffles.

1782. diuers] O1–O3 *subst*; diners

1786.1. varietie] O2–O3; varitie

1790. some without] O1–O3; soue without

1791–92. and some with none at all, some pleated] O1–O3 *subst*; and some pleated

1795. some] O1–O3; some some

1821. There is a certaine] *cor*; Ther is a ceitaine *uncor*

1826. heads,] O1–O3 *subst*; heads

1835–36. Hell, and sealed an Obligation] *cor*; hell, and sealed an an obligation *uncor*

1840. are layd down] O2 *subst*; or layd down

1876. their] O2–O3; their their

F2 PH. excesse] O1–O3; excesse

1962. Womens] *cor*; Womans *uncor*

1977. be] *cor*; be be *uncor*

F3 PH. England] *This ed.*; Englaud

2004.2. faces] *cor*; fnces *uncor*

2014. iealous] O1–O3 *subst*; iealons

2017–18. & a Cobbler should presume] *cor*; and a Cobler should presum *uncor*

F3ᵛ PH. Coloured] O1–O3 *subst*; Colonred

2093. creatures] O1–O3 *subst*; crearures

2100. that they which] O1–O3 *subst*; which they that

2118. and] O1–O3; ann

2119. prolixitie] O1–O3; prolixtie

2120. sapienti,] O1; sapientia

2130. fielde.] O2–O3 *subst*; fielde,

2149.1. Trimming] O1–O3 *subst*; Trtmming

2161. & cunningly] *cor*; and cunning- *uncor*

2170.3. frōtiers] O1–O3 *subst*; fɹōtiers

2179. faces] *cor*; faaces *uncor*

2182. an] O2–O3; and

2183. Pride, and] O1–O3; Pride. and

2189.2. colloured] O1–O3 *subst*; eolloured

2189.4. worne] O1–O3 *subst*; wotne

2199. in] O1–O3; in in

2200–1. owne natural Haire: and vppon ... Haire] *cor*; owne owne natural haire: and vpon ... haire *uncor*

2224–25. Veluet, some ... Wooll, some] O1–O3 *subst*; Veluet, some

2225–26. of that, and ... that, according] O1–O3 *subst*; of that, according

2230.2. Veluet] O2–O3 *subst*; Velret

2239. they haue filled] O1–O3 *subst*; they filled

2242.2. quenque] O1–O3; qnenque

2247. worst) wherwith] O1; worst wherwith

G2 PH. Great ruffes] O1–O3; Great rueffes

2327. fearful] O2–O3 *subst*; fearfnl

2347. Neckerchers] O2–O3; Neckerechers

2372. writhed] *This ed.*; writh

2387. away] O2–O3 *subst*; ɐway

2389. and woonder] O2–O3 *subst*; aud woonder

2408. vp the] O1–O3; vp to the

2417. degenerate] O1–O3 *subst*; degeneate

2419. written] O1–O3 *subst*; writted

2434. as] O2–O3; &

2451. most] O1–O3 *subst*; ɯost

2458. some of the] O1–O3; somem of the

2466. them.) Some] O1–O3; them) Some

2561. curiously] O1–O3; curionsly

2565–66. some of white] O1–O3; sdme of white

2566–67. yellow: some] O1–O3 *subst*; yellow some

2568. with silke] O1–O3 *subst*; with silke with silke

2569.2. innumerable] O1–O3; ɪnnumerable

2582.3. the] O1–O3; he

2602. Perfumes] O1–O3 *subst*; Persumes

2607. Gentlewoman] O1–O3; Geutlewoman

2612. except] O1–O3; excext

H1 PH. hurtfull] O1–O3; hurtfnll

2619. smelles] O1–O3 *subst*; swelles

2632. lighten] O1–O3; lighteu

2639–40. gingerlynesse] O1 *subst*; gingernesse

2641. and babishnesse] O1–O3 *subst*; aud babishnesse

2653. to allure] O1–O3; eo allure

2658. himselfe] O2–O3 *subst*; himfelfe

2665. the] O2–O3; thǝ

2693. busie] O1–O3; bnsie

2699.2. inuisories] O1–O3; inuisiories

2720. whosoeuer] O1–O3; whosouer

2722. authors] O1–O3; author

2769. naught] O1–O3; naughe

H2ᵛ PH. Womens] O1–O3 *subst*; vvomens

2796. hunting] O1–O3 *subst*; hnnting

2812. without] O1–O3; withut

2831. cared] O1–O3; careo

2834.3. former] O2–O3; formet

2848. weare] O1–O3 *subst*; weate

2853. himselfe] O1–O3 *subst*; hemselfe

H3ᵛ PH. Punishments] O1–O3; Punishmonts

2875. apparell (which] O2–O3 *subst*; apparell which

2887. Punishments] Furnivall; Punshments

2889. iudgments] O1–O3 *subst*; iudgmenɪs

2924. language] O1–O3; langnage

2925. we] O1–O3; me

2943. and] O1–O3; and and

H4ᵛ PH. iudgments] O1–O3 *subst*; iudgmcnts

2992. exasperate] O1–O3; exaseperate

2995. last. For] O1–O3; last, For

3001–2. the wayes] O1–O3 *subst*; the the wayes

3071. purpose. And] O2–O3; purpose, And

3073.1. Gardens] *This ed.*; Garden

3107. corruptions] O2–O3; corruptious

3145.1. Whoredome] O1–O3 *subst*; Whoredoms

3206. Lord, that] O1–O3 *subst*; Lord. that

3231. flying] O1–O3 *subst*; fly-

3258. some hang] O1–O3 *subst*; same hang

3279. sinne] O1–O3 *subst*; siune

I3ᵛ PH. Examples] O2–O3; Examples

3297. therfore] O2–O3 *subst*; thersore [long s]

3322. Leuiticus.18] O1 *subst*; Leuiticus.11

I4 PH. Whordome] O1–O3 *subst*; Wwordome

3333. liuing] O1–O3 *subst*; liuig

3350. delay] O1–O3 *subst*; de- / delay

3369. suffered] *This ed.*; suffer

3374.1. Numer.25] O1–O3 *subst*; Numer.24

I4ᵛ PH. Examples] O1–O3; Examplcs

3409.1. euils] O1–O3 *subst*; enils

3428. Bastardes] *This ed.*; Bastardes a peece

3436. ball] *This ed.*; hall

3501. feare it] *cor*; feare it it *uncor*

3507. as] O1–O3; as

K2 PH. Due] O1–O3; Dne

K2 PH. punishments] *This ed.*; punishmcnts

3543. maintenance] O2–O3 *subst*; maintenance

3543.1. dispence] O3; dispeuce

3555. polluteth] O2–O3; polluteh

3558. dispensations] O2–O3; dispensatious

3576. allowe, or] O2–O3; allowe) or

3586. punishment] O1–O3 *subst*; pudishment

3586. commaund] O1–O3 *subst*; commannd

K3 PH. excesse] O1–O3; excesse

K3 PH. delicate] *cor*; delicaɟe *uncor*

3650. hospitality] O1–O3 *subst*; hospitalily

3661. to] O1–O3; in

3661.1. of] O1–O3; of-

K3ᵛ PH. destruction] O1–O3 *subst*; destrnction

3704. but] Furnivall; bnt

3722. bring] O1–O3 *subst*; bringes

3722. Children] O1–O3; Chrilden

3725.1. 1.Reg 2] O1; 3.Reg 2

3728. sinne, as] O1–O3 *subst*; sinne. as

3733. pitifulie] O1–O3 *subst*; pititifulie

3754. chaunged] O1–O2; chaunced

3791. especially] O1–O3; efpecially

3814. euery] O1–O3; enery

3818. body?] O1–O3 *subst*; body⸴

3827. repugnancies] *This ed.*; repugnacies

3838.3. those] *cor*; ••those *uncor*

3838.5. daintie] O1–O3; daintiẽ

3841. from] O2–O3; srom [long s]

3880.2. qualities] O1–O3; qualitities

3887. man] O1–O3 *subst*; mau

3894. Doeth] O1–O3; *subst*; Doetb

3900. into] O1–O3; iuto

3928. thundereth] O1–O3; thundeereth

3941.1. Ioel.1] O1–O3; Ioel.2

3943. destruction of wickednesse] *This ed.*; wickednesse of destruction

3960. and] O1–O3 *subst*; aud

L2ᵛ PH. Drunkennesse] O1–O3; Drukennesse

4012–13. offensiue] O1–O3; offensine

4014. the] O1–O3; th

4026. our] O1–O3; onr

4031. in our] O1–O3; in onr

4044. Christi] O1–O3; Chrifti

4047. as we] O1–O3 *subst*; are we

4065. keeps] *This ed.*; keep

4084. Deuill] O2–O3; Deulll

4090. inconsiderately] O2–O3; incosiderately

4097. cold. But] O2–O3; cold But

4101. Hereupon] O2–O3 *subst*; Heeeupon

L3ᵛ PH. example] O3; example

4116. deliuerance] O2–O3; deliueronce

4126. Nekershofene] *This ed.*; Nekershofewe

4160. after] O3; aftr

4181. fulfilled] O2–O3; fulsilled [long s]

4192. little] O1–O3 *subst*; ltitle

4196. treasure] O1–O3; tceasure

4197. as the] O1–O3; as the

4197. wealthy] O1–O3 *subst*; weathy
4253. you] O1–O3; yon
4259. M1] *cor*, sig. missing *uncor*
4273. to liue] O1–O3 *subst*; to to liue
4290.1. Iniurie] O1–O3; Iuiurie
4290.4. iniurie] O1–O3 *subst*; iniuinrie
4323.3. Lawyers] O1–O3 *subst*; Lawyer
4338.3. Lawyers whẽ] O2–O3; Lawyers. whẽ
4338.5. haue] O1–O3; heue
4341. this President] O1–O3 *subst*; this Prcsident
4348. eares] O1–O3; earers
4352. summes] O1–O3 *subst*; suumes
4399. and] O1–O3; aud
4420.5.] against O1–O3; aginst
4421. the] O1–O3; thc
4426. seeke] O1–O3; feeke
4440. our hearts] O1–O3; onr hearts
4443. Kingdom] O1–O3 *subst*; Kindom
4464. the Lord] O1–O3 *subst*; tbe Lord
4464. turned] O1–O3; tnrned
4471.5. examples] O1–O3; examaples
4480. couetous] O1–O3; couecous
4511. couetousnes] O1–O3 *subst*; couetousues
4518. and] O1–O3 *subst*; aud
4527. extreame] O3; extrame
4527.4. euery] O1–O3; euey
4533. Maisters] O1–O3; Maistccs
4549. Sauiour] O1–O3 *subst*; Sauionr
4555–56. couetousnesse] O1–O3 *subst*; couetonsnesse
4597. beginning] O1–O3 *subst*; veginning
4599. If no] O1–O3; If uo
4624. aboue] O1–O3 *subst*; abone
4624. shillings] O1–O3 *subst*; shhillings
4628. &] *This ed.*; a
4629.5–6. commit mischiefe] O1–O3 *subst*; commit. mischiefe
4633. giue] O1–O3 *subst*; gine
4636. but] O1; aboue
4640. is it not] O1–O2; is not
4644. he] O1–O3 *subst*; hc

4648. heauen. If] O1–O3 *subst*; heauen If
4664.1. Psalme 15] O1–O3 *subst*; Psalme 16
4677. the] O1–O3; ehe
4690. in] O1–O3; iu
4695. children] O1–O3 *subst*; ehildren
4719. grace] O1–O3; gracc
4735. brethren] O1–O3 *subst*; brethen
4739. reuenge] O1–O3; reueng
4763. but] O1–O3; bnt
4767.2. then] O2; thcn
4771. indifferently] O1–O3; indifferenrly
4779. without] O1–O3; wlthout
N2 PH. Vsurie] O1–O3 *subst*; Vsurie
4809. true] O1–O3; trne
4828–29. Scriuener] O1–O3; Scrinener
N2ᵛ PH. Great] O2–O3; Great
4834. great deale more] O1–O3 *subst*; great more
4835. himselfe] O1–O3 *subst*; himselse [long s]
4836–37. money, than . . . mony. And] O1 *subst*; money. And
4841. without] O1–O3; witout
4843. inriched] O1–O3; inrinched
4848. disposition] O2–O3 *subst*; dispositiotion
4880. themselues] O2–O3; themselued
4921. speake] O2–O3; spake
4927. and sweare] O2–O3; aud sweare
4941. trueth] O2–O3 *subst*; tructh
4950. true, or] O2–O3; true. Or
5023. by his humanity] O2–O3 *subst*; be his humanity
5024–25. his power] O2–O3; hls power
5026. Whẽ] O2–O3 *subst*; whẽ
5033. any] O2–O3; any any
5035.2–3. creature is] O3; creature. is
5047. there] O2–O3; therc
5053. Were] Furnivall; Were
5075. death: For] O2–O3; death For
O1 PH. Examples] O2–O3; Examples
5094. God be] O2–O3; God to be
5109. thereof)] O2–O3 *subst*; thereof(
5135. leaue] O2–O3; lcaue

5146. after. Thus] O2–O3; after, Thus

5153. punished] O2–O3; puninished

5158. Merchandize] O2–O3 *subst*; Merchadize

5159. haue] O3; hane

5192. like. In] O1–O3; like, In

5219. all] O1–O2; call

5261. in] O1–O3; in in

5266. Sabboth] O1–O3 *subst*; Sabbod

5285. they] O1–O3 *subst*; the

5290. suffer] O2–O3; suffcr

5299. the] O2–O3; th

5325. haue] O1–O3; haoe

5328.3. Sabboth] O1–O3 *subst*; Sɐbboth

5328.4. consisteth] O1–O3; con.sɪsteth

5437. vertue] O2–O3; vertuc

5444. lust] O1–O3; lnst

5446.2. cap,11] O1–O2 *subst*; cap,1

5452. forcible] O1–O3; sorcible [long s]

5453.1. Writers] O2–O3; Waiters

5482.1. ground] O1–O3; groud

5482.2. of] O1–O3; os [long s]

5510.5. comparable] O1–O2; compasable

5552. playe] O1–O3 *subst*; ylaye

5559. slay] O1–O3 *subst*; flay

5569.1–2. Theaters, Schooles] O2–O3 *subst*; Theaters. Schooles

5585–86. liue. Therfore] O1–O3 *subst*; liue, Therfore

5614. against] O1–O3; agaist

5624. very] O1–O3; bery

5647–48. handkerchiefes] O1–O3 *subst*; handkerchiefe

5665. handkerchiefes] O1–O3 *subst*; handkechiefes

5684.2. Misrules] O1–O3 *subst*; Misɹules

5746. home] O1–O3; homc

5767.1. fruit] O1–O3 *subst*; fɹuit

5778. vse,] O1–O3; vse'

5788. quarters] O1–O3; qnarters

5812. swilling] O1–O3 *subst*; swillling

5841. and repairing] O1–O3 *subst*; aud repairing

5851. all] O1–O3; als

5875. erected] O1–O3; ereeted

5892. them?] O1–O3; them¿

5900.3. Wakesses] O1–O3 *subst*; Wakcsses

5932.3. feasts] O1–O3 *subst*; fcasts

5943. abhomination. For] O1–O3; abhomination, For

5954. and reuerence] O1–O3; aud reuerence

5974. it:) And] O3; it) And

5991. at the] O1–O3; at thc

6004–5. desireth] O1–O3; desisireth

6020. it] O1–O3; it it

6069. day of] O1–O3 *subst*; day of of

6072. nothing] O1–O3 *subst*; nothiug

6085. their] O1–O3; theic

6094.1. Math.14] O1–O3 *subst*; Math.1S

6097.1. Luke 7] O1–O3 *subst*; Luke k

6097.2. Eccle.3] O1–O3; Eccle.13

6106. life] O1–O3; lifc

6110. naturall] O1–O3; narurall

6115. falsly] O1–O3; fasly

6117–18. compendiously] O1–O3 *subst*; compendioufly

Q3 PH. examples] O1–O3 *subst*; examples

Q3 PH. followed] *cor*; followǝd *uncor*

6136. ballaunce] O1–O3 *subst*; ballaunc

6139. worde.] O1–O3 *subst*; worde:

6152. other] O2–O3; orher

6167. extream] O1–O3 *subst*; extram

6184. dexterity] O1–O3 *subst*; dexteriry

6194.9. triũphing,] O1–O3; triũphing.

6200. praise] O1–O3 *subst*; praist

6230. any] O1–O3 *subst*; auy

6233. thinke] *cor*; tinke *uncor*

6234. dances] *cor*; daunces *uncor*

6296.1 sixt] O2–O3; siκt

6330. plainly] O1–O3 *subst*; plainiy

6374. exercising] O1–O3 *subst*; exercisiug

6386. Baptist] O1–O3; Babtist

6414.4. of] O1–O3; os [long s]

6462. dauncing] O1–O3 *subst*; dauncig

6466. and] O1–O3 *subst*; aud

6469. condemne] O1–O3 *subst*; condeme

6489. praise and] O1–O3; praise aud
6532. woonderfull] O1–O3 *subst*; woondefull
6572. whoredome.] O1–O3 *subst*; whoredome,
6581. great] O1–O3; gxeat
6613. opinion] O1–O3; opinon
6624. of] O1–O3; of of
6627. Truculent] O1–O3 *subst*; Turculent
6632. Sicilians] O1–O3; Scicilians
6660.1–2. comparison betwixt] O1–O3; compari- betwixt
6669. dulled) by] O1–O3; dulled by
6670. soft] O1–O3 *subst*; soft
6676. Tirus] O1 *subst*; Titus
6678. Clytomachus] O1–O2; Clycomachus
6698. Dauid] O1–O3; Danid
6701.1. musick] O1–O3 *subst*; uusick
6701.3. assemblies,] O1–O3; assemblies.
6716. were] O1–O3; wece
6743. your] O1–O3; you
6745. filthy] O1–O3 *subst*; silthy [long s]
6748. whordome] O1–O3 *subst*; whordrme
6748–49. abhomination,] O1–O3 *subst*; abhomination.
6769.5. exercise] O1–O3 *subst*; exreise
6847. great] O1–O3; greae
6865. sleight] O1–O3 *subst*; fleight
6883. rule, if] O2–O3; rule. if
6922. there] O1–O3; thexe
6924. misliked] O1–O3; mifliked
6940. league] O1–O3; lcague
6955. openly.] O1–O3; openly,
6991. Faires, Courts] O1–O3 *subst*; Faires. Courts
7011–12. be bloudy] O1–O3 *subst*; bloudy be
7015. notwithstanding] O1–O3 *subst*; notwistanding
7018. magnificence] O1–O3; magnisicence [long s]
7044. al. A] O1–O3 *subst*; al, A
7046. reputation] O1–O3; xeputation
7060. (for] O1–O3;)for
7065. building] O1–O3 *subst*; buiiding
7079. spectacle] O1–O3; spectable
7089. shewed] O1–O3; shewcd
7090. iudgment] O1–O3 *subst*; iudginent

7092. and] O1–O3; aud

7107. places] O1–O3; plaecs

7120. set] O1–O3; seŧ

7124. purpose, Flags] O1–O3 *subst*; purpose. Flags

7125. notice] O1–O3; noitce

7130. England.] O2–O3; England,

7131.3. the] O1–O3; she

7147.3. scripture] O1–O3; cripture

7162. themselues] O1–O3; themselus

7173. Lord] O1–O3 *subst*; Iord

7174. shedding] O1–O3 *subst*; sheddiug

7176. after] O1–O3; eafter

7196. vs, &] O1–O3 *subst*; vs,, &

7215. strength] O1–O3 *subst*; strengh

7240. there] O1–O3; the

7256. exercise] O1–O3; exrcise

7258. forbidden] O1–O3 *subst*; forbidded

7274–75. broken, sometymes their backes, somtimes] O1–O3 *subst*; broken, somtimes

T2 PH. wicked] O1–O3; wtcked

7306. dishonor] O1–O3 *subst*; dishouor

7313. not present] O1–O3; not

7322. godliest] O1–O3 *subst*; godliesi

7346–47. themselues] O1–O3; themseues

7377. executed] O1–O3; excuted

7392. much] Furnivall; mnch

7424. of] O1–O3; of of

7424–25. appeare, as] O1–O2; appeare as,

7426. Philo.] O1–O2; Spud.

7427. certain: For] O1–O3 *subst*; certain For

7432. to remooue] O1–O3; co remooue

7473.1. materiall] O3; mareriall

7473.3. this] O3; this this

7477. think] O1–O3 *subst*; thiuk

7507. must] O1–O3; mnst

7532. ynough] O1–O3 *subst*; ynongh

T4ᵛ PH. Protestation] O1–O3 *subst*; Protestatian

7555–56. not to deferre] O1–O3; did not deferre

7568. needs] O1–O3 *subst*; ueeds

7591. thus] O1–O3; thns

Appendix Collation

Passage A:
19. than] O1–O2 *subst*; than thẽ
24. (Cum] O1–O2; Cum
56. willing] O1–O2; wiliing
89. complices] O1–O2 *subst*; complies

Passage B:
75. because] Furnivall; be-
78. women] Furnivall; womeu

Passage C:
2. CANDIDO] O1–O2; CADIDO

Passage D:
32. Author] Furnivall; Aurhor

Passage F:
10. mean,] *This ed.*; mean.

Variant Catchwords

This list records Q1 catchwords that fail to agree substantively with the word that opens the page immediately following:

Signatures	Last Word	Catchword	Opening Word	Line Reference
C4–C4ᵛ	ex-	cellentest	excellentest	945
E3ᵛ–E4	confuted.	Nether	Costly	1704–5
H2–H2ᵛ	passe.	Spud.	The	2770–71
S4–S4ᵛ	England,	————	And	7130–31

Appendix III:
Record of Ambiguous
Line-End Word Breaks

AMBIGUOUS LINE-END HYPHENATION IN MODERN EDITION

The following list records line-break hyphenations in the modern edition that should be quoted with the hyphen:

148–49: women-kind
5777–78: Church-ales

AMBIGUOUS Q1 LINE-END HYPHENATION

The following list records ambiguous Q1 line-break hyphenation:

2222: French-hood (hyphen preserved in modern edition)
2318: gew-gawes (hyphen not preserved in modern edition)

AMBIGUOUS Q1 LINE-END WORD BREAKS

The following list records the words and potential compound words in Q1 which are split over a line break without a hyphen. Where these instances have been silently elided in the modern edition, a slash indicates where the break occurs in the original text. Examples quoted without a slash have not been elided.

67: confer/red
78: con/tribute
92: com/mitteth
425: Demp/ta

470.1–2: three fold
539–40: our selues
686.4: accor/ding
1184: bo/some
1446: French men
1449: Notwith/standing
1687–88: euery one
1764.2: vn/easie
1912: a peece
2013.4: workman/ship
2034.2: co/lour
2055.2: con/demnatory
2111: for euer
2163: any thing
2318.2: cu/riositie
2407.2: wea/ring
2494.3: ex/cesse
2501: Noble woman
2558: any time
2643.9: glas/ses
2653: consequent/ly
2663.2: glas/ses
2676: sun/burning
2676.3: wea/rers
2683: can not
2696: it selfe
2720: com/mitted
2968: him selfe
3048.4: gentlewo/men
3092: garden houses
3239.3: vnreasona/ble
3275.5: whor/dome
3414: coun/tenance
3459: ouer great
3670: can not
3838.5: dain/tiẽ
4010: for euer
4049.2: dread/ful
4237.3: pro/uide

4359.3–4: Marchant men
4471.3: coue/tousnes
4579: euery one
4870: contem/ning
4885.2: wicked/nes
4939.3: law/full
4952–53: thy selfe
5008: blame worthy
5019.4: any thing
5128.2: dread/ful
5141.3: an other
5188: Church Ales (hyphenated form more usual in Q1: cf. 5777–78, 5780, 5783.2, 5870, 5881; hyphenated over a line break at 5822.5)
5189.2: ex/ercises
5223–24: our selues
5328.4: con/sisteth
5453.3: pro/phane
5555.3: lear/ned
5673: Church yard
5684.3: cog/nizances
5822.2: mo/ney
5974: notwith/standing
6031: it selfe
6070.2: ren/der
6465: other some
6736.2: marchan/dize
6815.3–4: Christmas time
6895.2: hou/ses
7269.1–2: Foot ball
7309.2: com/ming
7315: a dayes
7534: in deed

Appendix IV:
List of Chapter Titles in
The Anatomie of Abuses

Works Cited

EDITIONS OF *THE ANATOMIE OF ABUSES*

C[ollier], J. P., ed. *The Anatomie of Abuses*. By Philip Stubbes. *Miscellaneous Tracts Temp. Eliz. & Jac. 1*. London, 1870.

Furnivall, F. J., ed. *Phillip Stubbes's Anatomy of the Abuses in England in Shakspere's Youth, A.D. 1583. Part 1*. New Shakspere Society, 6th ser., nos. 4 and 6. 2 vols. London: N. Trübner & Co., 1877–1879.

Stubbes, Philip. *The Anatomie of Abuses*. London, 1583.

———. *The Anatomie of Abuses*. 1 May 1583. Facsimile reprint. The English Experience 489. Amsterdam: Theatrum Orbis Terrarum Ltd., 1972.

———. *The anatomy of abuses*. 1 May 1583. Facsimile reprint. With an introductory note by Peter Davison. New York: Johnson Reprint Corp., 1972.

———. *The Anatomie of Abuses*. 1 May 1583. Facsimile reprint. The English Stage: Attack and Defense 1577–1730. With a preface for the Garland edition by Arthur Freeman. New York: Garland Publishing Inc., 1973.

Turnbull, William B. D. D., ed. *The Anatomie of Abuses*. By Philip Stubbes. Edinburgh: W. & D. Laing, 1836.

OTHER WORKS BY STUBBES

Stubbes, Philip. *A Christal Glasse for Christian Women*. London, 1591.

———. "In sanguisugas Papistas." In *Actes and Monuments*, by John Foxe. 4th ed. London, 1583.

———. *The Intended Treason, of Doctor Parrie: and his Complices, Against the Queenes moste Excellent Maiestie*. London, 1585[?].

———. *A motiue to good workes. Or rather, To true Christianitie indeede*. London, 1593.

———. *A perfect Pathway to Felicitie, Conteining godly Meditations, and praiers, fit for all times, and necessarie to be practized of all good Christians*. London, 1592.

———. Preface. *A Godlie and fruitfull Treatise of Faith and workes. Wherein is confuted a certaine opinion of merit by workes, which an aduersary to the Gospell of Christ Iesu, held in the conference, had in the Tower of London.* By H. D. London, 1583. Sig. A4.

——. *The Second part of the Anatomie of Abuses, Conteining the display of Corruptions.* London, [1583].

——. *The Theater of the Popes Monarchie.* 1584. London, 1585.

——. *Two wunderfull and rare Examples. Of the vndeferred and present approching iudgement, of the Lord our God.* London, [1581].

1: Ancient, Patristic, and Medieval Sources

Aelian (Claudius Aelianus). *Historical Miscellany (Varia Historia)*, trans. N. G. Wilson. Loeb Classical Library. London: William Heinemann Ltd., 1997.

——. *A registre of Hystories.* Trans. Abraham Fleming. London, 1576. STC 164.

Alan of Lille. *Anticlaudianus.* In *Opera Omnia*, vol. 1. *Patrologiae cursus completus*, ed. J. P. Migne, Series Latina, 210:483–576. Paris, 1855.

Ambrose, Saint. *De Tobia.* In *Opera Omnia*, vol. 1.1. *Patrologiae cursus completus*, ed. J. P. Migne, Series Latina, 14:759–94. Paris, 1845. Trans. Lois Miles Zucker, *S. Ambrosii: De Tobia*. Washington: The Catholic University of America, 1933.

——. *De Virginibus.* In *Opera Omnia*, vol. 2.1. *Patrologiae cursus completus*, ed. J. P. Migne, Series Latina, 16:187–232. Paris, 1845. Trans. H. de Romestin, with E. de Romestin, and H. T. F. Duckworth, in *Some of the Principal Works of St. Ambrose*, Second Ser., 10:361–87. A Select Library of Nicene and Post-Nicene Fathers of the Christian Church. Oxford: James Parker and Company, 1896.

——. *De Bono Mortis.* In *Opera Omnia*, vol. 1.1. *Patrologiae cursus completus*, ed. J. P. Migne, Series Latina, 14:539–68. Paris, 1845. Trans. Michael P. McHugh, in *Seven Exegetical Works*, 65:69–113. *Fathers of the Church.* Washington: The Catholic University of America Press, 1972.

——. *Sermones.* In *Opera Omnia*, vol. 2.2. *Patrologiae cursus completus*, ed. J. P. Migne, Series Latina, 17:603–762. Paris, 1845.

Aristotle. *Meteorologica.* Trans. E. W. Webster. *The Works of Aristotle*, gen. ed. W. D. Ross, 3. Oxford: Clarendon Press, 1931.

——. *Ethica Nicomachea.* Trans. W. D. Ross. *The Works of Aristotle*, gen. ed. W. D. Ross, 9. Oxford: Clarendon Press, 1925.

——. *Politics.* Trans. Benjamin Jowett. *The Works of Aristotle*, gen. ed. W. D. Ross, 10. Oxford: Clarendon Press, 1921.

——. *De Partibus Animalium.* Trans. William Ogle. *The Works of Aristotle*, gen.

eds. J. A. Smith and W. D. Ross, 5. Oxford: Clarendon Press, 1912.

Augustine, Saint. *Contra Faustum*. In *Opera Omnia*, vol. 8. *Patrologiae cursus completus*, ed. J. P. Migne, Series Latina, 42:207–518. Paris, 1841.

———. *De Civitate Dei*. In *Opera Omnia*, vol. 7. *Patrologiae cursus completus*, ed. J. P. Migne, Series Latina, 41:13–804. Paris, 1841.

———. *De Doctrina Christiana*. In *Opera Omnia*, vol. 3.1. *Patrologiae cursus completus*, ed. J. P. Migne, Series Latina, 34:15–122. Paris, 1841.

———. *Enarrationes in Psalmos*. In *Opera Omnia*, vol. 4. *Patrologiae cursus completus*, ed. J. P. Migne, Series Latina, 36. Paris, 1841.

———. *Epistolarum Classes Quatuor*. In *Opera Omnia*, vol. 2. *Patrologiae cursus completus*, ed. J. P. Migne, Series Latina, 33. Paris, 1841.

———. *In Epistolam Joannis ad Parthos*. In *Opera Omnia*, vol. 3.2. *Patrologiae cursus completus*, ed. J. P. Migne, Series Latina, 35:1977–2062. Paris, 1841.

———. *In Joannis Evangelium Tractatus CXXIV*. In *Opera Omnia*, vol. 3.2. *Patrologiae cursus completus*, ed. J. P. Migne, Series Latina, 35:1379–1976. Paris, 1841.

Bernard, Saint. "In Festo Omnium Sanctorum." In *Opera Omnia*, ed. Jean Mabillon, vol. 2. *Patrologiae cursus completus*, ed. J. P. Migne, Series Latina, 183:453–82. Paris, 1854.

The Geneva Bible: A Facsimile of the 1560 Edition. With an introduction by Lloyd E. Berry. Madison: University of Wisconsin Press, 1969.

The 1599 Geneva Bible. Facsimile. 3rd ed. The Samuel Henson Simpson Memorial Edition. With an introduction by Michael H. Brown. Pleasant Hope, Missouri: L. L. Brown Publishing, 1993.

Boethius. *The Consolation of Philosophy*. Trans. S. J. Tester. London: William Heinemann Ltd, 1973. 130–435.

———. *De Consolatione Philosophiae*. In *Opera Omnia*, vol. 1.1. *Patrologiae cursus completus*, ed. J. P. Migne, Series Latina, 63:547–862. Paris, 1847.

Chaucer, Geoffrey. *The Riverside Chaucer*, gen. ed. Larry D. Benson. Oxford: Oxford University Press, 1988.

Chrysostom, John, Saint. *The Homilies of S. John Chrysostom, Archbishop of Constantinople, on the Gospel of St. Matthew*, trans. by members of the English Church. 3 vols. A Library of Fathers of the Holy Catholic Church, Anterior to the Division of the East and West. Oxford: John Henry Parker, 1851–1854.

———. *In Matthaeum Homilia*. In *Opera Omnia*, vol. 7.1. *Patrologiae cursus completus*, ed. J. P. Migne, Series Greca, 58:471–794. Paris, 1860.

Cicero, Marcus Tullius. *De Officiis*, trans. Walter Miller. Loeb Classical Library. London: William Heinemann Ltd., 1913.

————. *Philippics*, trans. Walter C. A. Ker. Loeb Classical Library. London: William Heinemann Ltd., 1926.

————. *Pro Murena*, in *The Speeches*, trans. Louis E. Lord, 143–255. Loeb Classical Library. London: William Heinemann Ltd., 1937.

————. *Rhetorica ad Herennium*, trans. Harry Caplan. Loeb Classical Library. London: William Heinemann Ltd., 1954.

Cyprian, Saint. *De Habitu Virginum*. In *Opera Omnia*, vol. 1. *Patrologiae cursus completus*, ed. J. P. Migne, Series Latina, 4:439–64. Paris, 1844.

————. "On the Dress of Virgins." In *The Writings of Cyprian, Bishop of Carthage*, trans. Robert Ernest Wallis, 1:333–50. Ante-Nicene Christian Library 8. Edinburgh: T. & T. Clark, 1868.

Diogenes Laertius. *Lives of Eminent Philosophers: Books 1–5, 6–10*, trans. R. D. Hicks. Loeb Classical Library. London: William Heinemann Ltd, 1925–1938.

Erasmus, Desiderius. *Adagia*, ed. M. L. van Poll-van de Lisdonk and M. Cytowska, et al., in *Opera Omnia Desiderii Erasmi Roterodami*, 2:1–8. Amsterdam: Elsevier, 1981–1999. Trans. Margaret Mann Phillips and R. A. B. Mynors, in *Collected Works of Erasmus*, vols. 31–34. Toronto: University of Toronto Press, 1982–1992.

————. *De Contemptu Mundi*, ed. S. Dresden. In *Opera Omnia Desiderii Erasmi Roterodami*, V.1. Amsterdam: North-Holland, 1977, 39–86. Trans. E. Rummel, in *Collected Works of Erasmus*, vol. 66, *Spiritualia*, ed. J. W. O'Malley (Toronto: University of Toronto Press, 1988), 134–75.

Galen, Claudius. *Claudii Galeni Pergameni medicorum omnium facile principis de sanitate tuenda libri sex*. Trans. T. Linacre. Tübingen, 1541.

Gratian. *Decretum*, ed. Emilius Lewis Richter. *Patrologiae cursus completus*, ed. J. P. Migne, Series Latina, 187. Paris, 1855.

Guillelmus. *Expositio in Epistolam ad Romanos*. In *Eugenii III: Romani Pontificis: Epistolae et Privilegia*. *Patrologiae cursus completus*, ed. J. P. Migne, Series Latina, 180:547–694. Paris, 1855.

Horace. *Satires, Epistles and Ars Poetica*, trans. H. Rushton Fairclough. Loeb Classical Library. London: William Heinemann Ltd., 1929.

Inscriptionum Latinarum Selectarum. Ed. J. C. Orelli, 3 vols. Turin, 1828–1856.

Isodorus, Saint. *Concilia*. In *Opera Omnia*, vol. 8. *Patrologiae cursus completus*, ed. J. P. Migne, Series Latina, 84:93–626. Paris, 1850.

Jerome, Saint. *Epistolae*. In *Opera Omnia*, ed. John Martian, vol. 1. *Patrologiae cursus completus*, ed. J. P. Migne, Series Latina, 22:325–1224. Paris, 1845.

John of Salisbury. *Policraticus*. Ed. K. S. B. Keats-Rohan. Corpus Christianorum Continuatio Mediaevalis 118. Turnhout: Brepols, 1993.

Josephus, Flavius. *Jewish Antiquities: Books 12–14*, trans. Ralph Marcus. Loeb

Classical Library. London: William Heinemann Ltd., 1943.

Justinian. *Corpus Juris Civilis*. Vol. 2. Ed. P. Krueger. 11th ed. Berlin: Weidmann, 1954.

Juvenal. *The Satires of Juvenal*. In *Juvenal and Persius*, trans. G. G. Ramsay, 1–307. Loeb Classical Library. London: William Heinemann Ltd., 1940.

Lactantius. *Divinarum Institutionum*. In *Opera Omnia*, vol. 1. *Patrologiae cursus completus*, ed. J. P. Migne, Series Latina, 6:111–822. Paris, 1844. Trans. E. H. Blakeney, *Epitome of the Divine Institutes*. London: S. P. C. K., 1950.

Livy, Titus. *Livy: Books 31–34*, trans. Evan T. Sage. Loeb Classical Library. London: William Heinemann Ltd, 1935. 9 of *Works*.

Maximus Tyrius. *The Dissertations of Maximus Tyrius*, trans. Thomas Taylor. 2 vols. London: R. H. Evans, 1804.

Ovid. *Heroides and Amores*, trans. Grant Showerman. Loeb Classical Library. London: William Heinemann Ltd, 1914. 1 of *Works*.

Paulinus, Saint. *Dissertatio Quarta*. In *Opera Omnia*, vol. 1. *Patrologiae cursus completus*, ed. J. P. Migne, Series Latina, 99:557–90. Paris, 1851.

Plato. *Epistles*, trans. R. G. Bury. Loeb Classical Library. London: William Heinemann Ltd., 1929.

———. *Laws*, trans. R. G. Bury. Loeb Classical Library. 2 vols. London: William Heinemann Ltd., 1926.

———. *The Republic: Books 1–5, 6–10*, trans. Paul Shorey. Loeb Classical Library. London: William Heinemann Ltd., 1937.

Pliny. *Selections from the History of the World Commonly Called The Natural History of C. Plinius Secundus*, trans. Philemon Holland, ed. Paul Turner. London: Centaur Press Ltd., 1962.

Plutarch. "Table-Talk: Books 7–9." In *Moralia* 9, trans. Edwin L. Minar, F. H. Sandbach, and W. C. Helmbold, 1–299. Loeb Classical Library. London: William Heinemann, 1961.

———. "On Music." In *Moralia* 14, trans. Benedict Einarson and Phillip H. de Lacy, 343–455. Loeb Classical Library. London: William Heinemann Ltd., 1967.

Publilius Syrus. *Sententiae*. In *Minor Latin Poets*, trans. J. Wight Duff and Arnold M. Duff, 1–111. Loeb Classical Library. London: William Heinemann Ltd., 1935.

Quintilian, M. Fabius. *Institutio Oratoria*, trans. H. E. Butler. Vol. 3. Loeb Classical Library. London: William Heinemann Ltd., 1921.

Sallust. *The War with Catiline*. In *Sallust*, trans. J. C. Rolfe, 1–130. Loeb Classical Library. London: William Heinemann Ltd., 1931.

Salvian. "De Gubernatione Dei." In *Opera Omnia*, ed. Franciscus Pauly, 1–200.

Corpus Scriptorum Ecclesiasticorum Latinorum 8. Vienna, 1883.

Scriptores Historiae Augustae. "Lampridius, Aelius," *Severus Alexander*, trans. David Magie, 2:178–313. Loeb Classical Library. London: William Heinemann, 1924.

Suetonius. "The Deified Augustus." In *Suetonius*, trans. J. C. Rolfe, 1:121–287. Loeb Classical Library. London: William Heinemann Ltd., 1951.

Terence. *Andria* and *Eunuchus.* In *Terence*, trans. John Sargeaunt. Loeb Classical Library. London: William Heinemann Ltd., 1912. 1 of *Works.*

Tertullian. *De Cultu Feminarum.* In *Opera Omnia*, vol. 1.2. *Patrologiae cursus completus*, ed. J. P. Migne, Series Latina, 1:1303–34. Paris, 1844. Trans. S. Thelwall, in *The Writings of Tertullian* 11:304–32. Ante-Nicene Christian Library. Edinburgh: T. & T. Clark, 1869.

———. *De Spectaculis.* In *Opera Omnia*, vol. 1.1. *Patrologiae cursus completus*, ed. J. P. Migne, Series Latina, 1:627–62. Paris, 1844.

Theophylact. *Argumentum in Evangelium secundum Marcum.* In *Theophylacti Archiepiscopi Bulgariae, in quatuor Euangelia enarrationes, denuo recognitae.* Johanne Oecolampadio Interprete. Cologne, 1525. I3–N4v.

Valerius Maximus. *Factorum et Dictorum Memorabilium*, ed. Carol Kempf. 2nd ed. Stuttgart: Teubner, 1964.

Vergil. *The Aeneid*, ed. J. W. Mackail. Oxford: Clarendon Press, 1930.

———. *Eclogues*, trans. H. Rushton Fairclough. Loeb Classical Library. London: William Heinemann Ltd., 1967.

2: Renaissance and Early Modern Sources

Arber, Edward, ed. *A Transcript of the Registers of the Company of Stationers of London; 1554–1640 A.D.* 5 vols. London and Birmingham: Privately Printed, 1875–1894.

Averell, William. *A meruailous combat of contrarieties.* London, 1588.

———. *A wonderfull and straunge newes, which happened in the Countye of Suffolke, and Essex, the first of February . . . where it rayned Wheat, the space of vi. or vii. miles compas.* London, 1583.

Bateman, Stephen. *The Doome warning all men to the Iudgemente.* London, 1581.

The Booke of Wysdome . . . Following the Authority of auncient Doctoures and Philosophers, deuyding and speaking of Vices and Vertues. 1532. London, c. 1580.

The Book of Common Prayer 1559: The Elizabethan Prayer Book, ed. John E. Booty. Washington: Folger Shakespeare Library, 1976.

Brome, Richard. *The Court Begger.* In *The Dramatic Works*, 1:181–272. London: John Pearson, 1873.

Bullinger, Heinrich. *Fiftie godlie and learned sermons, diuided into fiue decades.* Trans. H. I. London, 1577.

Calvin, John. *Sermons of Master Iohn Caluin, vpon the Booke of IOB.* Trans. Arthur Golding. London, 1584.

Carew, Richard. *The Survey of Cornwall.* 1602. The English Experience Series 100. Facsimile reprint. New York: Da Capo Press, 1969.

Cartwright, William. *The Ordinary.* In *The Plays and Poems of William Cartwright,* ed. G. Blakemore Evans, 257–351. Madison: University of Wisconsin Press, 1951.

Cay, John, ed. *The Statutes at Large, from Magna Charta, To the Thirtieth Year of King GEORGE the Second, inclusive.* 6 vols. London: Thomas Baskett and Henry Lintot, 1758.

Certain Sermons or Homilies Appointed to be Read in Churches in the Time of Queen Elizabeth of Famous Memory. London: Society for Promoting Christian Knowledge, 1851.

Churchyard, Thomas. *A warning for the wise, a feare to the fond, a bridle to the lewde, and a glasse to the good. Written of the late Earthquake chanced in London and other places, the 6. of April 1580. for the glorie of God, and benefite of men that warely can walke, and wisely can iudge.* London, 1580.

Collier, J. P. *Broadside Black-letter Ballads, Printed in the Sixteenth and Seventeenth Centuries.* [London]: Thomas Richards (for private circulation), 1868.

Cooke, John. *Greene's Tu Quoque or, The Cittie Gallant* (1611), ed. Alan J. Berman. The Renaissance Imagination 8. New York: Garland Publishing Inc., 1984.

The Defence of Conny-Catching. By Cuthbert Cony-Catcher. London, 1592.

Dekker, Thomas. *The Gull's Hornbook* (1609), ed. R. B. McKerrow. London: De La More Press, 1904.

Elyot, Sir Thomas. *The Boke Named the Gouernour* (1531), ed. Henry Herbert Stephen Croft. 2 vols. London: Kegan Paul, Trench, & Co., 1883.

Fetherston, Christopher. *A Dialogue agaynst light, lewde, and lasciuious dauncing.* London, 1582.

Field, John. *A godly exhortation, by occasion of the late iudgement of God, shewed at Parris-garden.* London, 1583.

Fleming, Abraham. *A Bright Burning Beacon … A commemoration of our late Earthquake, the 6. of April, about 6. of the clocke in the euening 1580.* London, [1580].

Furnivall, F. J., ed. *Child-Marriages, Divorces, and Ratifications, &c. in the Diocese of Chester, A.D. 1561–66.* Early English Text Society, Original Ser. 108. London: Kegan Paul, Trench, Trübner & Co., 1897.

————. *The Second Part of the Anatomie of Abuses*. By Philip Stubbes. New Shakspere Society, 6th ser., 12. London: N. Trübner & Co., 1882.

G., I. [John Greene]. *A Refutation of the Apology for Actors*. London, 1615.

Gascoigne, George. *A delicate Diet, for daintiemouthde Droonkardes* (1576). In *The Complete Works of George Gascoigne*, ed. John W. Cunliffe, 2:451–71. Cambridge: Cambridge University Press, 1910.

Golding, Arthur. *A discourse vpon the Earthquake that hapned throughe this Realme of Englande, and other places of Christendom, the sixt of Aprill.1580. betwene the houres of fiue and six in the Euening*. London, [1580].

Gosson, Stephen. *Playes Confuted in Fiue Actions* (1582). In *Markets of Bawdrie: The Dramatic Criticism of Stephen Gosson*, ed. Arthur F. Kinney, 138–97. Salzburg: Institut für Englische Sprache und Literatur, Universität Salzburg, 1974.

————. *The Schoole of Abuse* (1579). In *Markets of Bawdrie: The Dramatic Criticism of Stephen Gosson*, ed. Arthur F. Kinney, 69–137. Salzburg: Institut für Englische Sprache und Literatur, Universität Salzburg, 1974.

Granville, Henry, Duke of Norfolk, ed. *The Lives of Philip Howard, Earl of Arundel, and of Anne Dacres, His Wife*. London: Hurst and Blackett, 1857. Repr. as *The Life of Saint Philip Howard*, ed. Francis W. Steer, with a foreword by Bernard, 16th Duke of Norfolk. London: Phillimore & Co. Ltd., 1971.

Greene, Robert. *The Second Part of Conny-Catching* (1592), ed. G. B. Harrison. London: John Lane The Bodley Head Ltd., 1923.

Grindal, Edmund. *The Remains of Edmund Grindal, Successively Bishop of London, and Archbishop of York and Canterbury*, ed. William Nicholson. Parker Society 29.9. Cambridge: Cambridge University Press, 1843.

Hakluyt, Richard. *The Principal Navigations Voyages Traffiques & Discoveries of the English Nation* (1589). 12 vols. Glasgow: James MacLehose and Sons, 1903–1905.

Hall, Joseph. *Vergidemiae* (1597). In *The Collected Poems of Joseph Hall, Bishop of Exeter and Norwich*, ed. A. Davenport, 5–99. Liverpool: Liverpool University Press, 1949.

Harrison, William. *Harrison's Description of England in Shakspere's Youth: Being the Second and Third Books of his Description of Britaine and England. Edited from the first two editions of Holinshed's Chronicle, A.D. 1577, 1587. Part 1: The Second Book*, ed. F. J. Furnivall. The New Shakspere Society, 6th ser., 1. London: N. Trübner & Co., 1877.

Holinshed, Raphael. *Holinshed's Chronicles of England, Scotland, and Ireland* (1577, rev. and repr. 1587). 6 vols. London: J. Johnson et al., 1808.

Hughes, Paul L., and James F. Larkin. *Tudor Royal Proclamations*. 3 vols. New Haven: Yale University Press, 1964–1969.

Jewel, John. "An Exposition upon the two Epistles of St. Paul to the Thessalonians." In *Works of John Jewel, Bishop of Salisbury*, trans. John Ayre, 2:813–946. Parker Society 24. Cambridge: Cambridge University Press, 1847.

Jonson, Ben. *Euery Man out of his Humour*. 1599. In *Ben Jonson*, ed. C. H. Herford and Percy Simpson, 3:405–606. Oxford: Clarendon Press, 1927.

Lupton, Thomas. *Siquila. Too Good, to be True*. London, 1580.

Lyly, John. *Campaspe*. 1584. Ed. G. K. Hunter. In *Campaspe* with *Sappho and Phao*, ed. G. K. Hunter and David Bevington, 1–140. Manchester: Manchester University Press, 1991.

———. *Euphues: The Anatomy of Wit* (1579). In *John Lyly*, ed. Edward Arber, 31–198. Birmingham: n.p., 1868.

Macropedius, Georg. *Hecastus* (1539). In *Drei Schauspiele vom sterbenden Menschen*, ed. John Bolte, 63–150. Leipzig: Hiersemann, 1927.

Marlorat, Augustine. *A Catholike and Ecclesiasticall exposition of the holy Gospell after S. Mathewe*, trans. Thomas Tymme. London, 1570.

Munday, Anthony. *A view of sundry Examples*. London, 1580.

Nashe, Thomas. *The Works of Thomas Nashe*, ed. R. B. McKerrow, rev. F. P. Wilson. 5 vols. Oxford: Basil Blackwell, 1958.

Northbrooke, John. *The poore mans garden*. 1571. 3rd ed. London, [1575].

———. *A Treatise wherein Dicing, Dauncing, Vaine playes or Enterluds with other idle pastimes &c. commonly vsed on the Sabboth day, are reproued by the Authoritie of the word of God and auntient writers* (c. 1577), ed. J. P. C[ollier]. London: F. Shoberl, 1843.

Painter, William, trans. *The Palace of Pleasure*, ed. Joseph Jacobs. 3 vols. London: David Nutt, 1890.

Parker, R. B., ed. "A Critical Edition of Robert Greene's *A Quip for an Upstart Courtier (1592)*." Ph.D. Diss., University of Birmingham, 1958.

Prynne, William. *Histriomastix* (1633). Facsimile reprint. The English Stage: Attack and Defense 1577–1730. With a preface for the Garland edition by Arthur Freeman. New York: Garland Publishing Inc., 1974.

Saxey, Samuel. *A straunge and Wonderfull Example of the Iudgement of almighty God, shewed vpon two adulterous persons in London, in the parish of S. Brydes, in Fleetestreete, this thirde of Februarie. 1583*. London, [1583].

Shakespeare, William. *The Complete Works: Compact Edition*, ed. Stanley Wells and Gary Taylor, with John Jowett and William Montgomery. Oxford: Clarendon Press, 1988.

Stationers' Company. *Court Book B: 1576–1595*. Stationers' Hall, London, n.d.

Stockwood, John. *A Sermon Preached at Paules Crosse on Barthelmew day, being the 24. of August. 1578*. London, 1578.

Stow, John. *The Annales, or Generall Chronicle of England . . . continued and augmented with matters forreyne, and domestique, auncient and moderne, vnto the
ende of this present yeere 1614 by Edmund Howes, gentleman.* London, 1615.

———. *The Chronicles of England, from Brute vnto this present yeare of Christ
1580.* London, 1580.

———. *A Survey of London.* 1603. Ed. Charles Kingsford. 2 vols. Oxford: Clarendon Press, 1908.

Stubbes, John. *The discouerie of a gaping gulf.* London, 1579.

Taverner, Richard, trans. *The fyrst and second bookes of the garden of wysedome.*
London, 1547[?].

Vives, Juan Luis. *A very fruteful and pleasant boke called the Instruction of a christen woman.* [*De Institutione Feminae Christianae,* 1523.] Trans. Rychard
Hyrde. 1529[?]. London: 1557.

———. *Tudor School-Boy Life: The Dialogues of Juan Luis Vives.* [*Linguae Latinae
Exercitatio,* 1539.] Trans. Foster Watson. London: J. M. Dent and Co., 1908.

Walther, Rodolph. *Rodolphi Gualtheri Tigurini in Evangelium Iesu Christi Secundum Marcum Homiliae CXXXIX.* Heidelberg, 1608.

Whetstone, George. *A Mirour for Magestrates of Cyties* with *A Touchstone for the
Time.* London, 1584.

White, Thomas. *A Sermō Preached at Pawles Crosse on Sunday the thirde of Nouember 1577, in the time of the Plague.* London, 1578.

à Wood, Anthony. *Athenae Oxonienses. An Exact History of all the Writers and
Bishops who have had their Education in the University of Oxford* (1691). Ed.
and revised by Philip Bliss. 1813–1820. 4 vols. London: Johnson Reprint Corporation, 1967.

3: Modern Scholarly Works

Abbott, E. A. *A Shakespearian Grammar: An Attempt to Illustrate some of the Differences Between Elizabethan and Modern English.* New ed. London: Mac-
Millan and Co., 1883.

Archer, Ian W. *The Pursuit of Stability: Social Relations in Elizabethan London.*
Cambridge: Cambridge University Press, 1991.

Arnold, Janet. *Patterns of Fashion: The Cut and Construction of Clothes for Men
and Women c. 1560–1620.* London: Macmillan Ltd., 1985.

———. *Queen Elizabeth's Wardrobe Unlock'd.* London: W. S. Maney & Son Ltd.,
1988.

Ashley, Clifford W. *The Ashley Book of Knots.* Garden City, NY: Doubleday,
Doran & Company Inc., 1944.

Baldwin, Elizabeth Frances. *Sumptuary Legislation and Personal Regulation in England*, 1–282. Johns Hopkins University Studies in Historical and Political Science 44.1. Baltimore: The Johns Hopkins University Press, 1926.

Barish, Jonas. *The Antitheatrical Prejudice*. Berkeley: University of California Press, 1981.

Barnes, Thomas G. "County Politics and a Puritan Cause Célèbre: Somerset Churchales, 1633." *Transactions of the Royal Historical Society*, 5th ser, 9 (1959): 103–22.

Bertram, Paul, and Bernice W. Kliman, eds. *The Three-Text Hamlet: Parallel Texts of the First and Second Quartos and First Folio*. New York: AMS Press, 1991.

Binns, J. W. *Intellectual Culture in Elizabethan and Jacobean England: The Latin Writings of the Age*. Leeds: Francis Cairns, 1990.

Brand, John. *Observations of the Popular Antiquities of Great Britain*, rev. and enlarged by Henry Ellis. 3 vols. London: Henry G. Bohn, 1849.

Bray, Alan. *Homosexuality in Renaissance England*. London: Gay Men's Press, 1982.

Chambers, E. K. *The Elizabethan Stage*. Rev. ed. 4 vols. Oxford: Clarendon Press, 1951.

———. *The Mediaeval Stage*. 2 vols. London: Oxford University Press, 1903.

Clark, Sandra. *The Elizabethan Pamphleteers: Popular Moralistic Pamphlets 1580–1640*. London: The Athlone Press, 1983.

Collinson, Patrick. "Ecclesiastical Vitriol: Religious Satire in the 1590s and the Invention of Puritanism." In *The Reign of Elizabeth I: Court and Culture in the Last Decade*, ed. John Guy, 150–70. Cambridge: Cambridge University Press, 1995.

———. *The Puritan Character: Polemics and Polarities in Early Seventeenth-Century English Culture*. William Andrews Clark Memorial Library Paper. With an introduction by Karen E. Rowe. Los Angeles: University of California Press, 1989.

———. "William Shakespeare's Religious Inheritance and Environment." In idem, *Elizabethan Essays*, 219–52. London: The Hambledon Press, 1994.

Colvin, H. M., gen. ed. *The History of the King's Works*. Vol. 4. London: Her Majesty's Stationery Office, 1982.

Cox, J. Charles. *Churchwardens' Accounts from the Fourteenth Century to the Close of the Seventeenth Century*. London: Methuen & Co. Ltd., 1913.

Cox, Virginia. *The Renaissance Dialogue*. Cambridge Studies in Renaissance Literature and Culture 2. Cambridge: Cambridge University Press, 1992.

Cragg, Gerald R. *Puritanism in the Period of the Great Persecution 1660–1688*.

Cambridge: Cambridge University Press, 1957.

Cunnington, C. Willett, and Phillis Cunnington. *Handbook of English Costume in the Sixteenth Century*. Rev. ed. London: Faber and Faber Ltd., 1970.

de Courtais, Georgine. *Women's Headdress and Hairstyles in England from AD 600 to the Present Day*. London: B. T. Batsford Ltd., 1973.

Dent, R. W. *Proverbial Language in English Drama Exclusive of Shakespeare, 1495–1616: An Index*. Berkeley: University of California Press, 1984.

Earnshaw, Pat. *Lace in Fashion from the Sixteenth to the Twentieth Centuries*. London: B. T. Batsford Ltd., 1985.

Emmison, F. G. *Elizabethan Life: Disorder*. Essex Record Office Publications 56. Chelmsford: Essex County Council, 1970.

Frye, Northrop. *Anatomy of Criticism: Four Essays*. 1973. Princeton: Princeton University Press, 1957, repr. 1973.

———. "Varieties of Literary Utopias." In *Utopias and Utopian Thought*, ed. Frank E. Manuel, 25–49. Boston: Beacon Press, 1965.

Gabler, Hans Walter, with Wolfhard Steppe and Claus Melchior, eds. *Ulysses: A Critical and Synoptic Edition*. By James Joyce. 3 vols. New York: Garland Publishing, 1984.

Garber, Marjorie. *Vested Interests: Cross-Dressing and Cultural Anxiety*. New York: Routledge, 1992.

Genders, Roy. *A History of Scent*. London: Hamish Hamilton, 1972.

Goldberg, Jonathan. *Sodometries: Renaissance Texts, Modern Sexualities*. Stanford: Stanford University Press, 1992.

Gotch, J. Alfred. *Early Renaissance Architecture in England*. London: B. T. Batsford, 1901.

Graham-White, Anthony. *Punctuation and Its Dramatic Value in Shakespearean Drama*. Newark, DE: University of Delaware Press, 1995.

Gunn, Fenja. *The Artificial Face: A History of Cosmetics*. Newton Abbot: David & Charles, 1973.

Gurr, Andrew. *The Shakespearean Stage 1574–1642*. 3rd ed. Cambridge: Cambridge University Press, 1992.

Hajnal, J. "European Marriage Patterns in Perspective." In *Population in History: Essays in Historical Demography*, ed. D. V. Glass and D. E. C. Eversley, 101–43. London: Edward Arnold Ltd., 1969.

Harleian Society Publications. Vol 25: "Allegations for Marriage Licences Issued by the Bishop of London, 1520–1610." Extracted by Col. J. L. Chester, ed. G. J. Armytage. London: Harleian Society, 1887.

Hazlitt, W. Carew. *Collections and Notes 1867–1876*. London: Reeves and Turner, 1876.

———. *Hand-Book to the Popular, Poetical, and Dramatic Literature of Great Britain, From the Invention of Printing to the Restoration.* London: John Russell Smith, 1867.

———. *Second Series of Bibliographical Collections and Notes on Early English Literature 1474–1700.* London: Bernard Quaritch, 1882.

Heal, Felicity. *Hospitality in Early Modern England.* Oxford: Clarendon Press, 1990.

———. "The Idea of Hospitality in Early Modern England." *Past and Present* 102 (1984): 66–93.

Hefele, Charles Joseph. *A History of the Councils of the Church, from the Original Documents,* trans. Henry Nutcombe Oxenham. Vol. 2. Edinburgh: T. & T. Clark, 1896.

Hill, Christopher. *Society and Puritanism in Pre-Revolutionary England.* London: Secker & Warburg, 1964.

Hodges, Devon L. *Renaissance Fictions of Anatomy.* Amherst, MA: University of Massachusetts Press, 1985.

Honigmann, E. A. J. *The Stability of Shakespeare's Text.* London: Edward Arnold (Publishers) Ltd., 1965.

Howard, Jean E. *The Stage and Social Struggle in Early Modern England.* London: Routledge, 1994.

Jacob, Giles. *A New Law-Dictionary.* 5th ed. London, 1744.

Jardine, Lisa. *Still Harping on Daughters: Women and Drama in the Age of Shakespeare.* Brighton: Harvester Press Ltd., 1983.

Jones, Ann Rosalind, and Peter Stallybrass. *Renaissance Clothing and the Materials of Memory.* Cambridge Studies in Renaissance Literature and Culture 38. Cambridge: Cambridge University Press, 2000.

Jones, Norman. *God and the Moneylenders: Usury and Law in Early Modern England.* Oxford: Basil Blackwell, 1989.

Kerridge, Eric. *Agrarian Problems in the Sixteenth Century and After.* Historical Problems: Studies and Documents 6. London: George Allen and Unwin Ltd., 1969.

Kidnie, Margaret Jane. "Evidence of Authorial Revision in the Earliest Edition of *The Anatomie of Abuses.*" *The Papers of the Bibliographical Society of America* 92.1 (1998): 75–80.

———. "Printer's Copy Underlying the Four Editions of Philip Stubbes's *Anatomie of Abuses.*" *Analytical and Enumerative Bibliography* n.s. 8 (1994): 159–75.

Klein, Joan Larsen, ed. *Daughters, Wives, and Widows: Writings by Men about Women and Marriage in England, 1500–1640.* Urbana: University of Illinois Press, 1992.

Lachmann, Richard. *From Manor to Market: Structural Change in England, 1536–1640*. Madison: University of Wisconsin Press, 1987.

Lake, Peter. "Puritan Identities." *Journal of Ecclesiastical History* 35 (1984): 112–23.

Laroque, François. *Shakespeare's Festive World: Elizabethan Seasonal Entertainment and the Professional Stage*. Trans. Janet Lloyd. Cambridge: Cambridge University Press, 1991.

Laslett, Peter. *The World We Have Lost Further Explored*. 3rd ed. London: Methuen & Co. Ltd, 1983.

Lavin, J. A. "John Danter's Ornament Stock." *Studies in Bibliography* 23 (1970): 21–44.

Levine, Laura. *Men in Women's Clothing: Anti-Theatricality and Effeminization, 1579–1642*. Cambridge Studies in Renaissance Literature and Culture 5. Cambridge: Cambridge University Press, 1994.

Linthicum, M. Channing. *Costume in the Drama of Shakespeare and His Contemporaries*. Oxford: Clarendon Press, 1936.

Macquoid, Percy. "Costume." In *Shakespeare's England: An Account of the Life and Manners of his Age*, 2 vols., 2:91–118. Oxford: Clarendon Press, 1917.

Manley, Lawrence. *Literature and Culture in Early Modern London*. Cambridge: Cambridge University Press, 1995.

Marcus, Leah S. *The Politics of Mirth: Jonson, Herrick, Milton, Marvell, and the Defense of Old Holiday Pastimes*. Chicago: University of Chicago Press, 1986.

McKerrow, R. B. *Printers' & Publishers' Devices in England & Scotland 1485–1640*. London: The Bibliographical Society, 1949.

Moore, J. K. *Primary Materials Relating to Copy and Print in English Books of the Sixteenth and Seventeenth Centuries*. Occasional Publication 24. Oxford: Oxford Bibliographical Society, 1992.

Moulton, I. F. *Before Pornography: Erotic Writing in Early Modern England*. Oxford: Oxford University Press, 2000.

Mullaney, Steven. *The Place of the Stage: License, Play, and Power in Renaissance England*. Chicago: University of Chicago Press, 1988.

Norris, Herbert. *Costume and Fashion*. Vol. 3: "The Tudors, Book II: 1547–1603." London: J. M. Dent and Sons Ltd., 1938.

Orgel, Stephen. *Impersonations: The Performance of Gender in Shakespeare's England*. Cambridge: Cambridge University Press, 1996.

———. "Nobody's Perfect: Or Why Did the English Stage Take Boys for Women?" *South Atlantic Quarterly* 88 (1989): 7–29.

Otto, A. *Die Sprichwörter und sprichwörtlichen Redensarten der Römer*. Leipzig: B. G. Teubner, 1890.

Oxford English Dictionary. Compact Edition. 2nd ed. Oxford: Clarendon Press, 1991.

Palliser, Bury. *History of Lace*, revised M. Jourdain and Alice Dryden. London: Sampson Low, Marston & Company, 1902.

Palliser, D. M. *The Age of Elizabeth: England under the Later Tudors 1547–1603*. 2nd ed. London: Longman Group UK Ltd., 1992.

Parkes, M. B. *Pause and Effect: An Introduction to the History of Punctuation in the West*. Aldershot: Scolar Press, 1992.

Pearson, Terry. "The Composition and Development of Phillip Stubbes's 'Anatomie of Abuses.'" *Modern Language Review* 56 (1961): 321–32.

———. "The Life and Works of Phillip Stubbes." M.A. diss., Westfield College, University of London, 1958.

Peter, John. *Complaint and Satire in Early English Literature*. Oxford: Clarendon Press, 1956.

Petti, Anthony G. *English Literary Hands from Chaucer to Dryden*. London: Edward Arnold (Publishers) Ltd., 1977.

Planché, J. R. *History of British Costume, from the Earliest Period to the Close of the Eighteenth Century*. 3rd ed. London: George Bell & Sons, 1893.

Pollard, A. W., and G. R. Redgrave. *A Short-Title Catalogue of Books Printed in England, Scotland and Ireland and of English Books Printed Abroad, 1475–1640*. 2nd ed. Revised W. A. Jackson, F. S. Ferguson, and Katharine F. Pantzer. 3 vols. London: The Bibliographical Society, 1976–1991.

Prescott, Anne Lake. "The Evolution of Tudor Satire." In *Cambridge Companion to English Literature 1500–1600*, ed. A. F. Kinney, 220–40. Cambridge: Cambridge University Press, 2000.

Richard, Jean. *Saint Louis: Crusader King of France*, trans. Jean Birrell, ed. and abridged by Simon Lloyd. Cambridge: Cambridge University Press, 1992.

Ringler, William. "The First Phase of the Elizabethan Attack on the Stage, 1558–1579." *Huntington Library Quarterly* 5 (1941–1942): 391–418.

———. *Stephen Gosson: A Biographical and Critical Study*. Princeton Studies in English 25. Princeton: Princeton University Press, 1942.

Rye, William Brenchley. *England as Seen by Foreigners in the days of Elizabeth and James the First*. London: John Russell Smith, 1865.

Schmitt, Charles, et al. *The Cambridge History of Renaissance Philosophy*. Cambridge: Cambridge University Press, 1988.

Shugg, Wallace. "Prostitution in Shakespeare's London." *Shakespeare Studies* 10 (1977): 291–313.

Simpson, Percy. *Shakespearian Punctuation*. Oxford: Clarendon Press, 1911.

Spear, Gary. "Shakespeare's 'Manly' Parts: Masculinity and Effeminacy in *Troilus and Cressida.*" *Shakespeare Quarterly* 44 (1993): 409–22.

Stone, Lawrence. "The Anatomy of the Elizabethan Aristocracy." *Economic History Review* 18.1–2 (1948): 1–53.

———. *The Crisis of the Aristocracy 1558–1641.* Oxford: Clarendon Press, 1965.

Tawney, R. H. *The Agrarian Problem in the Sixteenth Century.* London: Longmans, Green & Co., 1912.

Thirsk, Joan. "The Fantastical Folly of Fashion: The English Stocking Knitting Industry, 1500–1700." In *Textile History and Economic History: Essays in Honour of Miss Julia de Lacy Mann,* ed. N. B. Harte and K. G. Ponting, 50–73. Manchester: Manchester University Press, 1973.

———. "Tudor Enclosures." *Transactions of the Historical Association,* gen. ser. 41 (1958): 1–23; repr. in Joan Thirsk, *The Rural Economy of England: Collected Essays,* 65–83. London: Hambledon Press, 1984.

Thomas, Keith. "Age and Authority in Early Modern England." *Proceedings of the British Academy* 62 (1976): 205–48.

———. *Religion and the Decline of Magic: Studies in Popular Beliefs in Sixteenth and Seventeenth Century England.* London: Weidenfeld and Nicolson, 1971.

Tilley, Morris Palmer. *A Dictionary of the Proverbs in England in the Sixteenth and Seventeenth Centuries.* Ann Arbor: University of Michigan Press, 1950.

Trayner, John. *Latin Maxims and Phrases.* 2nd ed. Edinburgh: William Green, 1876.

Walsham, Alexandra. "'A Glose of Godlines': Philip Stubbes, Elizabethan Grub Street and the Invention of Puritanism." In *Belief and Practice in Reformation England: A Tribute to Patrick Collinson,* ed. S. Wabuda and C. Litzenberger, 177–206. Aldershot: Ashgate, 1998.

Walther, Hans. *Proverbia Sententiaeque Latinitatis Medii Aevi.* Carmina Medii Aevi Posterioris Latina. 5 vols. Göttingen: Vandenhoeck & Ruprecht, 1963–1967.

———. *Proverbia Sententiaeque Latinitatis Medii ac Recentioris Aevi.* Carmina Medii Aevi Posterioris Latina. Nova series. 3 vols. Göttingen: Vandenhoeck & Ruprecht, 1982–1986.

Warren, Michael, ed. *The Complete "King Lear" 1608–1623: Texts and Parallel Texts in Photographic Facsimile.* Berkeley: University of California Press, 1989.

Watt, Tessa. *Cheap Print and Popular Piety 1550–1640.* Cambridge: Cambridge University Press, 1991.

White, Helen C. *Social Criticism in Popular Religious Literature of the Sixteenth Century.* New York: Macmillan, 1944, repr. New York: Octagon Books, 1965.

Woodbridge, Linda. *Vagrancy, Homelessness, and English Renaissance Literature.* Urbana: University of Illinois Press, 2001.

Wrightson, Keith. *English Society 1580–1680*. New Brunswick, NJ: Rutgers University Press, 1982, repr. London: Routledge, 1993.

———. "Estates, Degrees, and Sorts: Changing Perceptions of Society in Tudor and Stuart England." In *Language, History and Class*, ed. Penelope J. Corfield, 30–52. Oxford: Basil Blackwell, 1991.

Zeller, Hans. "A New Approach to the Critical Constitution of Literary Texts." *Studies in Bibliography* 28 (1975): 231–64.

Zitner, S. P. "Gosson, Ovid, and the Elizabethan Audience." *Shakespeare Quarterly* 9 (1958): 206–8.

Index

PROPER NAMES

BIBLICAL NAMES

SUBJECTS

Renaissance English Text Society

The Renaissance English Text Society was established to publish literary texts, chiefly nondramatic, of the period 1475–1660. Dues are $35.00 per annum ($25.00, graduate students; life membership is available at $500.00). Members receive the text published for each year of membership. The Society sponsors panels at such annual meetings as those of the Modern Language Association, the Renaissance Society of America, and the Medieval Congress at Kalamazoo.

General inquiries and proposals for editions should be addressed to the president, Arthur F. Kinney, Massachusetts Center for Renaissance Studies, PO Box 2300, Amherst, Mass., 01004, USA. Inquiries about membership should be addressed to William Gentrup, Membership Secretary, Arizona Center for Medieval and Renaissance Studies, Arizona State University, PO Box 872301, Tempe, Ariz., 85287-2301.

Copies of volumes X–XII may be purchased from Associated University Presses, 440 Forsgate Drive, Cranbury, N.J., 08512. Members may order copies of earlier volumes still in print or of later volumes from XIII, at special member prices, from the Treasurer.

FIRST SERIES

VOL. I. *Merie Tales of the Mad Men of Gotam* by A. B., edited by Stanley J. Kahrl, and *The History of Tom Thumbe*, by R. I., edited by Curt F. Buhler, 1965. (o.p.)

VOL. II. Thomas Watson's Latin *Amyntas*, edited by Walter F. Staton, Jr., and Abraham Fraunce's translation *The Lamentations of Amyntas*, edited by Franklin M. Dickey, 1967.

SECOND SERIES

VOL. III. *The dyaloge called Funus*, A Translation of Erasmus's Colloquy (1534), and *A very pleasaunt & fruitful Diologe called The Epicure*, Gerrard's Translation of Erasmus's Colloquy (1545), edited by Robert R. Allen, 1969.

VOL. IV. *Leicester's Ghost* by Thomas Rogers, edited by Franklin B. Williams, Jr., 1972.

THIRD SERIES

VOLS. V–VI. *A Collection of Emblemes, Ancient and Moderne*, by George Wither, with an introduction by Rosemary Freeman and bibliographical notes by Charles S. Hensley, 1975. (o.p.)

FOURTH SERIES

VOLS. VII–VIII. *Tom a' Lincolne* by R. I., edited by Richard S. M. Hirsch, 1978.

FIFTH SERIES

VOL. IX. *Metrical Visions* by George Cavendish, edited by A. S. G. Edwards, 1980.

SIXTH SERIES

VOL. X. *Two Early Renaissance Bird Poems*, edited by Malcolm Andrew, 1984.

VOL. XI. *Argalus and Parthenia* by Francis Quarles, edited by David Freeman, 1986.

VOL. XII. Cicero's *De Officiis*, trans. Nicholas Grimald, edited by Gerald O'Gorman, 1987.

VOL. XIII. *The Silkewormes and their Flies* by Thomas Moffet (1599), edited with introduction and commentary by Victor Houliston, 1988.

SEVENTH SERIES

VOL. XIV. John Bale, *The Vocacyon of Johan Bale*, edited by Peter Happé and John N. King, 1989.

VOL. XV. *The Nondramatic Works of John Ford*, edited by L. E. Stock, Gilles D. Monsarrat, Judith M. Kennedy, and Dennis Danielson, with the assistance of Marta Straznicky, 1990.

Special Publication. *New Ways of Looking at Old Texts: Papers of the Renaissance English Text Society, 1985–1991*, edited by W. Speed Hill, 1993. (Sent *gratis* to all 1991 members.)

VOL. XVI. George Herbert, *The Temple: A Diplomatic Edition of the Bodleian Manuscript (Tanner 307)*, edited by Mario A. Di Cesare, 1991.

VOL. XVII. Lady Mary Wroth, *The First Part of the Countess of Montgomery's Urania*, edited by Josephine Roberts. 1992.

VOL. XVIII. Richard Beacon, *Solon His Follie*, edited by Clare Carroll and Vincent Carey. 1993.

VOL. XIX. An Collins, *Divine Songs and Meditacions*, edited by Sidney Gottlieb. 1994.

VOL. XX. *The Southwell-Sibthorpe Commonplace Book: Folger MS V.b.198*, edited by Sr. Jean Klene. 1995.

Special Publication. *New Ways of Looking at Old Texts II: Papers of the Renaissance English Text Society, 1992–1996*, edited by W. Speed Hill, 1998. (Sent *gratis* to all 1996 members.)

VOL. XXI. *The Collected Works of Anne Vaughan Lock*, edited by Susan M. Felch. 1996.

VOL. XXII. Thomas May, *The Reigne of King Henry the Second Written in Seauen Books*, edited by Götz Schmitz. 1997.

VOL. XXIII. *The Poems of Sir Walter Ralegh: A Historical Edition*, edited by Michael Rudick. 1998.

VOL. XXIV. Lady Mary Wroth, *The Second Part of the Countess of Montgomery's Urania*, edited by Josephine Roberts; completed by Suzanne Gossett and Janel Mueller. 1999.

VOL. XXV. *The Verse Miscellany of Constance Aston Fowler: A Diplomatic Edition*, by Deborah Aldrich-Watson. 2000.

VOL. XXVI. *An Edition of Luke Shepherd's Satires*, by Janice Devereux. 2001.

VOL. XXVII. Philip Stubbes, *The Anatomie of Abuses*, edited by Margaret Jane Kidnie. 2002.